A Pentecostal Commentary on
THE PASTORAL EPISTLES

The Pentecostal Old and New Testament Commentaries

Series Preface

Over the last century, the Pentecostal movement has transformed the face of global Christianity. Nevertheless, Pentecostal voices continue to be underrepresented in biblical scholarship. Therefore, we would like to introduce *The Pentecostal Old and New Testament Commentaries*. The Pentecostal authors of this series come to the text with a high view of Scripture; however, we desire to say more than has already been said by non-Pentecostals. Thus, the contributors to this series have been charged with the task of articulating a truly Pentecostal perspective on every verse of the Bible.

This grand vision began in the heart of our series founder, Eun Chul Kim. He spent nearly a decade tirelessly advocating for this Pentecostal commentary and recruiting authors. However, like so many of God's servants, it was not given to him to see the fulfillment of the promise. On September 22, 2018, Kim succumbed to cancer, but his vision continues.

The commentaries themselves target the educated layperson, Pentecostal pastor, and student of the Bible and focus their attention on the exegesis and translation of the Greek (NA28) and Hebrew (BHS and BHQ) texts. In keeping with the diversity that characterizes Pentecostals and Charismatics themselves, we have left the authors with a great deal of liberty regarding their approaches. As the editors, we highly value academic freedom. Consequently, although all the authors identify as Pentecostals and greatly esteem the authority of Scripture, we have not required them to espouse any particular theological viewpoints or to take any prescribed theological positions. Accordingly, each author is responsible for what he or she has written and not the editors. Although the approaches of the various authors vary widely, two things have been deemed essential: a rigorously critical approach and a distinctively Pentecostal contribution. This combination will certainly profit Pentecostal believers whether in the pew, the pulpit, or the classroom.

It is our sincere prayer that God will use this commentary series to encourage Pentecostals everywhere to read the Bible *as Pentecostals*.

CHRISTOPHER L. CARTER—New Testament Editor
DAVID C. HYMES—Old Testament Editor

A Pentecostal Commentary on
THE PASTORAL EPISTLES

William K. Kay and
John R. L. Moxon

THE PENTECOSTAL OLD AND NEW TESTAMENT COMMENTARIES

Christopher L. Carter — New Testament Editor

WIPF & STOCK · Eugene, Oregon

A PENTECOSTAL COMMENTARY ON THE PASTORAL EPISTLES

Copyright © 2022 William K. Kay and John R. L. Moxon. All rights reserved. Except for brief quotations in critical publications or reviews, no part of this book may be reproduced in any manner without prior written permission from the publisher. Write: Permissions, Wipf and Stock Publishers, 199 W. 8th Ave., Suite 3, Eugene, OR 97401.

Wipf & Stock
An Imprint of Wipf and Stock Publishers
199 W. 8th Ave., Suite 3
Eugene, OR 97401

www.wipfandstock.com

PAPERBACK ISBN: 978-1-5326-4543-3
HARDCOVER ISBN: 978-1-5326-4544-0
EBOOK ISBN: 978-1-5326-4545-7

06/02/22

For WKK: George, Olivia, Joel, Ethan and Isaac
For JM: Annie and Zac

CONTENTS

Preface	ix
Note on Text and Translation	xiii
Abbreviations	xv

INTRODUCTION — 1

I. The Pastoral Epistles—What They are and Why They Matter	3
II. Recipients, Context, Purpose and Genre	8
III. Political, Social, Cultural and Religious Setting	15
IV. Questions Surrounding Date and Authorship	27
V. A Pentecostal and Charismatic Church	34
Excursus I. On the Problem of Style and Vocabulary in the Pastoral Epistles	35
Excursus II. On Church and Academy	41

1 TIMOTHY — 45

Outline	45
Commentary	47
I. Paul, Timothy, and The Mission to Ephesus	47
II. Prayer and Gender Roles	62
III. Overseers and Deacons	75
IV. Unhealthy and Healthy Teaching	87
V. Widows, Elders and Slaves	98
VI. Motivations and Judgements	112
Excursus III. On Spiritual Warfare	125
Excursus IV. On Holiness or Godliness	127

TITUS 129

Outline 129
Commentary 131
I. Paul, Titus, and Crete 131
II. Christian Living: A Rationale 146
III. Christian Living Outside the Church: A Rationale 160

2 TIMOTHY 173

Outline 173
Commentary 175
I. Paul from Prison 175
II. Paul Sets Out Future Plans 192
III. Paul Warns and Encourages 212
IV. Paul Unbowed 230
Excursus V. Time and Eternity 250

Bibliography 253
Index 269

PREFACE

We wish to make clear what kind of commentary this is and isn't. It is not intended to be a metacommentary, one that comments on all other commentaries in order to referee between them and arrive at a conclusion. This means that it will not provide an exhaustive listing of all the articles and commentaries that have been written on the Pastoral Epistles in the last 150 years.[1] Nor will it delve deeply into classical literature to pursue word meanings and points of grammar.[2] Rather, it is a commentary primarily written for *ministers* where the word is broadly conceived. These are people who share the Scriptures in Bible studies, from the pulpit, in home groups, youth clubs, in blogs, podcasts, or online discussions. We hope this commentary will especially benefit people in the huge, international, multi-ethnic, and vastly diverse Pentecostal and charismatic movements because it "speaks their language" by fastening onto the activities of the Holy Spirit, especially in Spirit baptism and the ministry gifts of Ephesians 4—apostles, prophets, evangelists, pastors, and teachers. We have countless times observed the laying on of hands, and we know how pertinent any discussion of the roles and qualifications of elders and deacons, or the ministry of women is. We have witnessed a "passion for the kingdom" and seen Pentecostal social action.[3]

---

1. There are big commentaries which have done this, or nearly so. We take William D. Mounce's Word Biblical Commentary on the Pastorals as being about as definitive and complete an engagement with the relevant literature as anyone could hope to publish in the covers of one book. For this reason, and because Mounce is a fair and vastly knowledgeable scholar, we quote or refer to him extensively in the pages that follow. We note, incidentally, that Mounce (*Pastoral Epistles,* p. x) salutes Gordon Fee, ordained into Pentecostal ministry with Assemblies of God, from whose scholarship we also have benefited greatly.

2. Though Mounce is no slouch in this type of classical and etymological investigation, we see Luke Timothy Johnson's and George W Knight III's commentaries as being more orientated in this direction, and we utilize these also while applauding Johnson's masterly historical overview of the interpretation of the Pastorals, 20–54.

3. Land, *Pentecostal Spirituality*; Kalu, *African Pentecostalism*; Miller and Yammamori,

We have heard African, Asian, and Latin American preachers and seen men and women "slain in the Spirit." We have many times heard prophetic and other charismatic "words" and been to house meetings or attended prayer gatherings focused on missionary outreach. Even so, across the world, Pentecostal and charismatic churches vary enormously. If we look for core beliefs and practices, we may find these in the itemized theology of denominational websites or more simply in the features revealed by the ten-country Pew survey. This showed the widespread importance of healing, vocal charismatic gifts, moral standards, and eschatological expectations, often in the form of an anticipation of the second coming of Christ.[4] Indeed, the Pentecostal "Fivefold Gospel" of Jesus as Savior, Sanctifier, Baptizer in the Spirit, and Soon-Coming King is one which can be drawn out from the text of the Pastorals.[5] We explore what the epistles have to say about these themes in the light of the kinds of things Pentecostals and charismatics regularly do (and not just believe).

Although we are interested in the general lines of interpretation of the Pastoral Epistles as they have developed over time, we think some lines are *cul de sacs* which end up without resolution: and here we have in mind the writers who date the epistles late and deny Pauline authorship.[6] The counter arguments in favor of Pauline authorship and a date between 64 and 68 AD are those we accept—as indeed they were accepted or assumed by the church for around eighteen centuries. We see little reason to engage in a kind of guerrilla warfare against the more critical or skeptical writers by constantly mentioning their views and then rebutting them on one ground or another and scattering our rebuttals throughout the commentary; a more detailed review of the long-running argument about authorship is given in the main body of the introduction (see also Excursus 2). The main thrust of

---

Global Pentecostalism. The huge diversity of the Pentecostal movement is well illustrated by *Brill's Encyclopedia of Global Pentecostalism* (edited by Michael Wilkinson et al., 2021, hereafter, *BEGP*).

4. No one knows how many Pentecostal denominations there are. Burgess and van der Maas, *NIDPCM* give a figure of 740 in addition to 6,530 charismatic denominations. The Pew Survey (Lugo, Stencel et al., *Spirit and Power*) is international (covering the United States, Brazil, Chile, Guatemala, Kenya, Nigeria, South Africa, India, The Philippines, and South Korea) and used the same data collection method in different countries to enable direct comparisons across the participating countries.

5. Savior (1 Tim 1:1; Titus 1:4), Sanctifier (Titus 2:3–6; 2:21), Baptizer in the Spirit (perhaps Titus 3:5–6) and Soon-Coming King (1 Tim 6:14–15).

6. We note Johnson's stricture, "For many contemporary scholars, indeed, the inauthenticity of the Pastorals is one of those scholarly dogmas first learned in college and in no need of further examination" (*Timothy*, 55).

what we have to say will look for the meanings of verses within the text itself and then within the broader context of the church and the life of Paul (see further in Excursus 1). In this sense, there is an *historical orientation* to this commentary as well as a Pentecostal and charismatic one.

We are interested in the position of the early church within the Roman Empire and, after 20 centuries, we can appreciate the courage and struggles of those early Christians in the light of the contempt and skepticism they faced. With a polytheistic civic culture endorsed by imperial militarism and with a cult of emperor worship designed to unify the many provinces and ethnicities within the borders of the empire, we note how these political and cultural forces outside the church criminalized Saint Paul. Inside the church we note the insidious presence of false teaching threatening the health and authenticity of the thriving Ephesian congregation or congregations. Without much imagination and, taking into account the many regimes and contexts where contemporary Christians find themselves, we can transpose aspects of these early troubles to today's globalized culture and today's church.

Because the Pentecostal and charismatic movements see themselves as raised up either to renew the church to its early vitality or to restore charismatic gifts that were once lost, Pentecostals and charismatics very much accept the canon of Scripture. In this respect, Pentecostals and charismatics are not revolutionaries seeking to supplant the text, but on the contrary, they are those whose love of Scripture is an essential part of their spirituality. The canon is that group of thirty-nine Old and twenty-seven New Testament writings accepted universally by the church after the final break with Judaism had taken place. The historical process by which this occurred is interesting but not part of this commentary. It is sufficient to say that we are glad to accept the canonicity of the Pastoral Epistles and the inference that the present-day church is therefore answerable to what they say.[7]

William K. Kay and John R. L. Moxon

---

7. Kruger, *Canon Revisited*, loc 701 "Scripture and canon . . . it seems difficult to imagine these two concepts being separated within the minds of, say, second-century Christians." See also, Childs, *Reading Paul*.

NOTE ON TEXT AND TRANSLATION

To ensure the widest access to the Greek New Testament, we have used the public domain SBL Greek text (Holmes, *Greek New Testament: SBL Edition* or *SBLGNT*), specially footnoted for non-specialists and others with limited Greek or experience of advanced forms of critical apparatus. This edition notes all the places where the more technical Nestle-Aland critical text (Aland et al., *Novum testamentum graece*, or NA28) has recently elevated a previously marginal reading to the position of "most likely" and thus now its *presented* reading. It is a convention of this commentary series that we use transliteration rather than a Greek font, following the scheme in Collins, *SBL Handbook of Style*, pp. 59–60.

    Our translation lies within the "literal," word-for word tradition, which will provide many resonances with those used to KJV, RSV, ASV, NRSV, NIV and ESV. Occasional places where our translation appears to follow one of these versions directly is inevitable but almost always occurs when the underlying words happen to follow English word order and traditional renderings are the most natural. Beyond this, we follow a number of conventions which include (i) changing word order where English grammar requires it (ii) omitting "a" or "the" with proper names, concepts, body parts etc. and/or inserting appropriate articles where usage in English differs (iii) eliminating unnatural repeated conjunctions or negations in lists.

    The above changes are not footnoted; however, we have preserved the KJV's use of italics to show words that are added to aid sense, but not where they are simply and properly implied by the Greek. Where other translations are possible for a Greek term, then these are footnoted. Occasionally, we indulge in a little paraphrasing when this seems required to communicate an important nuance or connotation of the Greek. This is always footnoted but can help readers pick up important overtones not otherwise evident.

We have tried to be reasonably consistent in the translation of words that appear frequently, but do not wish to fall into the "word study" fallacy classically underscored by Barr's *Semantics of Biblical Language*. Thus, depending on context, *oikos*, can be rendered by "home," "family" or "wider family," and although *eusebeia* is usually translated by "godliness," other options are sometimes used. Other words are handled in a similar manner, as appropriate.

We have opted for gender-neutral language where *anthrōpos* is used, and particularly where the masculine plural might be reasonably understood to refer to all those present in a mixed group. Where unknown individuals are in view, we have used the pronouns "they," "them," "their" etc. instead of "he or she," "him or her," "his or her" etc. to prevent awkwardness, but certainly with the intention of emphasising that a man or a woman might be in view. All this allows specific references to men as males (*anēr*, pl. *ăndres*), and women as females (*gynē*, pl. *gynaikes*), to stand out. Where possible, and certainly where the text itself does not suggest it, we have tried to eliminate subtle overtones in relation to qualities, roles and activities that might be regarded as gender stereotypical.

ABBREVIATIONS

1 Clem.	1 Clement
1 En.	1 (Ethiopic) Enoch
2 Apol.	Justin, *Second Apology*
2 Bar.	2 (Syriac) Baruch
4 Ezra	4 Ezra (1 Esdr 3–14)
A.J.	Josephus, *Antiquities of the Jews*
AB	Anchor Yale Bible Commentary
ABC	Africa Bible Commentary
ABD	*Anchor Bible Dictionary.* 6 vols. Edited by David Noel Freedman. New York, NY: Doubleday, 1992.
AD	Anno Domini (equivalent to CE)
ANE	Ancient Near East
ANF	*Ante-Nicene Fathers.* 10 vols. Edited by Alexander Roberts, James Donaldson et al. Grand Rapids, MI: Eerdmans, 1979.
Ann.	Tacitus, *Annals*
Anvil	*Anvil: Journal of Theology and Mission*
Apol.	Tertullian, *Apology*
As. Mos.	Assumption of Moses/Testament of Moses
ASV	American Standard Version
AWE	*Ancient West and East*
B.J.	Josephus, *War of the Jews*

BC	Before Christ (equivalent to BCE)
BCE	Before Common Era
BDAG	Walter Bauer, Frederick W. Danker, W. F. Arndt, and F. W. Gingrich. *Greek-English Lexicon of the New Testament and Other Early Christian Literature*. 3rd ed. Chicago, IL: University of Chicago Press, 2000.
BEGP	*Brill's Encyclopedia of Global Pentecostalism*. Edited by Michael Wilkinson, Connie Au et al. Leiden: Brill, 2021.
BST	Bible Speaks Today
BT	*Bible Translator*
CE	Common Era
Cels.	Origen, *Against Celsus*
CHum	*Computers and the Humanities*
Claud.	Suetonius, *Life of Claudius*
Comput. y Sist.	*Computación y Sistemas*
Conj. praec.	Plutarch, *Advice to the Bride and Groom*
CurBR	*Currents in Biblical Research*
ECF	*Early Christian Fathers*. Edited by Henry Bettenson. London: Oxford University Press, 1969.
Ep.	Pliny the Younger, *Letters*
ESV	English Standard Version
ET	English Translation
ExpTim	*Expository Times*
Haer.	Irenaeus, *Against Heresies*; Hippolytus, *Refutation of All Heresies*
Hist. eccl.	Eusebius, *History of the Church*
Ign. *Magn.*	Ignatius, *Letter to the Magnesians*
Ign. *Trall.*	Ignatius, *Letter to the Trallians*
J. Pentecostal Theol.	*Journal of Pentecostal Theology*

JBL	*Journal of Biblical Literature*
JRS	*Journal of Roman Studies*
JSNT	*Journal for the Study of the New Testament*
JSP	*Journal for the Study of the Pseudepigrapha*
KJV	King James Version
Latomus	*Latomus: Revue d'Etudes Latines*
LCL	Loeb Classical Library
Legat.	Philo, *On the Embassy to Gaius*
LSJ	Henry George Liddell, Robert Scott, Henry Stuart Jones et al. *A Greek–English Lexicon with Revised Supplement*. 9th ed. Oxford: OUP, 1996.
Lutheran Theol. J.	*Lutheran Theological Journal*
LXX	Septuagint
Marc.	Tertullian, *Against Marcion*
Med.	Aulas Cornelius Celsus, *On Medicine*
MM	James Hope Moulton and George Milligan. *The Vocabulary of the Greek Testament: Illustrated from the Papyri and Other Non-literary Sources*. Peabody, MA: Hendrickson, 2004.
MS	Manuscript
MS(S)	Manuscript(s)
MSS	Manuscripts
MT	Massoretic Text
NA28	*Novum testamentum graece*, 28. revidierte Auflage. Edited by Barbara Aland et al. Münster: Deutsche Bibelgesellschaft, 2012.
NCB	New Clarendon Bible New Testament
NDCT	*New Dictionary of Christian Theology*. Edited by Alan Richardson and John Bowden. London: SCM, 1983.
NEB	New English Bible
Neot	*Neotestamentica*

NIBC	New International Bible Commentary
NICNT	New International Commentary on the New Testament
NICOT	New International Commentary on the Old Testament
NIDPCM	*New International Dictionary of Pentecostal and Charismatic Movements.* Revd. ed. Edited by Stanley M. Burgess and Ed M. Van der Maas. Grand Rapids, MI: Zondervan, 2002.
NIGTC	New International Greek Testament Commentary
NIV	New International Version
NPNF	*Nicene and Post-Nicene Fathers,* 1st and 2nd Series. 28 vols. Edited by Philip Schaff and Henry Wace. Peabody, MA: Hendrickson, 1994–1995.
NRSV	New Revised Standard Version
NT	New Testament
NTS	*New Testament Studies*
Opif.	Philo, *On the Creation*
OT	Old Testament/Hebrew Bible
OTP	*Old Testament Pseudepigrapha.* 2 vols. Edited by James H. Charlesworth. NY: Doubleday, 1983.
Pneuma	*Pneuma: Journal of the Society for Pentecostal Studies*
PNTC	Pillar New Testament Commentary
Pol. *Phil.*	Polycarp, *Letter to the Philippians*
Popul Stud (Camb)	*Population Studies*
Priscilla Pap.	*Priscilla Papers*
RB	*Revue Biblique*
RSV	Revised Standard Version
SBLGNT	*Greek New Testament: SBL Edition.* Edited by Michael William Holmes. Atlanta, GA: SBL, 2010.
Sociol. Relig.	*Sociology of Religion*

Spec.	Philo, *Special Laws*
SRC	Socio-Rhetorical Commentary
Strom.	Clement of Alexandria, *Miscellanies*
Studies	*Studies: An Irish Quarterly Review*
TDNT	*Theological Dictionary of the New Testament*. 10 vols. Edited by Gerhard Kittel and Gerhard Friedrich. Grand Rapids, MI: Eerdmans, 1964.
THNTC	Two Horizons New Testament Commentary
TNTC	Tyndale New Testament Commentary
VC	*Vigiliae Christianae*
VE	*Vox Evangelica*
Vit.	Josephus, *Life*
WBC	Word Biblical Commentary

For early Jewish and Patristic texts listed above, we refer the reader to useful translations as follows: 1 Enoch, *OTP* 1:5–90; 2 Baruch, *OTP* 1:615–652; 4 Ezra, *OTP* 1:517–560; Assumption of Moses (Testament of Moses), *OTP* 1:919–934; 1 Clement, *ANF* 1:1–21; Ignatius, *Letter to the Magnesians*, *ANF* 1:59–65; *Letter to the Trallians*, *ANF* 1:66–72; Polycarp, *Letter to the Philippians*, *ANF* 1:33–36; Tertullian, *Apology*, *ANF* 3:17–60; *Against Marcion*, *ANF* 3:271–476, Justin, *Second Apology*, *ANF* 1:188–193; Origen, *Against Celsus*, *ANF* 4:395–669; Irenaeus, *Against Heresies*, *ANF* 1:315–567; Hippolytus, *Refutation of All Heresies*, *ANF* 5:9–153; Eusebius, *History of the Church*, *NPNF* 2.1:81–387; Clement of Alexandria, *Miscellanies*, *ANF* 2:299–568. Selected portions from some of these texts are also available in Bettenson's *ECF*. LCL editions for Josephus, Philo, Tacitus, Suetonius and Aulas Cornelius Celsus are listed in the bibliography under the ancient author's name, followed by the relevant translators.

INTRODUCTION

I. THE PASTORAL EPISTLES—WHAT THEY ARE AND WHY THEY MATTER

II. RECIPIENTS, CONTEXT, PURPOSE AND GENRE

III. POLITICAL, SOCIAL, CULTURAL AND RELIGIOUS SETTING

IV. QUESTIONS SURROUNDING DATE AND AUTHORSHIP

V. A PENTECOSTAL AND CHARISMATIC CHURCH

I. THE PASTORAL EPISTLES—WHAT THEY ARE AND WHY THEY MATTER

The Pastoral Epistles (abbreviated, "PE" or "the Pastorals") form part of the Pauline corpus and comprise 1 & 2 Timothy and Titus. The term "Pastoral Epistles" has been used since the eighteenth century and indicates simply that the letters are addressed to individuals rather than entire congregations and that, at the time, Timothy and Titus were involved in church work of one sort or another. As with other letters of Paul, details in the letters are not always easy to relate to the narrative of Acts but are compatible in general terms.[1] Because the letters are short and show strong stylistic and thematic similarities, it is common for studies to address them together.

This sense of a distinct grouping is borne out in the manuscript evidence for the PE, which do not feature amongst the earliest papyrus fragments of the NT, and also do not feature in the earliest known list of Paul's epistles.[2] When they do appear, (in the Muratorian Canon[3]), they are precisely noted as a separate group, written to individuals rather than churches.[4] Trobisch sees their addition as the third and final phase in the development of Pauline letter collections, included some time in the second century[5] and known to the church fathers from ca. AD 180 onwards.[6] That personal letters of this kind had a somewhat different preservation history compared to the "public" church letters is not surprising, and reminds us

---

1. There is room for activities either during gaps in the Acts narrative or after it if Paul is released from his Roman house arrest (on this see further below). Note the difference between house arrest (Acts 28:16, 23) and actual imprisonment (2 Tim 1:16).

2. Cf. Parker, *Introduction to the New Testament Manuscripts*, 246–82.

3. This is a fragment of writings, discovered in about AD 1740 by Ludovico Muratori, that contains a list of all the works that were accepted as canonical. The list was probably written in Greek in about AD 180.

4. Parker, *Introduction to the New Testament Manuscripts*, 252.

5. Trobisch, *Paul's Letter Collection*, 50.

6. I.e., about the same sort of time that they become aware of our four canonical Gospels. Cf. Hutson, *First and Second Timothy and Titus*, 9–10.

that it may be misleading to compare them too simply with other texts from the Pauline corpus.[7]

This commentary on the Pastoral Epistles is unusual in giving special attention to the typical interests and questions of Pentecostal and charismatic readers. But it does so with a strong sense of letting the letters speak for themselves. It seeks to make sense of what they say with reference to their own distinctive language, ideas and emphases, and their shared cultural, social, and literary context. If the church we see in the PE, and indeed Paul himself, seem a little unfamiliar, then we do not immediately seek to make the PE fit perfectly with other texts, but rather locate their distinct voice within the diversity and development seen across the NT as a whole (for fuller discussion see Excursus I).

Indeed, the Pastoral Epistles remain somewhat neglected amongst evangelicals and Pentecostals, eclipsed by the heavy-weight theology of Romans or the charismatic fervor of 1 Corinthians. These longer and more familiar Pauline epistles are the chief reason why the Pastorals feel "different." Compared to Romans, readers might notice a striking absence of longer themes and flowing theology. Compared to 1 Corinthians, with its focus on spiritual gifts, prophecy, and tongues, we see instead a developing sense of church organization and even ritual that sometimes feels like the informal, dynamic life of the earliest church is somehow degenerating into a form of institutionalism.[8] If that were not enough, others are disappointed by the way that the PE seem to pull back from a full role for women suggested by earlier epistles.[9]

While the exact reason for these differences and the more technical questions about authorship and date are dealt with further below, it is important not to react to these letters negatively simply because they are not *like* other epistles (or worse, that they feel less "dynamic"). In fact, in terms of the great questions facing us today about church planting, mission,

---

7. The Muratorian Canon contains distinct apologetic notes as to why letters to churches and to individuals might be considered canonical. Thus, in his letters to churches, Paul "follows the example of . . . John" (in Revelation), and though they write to churches, they nevertheless "speak to all." In a separate note, the text adds "He also wrote one letter to Philemon, one to Titus and two to Timothy out of fondness and love. They are sanctified with honor by the Catholic Church in the ordination of ecclesiastical discipline."

8. The term "routinization of charisma," which goes back to 1946 with Weber's, "Meaning of Discipline," 253–64 (cf. his "Social Psychology"), was first brought to the attention of New Testament Scholars in 1967 by Berger and Luckmann's *Social Construction of Reality* and later applied to the Pastoral Epistles by MacDonald, in *The Pauline Churches*.

9. E.g., the programmatic "no male and female" of Gal 3:28 and the equally distributed spiritual gifts of 1 Corinthians.

leadership and "next generation" church, these epistles could count as amongst the most significant and exciting of the New Testament. And ironically, of course, they are the place where we are reminded that *all* Scripture is inspired by God (2 Tim 3:16). Some really positive reasons to take note of the Pastorals are the following.

First, the epistles tell us about some of the important "second phase" activities that were needed in early mission work. At the time of writing, Timothy and Titus are helping in churches founded earlier by one or more of Paul's mission teams. Titus faces a network of home groups that have no formal governance yet and needs to "finish the job" by appointing elders (Titus 1:5). Timothy has been sent to a church that probably has elders, but which needs additional oversight to help combat false teaching (1 Tim 1:3). That neither Timothy nor Titus was a local Christian but had been sent to stabilize and consolidate communities that were not quite ready to "go it alone," reveals something extremely interesting about early mission, namely that the process of church planting was not as fast or as perfect as we imagine. In the quest to ensure viable long-term congregational life, securing a proper continuity of ministry, establishing clear procedures and good traditions become surprisingly important. It is no coincidence that in our own day, hot topics in second generation Pentecostal and Charismatic contexts include sustainability and succession.

Secondly, the epistles help us to realize how the early church organized its ministry in practical terms. Thus, although 1 Corinthians and Ephesians enumerate several broad ministry roles such as apostle, prophet, teacher etc.,[10] these are not linked to formal positions such as overseer, elder and deacon, which are mentioned in passing elsewhere in the Pauline corpus and the NT more widely[11] but which feature prominently in the PE. Al-

---

10. While Rom 12:4–8 and 1 Cor 12:7–11 speak of a number of general gifts and activities, 1 Cor 12:27–31 speaks of apostles, prophets, teachers, workers of miracles, those with gifts of healing, assistance, leadership and tongue-speaking. This list appears in a different form in Eph 4:11, where we hear of *apostles, prophets, evangelists, pastors, and teachers*. This five-fold pattern has been adopted as a standard or ideal model for ministry roles in many churches, although it is not clear any of these should be understood as "offices."

11. Overseers and deacons are mentioned in Phil 1:1 with Phoebe designated a deacon in Rom 16:1 but are otherwise absent. Outside of the Pauline corpus, overseer and deacon are unknown, but "elder" is visible. Luke speaks of "apostles and elders" at Jerusalem (e.g., Acts 16:4; 21:18) and significantly believes that it was Paul's idea to use this word for the leaders of the new mission churches (Acts 14:23; cf. 20:17). And this is not surprising since synagogues were run by elders which suggests Paul simply adapted the Jewish model of organization. Beyond Acts, the word is used in Jas 5:14; 1 Pet 5:1, 5 and possibly in the opening lines of 2 and 3 John. For

though this probably implies that ministry structures and terminology were still in a state of flux, the hints we get prove fascinating and do not seem to be "late developments" or retrograde provisions. In Pentecostal churches, where pastors have all too often emerged out of a split over "vision," many are longing to recover some sense of *governance* and *accountability* but are not sure how this should happen. The PE at least give some glimpse of how this might be realized.

Thirdly, and closely related to the above, is the issue of how one even enters a ministry. If 1 Corinthians were our sole guide, we might imagine this happened by a self-evident spiritual gift or anointing. It perhaps comes as a surprise therefore when in the PE, Paul speaks of "aspiring" to a ministry role (1 Tim 3:1), of the "testing" of candidates (1 Tim 3:10), and a fact often missed, that ministry always occurred in teams (cf. 1 Tim 4:14[12]). The PE certainly know about gifts, prophecy, and discerning spirits (1 Tim 4:1, 14), yet procedures and structures clearly appear alongside them. Equally disarming, of course, is the idea of a disciplinary process (run by the congregation?) that could, we assume, lead to the *removal* of an elder (1 Tim 5:19), contrary to the oft-cited Ps 105:15.

Another eye-catching emphasis in the PE is the theme of holiness (in the PE, godliness or *eusebeia* in Greek[13]). Whilst imagined in some Pentecostal contexts to be the more or less inevitable consequence of receiving the Spirit, the emphasis in the PE lies on training, formation, safeguarding and accountability. Again, as our movement and other churches too reel from scandals of a sexual, financial, power-based, or pastoral nature, the question of how to form and maintain Christian character (for ourselves *and our pastors*) is to the fore. The PE are suddenly starting to sound like texts for our time. While a clear experience of the Spirit is still central (Titus 3:5–6), we all need the Spirit's help not to end up losing the "treasure" of the Gospel through sheer lack of vigilance (2 Tim 1:12–14). The Spirit, formation and careful oversight are not enemies.

---

further background on the use of this term, see Campbell, *The Elders*.

12. Cf. 1 Tim 5:17; Titus 1:5 and the similar assumption of plurality in Acts 14:23; Jas 5:14, and 1 Pet 5:1.

13. This is a classic example of a theological term that is common in the PE but absent elsewhere in Paul, even though it clearly corresponds to something Paul "believed in." It does appear elsewhere in the NT, but not frequently, e.g., Acts 3:12 and 2 Pet 1:7, but becomes particularly common in second century Hellenistic moral exhortation by Stoics and others (cf. Foerster, "σέβομαι etc.," 175–85). It is observations like this that call forth some sort of explanation of the context in which and the exact way these letters came to be written.

When these thematic differences are combined with differences in style and vocabulary, to say nothing of details which are not easy to correlate with Acts, it is perhaps not surprising that some scholars have felt that these works really originate after Paul's death in the very different atmosphere of the second century. Indeed, many do not imagine the real "Paul" would have entirely recognized the change of emphasis (cf. 1 Cor 2:2–5, "I resolved to know nothing except Jesus Christ, and him crucified"). For more on these challenging suggestions, see "Questions about date and authorship" below.

However, the view taken by this commentary is that the special character and concerns of these texts are already present in some measure for other NT writers and that they can be explained by (a) a clear second-generation, future-facing orientation, (b) one or more amanuenses or assistants, and (c) a decision to use new, more specifically Hellenistic religious language. This is explained in part by the background of Timothy and Titus themselves, but also by the new, younger and educated believers that will find themselves the future of the church after Paul has gone.[14]

As for the historical difficulties mentioned above, it was quickly recognized by the early church that the letters imply that Paul must have been released from his house arrest in Rome and able to resume his travels—as found in 1 Timothy and Titus[15] but that three of four years later, he was arrested again and eventually martyred in AD 67 or 68. This would have given time for the promised mission to Spain (cf. Rom 15:23–24) as well as the further work in Crete and Macedonia that the Pastorals themselves imply.[16]

---

14. The term *neōterikos* in 2 Tim 2:22 ("youthful") would normally mean young adult, but in terms of public and professional life in the Graeco-Roman world, might imply anyone up to their early to mid-thirties. In terms of Paul's address to this next generation, 2 Tim 4:6–8 implies that Paul realizes his time is short and explain some of his concern with the future sustainability of the church (2 Tim 2:2 "what you have heard from me . . . entrust to faithful people").

15. Eusebius, *Hist. eccl.* 2:22.

16. 1 Clem. 5:7. Clement writing from Rome only about 30 years after Paul's death speaks of the apostle as reaching "to the limit of the west," an expression applicable to Spain. See also Eusebius, *Hist. eccl.* 2:22, "there is evidence that, having been brought to trial, the apostle again set out on the ministry of preaching, and having appeared a second time in the same city found fulfilment in his martyrdom. In the course of his imprisonment, he composed the second Epistle to Timothy . . ." Regarding the journey east N. T. Wright in *Paul: A Biography*, loc 4012 admits "as with Paul's putative trip to Spain, I have become more open to the possibility of a return visit to the East after an initial hearing in Rome."

II. RECIPIENTS, CONTEXT, PURPOSE AND GENRE

a. Timothy and Titus as faithful co-workers

Besides their other content, the Pastoral Epistles are important for the way they remind us about the team-work behind the early Christian missions, and for what they reveal about Paul's relationships with his numerous co-workers who, besides Timothy and Titus, included Priscilla and Aquila, Urbanus, Epaphroditus, Philemon, Markus, Aristarchus, Demas, Luke, and others.[17] At a time when team-building and mentoring have assumed an important role once again in church leadership discussions, that we have letters written to such co-workers becomes doubly important.

Of these various colleagues, Timothy is attested in Pauline and other NT texts perhaps more than any other individual, including special notes of appreciation in Phil 2:20–22 and 1 Cor 4:17. After his initial apprenticeship on the Macedonian mission, he helps Paul plant the churches at Corinth and Ephesus. More remarkable from the perspective of traditional independent church practice, is the fact that Timothy is also put into a series of emergency pastoral roles back in those same churches after they had notionally achieved autonomy,[18] a function he also performed in Corinth.[19] In

---

17. Priscilla and Aquila (Rom 16:3), Urbanus (Rom 16:9), Epaphroditus (Phil 2:25), Philemon (Phlm 1:1), Markus, Aristarchus, Demas, Lukas (Phlm 1:24), plus un-named others (Phil 4:3). This does not include a larger number of relatives, friends and acquaintances who helped more occasionally, such as many in the list in Rom 16. For an excellent review, see Strelan, "Paul's Work and his Co-Workers."

18. I.e., even though they technically had their own elders by this time. In 1 Thess 3:1–2 he is apparently sent back to help the Thessalonians; in Acts 19:22 he forms part of the advance party for a planned follow-up visit by Paul to Philippi; in 1 Cor 4:17, he is sent back to the Corinthian church, now more as an official apostolic representative ("to remind you of my ways in Christ Jesus"), although again, possibly as part of an advance party prior to an apostolic visit (vv. 18–21); in Phil 2:19–24 we learn of another visit to Philippi (possibly but not necessarily the same as Acts 19:22), and in 1 Tim 1:3, we hear of an emergency pastoral placement back in Ephesus which appears to come with full apostolic authority to silence false teachers, implicitly, at least, in conjunction with the temporary suspension of the body of elders mentioned in 1 Tim 4:13–14. Note that none of these visits is clearly mentioned in Acts, nor indeed is this sort of activity discussed by Luke. For an important recent study on the contours of power in the Pauline churches, see Holmberg, *Paul and Power*, and on the use of delegates, see especially page 80.

19. In the case of Corinth, Timothy performed this function twice, in 2 Cor 7:6–7 (implicit) and 2 Cor 8:17 (a declared intention).

addition, Timothy helps Paul in writing to these and other churches, ending up as the co-author of six of the Pauline epistles.[20]

Timothy was born in Lystra in central southern Turkey, living according to one estimate from about AD 34 to 97.[21] His father was Greek and his mother Jewish, but he was not circumcised, presumably because of his father's objections, which implies that his upbringing was not confined to the synagogue although both his mother and his grandmother made sure he knew the Scriptures, presumably in the Septuagint version but perhaps also in Hebrew.[22] He was literate in an age when fewer than 20 percent of adult men had this capability, spoke and wrote Greek, possibly Latin and was presumably free-born.[23] His mother and grandmother were Christians although we do not know the circumstances of their conversion, nor whether, as a teenager, Timothy's own commitment was taken to a new level as a result of Paul and Barnabas' visit to the area in Acts 14:6–12. That Paul would later describe him as his "true-born child in the faith" (1 Tim 1:2) would make this possible, although just one year later, he is described as an established disciple, well-spoken of by other Christians in his native Lystra and neighboring Iconium, some 18 miles away and thus implying some reasonable pre-history.

The episode in Acts 16:3 where Paul is said by Luke to have circumcised Timothy remains massively controversial for traditional Pauline scholars because of its apparent clash with Galatians 5:2–4 and similar texts, although this action is not mentioned in the Pastoral Epistles as such. Indeed, the entire Jew-gentile problem that occupies so much of the earlier epistles seems to be missing, although tensions with non-Christian Jews receive brief mention in Titus. Interestingly, Paul himself specifically notes that he did not circumcise Titus in similar circumstances (Gal 2:3). The explanation here probably lies in Timothy's mixed heritage and the fact that he may have felt he had a true choice about his identity after, we presume, *paternal* objections were no longer relevant.[24]

---

20. 1 & 2 Thessalonians, 2 Corinthians, Philippians, Colossians, and Philemon. On the role of helpers in writing and passing on early Christian teaching, Loubser, "Media Criticism and the Myth of Paul."

21. Pierson, *Steps of Timothy*, 14.

22. Cf. 2 Tim 3:15, where Paul notes how Timothy had "known the sacred writings . . . from childhood." As a gentile (at least from a technical point of view), Timothy may have been able to attend a synagogue as a "Godfearing" associate member, common in this period and referred to frequently in the NT.

23. Beard, *SPQR*, 470. It makes no sense for Paul to include Timothy as a co-author unless he was literate in Greek.

24. Paul's rule normally appears to have been that Jews becoming Christians retain this identity, and that those coming to faith as gentiles, equally remain gentiles (1 Cor

Paul and Silas certainly felt he was able to join them on their second missionary journey (Acts 16:1–3) and thereafter Timothy remained a close and trusted companion to Paul who, as noted above, besides using him in his church planting teams, also sent him on difficult assignments to recalcitrant or troubled churches. As someone who knew Paul intimately, and could be sent in Paul's absence to reinforce his example and teaching (1 Cor 4:17), Timothy has sometimes been called an "apostolic delegate." When they are together, he preaches alongside Paul (2 Cor 1:19) and later acts as the co-author of 1 and 2 Thessalonians, Philippians, Colossians, Philemon, and 2 Corinthians. No wonder Paul would later say "I have no one like him who will show genuine concern for your welfare" (Phil 2:20; 1 Cor 4:17). Such words speak of his dedication and selflessness.[25]

That Timothy was young, sensitive, and timid is often presumed but can be questioned.[26] He was certainly reminded not to be fearful (2 Tim 1:7), and Paul's instruction to the Corinthians that Timothy be treated respectfully (1 Cor 16:10) as well as the medical advice to take a little wine for his stomach's sake (1 Tim 5:23) have suggested both physical weakness and lack of confidence. On the other hand, he was sent on difficult assignments like the one to Corinth when the church was in danger of turning its back on Paul and to Thessalonica when the apostolic team had left after being arrested and beaten following a run-in with the local magistrates. Courage and cowardice are matters of degree and the threats to any Christians proclaiming the Gospel in early classical culture within range of a hostile synagogue would be enough to deter any but the most determined. Timothy would have been aware that Paul himself had been stoned and left for dead since the attack that occurred in Lystra (Acts 15:19). To join Paul's staff, was to associate with danger.

Less is known about Titus, although he became involved in Christian mission at a similar time, and in similar ways to Timothy. He was part of

---

7:18). The story in Acts 21:17–26, although not mentioned in the epistles, is presented as an enacted denial by Paul of a malicious rumor that he forbade Jewish Christians to pass their identity on to their children. If Timothy's situation were understood in that manner, then a properly Jewish identity might be open to him in a way that it was not for Titus. The later "matrilineal" principle of Jewish descent had not clearly emerged in the NT period, so the situation is still in flux at best. For a recent review of the possible lines of development that may explain Acts 16, cf. Gabizon, "Matrilineal Principle."

25. He seems not to be married in the NT stories known to us, although this is nowhere commended as an example to follow, particularly as Paul later condemns those who enjoin singleness as a Christian norm in 1 Tim 4:3.

26. Youthfulness is suggested by the command to flee "youthful lusts" (2 Tim 2:22). Fee, *1 and 2 Timothy, Titus*, 2, is less taken with the traditional portrait and thinks of Timothy as being over 30 years old by the time of the first epistle.

the same team in Macedonia (2 Cor 7:6) and may later have been sent to work in Dalmatia (2 Tim 4:10). Perhaps most important is his status as a true gentile convert with a Greek cultural background and a Latin name. He had possibly come to faith in Antioch, as he was chosen by Paul and Barnabas to accompany them to Jerusalem to set out their approach to gentile Christianity (Gal 2:1).[27] Although this was still a matter of controversy, Paul was clear that since Titus had no Jewish heritage at all, he should neither be compelled nor even encouraged to be circumcised, a judgement endorsed by the later council.[28]

Unlike Timothy, Titus did not become the co-author of any of the Pauline epistles, but he is described by Paul as a "partner and co-worker" (2 Cor 8:23) and indeed, like Timothy, is called a "true son" (Titus 1:4). His integrity is recognized on all sides as he is chosen to organize the financial collection in Corinth and take it to Jerusalem (2 Cor 8:6, 16). He is probably also the carrier of Paul's "severe letter" (2 Cor 2.13 and 7.6) and thus involved in improving relations with the Corinthians. In this sense, he operates at an equivalent level of trust and in comparable ways to Timothy, with church tradition similarly believing him to have ended his days as a "bishop"—this time on Crete.[29]

b. Context, purpose and genre of the letters

1 TIMOTHY

As noted above, one of Timothy's later assignments was to fulfil an emergency pastoral role back at the church in Ephesus. Timothy had probably been on the original church planting team (implied by Acts 19:22), but he did not come from the area, nor did he act as a regular elder there after its foundation. This reveals something very interesting about the church planting concept in this early period insofar as churches started up through

---

27. Bruce, *Circle*, 58.

28. Bruce, *Circle*, takes "compelled" here at face value (p. 60), especially given the heated advocacy of this position reported in Acts 15. Much of Paul's argument in Galatians defends this point that gentiles do not have to become Jews in order to be saved but can come to Christ directly. It is not clear how the five visits to Jerusalem reported in Acts (9:26–30; 11:27–30; 15:1–30; 18:22; 21:15–17), align with three such trips mentioned in the epistles (Gal 1:18–20; 2:1–10; Rom 15:25–33; 1 Cor 16:1–4). Bruce has championed the view that the trip with Titus in Gal 2:1 is the visit of Acts 11:27–30, preceding the formal council of Acts 15.

29. Eusebius, *Hist. eccl.* 3:4 6. When one of the authors visited Crete in 2018, he was confidently told Titus has been their bishop.

sometimes all too short initial visits did not become viable overnight. Even after being constituted with their own leadership (as per Acts 14:23), they nevertheless remained under apostolic oversight for some time, and if they got into particular difficulty, might be sent special help.[30] We learn about such assignments and secondments mainly from the Epistles, although in general terms, such activities can be inferred from Acts.[31]

Although poor or confusing instruction on the part of some of the teachers and the possible appearance of dangerous ideas are certainly mentioned (1 Tim 1:3–7; 4:1–7a), much of the letter comprises a compendium of otherwise positive instruction about running a church. This suggests that a completely heretical turn is not in view, although some stabilization, pastoral instruction and succession planning is certainly required.[32]

Thus, although not a complete crisis, there is a sense of Ephesus needing some sustained input. By the time Paul writes, Timothy has already been in Ephesus for some time and is asked to remain longer. Paul, whose own location is not stated, intends to come soon, but knows a delay might be possible (1 Tim 3:14–15).

In terms of literary form, it is widely agreed that 1 Timothy, while in one sense a real letter, straddles the genres of church order and moral instruction (*paraenesis*) and is not dissimilar to letters sent by Hellenistic rulers to their cities.[33] The sense in which this represents a distinct and intentional combination, which together with the use of Greek moral-ethical terminology, creates the impression of something more sustained and developed than the practical sections of the earlier epistles.[34] The format is seen increasingly in the decades that follow the NT.[35]

---

30. While Paul apparently took pains to construe his apostolic ministry in collegial, even parental terms (2 Cor 1:24 and 1 Thess 2:7), there is evidence that underlying this was a real sense of authority hinted at in 1 Cor 4:18–21, and cf. the note in Acts 16:4.

31. In Acts 18:5, Timothy and Silas are left behind in Macedonia while Paul moves on to Corinth and catch up with him later. In Acts 19:22, while Paul is in Ephesus, he sends Timothy and Erastus ahead to Macedonia in anticipation of his forthcoming visit. See the excellent discussion in Johnson, *Timothy*, 135–136.

32. Cf. Hutson, *Timothy and Titus*, 13–14.

33. Cf. Hutson, *Timothy and Titus*, 6–8, Johnson, *Commentary*, 138–40. On moral instruction in letters, cf. Malherbe (ed.), *Moral Exhortation*, 79–84.

34. Cf. 1 Thess 4:1–12; 5:1–19; Gal 5:16–6:10; Rom 12:1–15:13; Phil 3:2–4:20; Col 3:1–4:6; Eph 4:1–6:20, etc. The so called "household codes", visible in Ephesians and Colossians, are also modelled on a popular format of Greek moral instruction, cf. Balch, "Household Codes," 318–20, but are contained within letters of an otherwise different character and would not in terms of what we find in the PE, count as so developed.

35. The similarities to Polycarp's epistle to the Philippians have been frequently

2 Timothy

The most marked contextual change in 2 Timothy is the news that Paul has now been imprisoned. If this had occurred only once, then this would place the letter with Philippians, Colossians, Ephesians, and Philemon as a "prison" epistle, although as noted, the difficulty in understanding the movements presupposed in 1 Timothy led some church fathers to infer a release after the events of Acts 28 followed by a second arrest, possibly at Troas and then imprisonment once more in Rome. The sense of resignation in 2 Tim 4:6 ("the time of my departure has come") certainly seems different from the more open, even optimistic tone of Phil 1:19–26, where he speaks of being reunited with his supporters.

At the practical level, in the second letter, Paul asks Timothy to come to support him in Rome (2 Tim 4:9) and promises to send Tychicus to Ephesus, presumably as cover. Whether Timothy managed this we do not know but, if he did, there is evidence he returned to Ephesus and remained there for the rest of his ministry.[36] The letter also changes focus somewhat from church practicalities and concentrates on the personal relationship between the two men (cf. the tone of 2 Tim 1:3–7) and what Paul may have believed would be his last opportunity to encourage and solemnly hold Timothy to a task he will now face alone (2 Tim 4:1–5).

In this sense, as regards genre, although points of church order are discussed, and the moral vision being set before Timothy remains strong, this letter no longer has the open tone of moral instruction for its own sake, but begins to read like a "testament," a particularly popular format amongst Greek-speaking Jews, and visible as a subtext in 2 Peter.[37]

Titus

The letter to Titus concerns mission work not reported in Acts at all; Paul and his team have managed to evangelize and start informal Christian groups on the island of Crete. In Acts, Paul calls into a harbor on Crete only

---

discussed, cf. Hutson, *Timothy and Titus*, 10–11.

36. The fourth century historian Eusebius, *Hist. eccl.* 3:4., tells us that Timothy became the first "bishop of Ephesus" and continued there for many years. The fifth century apocryphal *Acts of Timothy* claims Timothy was martyred in Ephesus at around the age of 80 under the emperor Nerva.

37. 2 Pet 1:13–15 ". . . to refresh your memory, since I know that my death will come soon." On Testaments as an increasingly popular format in Second Temple Judaism, see Collins, "Testaments," 325–55.

after his arrest and only in passing, during his journey to Rome (27:7–12). The situation described in the letter to Titus would certainly have needed some time to develop and might be best understood within the "release-and-further-work" scenario. In a pattern we have seen before, Paul has apparently had to move on and has left Titus in Crete to appoint elders for the new communities (Titus 1:5). Besides displaying important links to 1 Timothy via the discussions about the qualities and duties of elders and overseers, the situation provides a very important conceptual link to Acts, where the idea of appointing such officers and calling them "elders" is reported as Pauline practice (Acts 14:23).[38] This implies an earlier phase in the church planting process, compared to the more developed situation at Ephesus into which Timothy was sent. The request to "put in order what remains to be done" is particularly telling as it implies not only a work left temporarily in hiatus by Paul's departure, but also that establishing a clear structure of this kind was the normal goal of such work.[39]

As in 1 Timothy, unhealthy or misleading teaching clearly represented a threat to be wary of, but again, no impression is given of an imminent threat from leadership "claimants" or an identifiable heresy requiring urgent intervention. What is clear, however, is that the as yet porous boundaries of the communities and the lack of oversight means that self-appointed or freelance teachers known to church members and operating around and amongst them have an influence that is difficult to control (Titus 1:10–16; 3:9). This is not utterly unlike the situation described in 2 & 3 John.[40] What is different on Crete compared to Ephesus, is that several of these teachers appear to have a Jewish background (Titus 1:10b, 14, and implicitly, 3:9). While this can scarcely be problematic as such (since true of all the apostles and many others), there is something wrong with the *type* of teaching involved, and it is said to be having an undesirable and divisive influence on church families.

---

38. Cf. the later situation in Ephesus where established elders are in place by Acts 20:17. It is possible Paul took the term from its generic use in Judaism (cf. Acts 5:1), apparently used by the church in Jerusalem to signal a leadership group working alongside the apostles (Acts 15:2, 4, 6, 22, 23; 16:4).

39. Even if (as per Timothy's placements), this did not mean no further help would be required at all.

40. Cf. 2 John 7–11, leading, we presume to the full-blown problem of authority related in 3 John 9–10.

III. POLITICAL, SOCIAL, CULTURAL AND RELIGIOUS SETTING

While there are many excellent introductions to the Graeco-Roman context of the early Christian missions,[41] this background will be unfamiliar to many. Here we note aspects of particular relevance to the Pastoral Epistles, in each section drawing out points of commonality and tension, of belonging and difference.

a. Political and cultural context

In many ways, the Pastoral Epistles share the same general setting as we would need to make sense of Acts and the other epistles, namely the early Roman Empire. With Jesus living during the time of Augustus (31 BC–AD 14) and Tiberius (AD 14–37), the earliest gentile missions starting in the time of Claudius (AD 41–54) and continuing under Nero (AD 54–68), Vespasian (AD 69–79), Titus (AD 79–81) and Domitian (AD 81–96), the Roman Empire forms a continuous backdrop for early Christian experience and literature.[42] The towns and communities we meet in the PE lie in the eastern part of the empire which, before the NT period, had existed as a loose network of Greek or "Hellenistic" kingdoms following the campaigns of Alexander the Great (356–323 BC). These regions were later brought under Roman political rule[43] and divided into smaller areas run either directly by Roman governors or local elites (e.g., the Herods) as client "kingdoms."[44]

The eastern provinces were all added by military conquest and all of the emperors of the NT period had served as generals. Roman soldiers would not have been a common sight in most towns, but were maintained in huge concentrations at a few strategic and frontier locations with a much smaller

---

41. Jeffers, *Greco-Roman World*; Ferguson, *Backgrounds*, esp. chs. 1–4; Klauck, *Religious Context*; Johnson, *Among the Gentiles*.

42. At the point when the church began, Rome was perhaps at the height of its power: it certainly had another four hundred years to run before its collapse. Rome was the immoveable superpower of its day and a reality the Western church had to deal with.

43. The exact causes of Roman expansion into territories beyond Italy and the advent of empire are still debated, but there is no doubt that it could be achieved only through a huge professional army, imposed tribute on conquered peoples, and slavery. See Erskine, *Roman Imperialism* and the excellent overview oriented towards students of biblical studies in Goodman, *The Roman World*.

44. On the use of these local elites in Judaea, cf. Goodman, *The Ruling Class of Judaea*, 29–50.

presence within the provinces to ensure regional stability.[45] However, it was soldiers attached to such units that could be drawn to local synagogues and churches and membership of these was not "illegal."[46] Although most Jews and Christians could not easily serve in the Roman military themselves,[47] soldiering as such was generally admired[48] with Paul telling Timothy to act as "good soldier of Christ Jesus" and not to get "entangled in civilian affairs" (2 Tim 2:1–4).

Unlike the Greeks who preceded them, the Roman expansion was not conceived of in such strongly cultural terms and did not lead to a change of language. This meant that Greek continued to operate as the language of trade, education and administration in the Eastern Empire, and thus became the language of the New Testament. Indeed, senior Roman officials such as Pilate, brought across from the West, would be expected to be able to speak Greek as well as Latin.[49] It was relatively common, therefore, for the inhabitants of the new provinces to know elements of at least three languages, their own regional tongue, Greek, and a smattering of Latin needed for written notices posted in garrison towns and centers of Roman provincial rule.[50]

In the empire, everyone belonged within a hierarchy that in Roman tradition ran from the imperial household, through the old aristocratic or *patrician* families dominating the senate, lower ranks of *equites,* often military veterans, down to the plebs or "ordinary" people.[51] As noted above, this Roman system was draped over the top of other sources of identity

45. Indeed, it was the threat of overwhelming force more than its actual use that kept subject nations in order. See the excellent article by Zeichmann, "Military Forces in Judaea 6–130 CE." At the more local level, however, there were no reservations about the public execution of criminals and rebels when necessary.

46. Cf. Luke 3:14; 7:1–10 and Acts 10:1–48.

47. Exceptions to this caution famously included Philo's nephew, Tiberius Julius Alexander, cf. Barclay, *Jews in the Mediterranean Diaspora,* 105–6.

48. Cf. the positive exchange between Jesus and the centurion in Luke 7:8–9 "I also am a man under authority . . ."

49. Suetonius reports the emperor's own energies in learning Greek, referring in one conversation to "our two languages" (*Claud.* 42).

50. In fact, bi- and sometimes trilingual notices were quite common. That John 19:20 notes that the sign affixed by Pilate to Jesus' cross was worded in Hebrew, Latin and Greek reflects this context perfectly. On other local languages noted in passing in the NT, cf. Acts 14:11, and for an instance where Paul switches languages, Acts 21:37–40.

51. Cf. Gill, "Acts and the Urban Elites," 106–8, cf. Holland, *Dynasty,* 261, "With great punctiliousness, the banks of seating in public venues had been divided up between various categories of Roman. Senators, naturally, had been awarded the best vantage points; women the worst."

and status, ranging from the cultural heritage of the Greek-speaking East[52] and/or citizenship of a Greek city state, membership of a leading family, or priesthood in a local cult.[53] It is significant that in order to help provincial inhabitants feel more "Roman," this period saw the increasing extension of citizenship, which could be conferred on a hereditary basis on individuals or entire communities by imperial edict.[54]

At the bottom of this hierarchy, and vital to the economy, labored a huge army of slaves, comprising up to 30 percent of the population. Either bred directly or pressed into service as captives of war,[55] slaves lay outside the norms of civil justice[56] until bought out or freed by their owners. Freedom at some point was not, however, unusual, particularly for those who had become literate or acquired useful skills.[57] Those so freed might remain within the household as servants or retainers, and in some cases as wives.[58] Although these "freedmen" sometimes assumed positions of responsibility, they were not automatically granted citizenship and constituted a distinct class that was still looked down upon by the free-born.[59] The PE and Pauline teaching generally sit within an early Christian approach that accepted slavery, but encouraged slaves to serve well, and masters to treat them

---

52. See the collection of essays in Goldhill, *Being Greek under Rome*.

53. Cf. Paul mentioning his citizenship of a Greek city in Acts 21:39a.

54. Cf. Lavan, "Foundation of Empire?," 21–54. Unlike Greek citizenship, which gave rights within particular cities only, Roman citizenship conferred rights across the empire as a whole.

55. Unlike eighteenth century American slavery, ancient slavery was multiracial because it covered any of the peoples conquered by Rome; cf. Madden, "Slavery in the Roman Empire," 109–28.

56. Slaves could legally be beaten (though not killed) by their owners.

57. For a comprehensive survey of manumission in the Greek tradition, cf. Zelnick-Abramovitz, *Not Wholly Free*.

58. Meeks, *Urban Christians*, 23 points out, "29% [of slave born women in one study] married their own patrons—one of the most common means for female slaves to gain freedom and upward and improved status."

59. In fact, former slaves *could* become citizens if manumitted by a citizen under Roman law; cf. Berthelot, and Price, *In the Crucible of Empire*, 3. However, for an example of the disdain with which a freedman might be held by a freeborn citizen, cf. Meeks on the Pliny the Younger's views of Pallas, a Claudian freedman in *Urban Christians*, 22.

properly,[60] a positive stance shared with Stoics, Jews, and others.[61] This was no doubt fueled in part by the presence of Christian masters and slaves in the same households. It may remain surprising to us that there is no immediate call for emancipation,[62] but Paul's insistence on the unity of slave and free *in Christ* and the use of "brother" for *both* clearly sows the seeds for change and modern egalitarian democracy.[63]

It is important to note that for much of this period, Christians were not known to the civic authorities as a separate religious group but were perceived as a part of Judaism.[64] Although negative stereotypes may have made this disadvantageous on occasions[65] this presumed identity generally worked well. Besides meriting a measure of respect for their *antiquity*,[66] Jews had adopted a relatively pro-Roman stance and had gained acceptance

---

60. Eph 6:5–9; Col 3:22–4:1; 1 Tim 6:1–2; Titus 2:9–10. Only Ephesians and Colossians add words to *masters*, (Eph 6:9; Col 4:1), although we should not read the omission in 1 Timothy and Titus as a specific retraction. On the "Slave" instructions in the Pauline "household codes," cf. Crouch, *Colossian Haustafel*, 117–9, 124–9.

61. Crouch, *Colossian Haustafel*, 117–9, and regarding Judaism, cf. Sir 4:30; 33:1; Philo *Spec.* 2:66–68, 89–91; 3:137–43.

62. Although very certainly calling for all masters to chart an intentional pathway to manumission, Jews and Christians would continue to own domestic slaves for several centuries to come, cf. Hezser, *Jewish Slavery* and De Wet, *Preaching Bondage*. In part, the evangelization of slaves prior to manumission was seen as a mission opportunity (Hezser, *Jewish Slavery*, 82–126).

63. Gal 3:28; Col 3:11, and for the term "brother," cf. Phlm 16. 1 Cor 7:21–24 encourages slaves to seek freedom (and by implication, masters to offer it), but also to feel that in Christ, this is already possessed. But this is not to accept slavery as a permanent reality. When in 1 Tim 1:10 Paul condemns *commercial* slave-trading, he may already be anticipating one of the first post-NT Christian "campaigns" on this issue, which by the fourth century, was also pressing families to reduce domestic ownership, with the goal of eradication. Cf. De Wet, *Bondage*, 83, 105–13. The first clear Christian call for emancipation is perhaps from Gregory of Nyssa, but this may draw upon earlier Jewish models; cf. Weisser, "Philo's Therapeutae." Regarding the influence of Christianity on modern human rights, see Holland, *Dominion*.

64. The Judgement of Gallio in Acts 18:14–17 and the letter Claudius Lysias in Acts 23:26–30 are typical in this regard (cf. Gill and Winter, "Acts and Roman Religion," 102). Although Tacitus (AD 56–120) implicitly claims in *Ann.* 15:4 that the name "Christian" was known in Rome at the time of Nero (AD 54–68), scholars increasingly suspect that awareness was only properly beginning towards the *end* of the first century, as suggested by Shaw, "Neronian Persecution."

65. Cf. Stern, *Greek and Latin Authors on Jews and Judaism*.

66. As underlined by Tertullian, "We [Christians] shelter ourselves only under the venerable pretext of this old religion" (*Apol.* 21).

in most localities.⁶⁷ Conditions for Jews did worsen after the failed revolt of AD 66–73, including via punitive taxation, and it is possible this contributed to the emergence of a separate "Christian" identity.⁶⁸ But in general, although there were inevitable clashes with local authorities, including the martyrdoms of Acts and a cluster in Asia Minor alluded to in the book of Revelation, it is wrong to think of continuous or widespread conflict with Rome throughout the NT period as a whole.⁶⁹ Thus, Luke and Paul take a relatively positive view of the Empire, even when the latter is imprisoned.⁷⁰

This means that the church in general, and particularly that of the Pastoral Epistles, was not, for the most part, an "underground" organization.⁷¹ Paul's congregations should be understood as *belonging* to the Graeco-Roman world, and he encourages them to contribute to society openly and positively, as implied by the requirement in 1 Tim 3:7 that overseers must be "well thought of by outsiders" and that the church as a whole in Titus 3:1 should be law abiding and "ready for every good work."⁷²

b. Domestic and community context

Besides the sense of belonging and tension experienced by Christians as citizens at the wider imperial and civic levels, it is particularly important that the two most vital local settings within which the Christian faith could be nurtured, the family and the church, were entirely recognizable and indeed valued structures within Graeco-Roman society. Christian families and households operated in very similar ways to those of their neighbors,

---

67. Cf. the important survey of Barclay, *Jews in the Mediterranean Diaspora*.

68. See Heemstra, *Fiscus Judaicus*.

69. Empire-wide persecutions first took place under Decius (AD 249–251), Valerian (AD 253–260) and Diocletian (AD 284–305).

70. The claim that Paul and indeed Silas were Roman citizens is known only from Acts 16:37 and is intriguingly never repeated in the Pauline Epistles. It is not, however, implausible amongst older, elite families from the eastern provinces, including Jews. Paul makes implicitly positive statements in Rom 13:1–7; Phil 1:12–14, even if his bold use of "Lord" in Phil 2:9–11 intends to show there is one greater than Caesar.

71. The sentiments of 1 Tim 2:1–4 "Pray for kings and all who are in authority, that we may lead a quiet and peaceable life" would be typical in this regard. The best tactic was to live peacefully within civic society, do good and keep on the right side of the law; cf. Chadwick, *The Early Church*, 55.

72. This feeling about the social context of the Pastoral Epistles led to German commentators coining the term *christliche Bürgerlichkeit* or Christian citizenship. For an excellent argument that aspects of this theme appear across Paul and other NT texts, cf. Winter, *Seek the Welfare of the City*.

and churches, too, took their place alongside the numerous social, charitable and religious associations present in every town.

The home was perhaps the most important shared structure, where all people, whether pagan, Jewish or Christian, lived, ate, slept, and often worked together, learning their identity and bonding with others. Living in more extended groups than we sometimes do, this would often include grandparents, other relatives, servants, and slaves, and thus be better understood as a *household*. The household was a fundamental organizational unit in society and had a legal status in regard to taxation and military conscription. For this reason, the father, the traditional head of the family, was publicly accountable for the running of the household, for the care of its members and the maintenance of order and piety.[73] If he became Christian, the entire household might reasonably have been expected to change religious affiliation,[74] but women and slaves converting on their own would find themselves in a delicate if not dangerous situation.[75] Safe all-Christian homes formed the basis of all the earliest churches whose gathering places were often just one of the larger properties within the network—in other words there were no stand-alone public church buildings in the early years of Christianity.[76]

Once the church connects more than one family, a broader structure is immediately brought into being, one that the surrounding society would immediately recognize. If the church held common funds and organized activities, then it would have been viewed as a kind of *voluntary association* (Gk. *thiasos*, Lat. *collegium*). Groups like this existed for a whole host of purposes, including trusts or charities, social clubs, trade guilds, professional colleges, social centers for immigrants from particular countries, and, of course, religious communities.[77] Indeed the word *synăgōgē* used by Jews and the earliest Christians,[78] and *ekklēsia*, rapidly adopted by the later

---

73. Meeks, *Urban Christians*, 23. "The hierarchical pattern of the family . . . was deeply entrenched in law and custom and its erosion constantly deplored by the rhetorical moralists and the satirists."

74. Cf. Acts 10:2, 10:24, 11:14 for repeated mention of the household in this regard.

75. The accusations noted in Origen, *Cels*. 3:55 and Justin *2 Apol*. 2 show the kinds of volatile sensitivities at work in such situations.

76. Note how Paul speaks of the "church" in his friend's house (Phlm. 1–2). Cf. Gehring, *House Church and Mission*. On the importance of women in such contexts, cf. Osiek and MacDonald, *A Woman's Place*.

77. See Kloppenborg and Wilson, eds., *Voluntary Associations*; Ascough et al., eds., *Associations in the Greco-Roman World*.

78. Intriguingly, a Christian gathering is called a *synăgōgē* in Jas 2:1. Given the later tensions between Jesus-believing and "ordinary" Jews, it is perhaps not

church were entirely routine words to use for local organizations of this kind. Much light is shed on the churches of the Pastoral Epistles by the numerous inscriptions and papyri now emerging, describing the officers, rules and constitutions of such associations, their membership dues and mutual care funds, and above all, their shared rituals and formal meals.[79]

The mention of the duty of care in both household and association contexts immediately highlights the issue of "welfare." Whilst the state could organize emergency food supplies in times of famine, and army officers certainly benefitted from medical care and a type of pension provision, the vast majority of people had only family, friends and local associations to fall back upon. The family played the primary role, and it is interesting that in 1 Timothy 5:8, Paul reminds Christians that their families should be their first line of defense, not the church, and, by extension, that their responsibility in this regard extended even to pagan relatives. However, for those with no other provision, associations often held community funds. The synagogues had long since given local expression to the mandate of Deuteronomy 14:29 to care for widows, orphans, and refugees, and in Acts 4:34–35, the Christians soon started their own fund on a large scale, with gifts ranging from ordinary weekly offerings through to the proceeds of property sales.[80] The appointment of special officers in Acts 6:1–2 (deacons?) and the discussion about "qualifying" widows in 1 Timothy 5:9–10 shows an early awareness of the need to operate such systems with care, but in later years, support not only for its members, but of the needy or sick more widely would become a major part of the church's witness.[81]

c. Religious context

Outside home or church, the earliest Christians would be immediately aware of a surprisingly complicated religious environment. There were

---

surprising that a different, but otherwise entirely equivalent word, *ekklēsia*, proved very useful for the church, even though it had in fact been used for the "assembly" of Israel in the Greek translation of the Old Testament.

79. For this point *in extenso*, cf. Harland, *Associations, Synagogues, and Congregations*.

80. In spite of much talk of "poverty," wealthier Christians, and especially homeowners played a significant role in early mission. Cf. Gill, "Acts and the Urban Elites," 110f.

81. Cf. the church's care for the victims of the epidemic of AD 165–180. The church's activities were praised personally by the emperor Julian as noted by Stark (*Rise*, 73, 76, 84). By AD 251, the church in Rome was said to be supporting "more than 1,500 widows and needy persons" (Chadwick, *The Early Church*, 57–58; Canavan, "Charity in the Early Church," 61–77).

minor deities associated with groves, springs, caves and mountains. There were demigods and heroes honored in local shines as well as the major gods associated with harvests, the sea, war, love, oracles, etc.[82] Cities would typically have patron deities, to whom prayers and sacrifices might be offered at seasonal or annual festivals. As a result of Alexander's conquests, however, foreign deities from Egypt, Syria and Persia started to be adopted on an elective basis in what many see as the advent of "personal religion."[83] Jewish and Christian worship was understood in this way and not opposed so long as the civic cult was not explicitly dishonored. While this Graeco-Roman respect for religion worked well in principle for Jews and Christians, their exclusivity in worship and social relationships could be seen rather negatively[84] and their avoidance of cultic images or statues sometimes led to their being accused of "atheism."

The refusal to participate in pagan sacrifices could occasionally be used to cast doubt on Christians' civic loyalty. And in the Roman context, the veneration of past and serving emperors as divine figures provided a potentially new pressure point.[85] This was not quite as problematic as one might expect, however. Started by Augustus, but promoted only patchily afterwards, participation was never compulsory. Jews were able to understand its primarily social and civic function with Herod even building such temples for his non-Jewish citizens.[86] Jews themselves were happy to offer sacrifices "on behalf of the emperor" and to pray for him in their synagogues.[87] While the issue sometimes provided local governors with a pretext for making life difficult,[88] Paul followed this Jewish lead by asking his members to "pray for kings and all in authority" (1 Tim 2:1–4; cf. Jer 29:7).

82. As Rome incorporated Greek speaking areas, a process of alignment occurred between Roman gods and the Greek Olympian pantheon, where, for instance Jupiter= Zeus, Juno= Hera, Neptune= Poseidon, Minerva= Athena etc. This jumble of gods and goddesses increased as the empire grew. Roman and Greek deities were more or less interchangeable, and this enabled Greek mythology to be absorbed into the Roman cosmos.

83. Cf. Instone, *Greek Personal Religion*.

84. On Greek and Roman reactions to Jews, cf. Stern, *Greek and Latin Authors on Jews and Judaism*. It is particularly striking that accusations that gentile Christians had abandoned their former Jewish religion and customs could be viewed with some alarm by Greeks and Romans.

85. Cf. Bowersock, "The Imperial Cult."

86. McLaren, "Jews and the Imperial Cult," 258–62.

87. Josephus, *B.J.* 2:197; Philo, *Legat.* 317; cf. McLaren, "Jews and the Imperial Cult," 271–3.

88. There were conflicts over the erection of statues of the emperor in places

In our quest to understand the background to early Christian writings, we should not underestimate the importance of busy urban environments like Ephesus for the sheer mixture of influences that could be brought together.[89] These ranged from Panhellenic and imperial cults, local temples for civic and patron deities and local groups linked to eastern religions, all the way down to the popular domains of magic, divination and sorcery. These were often completely entangled with each other. Thus, Ephesus' temple to the many-breasted goddess Diana, ministered to by an order of priestesses, was ranked as one of the seven wonders of the world.[90] At the level of popular religion, Paul famously upset the craftsmen who made images of Diana for the city's numerous visitors (Acts 19:23–41) and also clashed with Jewish exorcists and practitioners of "magic" (Acts 19:11–20). A place like Ephesus with its multi-cultural population and high volume of visitors was a breeding ground for every possible religious interest.[91]

It remains ironic that the greatest religious threat to church members was not from paganism, eastern religions or magic, but home-grown para-Jewish and/or Christian movements with characteristics that you may see referred to in older literature as "proto-Gnostic." Whilst our first evidence for Gnosticism "proper" is from c. AD 150, it is often assumed that tendencies later seen in this movement were at work in embryonic form within the NT period.[92] This would seem to comprise various philosophical ideas mixed with elements of biblical religion, emphasizing salvation through esoteric knowledge (or *gnōsis*) and the superiority of "spirit" to inferior matter

---

of worship under Gaius in the 30s and 40s AD, and Claudius in the 50s, McLaren, "Jews and the Imperial Cult," 262–71. We hear of Christians refusing to pray "to" such images in the second century, and hitting a new difficulty, insofar as they now did not sacrifice *at all* (cf. Pliny (Y), *Ep.* 10:96.5–6; Tertullian, *Apol.* 10, 28, 32). These difficulties, however, remained local and sporadic, and did not fundamentally compromise Christian citizenship. The *compulsory offering of a sacrifice* to the emperor as a tool of persecution did later occur under the emperor Decius in AD 249–51, a long time after the PE.

89. Ephesus itself was a major city close to the sea with the full range of Roman facilities such as a theatre, public baths and library.

90. There were priestesses associated with the cult of Diana; see Gill, "Acts and the Urban Elites," 116.

91. There was a Jewish colony and synagogue, but Jewish monotheism had made little impact on the city's mercantile spirit or its love of magic and charms.

92. They are often cited in connection with the discussion about "knowledge" (or *gnōsis*) and all things "spiritual" in 1 Corinthians and the false teaching in Colossians, where Paul warns of the dangers of "philosophy and empty deceit," noting that in Christ "the whole fullness (*plērōma*) of deity dwells bodily" (Col 2:8–9). *Plērōma* was later to become a major technical term in Gnosticism.

(including the human body). This latter "dualism" might result in asceticism (the harsh treatment of the body, denial of marriage etc. cf. 1 Tim 4:3), licentiousness (since what was done in the body could not harm the "spirit," cf. 1 Cor 6:12–13) or both. That some of Timothy's difficulties in Ephesus involved an ongoing struggle against such teaching is widely assumed.[93]

d. Marriage and morality

Many moral values in society were shared by all, especially those aimed at protecting the nuclear family.[94] However, Jews and Christians sought to champion higher standards wherever possible, taking a high and supportive view of marriage, a more restrictive approach to divorce and resolutely opposing abortion and infanticide. Overall, these stances were beneficial for women who could expect higher standards of fidelity from their husbands and the full support of the community in marriage and family life.

It is nevertheless important to note that the world of the early church was rather different from our own in its acceptance of very young brides. Girls were ready for marriage at the age of twelve although perhaps a third waited till they were eighteen or over. With men more often nearer thirty, later widowhood for women was almost inevitable.[95] The discussions in the PE about widows without relatives able to support them are thus entirely realistic and show precisely how a religious association would need to think about helping in such cases.[96]

The church also took a conservative approach to divorce. Responding to Jesus' own teaching, Christians permitted this only under particular circumstances.[97] And although, like Jews, they did their best to encourage marriage "within the faith," Christian mission appears to have created new problems with unconverted spouses divorcing their Christian partners or vice-versa, in some cases ending up in high-profile legal cases in which evangelists were accused of "breaking up families."[98]

---

93. For the churches of the PE, at least some of this may have involved a specifically Jewish form of Gnosticism (Titus 1:14).

94. "The . . . purity for which the Pauline Christians strive . . . is . . . defined in terms of values that are widely affirmed by the larger society," Meeks, *Urban Christians*, 101.

95. Stark, *Rise*, 107, quoting Hopkins, *Roman Girls*.

96. 1 Tim 5:3–16.

97. Matt 19:3–9's fairly clear concept of "fault" sets the general tone for the later church; cf. the excellent Instone-Brewer, *Divorce and Remarriage in the Bible*.

98. 1 Cor 7:15 refers to desertion by a non-Christian spouse, and 1 Pet 3:2 encourages Christian women to remain with pagan husbands as far as possible. But

Jewish and Christian opposition to abortion and the killing of unwanted babies was particularly striking. Abortion, a continued point of controversy in our own times, and detailed in a number of ancient medical texts, remained a grisly and dangerous procedure often leading to infertility or death.[99] It remains shocking that the safer alternative, and one that met with widespread approval, including by leading philosophers, was the abandonment of newborns on heaps of rubbish and elsewhere, a practice confirmed by archaeological finds.[100] It is quite possible that the general approach of the early church to family life was attractive to women, although this is obviously difficult to prove.[101]

Whether moral standards in society as a whole were different from our own is hard to judge. We do know that the behavior of several emperors—Tiberius, Caligula, and Nero—was far worse than would be expected of modern politicians. All three were guilty of rape, and in some instances male rape,[102] as well as the arbitrary execution of family members. Tiberius was said to have forced the children of certain senators into pornographic exhibitions,[103] and Nero, a persecutor of the church and a delusional psychopath, murdered his own mother.[104] The church along with other religious groups were quickly noted as committed to higher moral expectations and ideals.[105]

e. *Travel and communication*

As in his other epistles, the PE mention journeys by Paul and his teams. Paul was a seasoned traveler who, by one estimate, covered about 6,200 miles

---

occasionally things became more complicated, as in the legal case recounted by Justin (*Second Apology*) ca. AD 150–7. On the general requirement for Christians to marry within the faith, cf. 1 Cor 7:39.

99. Celsus, *Med.* 7:29 noted by Stark, *Rise*, 119–20.

100. Stark, *Rise*, 118, 121.

101. Cf. Lieu, "Attraction of Women," 5–22. For an excellent study of women in Acts and Paul in their Jewish and Graeco-Roman context, cf. Witherington, *Women in the Earliest Churches*.

102. Jennings, "Same-Sex Relations," 210.

103. Holland, *Dynasty,* loc 252, 253.

104. Holland, *Dynasty,* loc 214.

105. Pliny the Younger to the Emperor Trajan, ca. AD 112, *Ep.* 10:96.7 "They [the Christians] . . . bound themselves with an oath, not for any crime, but not to commit theft or robbery or adultery, not to break their word, and not to deny a deposit when demanded." All that Pliny could discover after torturing two deaconesses was that the Christian community pledged itself to live morally.

during the course of his life.[106] Much of this was on foot along Roman roads on which a fit person might cover 15–20 miles a day.[107] Although the major routes were relatively safe, travel as a whole remained a hazardous business, as we learn from Paul's note in 2 Cor 11:26 about his encounters with bandits. For certain routes in the Mediterranean area, it might make sense to secure passage on a merchant ship although this posed seasonal dangers from bad weather.[108] The account of Paul's shipwreck in Acts 27–28 reports heated discussions amongst the crew as to the advisability of continuing their journey at such a late stage in the year.[109]

Travel by sea and land was, of course, strongly involved in the conveyance of letters which were carried to their destination by couriers. This was usually a friend or family member who happened to be travelling to the destination but who could ensure safe delivery.[110] Writing letters required materials, skill, and time, and was laborious enough for even literate people to dictate their letters to a professional scribe, adding just a final greeting in their own hand (Rom 16:22; Gal 6:11).[111] Unless performed by a friend, this would not be a cheap process.[112] Dictation could be speeded up by making use of a system of shorthand from which the full text could be filled out later on, together with a copy for the sender's records. While the letter for

---

106. Richards, *Paul*, 190. On travel in the ancient world more generally, cf. Casson, *Travel in the Ancient World*.

107. Cf. Peter taking two days to cover forty miles in Acts 10:23–30. Routes were serviced by regularly spaced inns (cf. Luke 10:34), and typical rates of progress have been estimated from copies of letters bearing their date of posting and delivery, cf. Richards, *Paul*, 190.

108. The safest period was between the end of May and the middle of September. A trip from Corinth to Rome would only need ten days with a fair wind and Ephesus to Corinth, a week or two. Cf. Richards, *Paul*, 199.

109. Acts 27:9–12. The vivid shipwreck account has often been compared to Josephus' report in *Vit.* 13–16, also on a journey to Rome.

110. For private and domestic communication of this kind, the letter would be conveyed from end to end by a single courier. The only standing system for the delivery of letters was operated by the imperial civil service. Modeled on the equivalent system from Persia, this originally involved relays of couriers passing letters on from one to the other, until Augustus instituted a single-courier system but with changes of horses.

111. For older letter-writers (over forty!), dimming eyesight was another factor, making secretarial assistance doubly welcome. That Paul writes Gal 6:11 in "large letters" has sometimes been understood in these terms.

112. Estimating costs for materials and time, Richards calculates that "each of the Pastorals would take half a day [to complete] and might cost, including fees, between $200 and $500" (Richards, *Paul*, 169).

the recipient would normally be on a scroll, the private copy could be made on a re-usable codex or notebook. This convenient but informal form was eventually used for later edited collections of Paul's epistles, and accounts for our earliest Pauline manuscripts.[113] Paul's imprisonments would have made scribal assistance more difficult and urgent[114] and a probable cause of some stylistic variations.[115]

IV. QUESTIONS SURROUNDING DATE AND AUTHORSHIP

a. Traditional vs pseudepigraphal theories[116]

Within the humanities absolute certainty is impossible, and where events and situations are mentioned in a text like a letter, different interpretations are always possible. As noted in this introduction, the reconstruction that best seems able to account for the PE is that Paul was released from detention after the end of Acts and engaged in three or four additional years of ministry, during which all three letters were composed. This deduction is found in several ancient authors, including Clement, a Pauline associate who wrote his own letter from Rome only thirty years later.[117] There was no sense in which the date of Paul's martyrdom was so certain that doubt should be cast on this scenario. Indeed, Ignatius, Polycarp,[118] and Tertullian refer to the PE, a fact demonstrating the acceptance of these epistles by significant Christian leaders by the end of the first century or early in the second.[119]

---

113. Richards, *Paul*, 212ff.

114. The help of family and friends for all sorts of things, not least in bringing food, was the norm in prison life, and writing letters from such locations was surprisingly well attested.

115. Although there are clear differences in vocabulary, stylometric computer analysis finds little distinction between the Pastorals and other Pauline writings, cf. Kenny, *Stylometric Study*, 99–100, quoted by Richards, *Paul*, 144.

116. See Excursus I for more details.

117. Clement is mentioned in Phil 4:3. In 1 Clem. 5:7, the picture is primarily of *complexity* with numerous imprisonments and periods of missionary activity in both "East and West."

118. Polycarp cites them "in the same eclectic but authoritative way he does the other Pauline letters" (Fee, *1 and 2 Timothy, Titus*, 23). See also Berding, "Polycarp," 349–60.

119. Quinn, *The Letter to Titus*, 3. See also Mounce, *Pastoral Epistles*, pp. lxiv-lxix. They remained an unchallenged part of the canon until the beginning of the nineteenth century, as noted by Kelly, *Pastoral Epistles*, 4.

Paul's authorship of the PE was first questioned by German post-enlightenment scholars on the basis of style and vocabulary (see section below) and soon on other issues too.[120] The other issues concerned both the portrait of the church which emerges from the PE and the "Gnostic" or false teaching against which Timothy struggled. It was assumed by critics of Pauline authorship that the developmental stage of the church of the PE, and indeed of its "Gnostic" opponents, reflected the early second century more than AD 64–68.[121] Therefore, the letters were most likely by an unknown author writing in Paul's name anything up to about NINETY years later, a practice going by the name of "pseudepigraphy." An argument on this matter has dragged on for more than 150 years.[122] In the nineteenth century distinguished scholars (including Plummer and Lightfoot) affirmed Pauline authorship. In the first half of the twentieth century, at least nine commentators affirmed Pauline authorship, and in the second half of the twentieth and early twenty-first century, other distinguished commentators (including Guthrie, Hendricksen, Kelly, Fee, Mounce, Knight, Johnson, Towner, and Yarborough) also did so.[123]

The argument has ranged far and wide since it not only concerns the authenticity of the Pastorals themselves and all that they teach but also the extent of the biblical canon and therefore the settled judgements and uniformity of the early church. Plunging into the argument in greater detail, we note:

---

120. First raised in Germany by Fredrich Schleiermacher in 1807 who asserted, on linguistic grounds, that the same author could not have written 1 and 2 Timothy. J. G. Eichhorn in 1812 followed and extended Schleiermacher's argument although he thought all three epistles were "without doubt" by the same writer. De Wette in 1847 reviewed the scholarship until that point. For a summary and discussion of the history of modern interpretation until the 1980s, see Johnson, *Timothy*, 42–54.

121. Johnson, *Timothy*, 74–76. He adds, "although some version of this position [state of the church] is widely held, it is actually one of the weakest arguments against authenticity" (*Timothy*, 75).

122. The PE share many themes in common with other Pauline writings. Unfortunately, this commonality does not help resolve the dispute about authorship. Those who argue for pseudepigraphy find the overlapping themes give evidence of skillful imitation; those who argue for genuine Pauline authorship find the commonalities confirm Pauline authorship. The same thing happens with the differences. Those who argue for pseudepigraphy find differences confirm that Paul is not the author, and those who argue for genuine Pauline authorship can find many reasons why there are differences (situation, a new amanuensis and so on), and they point out that the differences are no greater than those already found across the rest of the Pauline corpus.

123. Knight, *Pastoral Epistles*, 22; Mounce, *Pastoral Epistles*, lxxxiv; Yarborough, *Timothy and Titus*, loc 2250–9.

(i) the presumption is that the lightly organized charismatic church of Paul turns over several decades into the formal, hierarchical, institutional, non-charismatic church of early Catholicism. In particular, the mobile apostle is replaced by a static bishop, elders become subsidiary, the exuberantly charismatic worship of 1 Corinthians becomes liturgical, and there is a drift away from the primacy of salvation by faith and vivid eschatology. It is argued that the PE show a departure from Pauline Christianity in the sense that charismatic worship is not prominent while other features of the letters are compatible with the direction of travel towards the less vigorous church of the second century. However, the church we find in the PE *is* compatible with the Corinthian congregation. There is reference to the activity of the Holy Spirit, to prophecy, to the importance of elders (as opposed to a ruling bishop), to salvation by faith, to other Pauline themes, to the return of Christ, and to dangerous days preceding this.

Kelly puts it this way, "It has been suggested that these arrangements [of elders and deacons] find their aptest parallel in Ignatius of Antioch's description of the churches of Asia Minor about 110" but actually "what in any case the Ignatian letters reveal is a closely articulated hierarchy, with the functions of each order and their relation to each other clearly defined. Of this there is not a breath in the Pastorals, the whole atmosphere of which is much simpler and less sophisticated and indicative of a rather early stage in the growth of the ministry."[124]

(ii) The beliefs of the teachers leading the Ephesian church astray are ill-defined and vague and unlike the full-blown Gnosticism of the second century. Moreover, the one reference to knowledge (*gnōsis*) in the Pastorals tells us little about the false teaching circulating Ephesus at the time of writing since the word *gnōsis* is used some twenty-two times elsewhere in Pauline writings when Gnosticism is not in view.[125] After extensive review of the evidence Mounce concludes, "One point is clear. The opponents' teaching was not developed Gnosticism and was much closer to the errors at Colossae and Corinth, mixed with portions of aberrant Judaism, speculative

---

124. Kelly, *Pastoral Epistles*, 14.
125. Knight, *Greek Testament Commentary*, 27.

superstition, and possibly magic. The nature of the opponents' teaching does not require dating the PE later than Paul.[126] And this is an opinion held equally plainly by Kelly.[127]

(iii) The writing of a text *as if it has come from the pen of someone else*, or pseudepigraphy, understandably rings alarm bells for modern Christians. It was, however, a surprisingly common practice and, although most Jewish examples use the name of long-dead biblical heroes, there are Christian texts purportedly from the hand of apostolic figures and their associates emerging in the second century.[128] What we should notice, however, is that the early church did exercise a process of discernment and was entirely capable of excluding questionable texts from the canon.[129] Johnson writes, "We note, for example, that all other literary productions associated with the name of Paul—such as 3 *Corinthians*, the *Letter to the Laodiceans*, and the *Letters of Paul and Seneca*—were as universally rejected from the developing NT canon as the Pastorals were universally accepted (with the certain exception of Marcion and the possible exception of Tatian and Valentinus)."[130] Similarly, as Eusebius points out, the *Gospel of Peter* was rejected.[131] As further evidence of the discernment of the early church and the detestation in which pseudepigrapha could be held, the bishop who composed the so-called

126. Mounce, *Pastoral Epistles*, lxxv.

127. Kelly, *Pastoral Epistles*, 12.

128. This practice is called "pseudepigraphy." As Kelly explains, "A large proportion of Jewish writings, both in the Bible and outside it, produced between 250 BC and AD 200 bear the names of Enoch, Daniel, the patriarchs, and others. Early Christian books like the *Didache* and the apocryphal gospels and acts claim to come from apostles and personages like Nicodemus" (Kelly, *Pastoral Epistles*, 5). But this is the point: it is the *apocryphal*, i.e., non-canonical gospels, gospels not admitted to the canon, which try to gain credibility by associating themselves with known historical figures.

129. The Muratorian Canon mentions the rejection of a letter to the Laodiceans and one to the Alexandrians.

130. Johnson, *Timothy*, 84. Further along these lines Johnson adds "a late dating must deal with Tertullian's explicit statement that Marcion 'rejected' (*recusavit*) the letters of Timothy and Titus (*Marc.* 5:21), signifying at the very least they were already written and able to be accepted or rejected on the grounds of their contents. In the light of these considerations, the question must be asked how likely it would be for these letters both to have been produced between 100 and 150 and to have been so widely distributed and accepted as Pauline." (*Timothy*, 85, reference format adapted).

131. *Hist. eccl.* 6.12.2–3.

Acts of Paul confessed his work was a forgery but was nevertheless condemned and removed from office.¹³²

In modern scholarship it remains entirely proper to continue to raise "common sense" practical and moral questions about a pseudepigraphic scenario.¹³³ One is why pseudepigraphal letters were needed when former associates were openly upholding Paul's teaching by writing under their own names.¹³⁴ Another concerns cynical immorality. Would a pseudepigraphal writer seeking to honor Paul write, "I am speaking the truth, I am not lying" (1 Tim 2:7) when lying is exactly what he was doing? Another is why an author would include so many details about people, places, and movements that risked being falsified by traditional accounts handed down in the churches themselves.¹³⁵ Yet another is why an author drawing on the authority of Paul would have included sentences showing Paul's authority was rejected in some quarters: he writes "all Asia has left me" (2 Tim 1:15). Yet another is why it would be necessary to write *three* letters in the PE. One would have been enough.¹³⁶ And finally, we can ask what the circumstances were in the second century which led a writer to pretend to be writing letters by Paul which purported to address problems in the Neronian period, but which were really directed at a period forty or more years later. More than this, we have to ask on what basis the author constructed the legal situation confronting Paul which emerges in 2 Timothy. Did the pseudepigraphic author have historical knowledge about the lapse in time between Paul's "first defense" (2 Tim 4:16) and his eventual execution? These considerations show just how weak the pseudepigraphic case is. Nevertheless, there is still a question to ask about vocabulary and style, to which we briefly now turn.

---

132. Mounce, *Pastoral Epistles*, cxxiv.

133. The case against pseudepigrapha was strong enough to lead some writers (Moffatt, Harrison, Hanson, et al.) to alter the received critical position to the extent of proposing there were fragments of Paul's own words included within the PE. One objection to the Fragment Hypothesis is that it is entirely speculative. There are no textual indications anywhere of genuine Pauline words being mixed with fictional ones. In addition, as Guthrie (*Introduction*, 591, n 1) points out, the proponents of the Fragment Hypothesis cannot agree which verses are genuinely Pauline and which are not (cited by Mounce, *Pastoral Epistles*, cxxi). The fragments are supposed to be mainly in Titus and 1 Timothy but oddly absent from 2 Timothy.

134. Cf. 1 Clem. 47 "Under the inspiration of the Spirit, [Paul] wrote to you concerning himself, and Cephas, and Apollos, because even then parties had been formed among you."

135. Kelly notes that the theory becomes "a tissue of improbabilities" (*Pastoral Epistles*, 29).

136. Fee, *1 and 2 Timothy, Titus*, 6; Mounce, *Pastoral Epistles*, lxxxiii.

b. Vocabulary and style

As noted above, the authorship of the PE was first questioned on the basis of linguistic analysis. This particularly seeks to respond to the fact that the PE have a number of new ethical and religious words that do not occur at all in the rest of Paul's writings (nor in a few cases, in the NT as a whole), and some of these are used instead of otherwise very distinctively Pauline terms found in all his earlier epistles. That many of these terms are well known from Hellenistic moral discourse from a *somewhat later period* certainly adds to this challenge.[137]

Although these observations have been taken by NT scholars following in the German tradition as pointing to a later (unknown) author, recent scholars are now ready to ask more open questions about what we see. A simple starting point is a clear acknowledgment that the PE do share a fair amount of common vocabulary with the earlier epistles.[138] Another is whether ancient writers *always* called on the same pool of vocabulary irrespective of context. As suggested earlier, authors were trained to be aware of what lexical resonances and literary allusions might be meaningful for particular audiences, and growing numbers of church members with Hellenistic educational backgrounds provides a plausible context for such a scattering of new words.[139] The apologetic and pastoral context can add further nuances here. When Paul has to deal with new types of false teaching, then he might very well need new words to describe them and new rallying calls to oppose them. It should be pointed out that painstaking analysis of the vocabulary of the PE has been carried out by several scholars who typically have counted and compared word usage across the whole Pauline corpus to discover if there are clues to be gained about authorship. Suffice it to say the results of these enormously time-consuming analyses have satisfied scholars that genuine Pauline authorship is either likely or perfectly plausible.[140] Even stylometric analysis using computer assisted assessment of the text finds no distinction between the Pastorals and other Pauline writings.[141]

---

137. Mounce, *Pastoral Epistles*, xcix.

138. Mounce, *Pastoral Epistles*, cx.

139. The use of *logos* in the opening verses of John's gospel is a clear example of this phenomenon.

140. Guthrie, *Pastoral Epistles*, 53–5, 224–40; Mounce, *Pastoral Epistles*, xcix-cxviii; Yarborough, *Timothy and Titus*, passim. Yarborough makes extensive use of Adolph Schlatter (1852–1938).

141. In his *Stylometric Study*, 99–100, Kenny writes, "there is no support given by [the data] to the idea that a single group of the Epistles (say the four major Tübingen Epistles [*Hauptbriefel*]) stand out as uniquely comfortable with one another; or that

But are any differences great enough to demand a different author?[142] We have already said that the imprisoned Paul would have needed an amanuensis, and while it is not a problem to suggest this may have introduced stylistic or linguistic innovation, it does raise the question of whether the resulting text was read out to and/or approved by Paul. If so, then Paul is happy with these choices, they become his own, and indeed part of his *mission*.

As we have said, the vocabulary of a text is determined by its subject matter and so, if Paul is addressing new situations, we should expect to find new words or new ways of expressing old ideas. And if the eyes of the original readers noticed these differences as they read Paul's letters (something we know was done even before the NT as a whole was complete)[143] then it becomes important to recapture something of how this key-shift might have "sounded." That these epistles complement, supplement, and illuminate what we have in the rest of the Pauline corpus should become evident in the commentary that follows.

c. Movements and events revisited

Insofar as several early church fathers deduce the events mentioned in the PE occurred *after* the end of the Acts narrative, we can say that efforts to harmonize the two are misplaced.

Acts ends with Paul under house arrest in Rome. But his "offence" is already regarded as somewhat marginal by Roman officials (Acts 25:25). If this happened in ca. AD 62 or 63 and we assume a martyrdom in the later part of Nero's rule (say, AD 66–68), then we have some four years of further activity on Paul's part. This would certainly allow him to fulfill his plan to go to Spain (Rom 16:24),[144] and after his return, revisit key church networks in the East and individual co-workers such as Timothy in Ephesus and Titus on Crete. On these visits he may have encouraged

---

a single group (such the Pastoral Epistles) stand out as uniquely diverse from the surrounding context" (quoted by Richards, *Paul*, 144).

142. In modern study, this remains a key challenge for such analysis, as can be seen when comparisons are made between one Shakespeare play and another, cf. Mounce, *Pastoral Epistles*, cxiv.

143. 2 Pet 3:16 presupposes that a collection of Pauline writings was circulating and could be spoken of in terms both of general tendencies and variations, e.g., "speaking of this in *all* his letters," cf. "*some* things, hard to understand".

144. The reference in 1 Clem. 5 to Paul reaching the "extreme limit of the west" is often taken as a reference to Paul completing his planned visit to Spain.

Timothy to excommunicate false teachers (1 Tim 1:20),[145] sent Titus off to his work on Crete, and possibly met up with Timothy again at Miletus (2 Tim 4:20) on his way back to Macedonia. Later we hear about a cloak and vital parchments that have been left behind (2 Tim 4:13), and of course the news that Paul was eventually arrested, *again*. It is from his new imprisonment that he wrote to Titus and after realizing the judicial "climate" had turned hostile (2 Tim 4:16)—probably as a result of the scapegoating of Christians for the great fire of Rome in AD 64.

V. A PENTECOSTAL AND CHARISMATIC CHURCH

As we have indicated above by reference to church governance and succession, the portrait of the church given in the PE is compatible with the worldwide Pentecostal and charismatic church of today. Although, as we have said in the Preface, this church is hugely diverse in its practice and, to a lesser extent, in its beliefs, it is worth emphasizing this point. The Pentecostal and charismatic churches given in the ten-country survey, *Spirit and Power*, organized by the Pew forum in 2006 and the *Brill Encyclopaedia of Global Pentecostalism* (2021) offer the nearest we currently have to a comprehensive picture. Pew shows speaking in tongues, divine healing, exorcism, answers to prayer, and revelations from God are all part of typical Pentecostal experience in the countries where the survey was conducted. Similarly, the PE contain reference to charismatic phenomena, especially prophecy (1 Tim 4:14), and other powerful encounters with the Spirit (Titus 3:5). The Christians of the PE still meet in homes rather than church buildings (2 Tim 1:16, 4:19). These arresting letters, then, can easily be imagined as speaking to the concerns of early church leaders, their congregations, and today's Christians. And beyond the church, these words bear the scrutiny of the academy (see Excursus II).

---

145. He could have excommunicated the ringleaders at a distance, as he did in Corinth (1 Cor 5:5).

EXCURSUS I.

On the Problem of Style and Vocabulary in the Pastoral Epistles

As noted in the introduction, the key issues that have played a role in the rejection of Pauline authorship of the Pastoral Epistles have been: (a) the Greek style and vocabulary of the letters, (b) the theological emphases and images of church life, and (c) the difficulty of locating the events alluded to within the framework of Acts. That both the language and theology seemed to belong to a later period has led to a long-standing consensus that the Pastoral Epistles were written by someone else, after Paul's death. While not impossible,[1] it is a very healthy sign that this conclusion is being questioned in modern research, with scholars from all parts of the theological spectrum reconsidering all three of these points and seeing the letters as genuinely "Pauline" again, albeit in some qualified sense.[2]

---

1. Some would hold to a benign version of this theory where, although the presentation as a Pauline letter remains a *device*, a genuine disciple was still seeking to honor the apostle's teaching, perhaps including a number of genuine sayings, the so-called "fragment" theory described in section IV of the introduction. The majority of scholars have been more pessimistic than this and feel that the letters ultimately undermine Pauline teachings and/or are simply claiming his endorsement for later church perspectives they wish to promote.

2. For the problem of Pauline pseudepigraphy in general, see the excellent collection of essays in Porter and Fewster, *Paul and Pseudepigraphy*. For a list of recent commentaries that have re-asserted Pauline authorship of the Pastorals, see Porter, "Pauline Chronology," 65 and n.1.

Of these three points of difficulty, the question of events (c) has no direct bearing on authorship in so far as Acts allows all sorts of other things to have happened, both inside and outside of its narrative framework.³ And as for (b), we note, too, growing support for a picture of the church revealing more organization than we might have expected, but which is certainly compatible with what we find in the other epistles.⁴ Nevertheless, the differences in style (a) do beg questions about writing and style variation in the ancient world, and of course, the possible contribution of a co-author or amanuensis. While the contribution of a helper has been something of a standard explanation, there are problems with this. Such helpers are clearly implied for several other Pauline letters, yet this does not seem to lead to particularly large deviations of style⁵ nor do the challenges of Paul's imprisonment appear to make their contributions more visible.⁶

The purpose of this excursus is to explore the issue of language and style at a greater length than was appropriate within our main text, and to point the reader towards some recent scholarship on this issue. The first question is whether this could actually *be* Paul but writing in a deliberately different style. In modern scholarly terms, this is no longer as naïve a question as it might appear. The second is, if an amanuensis is involved, how or why has this led to stylistic changes in *these epistles* and not others. Have they made this change independently, so to speak, or would it be possible for someone like Paul to *direct* a change of this kind? If Paul knew the sort of

---

3. The main conjectures about when the events mentioned in the PE occurred are discussed in the introduction, §IV "Questions Surrounding Date and Authorship"/ *"Movements and events revisited."* For a masterful survey of the strengths and weaknesses of the classic possibilities for this, see Porter, "Pauline Chronology."

4. See our introduction, §IV and our comments on relevant verses throughout the commentary.

5. For instance, the listing of Paul's co-workers follows this pattern: Romans, Galatians, and Ephesians name Paul only; 1 Corinthians names Paul and Sosthenes; 2 Corinthians, Philippians, Colossians, Philemon name Paul and Timothy, and 1 & 2 Thessalonians name Paul, Silvanus, and Timothy. Of these, we have noted that Ephesians and Colossians stand apart from the others, but less so than the Pastoral Epistles, which nevertheless, claim sole Pauline authorship. An amanuensis called Tertius explicitly names himself in Rom 16:22 and yet the style and vocabulary of Romans is regarded as quintessentially Pauline. The comment in Gal 6:11 is widely believed to imply Paul is using an amanuensis there too, perhaps even the same individual.

6. Of the Pastoral Epistles, only 2 Timothy has Paul in prison, yet all three epistles display a strong stylistic relationship. Amongst the other letters, Colossians, Ephesians, Philippians, and Philemon present as "prison" epistles, yet only Colossians and Ephesians assume a distinct style, with Philippians and Philemon more resembling the main group.

change he wanted, of course, this would get close to implying that he could have been capable of doing this himself and dictating the words we now see.

In an excellent recent reconsideration of these questions, van Nes[7] reminds us that the key publication that embedded the idea that the style and vocabulary of the PE were not just different, but post-first century, was Harrison's 1921 monograph, *The Problem of the Pastoral Epistles*.[8] An early, and pre-computational application of what we might now call stylometry,[9] Harrison's conclusion as to authenticity was critically dependent on the relative frequencies of words that do not appear in the other Pauline epistles or indeed, in the New Testament at all, the so-called *hapax legomena*.[10] Observing the higher frequency for these words in second century texts, however, supported the claim that the entire composition was simply from this later period.[11] Finally, Harrison agreed that certain short passages in the Pastorals showed a much higher alignment with the vocabulary and style of the uncontested epistles, and that this at the least might support the "fragment" theory.[12]

Far from wishing to discourage stylometric study, van Nes simply shows that Harrison's analysis may be flawed in various ways.[13] This ranges from the way hapaxes are defined and counted, how grouping the Pastorals together curiously exaggerates their difference from the other epistles, and how this difference is exacerbated by Harrison's way of diagramming the results.[14] The problem of grouping was specifically addressed in fresh stylometric assessments by Anthony Kenny in 1986, where each epistle in the standard corpus was analyzed separately using a more modern and larger set of stylistic metrics.[15] This brought the Pastorals much closer to the rest of the corpus and also uncovered greater differences between Paul's main letters.[16] This now suggests shifts in style and vocabulary are going on "all

---

7. van Nes, "Problem."
8. Harrison, *Problem*.
9. Cf. Holmes and Kardos, "Who was the Author?"
10. Cf. van Nes, "Problem," 155–6. Another group of words, the "indeclinables" are also involved in the analysis and are claimed to be particularly characteristic of Paul's writing and thus less frequent, or present with different relative frequencies in the writing of others.
11. van Nes, "Problem," 156.
12. van Nes, "Problem," 156.
13. van Nes, "Problem," 157–61.
14. van Nes, "Problem," 158.
15. Kenny, *Stylometric Study*.
16. van Nes, "Problem," 160. It proved particularly revealing that in an experiment

the time" in the Pauline corpus as changes in subject matter, audience or rhetorical purpose dictate.[17]

Finally, van Nes reviews both classic and more recent challenges to the basis upon which Harrison came to believe that the lexical stock of the Pastoral Epistles was more in line with the second century than the first.[18] This was crucially dependent on the selection of comparative texts and is considerably altered by the simple expedient of including the Septuagint, Jewish, and other Graeco-Roman writings from the late Hellenistic period through to the first century, work that was less easily done before the computer era. The conclusion is again that, while different in particulars—some of the word-choices still need explaining, the general positioning of the Pastoral Epistles in their ostensible period is much strengthened.

Is interesting that van Nes' conclusions are reflected in various ways in the advancing field of computer-based, forensic, and AI-assisted stylometry, where the questions of author identification, whether different contributing authors can be separately identified from a composite or team production, and, importantly for the present discussion, detecting when a single author is in fact responsible for works written in different styles, whether eclectically, or via different but settled approaches in different periods of their career.[19] This is still an imperfect science, and stylistic metrics in different languages, like Arabic, for instance, need defining very carefully.[20]

While the application of these modern computer-based approaches to ancient texts is necessarily limited via limited corpuses of writings reliably known to be by the same person, it raises the very interesting question as to whether authors in Paul's period may not have been more in command of their style and vocabulary than we given them credit for. Since the authorial unity of the Pauline corpus is itself contended, this can scarcely be used to settle the matter, but our insight into its possibility could be considerably helped by clearer examples from other ancient authors whom we can observe with some certainly working in different styles.

---

where 1 and 2 Thessalonians were "grouped" before analysis, then their "distance" from the rest of the epistles also increased, leaving them more "un-Pauline" than the Pastorals themselves.

17. van Nes, "Problem," 160–1.

18. van Nes, "Problem," 162–3, discussing Hitchcock, "Tests for the Pastorals"; Guthrie, *The Pastoral Epistles and the Mind of Paul*.

19. See, for instance Neal, Sundararajan, et al., "Surveying Stylometry"; Gómez-Adorno, Posadas-Duran, et al., "Detecting Writing Style Changes"; Daelemans, "Explanation in Computational Stylometry"; Can and Patton, "Writing Style"; Ashraf, Iqbal, et al., "Cross-Genre Author Profile Prediction."

20. Al-Yahya, "Stylometric Analysis of Arabic Texts."

This line of argument is precisely that pursued by Andrew Pitts in his article on "register" in ancient texts.[21] While this involves style in the general sense, the term "register" emerges from the relatively modern field of sociolinguistics and refers to the intended social location of a piece of writing, e.g., typically, formal vs. informal, family vs. strangers, older vs. younger readers, somber vs. humorous, straightforward vs. ironic, etc., and where register detection becomes an important part of communication in different contexts.[22] In biblical studies we are very used to the need to rightly identify genre, but because many biblical authors only write *in one genre*, biblical scholars very often never truly reckon with the question of "register."

Pitts notes how the overly simple stylistic metrics used by Harrison and others prior to the computational linguistics era were frequently caught out when tested on modern authors by unusual or outlier texts genuinely by those authors but somewhat different from what might be regarded as their main or classic texts, citing the problem of C. S. Lewis' posthumously published *Dark Tower*.[23] Even using more modern systems, software can still be caught out even by the difference between the narrative sections of novels and sections of quick-fire dialogue, so researcher awareness of the basic nature of a work and "what we might expect" is essential.[24]

Thus, even if meaningful analysis of a text group as small as the Pauline corpus is beyond machine-based approaches, a new awareness of the *question* of register variation in ancient writings, and what we might reasonably expect to be visible to a trained eye is surely welcome. Critically, sociolinguists point to register-adaptation drivers which have long been the center of quite independent study in Pauline studies, namely the social context of communication, which immediately distinguishes individual from group addressees,[25] and in a group context might involve questions of the overall balance of ethnicity, educational background or class, but also the present state of addressor-addressee *relations*. Pitt notes that recent research has thus spoken about *Audience Designed Style-Shift*,[26] a concept that could very usefully inform future consideration of New Testament writings.

Typically, contextual approaches of this kind have confined themselves to *rhetorical* analysis, asking what it is that Paul is trying to persuade his

---

21. Pitts, "Style and Pseudonymity."
22. Pitts, "Style and Pseudonymity," 117–22.
23. Pitts, "Style and Pseudonymity," 114–55.
24. Pitts, "Style and Pseudonymity," 117 and nn. 11–13.
25. A letter to one's spouse or child, for instance, could certainly differ in very significant ways from a community or business letter.
26. Pitts, "Style and Pseudonymity," 122–5.

audience to do or believe, and what (standard) devices does he employ to do this.[27] Ancient rhetoricians were in fact entirely aware that style variation was an important tool even within a single work,[28] but the addition of the insights reported by Pitts allows better nuancing of what we might see for a single author addressing different readers and contexts in different compositions, not just at the level of persuasion about slightly different issues, but about differences in register and style used for such projects informed by other audience-based, contextual and relational issues.

In conclusion, we suggested in our introduction that what we saw by way of style and vocabulary in the Pastoral Epistles could be explained by a clear second-generation, future-facing orientation and a decision to use new, more specifically Hellenistic religious language in framing the epistles, a language increasingly "natural" to the young, often mixed-race and metropolitan group represented by Timothy himself and the friends, associates, and families increasingly being drawn into the churches. An amanuensis may certainly have been involved, but as we also note, it becomes far more fruitful to conceive of this as a deliberate change of register and style that is Pauline in its intention and, ultimately, in its missiological vision. That Paul personally imagined the creation of an authentically Christian, yet integrated, public and contemporary language of virtue is a testament to aspects of Paul's genius perhaps sometimes under-appreciated.

---

27. Cf. the pioneering approach of Betz, "Composition of Galatians"; Anderson, *Ancient Rhetorical Theory and Paul*; Witherington and Hyatt, *Romans: A Socio-Rhetorical Commentary* and other examples from the Eerdmans Socio-Rhetorical Commentary series.

28. Garrison, *Rhetoric and Roman Poetry*, 35–45 on the importance of judicious use of poetic elements for register change in rhetorical writings and note that this affected those composing works of narrative fiction too, e.g., as discussed by Laird, "Style and Rhetoric."

EXCURSUS II.

On Church and Academy

While Pentecostals and charismatics are the main audience of this commentary, we recognize the importance of two large professional groups outside the church (although some members are inside it). The first is the great international community of biblical scholars. These are people who typically work in academic institutions and engage with the text of the New Testament not for the purpose of preaching but for other purposes related to the advancement of human knowledge. The academic community as a whole is intrinsically secular in orientation, and in the West, is driven by large intellectual movements that have made their way through universities since their foundation. It was not always so. In the Middle Ages, European universities were brought into being on a theological basis or with a Papal license with the aim of assisting the church so that, for instance, the Theology Department at the University of Oxford can date itself back to the tenth century. Later, at the time of the Reformation, the universities provided scholars whose learning enabled the translation of the Bible into English (in the case of Wycliffe) or German (in the case or Luther). But as the centuries passed, and especially after the Enlightenment of the eighteenth century, universities became secularized, dispassionate, places of teaching and research without any attachment to the gospel although, in the older universities in Britain, constituent colleges still include functioning chapels and chaplains as a consequence of their historical and pre-Reformation roots.[1] University-based theology may or may not have a connection with faith

---

1. Maxwell Lyte, *University of Oxford*; Asztalos, "Faculty of Theology"; Engel, "Academic Profession."

communities, a result that can lead to readings quite foreign to those held by the communities from which they originated.

In the United States, higher education grew differently. The USA fields a disparate set of institutions, some of which are faith-based and not dependent upon tax dollars or the imperatives of secularity. Even so, the Academy as a whole—European and North American—does not see itself as existing to serve the church, but rather operates as an alternative source of authority to the pulpit. Sometimes the church ignores the Academy and at others it is critiqued by the Academy, and, equally, the church, if it is doing its job, will have occasion to question the moral implications of the Academy's projects. There is, or can be, a creative tension between Academy and church that allows each to correct the other for the benefit of all. In Nazi Germany, it was the Confessing Church which most clearly saw and resisted the outrageous doctrines of Hitler's propagandists.[2] For a period just before and just after the WWII in Britain, it was the Anglican Church that most successfully moderated the soulless stipulations of government economists.[3] In the United States, it is from the Academy that we can expect critique of those Pentecostal and charismatic prophets who wrongly foretold Donald Trump's electoral victory in 2020.

The second scholarly community or movement within the Academy concerns Cultural Studies and the hermeneutical apparatus customarily applied to any text, and particularly literary ones.[4] A huge range of theoretical positions has developed, often driven by variants of Marxism informed by a type of existential philosophy uninfluenced by empiricism. The consequence of these theoretical positions is to provide numerous incompatible readings of any piece of writing by attaching it to, or prioritizing, one or other social group, especially those which have been historically repressed, women, ethnic groups, and so on. What we offer is a Pentecostal and charismatic reading—one that takes seriously the concerns and experiences of the Pentecostal and charismatic congregations across the world in the light of their self-understanding as communities raised up by God through the twentieth century outpouring of the Spirit. We seek to do this while continuing to give close attention to the text, to the way the words on the page connect or qualify each other. In short, what follows is not a piece of purely theoretical commentary that dissolves the text but, on the contrary, is a piece of writing attentive to the canonical words.

---

2. McGrath, *Christian History*, 301.
3. Iremonger, *William Temple*; Temple, *Christianity and Social Order*.
4. Cunningham, *Reading After Theory*, 29.

We can think of literary theory as prompting the reader away from a common sense understanding of a text towards more innovative or complex or reflective readings. If we think of the old literary theory dating back to classical times as including the trio of *writer*, *reader*, and *text*, the new literary theory unpacks or problematizes each member of the trio. The writer becomes representative of a class—if indeed he or she is actually allowed any independent existence outside the text itself. The reader is to engage with the text but also may use a text for purposes that run against the grain of its words; and we think this was customarily done by a string of scholars who saw the epistles as primarily designed to promote church discipline even to the extent of being a handbook on the topic.[5] The text becomes evidence for historical circumstances, oppression, exclusion, bias and prejudice to the extent that the intention of the writer is ignored or denied. Or it becomes evidence for second century preoccupations and developments as the rudiments of the Roman church emerged from the pristine days of Saint Paul and the first apostles. Thus, whereas the *meaning* of a text was seen to derive directly from the historical circumstances which gave rise to it and the intention of its writer whose own interpretation was the prime and authentic one, by literary theory, intention is deconstructed and dismantled and has no priority above that of any other reader—a position we would profoundly disagree with. Yes, we would say, the intention of the writer is primary and the circumstances in which the writer is placed are important to the extraction of meaning from the text. But here again the notion of meaning which is an interactive product of the reader's scrutiny of the text becomes polyvalent, subjective, uncertain, shifting with historical circumstances, and definitely not in any way fixed. Again, this is a position from which, in the main, we dissent. Of course, the text has meaning even if this meaning may be bigger than the meaning which inspired the writer to write the words in the first instance. And as for the *text itself*, this is in another language written in another time with words that must be translated into our own language and culture. So, the text is itself a matter of scrupulous investigation. When was it written? Are there significant differences between it and other comparable texts? Who wrote or copied it? Have word meanings changed over time or during translation? This is a task demanding long hours in the library or online with facsimiles of the manuscripts themselves.

In the end, though, when all this hard graft has been completed, we are still left with the need to interpret the text, and we take the view that literary theory, although it extends the range of interpretative possibilities, is a

5. Kümmel, *Introduction to the New Testament*, 367, 384, cited by Mounce, *Pastoral Epistles*, lviii.

double-edged sword: Marxist theory will detect class consciousness where none exists, psychoanalytic readings will detect unconscious motivations without further evidence, and so on. Insofar as theology *is* literary theory, we seek to prioritize Pentecostal and charismatic theology because it is drawn from the lived experience of Pentecostal and charismatic churches.

Chris Thomas[6] and Ken Archer[7] in writing about Pentecostal interpretation point to the importance of the interpretive community—and the Jerusalem Council in Acts 15 is often taken as a paradigmatic example.[8] We could therefore see the huge, multi-national and diverse Pentecostal church as one interpreter and the Academic community as another, very different one. However, their tasks and questions are not entirely distinct, as the church seeks to ensure its teaching remains a form of public discourse.[9] Might this commentary series, perhaps, help to find an accommodation between them?

---

6. Thomas, "Women, Pentecostals and the Bible."
7. Archer, *Pentecostal Hermeneutic*.
8. See also Yong, *Spirit-Word-Community*.
9. As implied by Yarborough, *Timothy and Titus*, loc 779 n.10.

1 TIMOTHY

OUTLINE

I. PAUL, TIMOTHY, AND THE MISSION TO EPHESUS (1:1–20)
   a. The basis of action and relationship (1:1–2)
   b. The urgent task: stop the false teaching (1:3–7)
   c. The proper function of the law (1:8–11)
   d. Paul remembers God's saving goodness (1:12–17)
   e. The urgent task: a war to be won (1:18–20)

II. PRAYER AND GENDER ROLES (2:1–15)
   a. Prayer (2:1–2)
   b. The purpose and scope of prayer (2:3–7)
   c. Men and women in the church (2:8–15)

III. OVERSEERS AND DEACONS (3:1–16)
   a. Overseers (3:1–7)
   b. Deacons (3:8–13)
   c. Reiteration of Pauline purpose with faith summary (3:14–16)

IV. UNHEALTHY AND HEALTHY TEACHING (4:1–5:2)
   a. Devilish inroads (4:1–3)
   b. Teaching the goodness of creation (4:4–6)
   c. Strenuous and exemplary godliness (4:7–11)

d. Following through (4:12–5:2)

V. WIDOWS, ELDERS AND SLAVES (5:3–6:2a)

   a. Widows (5:3–16)

   b. Elders (5:17–25)

   c. Slaves (6:1–2)

VI. MOTIVATIONS AND JUDGEMENTS (6:2b-20)

   a. The corruption of false teaching (6:2b-10)

   b. Timothy's battle (6:11–16)

   c. Warning to the rich (6:17–19)

   d. A final charge (6:20)

COMMENTARY

I. PAUL, TIMOTHY AND THE MISSION TO EPHESUS (1:1–20)
  a. The basis of action and relationship (1:1–2)
  b. The urgent task: stop the false teaching (1:3–7)
  c. The proper function of the law (1:8–11)
  d. Paul remembers God's saving goodness (1:12–17)
  e. The urgent task: a war to be won (1:18–20)

I. PAUL, TIMOTHY, AND THE MISSION TO EPHESUS

a. The basis of action and relationship (1:1–2)

> Paul, an apostle of Christ Jesus according to *the* command of God our savior and Christ Jesus our hope, to Timothy my true[1] child in *the* faith, grace, mercy *and* peace from God our[2] Father and Christ Jesus our Lord. (1 Tim 1:1–2)

1. The letter uses the conventions of classical letter-writing. First the sender is named, and then the recipient, and after that, greetings. It has been suggested that this letter follows the pattern of a *mandata principis*, an instruction from a senior to a junior rather than being a letter of encouragement and exhortation.[3] Certainly the beginning is more than a formality. Paul's apostleship is "according to the command" of God (*kat' epitagēn theou*) and Timothy is commissioned as his "true son" to carry out what Paul instructs. Today and in the light of their long relationship we would expect a warmer

---

1. The translations of "dear" or "genuine" are also possible.
2. Greek omits any article.
3. Johnson, *Timothy*, 157.

start, but this letter is likely to be read out in church (and carefully examined by church leaders), so Paul's words may well be intended to supplement and define Timothy's authority as he begins his demanding assignment.

Paul names himself as he does in other epistles without reference to his family or geographical origins and he begins unusually without giving thanks for the church—though this is understandable given the critical state into which it has sunk.

He refers to himself as an "apostle" (*apostolos*). This is not a title or a rank, but a special ministry commissioned and exercised in relationship to Christ, and in Paul's case, stemming entirely from his visionary encounter with him. The data on apostleship in the New Testament is extensive.[4] In Acts, Paul is dramatically confronted by Christ (Acts 9:4–6) and later sent out by him in a vision to the gentiles (Acts 22:21). In Galatians, Paul confirms his focus on the gentiles (Gal 2:7), and the speeches at the Council of Jerusalem (Acts 15:4; 7–11) tell how successfully he and Barnabas preached and formed new communities of believers, and the word "apostle" is applied to both of them in Acts 14:14. Acts also relates the beginnings of the Ephesian church from Paul's lengthy and eventful visit (Acts 19). Putting the data together, the function of the apostle as a church-planter more than an evangelist is well established.[5] The apostle has particular authority over a church he has planted (1 Cor 4:15), which raises the generic question of the apostle's authority over a church he has *not* planted, and here the data are inconclusive. In the case of Ephesus, the picture in Acts is unambiguous: Paul is the original church planter and presumably the apostle who ordained the first Ephesian elders. These elders come in a group at his summons to say goodbye to him as he journeys to Jerusalem (Acts 20:17–37). If we take church planting seriously and see it as one of the distinguishing marks of an apostle, we must ask whether those who claim to be apostles but have not planted churches are really apostles. Apostleship *per se* does not confer either absolute authority or unimpeachable standing. Jesus' principle of "by their fruits shall you know them" (Matt 7:16) always applies.

Apostleship is rooted in a relationship with Christ himself, as are all the ministries listed in Ephesians 4. The point here is important in the light of the false teachings permeating the Ephesian church. Paul is an apostle of Christ Jesus, sent out by Christ himself through and by the "command" of God. The word "command" carries military overtones, and is not speculative or tentative. Insofar as a theological distinction can be made, Paul's apostleship is from God and Christ. The coordinated action of Christ and

---

4. For a useful overview, see Clark, "Apostleship," 49–82.
5. Scott, *Apostles Today*, 59–65.

God provides a glimpse into the operation of the Godhead while the reference to God as "our Savior" (*sōtēros*) shows further coordination. In the New Testament, Jesus is the Savior (Luke 2:11) whereas in the Old Testament God is Savior (Deut 32:15; Pss 5; 24:5; 25:5; 42); so, Jesus acts as God does. And Christ himself is also "our hope." Any future expectations of good coming to believers are placed in Christ who is the source and ground of the church's hope always in any place, at any time, and certainly in respect to the trouble at Ephesus.

2. Timothy received his commission as a "true child" (*gnēsiō*), a word used to describe the legitimate descent of natural children. Timothy is a legitimate descendant of Paul "in the faith" though not Paul's actual physical son.[6]

The greeting Paul brings to Timothy (and the church) is close to the pattern of many of the other epistles. "Grace" (*charis*) is a particularly Christian word and concept implying, as has been said, the "free, unmerited favor of God." In this context, as in others, Paul has taken the conventional greeting of the time (*chairein*) and Christianized it.[7] He wishes Timothy and the church God's favor. "Mercy" (*eleos*) speaks of the suspension of righteous judgement. To receive mercy is to avoid sanction or punishment even though it is deserved—a relevant factor for a church in danger of veering into heterodoxy. Paul's reference to mercy should ring an alarm bell for his readers: it is not his customary greeting. And finally "peace" (*eirēnē*) is part of the normal Jewish blessing of *shalom*, or completeness and rest, without rebellion against God or subjugation by an enemy. And all this is wished from "God" the Father, the personal God in whom creation and salvation originate and "Christ Jesus our Lord," reminding Timothy and the church that Jesus, the Messiah, is also Lord of creation and head of the church.

b. *The urgent task: stop the false teaching (1:3–7)*

> I urge you[8] just as I did when I was on my way to Macedonia, to remain in Ephesus so that you may command certain

---

6. On the use of "family" language in the church, as in Rom 1:13, 1 Tim 5:1–2, see Hellerman, *The Ancient Church as Family*. The special use of "child" or my "child" for those one has evangelized, mentored or trained probably goes back to Jesus (Mark 5:34, Matt 18:6) and is visible in 1 Pet 5:13, 1 John 2:1 and elsewhere.

7. Johnson, *Timothy*, 158.

8. Or "request," "summon," "encourage," "exhort."

> people not to teach falsely[9] and not to pay attention to myths and endless genealogies which promote speculation[10] rather than divine stewardship[11] in *the* faith. But the goal of this[12] instruction is love *which comes* out of a pure heart[13], a good conscience and *a* sincere faith, from which some *people* have deviated, turning away into empty talk, wanting to be teachers of the law, but not understanding what they are saying or the things they assert. (1 Tim 1:3–7)

3. Here we come to the main purpose and occasion of the letter. Paul and Timothy have obviously met face-to-face while Paul was on his way to Macedonia and at that meeting Paul urged Timothy to remain at Ephesus. We do not know where the critical meeting between Paul and Timothy occurred, but we can deduce that Timothy was already working in the Ephesian church. He is to "remain" there and not to leave and join Paul or to desert his post. His task is to "command" (*paraggellein*, a military term with the meaning "to give strict orders" or a legal term covering a summons to court) "certain people" not to teach "falsely," departing from what Paul had taught. Timothy has sufficient credibility and status within the church—some commentators have called him "an apostolic delegate"—to confront "certain people," and, in this situation, only his clear and direct orders will stop the spread of false doctrine. Whether there is implicit criticism of Timothy's failure to halt the advance of the false teachers is a moot point which will surface occasionally in the commentary on particular verses.

The situation envisaged here follows neatly on from Paul's warning to the Ephesian elders that from "their own number fierce wolves" will arise leading the flock after themselves or, in other words, making disciples out of existing church members (Acts 20:29, 30). If the church was organized on a household basis as a network of home groups each presided over by one or more elders, the schismatic situation is easy to imagine and engineer.[14]

So, what is the false teaching? The short answer is that we do not know for sure though informed guesses have been made from our knowledge of church history, other New Testament passages (cf. Titus 1:4; 1 Tim 4:3, 7; 2 Tim 2:16–18; Gal 1:6–9), and the information in the following verses. The

---

9. Or "teach strange doctrines."
10. Greek, plural.
11. Or "training."
12. The Greek article, "the," could, this context, also be rendered "this" or "our."
13. Greek "and."
14. See, for example, Gehring, *House Church and Mission*.

most likely answer appears to be a distorted type of Judaism with Gnostic overtones and components.

4. "Myths and genealogies." The Greek term *mythos* could refer to a range of things, from heroic, even instructive tales of the distant past, to "tall tales" and falsehoods as contrasted with truth.[15] Here Paul's concern is with a mesmerizing ability to distract more than with falsehood as such.[16] In terms of content, para-biblical folklore and specifically gnostic material have both been imagined, categories that might also account for "genealogies."[17] That this material was valued by those who wanted to become "teachers of the law" (v 7) suggests it was of a specifically Jewish character. The trouble in Ephesus was different in character from that in Galatia or Colossae but similar in that, within a decade or so of the church's foundation, the purity and simplicity of the gospel had been compromised. The result of the Ephesian heresy was to divert sections of the congregation from "love" and "sincere faith" (v 5) until they became contentious communities rife with speculative hypotheses.

Instead of becoming side-tracked by speculative myths and genealogies the wayward leaders of the Ephesian church should have recognized their "stewardship" (*oikonomia*) from God to engage in ministry in keeping with divine order. The term "*oikonomia*" can be translated as "plan" in reference to divine purposes or "stewardship" which is another way of referring to a responsibility to communicate what God has revealed. Elsewhere Paul speaks of his responsibility to preach the gospel which has been entrusted to him (1 Cor 9:17) and the same idea is implicit here. The "stewardship" is "in the faith" and not a legal requirement. If there is a lesson for modern Pentecostal and charismatic ministers, it is that they should not allow themselves to be distracted by the flamboyant oddities that sometimes circulate in the church (e.g., stories of miraculous new gold teeth or the handing on of special clothes to which "the anointing" is connected) but instead exercise faith in sticking to their core tasks.

5. Paul explains the purpose and "goal" (*telos*) of his command is to ensure "love" (*agapē*). By this, we realize the baneful consequence of the false teaching was to drain love out of the church and turn it into a place of speculation and argument. Instead, it should be a place of sacrificial, self-giving love that comes from three sources: the heart, conscience, and faith.

15. Johnson, *Timothy*, 163.

16. That this "meaningless" material encouraged "speculation" and that it had the power to "turn people away" from more central concerns (v. 4–6) suggests as much.

17. The genealogies may have been either human or divine and were most likely laden with symbolic significance. Murphy-O'Connor suggests this may have involved allegorical readings of the patriarchal lineage (Murphy-O'Connor, "2 Timothy Contrasted with 1 Timothy and Titus," 403–18, 415–416).

"Heart" refers to the center of emotional life within the individual.[18] The anthropological or psycho-dynamic model of human beings within Scripture is very different from any contemporary account which may say human beings are social constructs, animals, political units, or some other formulation. For Paul, as for the rest of Scripture, the heart is the source and seat of action and motivation. When the heart has been purified by faith or transformed by God's loving grace, it becomes new in line with the promise of a new heart for those entering a new covenant (Jer 31:33; Ezek 36:26).

"Conscience," a term popular with Greek philosophers, refers to a person's "inner awareness of the moral quality" of their own actions.[19] Paul describes it as a guide to life (Rom 2:15). Elsewhere Paul writes of his conscience as bearing him witness "through the Holy Spirit" (Rom 9:1) with the meaning that the Spirit guides and shapes the conscience of a Christian. Thus, the inner life of the Christian is reflective and aware of what is right; the Christian is not merely an automaton thoughtlessly and unreflectively obedient to external regulation.

"Sincere faith" is inner confidence in the living God. It is not necessary to distinguish between different types of faith at this point (saving faith, prevenient faith, and so on).

6. By "deviating" from love, spurning conscience, and losing the sincerity of their faith, the false teachers have "wandered" off course into verbose and futile discourse probably connected with "wanting to be teachers of the law."

7. These false teachers want to be "teachers of the law" (*nomodidaskaloi*, cf. Luke 5:17, Acts 5:34), the standard Jewish term for a religious expert. However, this term may have carried over into Jewish-Christian communities with a less formal connotation.[20] If they were Jewish before conversion, they may have known the Torah well, but if they were gentiles, their knowledge would have been more limited. Either way, the people concerned were clearly unsuited to the task which Paul, as an expertly trained Jewish scholar and now Christian teacher, understood thoroughly. Having earlier understood and applied the Mosaic law as a Pharisee (Acts 23:6; Phil 3:5), upon his conversion, the apostle Paul came to see it afresh as a "schoolmaster to lead us to Christ" (Gal 3:24). On either account, Paul could

---

18. Cf. Smith "The Heart and Innards in Israelite Emotional Expressions."

19. Kelly, *Pastoral Epistles*, 47.

20. Cf. Matt 13:52 which speaks of "scribes" who have been "trained for the kingdom of heaven." "Teacher" (*didaskolos*) certainly appears very early in lists of Christian ministries, e.g., Acts 13:1, 1 Cor 12:28, Eph 4:11, cf. Jas 3:1.

c. The proper function of the law (1:8–11)

> For we know the law is good if a person uses it rightly[21]. We know, this, *at least*, that the law is not given for *the* righteous[22], but *the* lawless[23], *the* unruly, *the* impious and sinners, *the* unholy and profane, *murderers* who *would* kill even *their own* parents, *the* sexually immoral, men who take young boys, human traffickers, liars, perjurers, or *anyone who does* anything else contrary to healthy teaching that is in accordance with the gospel of the glory of *our*[24] blessed God, with which I was entrusted. (1 Tim 1:8–11)

8–11. "We know that the law is good if a person uses it rightly." And here is the point. The law is not designed to be used in the way the false teachers have taken it. It is not the basis for myth or abstruse speculation but rather designed to reveal and combat vice and a whole range of criminal behaviors such as murder, corruption, perjury, and the like. Nor is the law designed to prevent perfectly legitimate activities like getting married or eating certain foods (1 Tim 4:3). Paul is not attacking the law itself because it is *good* and gives us a general outline of the will of God for human society.

That the key "mission" of the law is to the "lawless and impious" rather than the "righteous" is a well-known Jewish commonplace (Ps 25:8, Mark 2:17, Luke 15:1–7). This re-appears in Paul's teaching for the church where he says that although the law is "good" and indeed "spiritual" (Rom 7:14–16), it cannot create, confer, or "organize" righteousness (Rom 7:7–25; Gal 2:16, 5:13–26), which is found instead by those who put their faith in Christ. This does not mean, however, that the law is not taught at all. "Healthy teaching," as the Ephesian Christians should know, emphasizes faith in Christ as the mainspring of their existence (cf. 1 Tim 1:14) yet certainly calls out unrighteousness as and when it appears. Three pairs of broad categories are listed: the "lawless and unruly, impious and sinners, unholy and profane"; the first

---

21. "Legitimately" or "appropriately" are also possible translations.
22. Greek singular.
23. Greek plural.
24. Greek "the."

pair refers to civic recklessness, the second to irreligious attitudes and behaviors, and the third to those whose lifestyles and words despise God.

All the next eight categories of offences have parallels with the Ten Commandments.[25] "Those who strike their fathers and mothers" contradicts "honor your father and mother" (Exod 20:12; Deut 5:16), "murderers" contradicts "you shall not murder" (Exod 20:13; Deut 5:17), "sexually immoral and men who practice homosexuality" echoes the command not to commit adultery (Exod 20:15; Deut 5:8), "enslavers" (kidnappers) contradicts the command not to steal (Exod 20:15; Deut 5:19), and "liars" and "perjurers" contradict the command not to bear false witness (Exod 20:16; Deut 5:20).

"Anything else contrary to healthy teaching." The list ends with a catchall statement connecting true doctrine with health (*hygiainousē* is translated "healthy," and the English word "hygiene" is connected with it) and by implication connects false doctrine with sickness. This is part of the polemical vocabulary of philosophical dispute and may be where Paul acquired it.[26] The medical metaphor implies that false doctrine does not necessarily make an immediate impact but, whether quickly or slowly, causes spiritual health to decline with the possibility of disfigurement or death; hence, the reference to gangrene in the later epistles (2 Tim 2:17; Titus 1:9; Titus 2:1).[27] Sound doctrine is "in accordance with the gospel of the glory of our blessed God." Thus, sound doctrine is formed "in accordance with" the good news of Jesus Christ. This news, this "gospel," is by grace and faith and has a more limited role for the law, as the previous verses show. Such a gospel displays "the glory of Christ" (2 Cor 4:4) and is given by the "blessed God," that is, the God who is the source of all blessing. And this gospel, says Paul in a characteristic reminder underscoring the line of authority found in the opening greeting, is the one with which "I was entrusted": Paul's sense of weighty personal responsibility for the proclamation of the gospel is repeated in Titus 1:3 and coheres with his own self-description as a steward and servant of Christ (cf. 1 Cor 9:17; Gal 2:7; Eph 3:2).

The train of thought within the epistle has moved from the false teachers who, employing myth and speculation, were setting themselves up as teachers of the law, to the proper function of the law as a bulwark against sin and from there, to a gospel centered around Christ himself whose power to transform the wicked, as the next verses will show, is exemplified in Paul himself.

---

25. This strongly suggests that biblical material of this kind remained a central part of Christian instruction.

26. Mounce, *Pastoral Epistles*, 41. Kelly, *Pastoral Epistles*, 50.

27. Health-related terms are visible elsewhere in Paul, e.g., Eph 4:16.

I. PAUL, TIMOTHY, AND THE MISSION TO EPHESUS

d. Paul remembers God's saving goodness (1:12–17)

> I thank Christ Jesus our Lord, who *has* strengthened me because he considered *me* faithful and put me into *his* service, even though I used to be a blasphemer, a persecutor, and an arrogant *man*. But I was shown mercy because I acted ignorantly and in unbelief, and the grace of our Lord abounded with faith and love in Christ Jesus. The saying is sure and worthy of complete acceptance that Christ Jesus came into the world to save sinners, of whom I am the foremost. But I was shown mercy for this reason, that in me, as the foremost, Christ Jesus might demonstrate complete forbearance as an example for those who would later believe in him for eternal life. Now to the king of *all*[28] ages, immortal, invisible, *the* only God, be honor and glory forever and ever. Amen. (1 Tim 1:12–17)

Luke has Paul testifying to his salvation through Christ on three occasions in Acts (22:1–21; 24:10–21; 26:1–23) because he knows how powerful his individual narrative is. In Acts 23:6 he is shown splitting a Sanhedrin composed of Pharisees and Sadducees by drawing attention to his Pharisaic credentials. So, in speaking of his salvation here, he is confronting the false teachers with their own feebleness because their nebulous doctrines cannot transform anyone's character for the better or draw anyone closer to God.

The paragraph (1:12–17) which follows might appear as a digression unconnected with the main purpose of the epistle. However, the reference to Paul's own amazing experience of salvation is relevant because, like all testimony to God's interventions, the implication is always that what has been has done once can be done again. In this instance, all those who have done wrong are reminded of God's transforming grace, and Paul's confession of his previous sinfulness shows how those in error can and should be prepared to admit their faults in the same unvarnished way as Paul himself. If Timothy and other church leaders (though not necessarily the false teachers) have done wrong, they should recall the reach of God's love and restoring grace.

12. Paul thanks Christ Jesus "who has strengthened" (*endounamōsanti*) him and for "considering" him "faithful" and "putting" him to his "service." The tenses used for strengthening, "considering," and "putting" are aorist implying Paul has a single event in the past in mind, presumably his

---

28. Greek "the."

encounter with Christ on the Damascus Road. A variant reading puts "who has strengthened" into the present tense implying divine strength is given continually as in Phil 4:13. Whatever the precise tense used, Paul speaks of "strengthening," the word describing the Holy Spirit's activity in the life of the believer. Christ promised the apostles they would "receive power" (Acts 1:8 *dunamis*, cognate with *endunamōsanti*) after the descent of the Holy Spirit. The Spirit empowers through a rich and practical diversity of charismatic gifts enabling Christians to do what, in their natural strength, would have been completely beyond them (1 Cor 12:4–11; Rom 12:3–8). This is Paul's experience and can be Timothy's.

It would be theologically incorrect to understand Paul is claiming to have been chosen on merit for his good qualities including his faithfulness because, as he freely admits, he was a sinner and only transformed by the abundance of God's grace (v. 14). Once entrusted with the gospel he was reckoned by God to be "faithful," and it is faithfulness that is the pre-eminent requirement of the minister or steward (1 Cor 4:2). Having been deemed faithful, he was appointed into "service" (*diakonia*) and ready to carry out the tasks he was assigned. And here is the paradox of apostleship: in essence it is and always remains a form of service though, by it, the apostle gains the church's respect which is accompanied by authority.

13. When Paul says he was a "blasphemer" he means he spoke against God and reviled him, and probably he did this as speaking against Christ since, as a Pharisee, he would hardly have spoken against the one whose law he kept.[29] When he admits that he was a "persecutor" he refers to his playing havoc with the early church by hauling men and women off to prison (Acts 8:3). His persecution of the church is poignantly raised by Jesus on the Damascus Road: "why do you persecute *me*?" is the question asked from the blinding light, a question demonstrating Christ's identification with his people: to persecute the church was to persecute Christ (Acts 9:4, 5). Paul confesses to over-reaching himself, being self-confident and "arrogant." And all this despite being a leading teacher of the law, exactly the status desired by the false teachers (v. 7).[30]

"But I was shown mercy because I had acted ignorantly and in unbelief." Here Paul is drawing on a conventional distinction within Judaism

---

29. This is very interesting evidence that the Christian movement had rapidly moved beyond mere *respect* for Christ. Note the blasphemy outcry during Jesus' trial in Mark 14:64, and how, in John 10:33, Jesus is accused of blasphemy for appearing to make himself "equal with God."

30. The value of such "autobiographical" fragments cannot be underestimated in corroborating information from other authors such as Luke; cf. also Gal 1:13–24; 1 Cor 15:9, and Phil 3:4–11.

between ignorance and willfulness (or presumption); both categories are culpable, but the former is less blameworthy than the latter (Lev 22:14; Num 15:22–31; cf. Acts 3:17, 17:30). When Paul says he received mercy, he is making a significant statement. He knows fearful divine judgement has been withheld.

14. "The grace of our Lord abounded." Instead of judgement the "grace" of God was poured out abundantly on him. The Greek word *hyperpleonazein* for "abounded" is a compound only once used in the New Testament, perhaps coined for this occasion but not in an unusual way since Paul adds the prefix *hyper* onto other words in other letters (e.g., Rom 5:20; 8:26, 26; 2 Cor 10:14). The "grace of our Lord abounds" and Paul's hard heart is filled with "faith" and "love." Whether faith and love are given by the Lord along with grace or whether they are Paul's response to the grace he has received cannot be determined from the grammar alone. And though Paul speaks of his own experience of overflowing grace, the giver of grace is *our* Lord. Timothy may anticipate grace to deal with the erring elders because he worships the same Lord as Paul.

15. Following on from the particular instance of his own salvation, Paul cites a striking "saying worthy of complete acceptance"—an apparently well-known formula used five times in the Pastoral Epistles but nowhere else in the New Testament.[31] Its affirmation is that "Christ Jesus came into the world to save sinners." In that he "came into the world," Paul affirms the incarnation. In that he came to "save sinners," Paul affirms the central purpose of Christ's mission. The additional words "of whom I am the foremost" look at first sight exaggerated unless we remember how, when we are convicted of sin by the Holy Spirit, we "give up all such comparisons" and only apprehend our own state.[32] Moreover, such humility is in line with Paul's evaluation of himself elsewhere as the "least of the apostles" because he "persecuted the church" (1 Cor 15:9).

16. Paul understands he received "mercy" (the same word as before, v. 13) so Jesus Christ might display his "forbearance," his willingness to put up with sinners as an *example* to others coming later. If Christ could be patient with Paul, he could be patient with any sinner. The patience of God is found in both Testaments (Exod 34:6, Num 14:18; Rom 2:4) and is a breathtaking quality or attribute which appears at variance with power and glory but is not. The God of Scripture wants people to come "to believe in him for

---

31. Cf. 1 Tim 3:1; 4:9; 2 Tim. 2:11; Titus 3:8. Kelly notes that the formula "has a solemn ring," and introduces or follows words probably drawn from early Christian teaching or worship (*Pastoral Epistles*, 54). Cf. also Mounce, *Pastoral Epistles*, 48–49.

32. Stott, *1 Timothy & Titus*, 53.

eternal (*aiōnios*) life," a life starting in this age and continuing into eternity in the presence of the "immortal" God.

17. Having recounted the grace and forbearance of Christ, Paul breaks into a doxology, words of praise to God, the "king of all ages." Paul, in his letters, has done this previously (Gal 1:5; Eph 3:21; Phi 4:20; Rom 11:33–36), and he will do so again here in 1 Tim 6:15–16. We can almost hear the voice of Paul the preacher as he breaks into such praise while leading worship in the congregation. We may, of course, be hearing not so much Paul as the early church itself, just as its own patterns of worship were developing— there is a liturgical moment at this point—so Paul may be quoting these words in the same way a preacher today might quote from a well-known worship song. There are also here elements of what will become an explicit doctrine of the Trinity: Christ has displayed forbearance and yet God, the king of the ages, is praised.

God is "king of all ages" (*aiōnōn*), this age and the next, within and beyond normal time and therefore eternal. God is "immortal," untouched by the effects of time, and incorruptible, and "invisible," as both Testaments show (Exod 33:18–20; Col 1:15) and the "only" God, as the Jewish Shema (Deut 6:4) states and stands in complete contrast to the polytheism of the Greek and Roman era. To this God "honor" and "glory" are due throughout all ages (*aiōnōn*). To this the only response is "Amen," a word of assent long spoken in the Jewish synagogue.

e. *The urgent task: a war to be won (1:18–20)*

> I set this exhortation before you, Timothy, *my* child, according to the prophecies made about you[33], so that by them, you may fight the good fight, holding on to faith and a good conscience. Some have rejected these, making a shipwreck of their faith, among whom are Hymenaeus and Alexander, whom I have handed over to Satan so that they may be taught not to blaspheme. (1 Tim 1:18–20)

The chapter ends with a return to the original charge given in verse 3, the same word is used each time. Again, as in verse 2, the filial relationship between Paul and Timothy is emphasized in the words "my child." Verses 8–18 could be misunderstood as a digression although, as we have seen, the discussion of law and Paul's own testimony of salvation are entirely relevant to the topic in hand.

33. Greek "previously."

The prophecies made about Timothy remind us of plentiful charismatic gifts within the early church and indeed the Spirit's assistance in recognizing or encouraging gifts in others. Exactly how this happened in Timothy's case is not entirely clear.[34] 1 Corinthians 14:3 tells us prophecy is given for "exhortation, edification, and comfort" (AV) so a prophecy could easily have been given to Timothy along these lines. A word of this kind might have been given privately but if 1 Timothy 4:14 is relevant, where the entire leadership team was present, then a shared setting might seem likely (cf. 1 Cor 14:29 where others "weigh" what is said).

As well as providing a fitting context for words relevant to the entire church (e.g., Acts 11:27–30, concerning a forthcoming famine[35]), Acts shows that even "personal" prophecies, such as the warning given by Agabus to Paul (Acts 21:10–12) could occur with others present. The scene depicted in Acts 13:1–3 contains helpful pointers. On this occasion, just prior to the first missionary journey, the Holy Spirit commands Paul and Barnabas be set aside to the work for which they "have been called." Given the text speaks of prophets in the congregation, it is reasonable to deduce the command was spoken prophetically. That said, the prophetic utterance concerns the timing of the journey rather than other details since the leaders in Antioch are told only to set aside Paul and Barnabas for the work to which they "have been called." The calling, at least from God's point of view, pre-dated the prophetic utterance. So, prophecy is not directive in any absolute sense, but operates in conjunction with other spiritual gifts and intuitions to discern the will of God.

So, what happened to Timothy? The most likely scenario is that, at a gathering of church leaders, powerful prophecies were given marking out Timothy's calling and gifts in respect of Ephesus. One suggestion that has its attractions is that a repetition of Acts 13:1–3 occurred in Timothy's home city of Lystra when he was originally released to work with Paul[36] though, if the situation was entirely analogous, the prophetic utterance in that case would similarly have confirmed a call Timothy already felt. But it is probably better to assume a more specific encouragement to Timothy containing

---

34. This would be the only reference in the New Testament to prophecy being used in this way, although Paul may be referring to the occasion(s) mentioned in 1 Tim 4:14 and 2 Tim 1:6 where gifts were not just revealed but *imparted*. See the discussion in Mounce, *Pastoral Epistles*, 70–2.

35. Interestingly, the utterance was non-directive in that it warned of a famine in Jerusalem without telling the Antioch church what it should do (this was not church government by prophecy); Antioch needed to help Jerusalem, but the precise form of help was in Antioch's hands.

36. Mounce, *Pastoral Epistles*, 71, quoting Hort, "Titus and Timothy," 183–84.

an explicit warning of battles ahead. This would then make better sense of the notion of "fighting the good fight" according to the prophecies that had been given.

"Fighting the good fight." This phrase may simply refer metaphorically to the struggle Timothy was about to begin. Alternatively, references to warfare in Scripture may speak of intense combat (in prayer) against invisible spiritual forces (see Excursus III). The letter to the Ephesians refers to this kind of battle and Christians are told their fight is not against flesh and blood but against "spiritual wickedness in high places" (Eph 6:12, 13). Similarly, in 2 Corinthians 10:4 Paul speaks of "pulling down strongholds" and "destroying arguments" and every "lofty opinion" raised against the knowledge of God. Timothy's defense of the gospel must be powered by more than debating skill or emotional appeal. The prophecies Timothy received may give him resilience as well as intellectual insight into the road to victory. If they touched upon the future state of the Ephesian church or his own future role, we can understand they gave Timothy confidence without fully understanding what sort of warfare he engaged in.

19. He is to hold "faith and a good conscience" in the battle since contests of this kind threaten the sweetness of Christian character. Timothy must maintain his integrity, and therefore his "conscience," and his "faith" and the faith of others. By losing these essential traits some leaders have already been "shipwrecked," a maritime disaster often accompanied by the loss of life and possessions.

20. "Hymenaeus and Alexander" are named. If these men were once leaders in the church, they will have caused considerable damage. If they lost their faith, they may have walked away from Christianity altogether and Paul's comment that he "handed" these men "over to Satan," would appear to suggest this.[37] The image may well reflect the way that recalcitrant individuals were "cut off from Israel" (e.g., Exod 12:15; Num 9:13), excluded from God's people and his protection (cf. Acts 8:21). That the judgement pronounced against Ananias and Saphira (Acts 5:1–5) led to their "deaths" might mean this always implied some permanent if not fatal conclusion. Curiously, however, the balance of usage would suggest that "handing over to Satan" functions as striking language about a serious but *temporary* exclusion. The use of this same phrase in 1 Cor 5:5 appears to offer some hope for the future, and 2 Cor 2:6–8 may refer to a resolution within a number of months, indicating in practice a temporary exclusion from fellowship and

---

37. A phrase whose meaning we cannot pin down and which may or may not have taken place when Paul was present. A similar procedure when Paul was not present is described in 1 Cor 5:1–5.

particularly communion. Such "punishments" were thus normally intended to be remedial and to bring about a change of behavior, as here where Paul hopes the pair will "be taught not to blaspheme."[38] Whether Alexander is the metal worker who did Paul a "great deal of harm" (2 Tim 4:14) or the man who tried to speak to the crowd in Acts 19:33 cannot be known.

The chapter began with a command, a charge, to Timothy to stay in Ephesus to deal with the false teachers, continued with a short account of their doctrinal errors over misuse of the Mosaic law, showed why these were harmful, considered the correct use of the law, recounted Paul's own amazing salvation, which had been a result of grace not law, and ended by reminding Timothy strongly of what he needed to do.

---

38. Acts 8:22 amazingly extends this hope even to Simon. Whether Hymenaeus and Alexander had literally spoken against Lord or had blasphemed through some more general departure from conscience is not clear.

II. PRAYER AND GENDER ROLES

    a. Prayer (2:1–2)

    b. The purpose and scope of prayer (2:3–7)

    c. Men and women in the church (2:8–15)

II. PRAYER AND GENDER ROLES

a. Prayer (2:1–2)

> First of all, therefore, I urge *that* petitions, prayers, requests *and* thanksgivings be made for all people, for kings and all those who are in authority, so that we may live a quiet and well-ordered life in all godliness and dignity. (1 Tim 2:1-2)

1. Paul "urges" prayer as a matter of priority, and his exhortation follows on from the epistle's purposes laid out in the previous chapter. Prayer "therefore" is the matter he encourages Timothy to correct "first of all" and by prayer, "love which comes out of a pure heart" and "good conscience" (1:5) will be fostered. There is no evidence here the text comes, as some commentators have suggested, from a manual of church liturgy and order.[1] The different types of prayer given in this verse are not set in any particular sequence or pattern as would be the case if they were arranged liturgically.[2] The intention is that prayers of any and every kind be offered both by individuals and together in the context of a prayer meeting. Paul wants the congregation to be turned from its useless disputing and speculation to the practice of intense and varied prayer, and moreover, this prayer is unlimited in its focus: it is to be made for "all people," both within the church and in wider society. This may imply that the false teachers of chapter 1 restricted the scope of prayer to a more exclusive group.

Although the three (or possibly four) types of prayer share similarities, there are genuine distinctions between them. "Petitions" (*deēseis*) are entreaties and can apply to urgent requests from one person to another although the word more usually refers to our requests to God. Here we ask God for any number of things covering any number of topics. "Prayers" (*proseuchas*) have an inclusive sense because the word also describes Jewish and pagan practice: this is calling out to God anywhere and at any time.[3]

---

1. Kelly, *Pastoral Epistles*, 59, 60.
2. Johnson, *Timothy*, 189.
3. MM, 547.

"Requests" (*enteuxeis*) can refer to intercessions where a specific request is made by one person to God on behalf of someone else.[4] "Thanksgivings" (*eucharistias*) may accompany all the other types of prayer or constitute a prayer of its own type.

2. "For kings and all those who are in authority." The prayer of the church is to be made for political leaders at all levels of the imperial system. No doubt the church took note of the example of the Jewish people who, while exempt from making sacrifices to other gods, showed their loyalty to the state by praying for the emperor.[5] Here, though, the explicit purpose of praying for the authorities was "so that we may live a quiet and well-ordered life in all godliness and dignity." Too often Christians have taken for granted the comforts and conveniences of modern life. War and civil strife are enemies of the gospel and prevent evangelism; Christians should not, therefore, feel guilty if they live in peaceful and prosperous conditions. Rather, they should thank God for their circumstances and take every opportunity to communicate the love of Christ. Critics have occasionally dismissed the idea of Paul calling for what appears to be a bourgeois church lacking radicalism but that is to ignore the precariousness of first-century Christianity and the practical benefits of a just and efficient social order, let alone of its intrinsic good.

The two pairs of words "quiet" (*ēremon*) with "well-ordered" (*hēsychion*) and "godliness" (*eusebia*) with "dignity" (*semnotēti*) convey not only desirable qualities of life in community and wider society but may imply these are specifically lacking in church members stirred up by the false teachers. All four of the qualities commended by Paul reduce the sense in which the church may come across as socially and politically suspect. Be that as it may, Pentecostal or charismatic congregations full of joy and loud praise have sometimes not sufficiently valued "quietness" and "dignity."

b. *The purpose and scope of prayer (2:3–7)*

> This *is* good and acceptable before our savior God who wants everyone to be saved and come to a knowledge of *the* truth. For there is one God and one mediator between God and humankind, the human being *that is* Christ Jesus, who

---

4. It is used in this sense in 3 Macc. 6.40, see MM, 218.

5. Cf. Josephus, *B.J.* 2:197, Philo, *Legat.* 317, noted in McLaren, "Jews and the Imperial Cult," 271–73.

> gave himself as a ransom for all, a testimony *born*[6] at exactly the right time. For this I was appointed a herald and apostle (I am speaking the truth; I am not lying)—a teacher of *the gentiles*[7] in faith and truth. (1 Tim 2:3–7)

3–4. Reiterating the thought in vv. 1–2, the prayers of the church should reach out in every direction to all peoples. In this way the wide and deep love of God is mirrored by the church. "This is good and acceptable before God our Savior," where "before" (*enōpion*) has the nuance of "in the opinion or judgement of"[8] and indicates the church stands primarily before God and not public opinion, even if public opinion must not be entirely neglected (1 Tim 3:7).

This text declares God is "our Savior." God, and no one and nothing else, saves people though in Luke 2:11 Christ is savior; the identical word used of God and Christ provides one further piece of canonical data supportive of the orthodox doctrine of the Trinity.

"God who wants everyone to be saved" expects the church to share this desire. God imparts this desire to his ministers (Paul and Timothy) as Paul's prayer about the breadth and height of God's love indicates (Eph 3:18, 19). Ministers can impart this wide vision of God's love to the church, and the church prays in expectation of a change in the spiritual and social climate as conversions occur. Paul's own conversion in 1:13–15 has already demonstrated what God can do for sinners.

There is no discussion in the text of predestination or limitations to the atonement, as Calvin acknowledges. He states, "the Apostle simply means, that there is no people and no rank in the world that is excluded from salvation,"[9] which is true, though the text itself goes beyond categories of kings and civic officials to the generality of the human race. That God "wants" (*thelei*) "everyone" (*pantas*) "to be saved" (*sōthēnai*) raises questions about universalism since, if God desires something, will it not inevitably come to pass? Yet we know from elsewhere in Paul's writings that not everyone will be "saved" not least through clear mentions of judgement and destruction (e.g., in 1 Tim 3:6, 5:24, or 6:9) as well as the need for faith. Additionally, it must be admitted "all" does not always mean all as when

---

6. Greek has no verb here, but implies "carried", "born" or similar.
7. Or "nations."
8. Knight, *Pastoral Epistles*, 119.
9. Calvin, *Timothy, Titus, Philemon*, on 1 Tim 2:4.

Jesus commands Paul to take the gospel to "all men." Yes, but Paul could not himself reach every human being in every country on the planet.[10]

The saving work of God involves a cognitive process as people "come to a knowledge of the truth." Coming to knowledge (*epignōsin elthein*) can imply a gradual realization rather than a flash of light. The intimate relationship between salvation and truth queries the notion that salvation is a "blind leap" of faith without any rational component. On the contrary, salvation involves the mind as well as the heart, and the mind may be well exercised as the extensive history of Christian theology shows.

5. "For there is one God." Here Paul asserts the monotheism of Christianity and echoes the Jewish Shema (Deut 6:4–9).[11] The one God stands over and against the multiplicity of Pagan gods. Paganism spawned a host of major and minor deities with charge of particular events or localities. Christianity, like Judaism, affirmed there is only one universal God, and, in this context, the affirmation provides a further reason why the Ephesian church should pray for everyone: everyone comes within the scope of the one God.

"One mediator between God and humankind." There is only "one mediator" or middleman or go-between with the right to speak or act on behalf of God towards humanity or speak and act on behalf of humanity towards God. The mediator can bring those who were opposed to each other together and reconcile them (2 Cor 5:19), and there is only one person who can do this and not, as Gnosticism and the false teachers are likely to have taught, a series of angelic or spiritual intermediaries spiraling all the way up from earth to heaven in a mystical and complex chain. Indeed, Towner has convincingly demonstrated that all these ideas can be explained more probably in terms of second temple Judaism and are not likely to be related to Gnosticism in any way.[12]

"The human being that is Christ Jesus." Elsewhere in the epistle Paul has implied the deity of Christ Jesus (1:2), but here he re-asserts his humanity. No special link here is made to his masculinity, however. Christ is first and foremost fully "human" (*anthrōpon*) and plunged himself into our situations and circumstances to stand alongside us all in our sorrows and joys. Though Christians have been accused of religious exclusivism in their proclamation of "one mediator," that mediator is one who gets down into the dirt of human existence and proves himself, in that sense, very far from "exclusive."

---

10. Stott, *1 Timothy & Titus*, 66, and referencing Acts 22:15, 21. Or see Col 3:11.

11. See the similar echo in 1 Cor 8:6, also moving in a "Christian" direction in its phrasing "one God . . . one Lord." Cf. here "One God . . . one mediator."

12. Towner, *Instruction*, 22–32.

6. "Who gave himself as a ransom for all." As mediator, Jesus, "gave himself" (*dous heauton*) indicating that his act was one of voluntary self-sacrifice. His mediation affects both parties, both God and humanity, and as with other descriptions of the death of Christ in the New Testament (Rom 5–7), a rich variety of concepts and metaphors is necessary to cover the multiple ways of understanding this unique and momentous event. As most commentators agree, the words here are an echo of the words of Jesus himself in Mark 10:45, thus showing how what Jesus said is carried forward into the later theology of the church. Jesus is a "ransom," and here the full force of the reality must be faced. A "ransom" is only paid to free a captive, and the term still applies today when terrorists seize innocent people and demand payment to release them. The ransom is *antilytron*, a composite word used only once in the New Testament and made up of *anti*, a preposition connoting "in place of," and *lytron*, a ransom. So, Jesus, in this compressed wording, is the self-giving substitutionary ransom. And he is the ransom for "all," which is another reason the church should pray for all.

"A testimony borne[13] at exactly the right time." This is an enigmatic statement referring back to the events of the crucifixion which occurred at "exactly the right time" in the history of the world or, alternatively, the testimony of Paul proclaiming the gospel occurred at precisely the right time for the church.

7. Paul writes of being appointed as a "herald," "apostle," and "teacher" of the gentiles. These three separate functions may refer to three overlapping but distinct activities. He was appointed by Christ as a herald, that is, to make an official announcement. The job of the herald was to announce from a higher authority the message, faithfully without alteration or comment. The word connects with *ekkēryssō*, the word used to describe the preaching of Jesus and apostolic preaching (Matt 12:41; Mark 1:7; Acts 8:5; Rom 16:25) or evangelism. The second function of "apostle" goes beyond announcement. The apostle remained in a location to look after, build up and organize the ongoing and sustainable Christian community. The third function of "teacher" goes further still and involves ensuring the new Christian community understands the breadth and basis of the Christian faith. We could argue that the three activities of heralding, being an apostle, and teaching occur in sequence, are illustrated by Paul's activities in Acts, and, indeed, are entirely in line with the revelatory visions Paul receives at his conversion and then later in the temple (Acts 22:17ff).

"A teacher of the gentiles": Paul's task of gentile mission entails prayer for the gentiles and is therefore another reason for the exhortation

---

13. Greek "made."

to wide-ranging prayer with which the chapter starts. As a teacher, Paul communicates "faith and truth." Although it is possible to read these three words to imply Paul should communicate faithfully and truthfully or even as "faithful truth," elsewhere in the Pastoral Epistles faith and truth refer objectively to the message being preached, and it seems best to presume that meaning here.[14]

"I was appointed." The personal pronoun here is emphatic and the appointment by Christ himself is consonant with the passage in Ephesians 4:11–13 speaking of the ascended Christ giving exceptional people in specialist roles to the body of the church.

"I am speaking the truth; I am not lying." By affirming that he is speaking the truth, Paul is increasing the pressure on his opponents and detractors. It is one thing to be mistaken and another thing to be a liar. The false teachers cannot claim to be teaching the truth in the same way as Paul is, especially because the very existence of the Ephesian church is evidence of Paul's truthfulness. If Paul had not been an apostle and a teacher of the gentiles, the church would not have existed. That Paul has used this kind of argument before (e.g., Rom 9:1, 2 Cor 11:31) is a further pointer to its genuineness.

c. Men and women in the church (2:8–15)

> I want men everywhere to pray, lifting up holy hands without anger and disputing, and women too, dressed respectably with modesty and self-control, not with braided hair, gold jewelry, pearls or expensive outfits, but rather *clothed in* what is suitable for women who profess godliness—good deeds. A woman should learn without distraction and in a disciplined manner[15.] I do not permit a woman to teach or exercise authority over a man, but she should remain silent. For Adam was made first, then Eve. *It was* not Adam *that* was deceived, but the woman who was deceived and fell into transgression. But she will be kept safe through childbirth[16] if she stands fast in faith, love and holiness with self-control. (1 Tim 2:8–15)

---

14. Mounce, *Pastoral Epistles*, 93.

15. Traditionally "in silence", but the Greek could imply ensuring women have proper opportunity for study.

16. The language could also mean something like "saved in and throughout her life of child-rearing etc."

8. "I want..." The structure of the chapter is shaped by the "I urge" of verse 1 and the "I want" of verse 8. In keeping with his prescription for the troubled Ephesian church, Paul turns to the men who are presumably spending more time disputing than praying and whose "hands" (in the sense of actions) lack holiness. Psalm 24.3-4 asks, "who may ascend to the hill of the Lord?" and answers "he who has clean hands and a pure heart." The precondition of approaching God is purity of heart and hands, the hand being the symbol of what we do. So here Paul wants the men (*andras*) to "pray" (*proseuchesthai*) "lifting up holy hands" and "without anger and disputing."[17] The picture is of the Mosaic position of prayer with raised hands (Exod 17:10-13). As the men pray, the disunited and disputatious congregation will come together and the effect of the false teaching will begin to fall away.

9-10 "and the women too." A natural way of taking this verse is to assume the "I want" carries over from the men to the women.[18] So the gist of the meaning would be "I want the men to pray without disputing and with holy deeds and the women to pray without ostentatious clothing and with good deeds." Consequently, Paul's desires reflect essential parity for both sexes but with some differences in detail. Although other readings are possible, the one we have chosen is less disjointed and makes sense within the context initiated in verse 1 with the general call for prayer to be made "for all people." Thus, the whole church, men and women, prays for the whole world—everyone from the civic authorities downwards.

The clothing of the women is to be "respectable" and not showy or extravagant. The actual details—"braided hair, gold jewelry, and pearls"— have cultural significance. There is nothing religiously wrong with gold (used in the OT tabernacle and temple) or jewelry (worn by the OT high priest) or pearls (used in the gates of the new Jerusalem Rev 21:21). The clothing of women is to be "modest" (or not *polytelei* or costly). There was a general concern in the early church not to introduce class distinctions on the basis of clothing, as James 2:2-4 reveals—a concern for men as well as women. However, within Roman society of this time, a new emphasis on *female* assertiveness and some of its attendant dress sense offended the sensibilities of Roman traditionalists to the extent that Augustus legislated against it.[19] Against these tendencies, women who "profess godliness" should

---

17. The fact that Paul immediately goes on to address the women in the next verse, may suggest that the disputes he is speaking of here are being considered in characteristically male terms.

18. Knight, *Pastoral Epistles*, 132. Barrett, *The Pastoral Epistles*, 55.

19. Towner, *Timothy and Titus,* 196. See also Winter, *Roman Wives*. Note the similar concern in 1 Pet 3:3-4 and on Roman sensibilities about adornment, see Wyke, "Woman in the Mirror," 134-151.

be "clothed with good deeds"—a classic theme of biblical wisdom and resonant with Roman culture too. Since good deeds are required of poor widows seeking financial support from the church (5:25) and wealthier women and men alike (6:18), the image is neither trivial nor specifically gendered.[20] As noted above, the reminder may also challenge the barren unproductiveness of those caught up in the ambit of the false teachers. In all this, Paul is urging the church at Ephesus to turn "love which comes out of a pure heart" (1:5) outwards to society at large (see also Excursus IV).

11. "A woman should learn without distraction and in a disciplined manner." Although also concerning women, this new thought brings something of a jolt as it switches away from clothing and prayer to the theme of teaching, learning, and speaking. Whilst some see this as an abrupt transition inherited from a church "rule" or early manual,[21] it is possible that there is a link if we discern further confusion caused by the false teachers.

The brief discussion of women's roles in the church which follows has been the focus of fierce disagreement among commentators and preachers. How readers respond to what is said here about teaching and learning depends to a large extent on two broader approaches to gender which may constrain their initial impressions: *complementarians* argue for men and women having equal but different roles while *egalitarians* argue for equality in every respect and without restriction.[22] Pentecostals have been instinctively egalitarian following the proclamation by Peter on the Day of Pentecost concerning the outpouring of the Spirit on men and women without distinction (Acts 2:17,18), and early Pentecostal churches as well as the revivals which preceded them freed women for ministry as evangelists, pastors, and missionaries.[23] In this, Pentecostals were following in the footsteps of Methodists who welcomed women preachers and the Salvation Army which did the same. More than this, some Pentecostals might point to Galatians 3:28 and the sweeping away of many conventional distinctions including those between the males and females. Even if the radicalism of Galatians 3:28 was nuanced in some way, Pentecostals and others would still

---

20. Johnson, *Timothy*, 200.

21. A judgement we consider unsatisfactory and improbable: "unsatisfactory" because it is unsystematic and fails to cover many aspects of church organization and conduct and "improbable" because it would be odd to write a personal letter to Timothy containing personal testimony and exhortation that was really intended to be an instructional manual for lots of congregations. The idea the Pastorals were "a handbook for church leaders" is referred to by Fee (*1 and 2 Timothy, Titus*, 21) and Kelly (*Pastoral Epistles*, 59, 60).

22. E.g., Archer and Archer, "Complementarianism and Egalitarianism," 66–90.

23. de Alminana and Olena, *Women*; Kay, *Pentecostalism*.

point to the instruction given to the older women to teach younger women (Titus 2:3, 4), that is, the impossibility of reading the restriction on women's teaching in verse 12 as being absolute.

The dispute between egalitarianism and complementarianism has played out in a different way recently. In the light of the #MeToo movement and the evidence of abuse against women in several industries, there have been calls for Pentecostalism to take a hard look at itself.[24] Has an insistence on male authority justified by Scripture led to, or made easier, the abuse of women in church-related situations? This is so in some places, and there are testimonies to this effect.[25] Yet, because violence against women has occurred in entirely secular situations and in contexts devoid of religion, it would be illogical to treat complementarian theology as a necessary cause. The World Health Organization connects violence against women with alcohol[26] which has nothing to do with theology or, rather, if there is a theological connection, it is because Scripture speaks *against* drunkenness and, according to some Pentecostals, in favor of teetotalism.

Regarding more insidious forms of abuse including the manipulation of women by powerful patriarchal forces within the church, we can only say that Scripture, as we read it, is against the mistreatment of women in any way whatsoever. The command to husbands to love their wives or to shepherds to self-sacrificially care for their flocks indicates how power within the church ought to be manifested (Eph 5:25; 1 Pet 5:1–3). In the words of Jesus himself, leaders within the church ought to sharply contrast with the exploitative and ostentatious leaders of the world: "You know that the rulers of the gentiles lord it over them, and their high officials exercise authority over them. Not so with you. Instead, whoever wants to become great among you must be your servant, and whoever wants to be first must be your slave" (Matt 20:26). Within marriage sexual relations are a matter of consent (1 Cor 7:5).

"A woman (*gynē*) should learn." In contrast with Judaism, which excluded women from the study of the Torah, Christian women were expected to learn, and do so "without distraction" (*hēsychia*) "and in a disciplined manner" (*hypotagē*) or in a formal and sustained way rather than by interruption with uninvited questions as appears to have occurred in Corinth (1 Cor 14:35). The importance of Paul's statement in favor of female learning

---

24. See also #pentecostalsisterstoo and #churchtoo

25. "This Is My Body: Addressing Global Violence against Women." Society for Pentecostal Studies 50th Anniversary Meeting, The King's University, Southlake, TX, March 18th–20th 2021 provided opportunities for personal testimonies.

26. World Health Organization, "Intimate Partner Violence."

can hardly be overstated.[27] From the very beginning Christianity was concerned with education and with the education of women. Whatever brickbats were thrown at the church by its detractors and critics, and whatever criticisms were and are made of Paul himself by those offended by one or other elements of his teaching—it was too narrow, too patriarchal, too exclusive in its doctrine of salvation—his endorsement of female education stands to his credit.

12. "I do not permit (*epitrepō*) a woman (singular) to teach (*didaskein* [infinitive]) or exercise authority (*authentein* [infinitive]) over a man." Paul restricts the Ephesian women by a similar statement (*epitrepō*) in the present indicative ("I am not permitting") and continues with the requirement that they "should remain silent" (*hēsychia*). This statement should be set in context. Speaking and remaining silent occur together in complex, sometimes unobvious, ways in different Pauline passages where the situations may not always be clear. In 1 Cor 14:34 women are apparently commanded to be silent in churches at all times, yet only a few chapters earlier, clear permission is given for them to pray and prophesy (1 Cor 11:5).

Two sorts of issue might affect the exercise of speech, one arguably where "order" is threatened and the second involving gender and culture issues more formally. These could, in different circumstances, limit the speech of both men and women.[28] Such observations will be relevant in this epistle too.

On the first point, in principle anyone may speak in church but to maintain order in many situations, people need to give way to others and remain quiet. This can be seen when prophecies and revelations are given in a group context ("if a revelation comes to someone who is sitting down, the first speaker *should stop*," 1 Cor 14:30), and the same applies to tongue-speakers where no interpretation can be offered (1 Cor 14:28). Both these contexts affect men and women alike. We should not, therefore, assume that the command for women to be silent applies all the time and in all circumstances. This is particularly clear in view of the outpouring of the Spirit on the whole church regardless of gender (cf. Acts 2:18 "and they shall [all] prophesy") and because of evidence from elsewhere in the Pauline Epistles (e.g., Phoebe, Priscilla, Mary, Junia, Tryphena, Tryphosa, Persis, Julia, the sister of Nereus in Rom 16, Euodia, and Syntyche in Phil 4:2–3) as well as

---

27. Readers will notice how translation here moves away from the frequent implication that women learners are *routinely* noisy or disruptive (cf. NRSV, NIV, et al.). For an excellent overview of all the relevant passages, see Bailey, "Women in the New Testament," 7–24.

28. On the latter point, which we shall turn to further below, the disciples are amazed in John 4:27 to find Jesus "talking with a woman" in a public place.

Acts where women like Lydia or Priscilla (*again*) could take leading, speaking roles (Acts 16:15, 40; 18:26). We believe Christian women would have spoken in the assembly—how could they pray or prophesy silently? (1 Cor 14:5, 31, 39)—even if there were occasions when it was right to remain silent. As elsewhere in the verses above, it is possible that moments of disruption occurred more often under the ministrations of the false teachers.

On the second point about the restriction of women's speech in some instructional contexts, we do not know exactly what was meant by "teaching" but assume from the wider context of these epistles the word denotes exposition of Scripture and communication of doctrine (1 Tim 3:1–7, especially v. 2; Titus 1:9). *Authentein* only occurs here in the New Testament and a huge amount of ink has been spilt on researching its usage in secular Greek texts in the years before and after the composition of the Pastoral Epistles.[29] Options boil down to a positive sense of "have authority" and a negative one of "domineer." If teaching and a negative version of *authentein* are taken together we could end up with a composite meaning that forbids domineering teaching and by implication allows other types of teaching. If teaching and *authentein* are kept apart we end up with two activities: women are forbidden to teach and to have any (domineering) authority over men. The option to narrow this interpretation to "wives" and "husbands" through the double meanings of *gynē* and *andros* is not convincing since it would suddenly shift the focus of the passage from the public setting of the church to the private setting of the home. Given the wide range of activities women have performed in Pentecostal and charismatic churches in terms of testimony, Sunday school teaching, leading worship, evangelism, prophecy, prayer, and exhortation, it is evident that Pentecostals really do take seriously the promised empowerment of women by the Holy Spirit (Acts 2:17:18).

In actual practice in Pentecostal and charismatic churches, the wives of ministers will, according to their gifting, often speak to congregations but do so as being under the authority of their husbands, even if this proviso is not made explicit. This, of course, implies some Pentecostal churches pay lip service to male authority and limitations on female teaching but look for ways to get around the restriction. In actuality, practice is less easy to categorize than theory since female testimony to healing or answered prayer or prophecy may also include teaching elements so that, even where Pentecostal and charismatic churches are influenced by latent complementarian or anti-female tendencies, the voices of women are still heard.

13. "For Adam was made first, then Eve." Supporting his argument in favor of male authority, Paul alludes to the Genesis 2 narrative of Adam's

---

29. Hübner, "Translating *authenteō* in 1 Timothy 2:12."

prior creation. There is nothing in Genesis 2 indicating Adam's authority over Eve (this waits until after the fall, Genesis 3:16) and in 1 Corinthians 11:11–12 Paul teaches the interdependence of Christian men and women on the basis of the relationship between Adam and Eve. Nevertheless, here in 1 Timothy 2:13, Paul does use the creation account to explain his interdiction on the domination of men by women, and he goes on to give a further reason against teaching by women. 14 "It was not Adam that was deceived, but the woman who was deceived and fell into transgression." So, the implication here is that the Ephesian women have been deceived just like Eve whereas the men like Adam were not.[30] That both sinned implies the men are not excused: they have sinned knowingly while the women have sinned unknowingly. In any case, Romans 5:14 states sin came on the whole human race through Adam's sin, making Adam (not Eve) the representative and blameworthy human being.

Some commentators have argued that Paul, by referring to the creation account in Genesis, is establishing a universal and unbreakable principle forbidding female teachers in the church on the grounds that they are created second and prone to deception.[31] This argument is not one we can accept for the reasons implied above. Prior to the fall the human pair enjoy mutuality and a joint commission to care for creation (Gen 2:15, 18). At the fall, the sin of Adam is greater than that of Eve since he acts knowingly and deliberately—he is undeceived, which is why he is singled out in Romans 5 and 1 Corinthians 15:22. Our reading of these controverted texts is that in the context of pervasive false teaching, which may have made disproportionate inroads among largely untaught and gullible women, Paul expects Timothy to introduce severe corrective measures: the Ephesian women are not to teach and must learn in quietness.

15. "But she will be kept safe through childbirth." This also is a statement attracting several interpretations. It is presumably given as a kind of counterbalance to restrictions placed on women in the earlier verses. The first interpretation is literally to do with giving birth and asserts the lives of Christian women will be kept safe as they give birth to babies.[32] The trouble with this view is that good Christian women sadly do die in childbirth

---

30. Bailey points out that the somewhat special Ephesian context of Artemis worship hypothesized here leads to the only mention of the deception of Eve in the whole of the New Testament. This may rightly add to our suspicions that quite disruptive claims to female spiritual authority may be at play here as nowhere else.

31. Implied by Barrett, *The Pastoral Epistles*, 56. See also Packer, *Differences*, 299, quoted by Stott, *1 Timothy & Titus*, 77; also, Knight, *Pastoral Epistles*, 144. At least some Jews did think this, as seen in Philo, *Opif.* 165–66; *QG* 1:46; *Leg.* 2:24–25.

32. Fee, *1 and 2 Timothy, Titus*, 75.

from time to time. A second view interprets childbirth metaphorically to mean women will be saved to give birth to the virtues of "faith, love, and holiness with self-control." Despite extensive defense, this seems a strained reading.[33] The third possibility asserts that women will be able to live full and spiritual Christian lives in and through the working context of household management and motherhood. Support for this position comes from the encouragement later in the Pastorals to women to take on such roles and the fact that the false teachers derided and suppressed such a vision, to the extent of forbidding marriage altogether (1 Tim 4:3; 5:14). Fourth, childbirth or "the childbirth" refers to the birth of Christ which some early exegetes believed to be foreshadowed by Genesis 3:15 where the offspring of the woman "crushes the serpent's head." If this functions as a theological overtone to the already huge importance of mothers for the life and mission of the church[34], then the third and fourth suggestions can work together as a doubly convincing reading. It remains significant that Paul closes his argument here with a reminder that the key goals for women disciples are the same as for men, namely that they "stand fast in faith, love, and holiness with self-control." In this sense, the whole community is involved in offering a powerful and living denial of the false teaching.

Our reading of these verses condones the participation of women in the life of the church as actors and not merely spectators. This said, these verses affirm again and again the unique, saving and redeeming work of Christ. The crucial issue is not the gender of the teacher but the doctrine the teacher expounds.

---

33. Waters, "Saved through Childbearing," 703–35.

34. As, of course, particularly emphasized in Timothy's own case in 2 Tim 1:5. For an excellent study on both the opportunities and the constraints facing women in the domestic sphere in early Christianity, see Osiek, *A Woman's Place*, 6.

III. OVERSEERS AND DEACONS
   a. Overseers (3:1–7)
   b. Deacons (3:8–13)
   c. Reiteration of Pauline purpose with faith summary (3:14–16)

III. OVERSEERS AND DEACONS

a. Overseers (3:1–7)

> The saying is sure, "if anyone aspires to be an overseer, they desire a noble task." An overseer must be irreproachable, the husband of just one wife, sober, self-controlled, respectable, welcoming newcomers, an experienced teacher[1], not *someone* with a drink problem *or* a bully, a capable[2], peaceful *person*, not always thinking about financial rewards, looking after their own household well[3], keeping their children in order by being truly worthy of respect[4]. For if someone does not know how to manage their own household, how will they take care of God's church? They should not be a new convert[5] or they may become conceited[6] and fall into the condemnation of the devil. Rather, they should have a good reputation amongst those outside the church and not be in danger of[7] falling into disgrace and the devil's trap. (1 Tim 3:1–7)

This chapter describes the sort of people who should be in office in the church. The first section deals with "overseers" (*episkopēs*) and the second with "deacons" (*diakonous*). Acts 20:17, 28 show overseers (and the word

---

1. Himes, "Rethinking the Translation of Διδακτικός," 189–208.

2. Alternative translations might include: "respectable," "fair," or "kind."

3. The "household" would have included the nuclear family, probably grandparents, possibly other relatives, and potentially servants and slaves.

4. Greek "in all dignity."

5. *neophytos*, "recent convert" (lit. "newly planted") is used just here in the NT, cf. BDAG, 536.

6. Other possible translations include: "deluded" or "conceited." A more colloquial translation might be "end up with his head in the clouds," if a smoke etymology is to be accepted (Mounce, *Pastoral Epistles*, 181).

7. Greek "in order that they may not . . ."

has also been translated "bishops") are the same as elders (*presbyterous*). Deacons are those who serve and, if we take Acts 6 to describe the appointment of the first deacons, we then have a two-tier model where the elders deal with the spiritual life of the church including teaching and the deacons deal with practical and community matters. Such a model stems directly from Acts 6 where the apostles find themselves unable to function efficiently because they need to distribute food to the many widows in the Jerusalem church. They ask the church to choose seven men full of the Holy Spirit and wisdom (6:3) whom they can set over this duty. The church makes its choice, and the apostles complete the appointment with laying on of hands and prayer. Once the apostles have been freed up, the church goes through a further phase of growth (6:7). We assume the pattern established in the large church in Jerusalem is followed by smaller churches elsewhere—though with the variation that elders (or bishops or overseers) take on the spiritual and teaching role originally performed by the apostles.

Ignatius exhorts the second-century church to set a sole "bishop" over a large geographical area covering many separate congregations.[8] This would seem to represent a departure from the earliest situation where Paul appointed elders for local churches and left them in charge while he traveled and planted new congregations (Acts 14:23). The situation presupposed by the Pastoral Epistles is still like this, where a group of elders is in charge of each congregation, though the network as a whole is still overseen in some sense by the original founding apostle or his delegate. The kind of situation depicted here is fully in line with what we should expect of an epistle written towards the end of Paul's life: the Ephesian church is governed by a plurality of elders and can only be brought back to the right path by one of the final undertakings of the elderly apostle.

The solid and stable character of elders and deacons spelled-out in this chapter is crucial to the righting of the Ephesian church. The stipulations "seem to me to be forged on the anvil of the Ephesus crisis (hence the emphasis on reputation, the test of time, etc.)."[9]

1. "The saying is sure." Although some scholars assume these words belong with the maxim on women's faith at the end of the preceding chapter, they can also make sense introducing a saying about ministry at the start of this new section. It is possible that the saying arose in a secular context as an encouragement to civic leadership. This could be expensive to the holder who might be expected to erect buildings or in other ways benefit

---

8. Ign. *Magn.* 6–7, *Trall.* 2–3; Chadwick, *The Early Church*, 46. See also Lightfoot, "The Christian Ministry," 181–269, and Kelly, *Pastoral Epistles*, 73.

9. As Lance Pierson put it to us (private communication, 2020).

the populace. The word *over-seer* is a literal translation of *epi-skopos* and so could apply to any managerial role. In the current context, Paul may be encouraging new leaders to come forward to replace the false elders who have caused so much harm.

"If anyone aspires to be an overseer, they desire a noble task" (*kalou ergou*, literally *good work*). The task is *noble* (or good) and an ambition to become an overseer is acceptable and should be fostered. Existing church leaders should encourage their flock to grow and take on new responsibility in the leadership realm: the suppression of new talent by leaders only concerned about protecting their own positions is reprehensible.

2. "An overseer must be irreproachable." What follows is not a list of tasks as is found in a job description but a list of character traits. The requirement is strictly necessary, as the Greek *dei* (*must be*) indicates. The word "irreproachable" (*anepilēmpton*) heads the list and the qualities given in the next few verses point to the behaviors that mark out an overseer. Irreproachability like the "breastplate of righteousness" (Eph 6:14) indicates the overseer is not vulnerable to accusations arising inside or outside the church. This is a person who has done what is right over an extended period of time.

The first area of life is marriage. The overseer is "the husband of just one wife" (*mias gynaikos andra* or literally a *one-woman man*). Four interpretations of this unusual phrase have been offered. The overseer must (i) must be married or (ii) have only had one wife during his entire life or (iii) be monogamous, i.e., not polygamous or married to several wives at the same time or (iv) faithful to his one wife. Of these options, (i) founders on the strong likelihood that neither Paul nor Timothy was married and, moreover, the later words about managing children would rule out married men without children; (ii) is unlikely because it would rule out remarriage after the death of a spouse, something Paul specifically allows and accepts elsewhere both in the Pastorals (1 Tim 5:11–15) and in his other epistles (1 Cor 7:39; Rom 7:1–3); (iii) is supported by the social conditions of the day: polygamy occasionally occurred in the elite strata of the Jewish community[10] and (iv) fidelity to one wife, in keeping with the mainstream of Christian tradition; this would rule out sexual promiscuity, "open marriages," "affairs," and other forms of adultery. Options (iii) and (iv) are supported by the most evidence. The words *one-woman-man* anticipates the overseer will be faithful to his wife, but the phrase does not have an obvious bearing in the realm of divorce and remarriage. Those denominations which accept divorce on

---

10. Knight references Josephus *A.J.* 17:14 and *B.J.* 1:477 and also points out that in AD 212 "*lex Antoniana de civitate* made monogamy the law for Romans but Jews were excepted" (*Pastoral Epistles*, 158).

the grounds of adultery or separation and the consequent remarriage of the innocent partner would not find 1 Timothy 3:2 an obstacle to church office.

"Sober" (*nēphalion*), "self-controlled" (*sōphrona*), "respectable" (*kosmion*) all add to the picture of the overseer as a prudent, thoughtful, clear-headed, and orderly, virtuous person. Welcoming newcomers (*philoxenon*, literally *loving foreigners*) draws attention to hospitality in the early church, to the welcome of local visitors as well as itinerant ministers.[11] "An experienced teacher" (*didaktikon*, from which we derive the English word "didactic") is a crucial qualification which is amplified, as are most of the words in the list, in a parallel passage in Titus (1:6–10). In Titus 1:9 the overseer must be able to "exhort in sound doctrine and refute those who contradict," a positive expository ministry to edify the congregation and a negative critical capacity to expose error and resist it. Rational argument and expository skill are needed to bring down false teaching and defeat it.[12] The overseer does not shout or use physical threats or force but as a calm self-controlled person can return the congregation to sound doctrine by arguments directly taken from a broad understanding of Scripture.

3. "not someone with a drink problem or a bully." The overseer is not alcoholic or veering in this direction but, at the same time, the word (*paroinon*) does not imply teetotalism. Additionally, they are not a "bully" (*plēktēn*), a brawler, prone to physical violence; quite the opposite, they are "peaceful" (*epieikē*), forbearing, and "capable" (*amachon*) as well as kind. This peaceful and gracious disposition avoids obsessional love of money found in those "always thinking about financial rewards" (*aphilargyron*). 4. More than this these qualities are practically realized in the overseer's household, which is properly managed. They look "after their own household well," a social unit that might include grandparents as well as servants, slaves, and children. The overseer's relationship with their children is the surest sign of their parental (here, fatherly) qualities and their suitability for responsibility within the church. Their children are *kept in order* with dignity and "respect" (*semnotētos*). 5. The connection between home and church is explicit: "For if someone does not know how to manage their own household, how will they take care of God's church?" The same combination of love, authority, wisdom, and skill that is required to bring up respectful children is necessary in the congregation because the church is a family, a household of faith, a place of brotherhood and sisterhood, an organic all-age social group. By contrast, then, the church is not an institution or a

---

11. See Arterbury, *Entertaining Angels*.

12. It is intriguing that in 2 Cor 10:4–5 Paul uses the language of spiritual warfare to describe this task.

business organization ruled over by a chief executive and their staff. Nor is it a fiefdom bullied into subjection through the threat of violence by money-grabbing pastors.

6. If they are read in their most natural way, the next two verses highlight two dangers with appointing the wrong people as overseers. New converts are in danger of becoming proud of their position and then abruptly falling (into sin), and men without a good reputation in the community are in danger of falling into devilish traps and so bringing disgrace on the church. This double warning is put in place to caution against the appointment of men who, though they fulfill all the other criteria, are ultimately unsuitable.

The overseer is not to be a "new convert" (*neophyton*), literally one newly "planted" in the faith. Such a person may become "conceited" (*typhōtheis*). This word derives from a word denoting being "enveloped in smoke," or out of touch with reality, living in cloud-cuckoo-land,[13] and caught up in fantasy. How many young leaders have we seen launching into grandiose building projects only to find themselves empty handed and embarrassed? The danger here is of a false vision fueled by naïve teaching on visualizing the object of faith or a superficial faith doctrine about speaking things into existence without fulfilling any other conditions.

"And fall into the condemnation of the devil." The devil's pride was judged by God and the conceited overseer or elder will suffer the same fate unless he maintains humility. The mechanism typifying this sort of event is likely to vary. We may be helped by considering the contrast between tentative Moses, reluctant to take up his commission at the burning bush (Exod 4:10, 13), and resentful Miriam who feels her voice is not being heard, "hasn't he [the Lord] also spoken through us?" (Num 12:2). For her arrogance she experienced a week of divine judgement and shame (Num 12:9–15).

7. The overseer or elder should have a "good reputation" (*martyrian kalēn*) "amongst those outside the church" which implies the elder is known in the secular community and respected. He is not an isolated individual without any dealings with the outside world but, on the contrary, pays his bills, behaves courteously to others, and is trusted by non-Christians. The early Quakers and Methodists built up their businesses and prospered because customers knew they would not be cheated. It takes wisdom, time, and patience to build up such reputations and the leaders of the early church must have worked hard to gain this level of esteem.[14] Appointing men without a good track record is risking trouble.

---

13. Stott, *1 Timothy & Titus*, 98.

14. On the positive sense of social engagement, integrity, and public "belonging"

"Not be in danger of[15] falling into disgrace and the devil's trap." The picture here is of the devil trying to ensnare Christian leaders with a tasty temptation which, if surrendered to, will expose them to *oneidismon* or reproach and negative publicity. The trap (*pagida*) speaks of snares to catch birds.[16] In an age of social media, the sins of the clergy can be halfway round the world in hours bringing disrepute on the whole Christian community.

Because the word *diabolos* or devil means "slanderer," the references in these verses might conceivably refer to a human slanderer but the context points to the personal devil most certainly believed in by the authors of the New Testament. The earlier reference to Hymenaeus and Alexander being handed over to Satan (1:20) as well as later the later allusion contained in the phrase "doctrines of demons" (4:1) show Paul understood the Ephesian church's situation as endangered by occult powers, a concept disturbing to the contemporary mind.

The character and attributes of Christian leaders are firmly rooted in their godly behavior established over considerable periods of time—long enough for the results to be seen in the sort of children they are raising. Of course, no parent can be held responsible for the sins of their children, especially when these children are grown-up (Ezek 18:20; 1 Sam 8:1–3), but the general principle that true character is revealed behind the closed doors of the home and seen by family members remains a good one. There is no reference in this chapter to the need for church leaders to exercise spiritual gifts, and some commentators have found this odd. However, Paul has already made reference to prophecies uttered by the body of elders who ordained Timothy and so he obviously recognizes elders are likely to manifest *charismata* (1:18). We should best understand the first verses of this chapter as underlining the primary importance of character and integrity without assuming spiritual gifts are unnecessary or unimportant. Although several early Pentecostals attempted to correlate the spiritual gifts of 1 Corinthians 12 with the ministry gifts of Ephesians 4, the linkages were never exact or invariable. Donald Gee concluded that elders who were expected to teach would manifest the "word of knowledge" (1 Cor 12:8) rather than any of the power gifts involving signs and wonders.[17] By contrast healing in the church stemmed from the Holy Spirit's response to the prayer of faith (Jas 5:14–16) rather than to the "gifts of healing" listed in Corinthians (1 Cor 12:9).

---

suggested here, see Winter, *Seek the Welfare of the City*.

15. Greek "in order that they may not . . ."
16. Knight, *Pastoral Epistles*, 165.
17. Gee, *Concerning Spiritual Gifts*, 34. Gee, *The Ministry Gifts of Christ*, 65.

When totaled up, overseers meet ten criteria: faithfulness in marriage; clear headedness; hospitality; teaching ability; moderation in drinking; a cool temper and balanced temperament; not money-grubbing; managing the home well; spiritual maturity and having a good reputation outside the church.

b. Deacons (3:8–13)

> In the same way, deacons *should also be* worthy of respect, not duplicitous, not given to too much *alcohol*[18], not financially corrupt, holding to the mystery of the faith with a clear conscience. Such people should first be tested, then if they *prove themselves* blameless, let them serve. In just the same way, female *deacons*[19] should be equally worthy of respect, not slanderous, not problem drinkers *and* faithful in all things. *Male* deacons should be married to only one woman, manage their own homes and *bring up their* children well[20]; for *all* those who serve well gain a good standing for themselves and great confidence[21] in *their*[22] faith in Christ Jesus. (1 Tim 3:8–13)

The next section focuses on deacons. We assume that deacons handle practical and community matters because the main difference between the verses dealing with them and with elders is that there is no requirement for deacons to be able to teach. There might be confusion between elders and deacons on the grounds that Paul many times refers to himself as a servant using the Greek word also translated as "deacon" (e.g., 1 Cor 3:5, 2 Cor 6:4; Eph 3:7; Col 1:23), and, in fact, all those with any form of ministry within the church are strictly speaking servants. However, if we take Acts 6 as our template, then there is a distinction between the practical and the pastoral roles. We know the early church developed two orders of ministry: elders/overseers on the one side and deacons on the other.[23] We also know the huge

18. Greek "wine."
19. Or "*deacons*' wives."
20. The Greek word "manage," unnaturally to us, applies to both home and *children*.
21. Or "boldness."
22. Since the Greek article "the" appears here, Paul could be referring to "*the* Christian faith" as a social context.
23. "The epistle of Clement of Rome to the Corinthians implies the existence of two distinct orders of ministry, bishops *or* presbyters (the titles are applied to the

and wide-ranging practical and community-facing effort of the early church resulted in charitable acts in a Roman society lacking any centrally directed form of welfare. "By 251 the resources of the church in Rome had grown so much that it was supporting from its common purse not only the bishop, 46 presbyters, seven subdeacons, 42 acolytes, and 52 exorcists, readers and doorkeepers, but also more than 1,500 widows and needy persons all of whom were 'fed by the grace and kindness of the Lord.'"[24]

8. "In the same way" (*hōsautōs*), introduces this next section and makes it parallel to the requirements for overseers. "Deacons (*diakonous*) should also be worthy of respect (*semnous*)," serious, grave, and even venerable people who are obviously trustworthy and reliable. They are not "duplicitous (*dilogous*)" or double-tongued, saying one thing and doing another or "given to too much alcohol," a phrase that would exclude total abstinence or teetotalism by implying moderate drinking (but not drunkenness) is permissible. Nor are they "financially corrupt" (*aischrokerdeis*) or greedy for dishonest gain for the very obvious reason that they will administer or distribute money from the church.

9. "Holding the mystery (*mystērion*) of the faith." Not only is the deacon a man of integrity, he holds the faith honestly. The New Testament term "mystery" refers to a previously concealed truth that has now been revealed by God. Jesus himself speaks of the "mystery of the kingdom" (Mark 4:4), and Paul speaks of the "mystery of the gentiles" (Rom 11:25), "of the faith" (1 Cor 2:1), and of "the resurrection of the body" (1 Cor 15:51). With "a clear (*kathara*) conscience (*syneidēsei*)," again as in 1:5, 19 "conscience" refers to the inner self-knowledge of the believer, an important clue as to the way Paul thought of people not as robotic mechanisms but with self-consciousness and a capacity to evaluate their own beliefs and actions.

10. Paul instructs the church to test potential deacons ("such people should first be tested") before being allowed to serve. We do not know what sort of testing occurred, but it shows how early Christians considered serving Christ was a privilege. Ostensibly, there were more candidates than places, so some would have failed the test and been turned down. It is striking that a *claim* to be called and/or gifted for this work was not enough. Only "if they prove blameless (*anenklētoi*, repeated also in Titus 1:6–7), should they serve."

11. "In just the same way (*hōsautōs*), female deacons . . ." This introduces a new group set in parallel to those addressed previously, who would most naturally be understood as women deacons. It is true the interpretation

---

same people) and deacons," Chadwick, *The Early Church*, 46.

24. Chadwick, *The Early Church*, 57, 58.

of this sentence is not entirely straightforward, not only because the word *diakonoi* from v. 8 is not repeated[25] but also because the word *gynaikas* can mean "wives" as well as "women." However, although a reference here to deacons' wives is possible, the absence of a similar requirement for the wives of overseers or elders would make this unlikely. It would be odd if the wives of deacons were to be irreproachable, but the wives of elders need not reach the same standard! Because each new category is introduced by *hōsautōs*, "in the same way," we take verse 11 to refer to female deacons. The criteria are: being (1) "worthy of respect" (*semnas*[26]), (2) "not slanderers" (*diabolous*), (3) "not problem drinkers," i.e., temperate (*nēphalious*), and (4) "faithful in all things." The first requirement is exactly the same as for the men, the second is very similar, and the third is also paralleled.

An historical snapshot is found in the correspondence of the obsequious Roman administrator, Pliny, in about AD 112. Investigating reports of Christianity in the province of Bithynia, he found two female "servants" of the church[27] and had them tortured to discover more about the Christian community in his vicinity. The two unfortunate women confirmed what he already knew, namely that Christians had no evil or immoral intent towards wider Roman society.[28]

12. The text then awkwardly returns to male deacons and specifies the same need for faithfulness in marriage and well-managed homes as was found in the list of requirements for overseers. 13. Those who served well in a diaconal capacity gained "good standing for themselves" which must have been in addition to the exemplary character they had demonstrated prior to their appointments and "great confidence in their faith," presumably because the period of service fortified their Christian beliefs as they saw close up how the teaching of Jesus impacted impoverished lives for the better. In short, arduous practical service for Christ will be rewarding.

---

25. *Diakonos* can be used for both male and female servants (LSJ, 398). Famously, in Rom 16:1, Paul calls Phoebe a *diakonos tēs ekklēsias*.

26. The feminine form of the word applied in verse 8 to men.

27. That female deacons are intended is fairly likely, although Pliny is clearly struggling to understand their status: "duae ancillae, quae ministrae dicebantur," two female slaves said to be "attendants"; *ministra* could easily translate the Greek *diakonos*.

28. Plin. (Y) *Ep.* 10:96 in Stevenson, *A New Eusebius*, 19.

c. Reiteration of Pauline purpose with faith summary (3:14–16)

> I hope to come to you very soon, but if I am delayed, I am writing these things to you[29] so that you may know how everyone should conduct themselves in God's household which is the church of the living God, the pillar and mainstay of the truth. Without question, the mystery *at the heart* of our religious devotion is great:
>
> "He was manifested in the flesh,
>
> vindicated by the Spirit,
>
> seen by angels,
>
> proclaimed among the gentiles[30],
>
> believed upon in the world,
>
> *and* taken up in glory." (1 Tim 3:14-16)

The chapter affirms Paul's intention to come to Ephesus to enforce the instructions he has given Timothy in the light of the church's critical role in support of the truth. What is particularly interesting about all these words is that they show Paul's strategy for dealing with the desperate problems within the Ephesian church. Not only will he rebut the false teaching (chapter 1) and encourage fervent prayer (chapter 2), but he will also re-assess the suitability of existing elders and deacons—and presumably look for others (3:1)—because he needs to ensure the leadership of the church is sound (chapter 3). Only if he is delayed will the work fall to Timothy, but, even here, his general stipulations are such as to show the errant leaders in the church what is wrong, and the direction they should take to reform themselves and their teachings. The chapter then ends on a high note and in this respect is similar to other chapter endings elsewhere in the epistles (Rom 11:33-34; 1 Cor 15:58-16:1; Eph 3:20-21; 1 Tim 1:17-18).

14-15. "I hope to come to you very soon." Still hopeful of opportunities to travel, Paul intends to sort out the Ephesian church himself. In the interim, and if he is "delayed," the epistle directs Timothy and is intended to have an impact on the congregation(s) as it is read out to them. Here is instruction on "how everyone should (*dei*) conduct themselves." They are "in God's household (*oikō Theou*)" and as a consequence should (*dei*, or must) behave appropriately. The notion of a household is present in this epistle and elsewhere in the New Testament since it was the basic social unit

---

29. Word order altered here to make better sense in English.
30. Or "nations."

of Roman society.³¹ It represented not only the nuclear and extended family living under one roof but also slaves and retainers of the home who would have had sleeping quarters in the property and been fed and clothed as part of their pay or conditions of service. There would have been variations in the composition of the household according to wealth and social status, but the concept was the same. So, the people of God within the church are part of the household of God where God is the head of the household and provides for his family. In God's household, there should be godly attitudes and behavior. In a secular Roman household, disobedient and rebellious members would eventually find themselves excluded and the same threat hangs over the false teachers damaging the Ephesian church (cf. 1:20).

God's household is none other than the "church (*ekklēsia*) of the living God."³² We are so accustomed to the word "church" that we skip over its origins. It was originally used in a secular sense of a gathering or people called out for a particular purpose, and the New Testament has taken this word and adapted it to the reality of Christianity.³³ There is in the gathering of Christians for worship or teaching or other purposes a special solemnity and order that creates conditions for God to dwell in his people. The Old Testament saw the manifestation of God's presence within the magnificent Jerusalem temple, but here, in the New Testament, this manifestation is in the gathered people of God (though that does not mean God fails to dwell in individual Christians in a solitary condition). And God is the "living God," active, awesome, and willing to speak and manifest his presence through charismatic gifts which are gifts of the Holy Spirit. By using the metaphor of the household and the metaphor of the church, Paul is able to demonstrate the rich multi-functionality of Christian communities, and to these, he adds a further key function. The church is to be the "pillar and mainstay of the truth" in the sense that the church is the protector and embodiment of the truth of the gospel. Truth in this epistle (e.g., 2:4) and elsewhere in Paul's writing tends to refer to the gospel rather than to an abstract philosophical concept although, undoubtedly, speaking the truth and acting with integrity are part of the gospel's outworking in any community of Christians. By making a fluid transition from the metaphor of household to the formal gathering (church) to a building with a pillar and mainstay (or foundation?), Paul

---

31. See Introduction.

32. We note absence of the definite article here implies the church denoted in this phrase is local (i.e., Ephesian) rather than universal, but the meaning is the same since lots of local churches when added together comprise the universal church.

33. MM, 195. The word "meant originally any public assembly of citizens summoned by a herald."

recognizes the structural solidity of the church as a visible testimony in its own right. There may be institutional aspects to the church but these by no means negate the household aspects or hide the imperatives of the gospel.

16. Paul does not disguise "the mystery at the heart of our religious devotion (*eusebeias*)." "Mystery" is revealed truth from God and should never be confused with the rationally derived propositions of Greek philosophy. Our "religious devotion" or piety can be expressed in what appears to be an early Christian hymn or fragment of a hymn arranged in six lines. These have been variously analyzed, but they all start with aorist passive verb ending in *ōthē* followed by a prepositional phrase beginning with *en*. The simplest way to understand these lines is as a stylized account of the coming, mission and exaltation of Christ. "He was manifested in the flesh (born, incarnated), vindicated by the Spirit (either at his baptism or resurrection), seen by angels (either at his birth or resurrection), proclaimed among the gentiles (preached by the early church), believed upon in the world (as a result of preaching), and taken up in glory (at his ascension)." The contrast between flesh and Spirit in the first pair of lines and angels and gentiles in the second pair and the world and glory at the end is deliberate and intended for literary as well as theological effect.

IV. UNHEALTHY AND HEALTHY TEACHING

    a. Devilish inroads (4:1–3)

    b. Teaching the goodness of creation (4:4–6)

    c. Strenuous and exemplary godliness (4:7–11)

    d. Following through (4:12–5:2)

IV. UNHEALTHY AND HEALTHY TEACHING

After the highpoint of the ancient hymn the letter returns to the enormous challenges ahead. The words "teach these things" (v. 6) and "command these things and teach them" (v. 11) provide a structure to what Paul says next. Beginning with two pithy and pointed verses about the current onslaught on the church at Ephesus, he spends the best part of the chapter with a mixture of instruction and encouragement to Timothy. The created order in Genesis and godly living are key to what follows.

a. Devilish inroads (4:1–3)

> Now the Spirit clearly says that in later times, some will depart from the faith, giving credence to deceitful spirits and *the* teachings of demons *thanks to the* hypocrisy of *certain* liars, whose consciences are seared. They forbid marriage *and insist on* abstinence from foods which God created for partaking in with thankfulness by the faithful who know the truth. (1 Tim 4:1–3)

1. The current wave of false teaching afflicting the Ephesian church should come as no surprise. The "Spirit" has already warned of defections "in later times." How the Spirit spoke is unknown to us although we have examples in Acts of the ministry of Agabus who warned the Antioch church of impending famine (Acts 11:28). We already know that Jesus himself in Mark 13:6 outlined a period of spiritual confusion: "many will come in my name . . . they will lead many astray." To the church in Thessalonica, Paul had warned of a "wicked deception" and the appearance of the "son of perdition." The result of all this is "some will depart from the faith" meaning that they had once been in the faith. This is not persecution of the church but loss. Ex-Christians who had once rejoiced in their salvation and taken Holy Communion have now reverted to their pagan way of life. And why did

they do so? They have done so because they have listened to deceitful spirits (perhaps in the cultural realm) and the "teaching of demons" (perhaps emanating from cultic oracles in the nearby temple of Artemis (also known as Diana). (See also Excursus III).

2. The mechanism by which these doctrines have been implanted in the church is now addressed. Paul could hardly be more dismissive or curt about the perpetrators of these fatal errors. Errors have come into the church through "certain liars," that is, individuals who speak all kinds of dangerous rubbish and whose own "consciences are seared." The individuals concerned are "liars," speaking things that are false, and whose own consciences have been "seared (*kekaustēriasmenōn*)" or cauterized or in other words burned till they are dead. Here again (1:5, 19; 3:9), we have reference to conscience as the internal monitor of moral behavior. These "liars" have no consciences and do not reflect on their actions. In this sense they are superficial and shallow individuals however forceful they may be.

3. The false teachers "forbid marriage." This shows how arrogant and misguided they are.[1] Their commands and rules are "hypocritical" because they allow those who are already married to remain in this state; there is no hint of a demand for forced divorce. Marriage services were presumably conducted at a ceremony in front of the congregation with the result that the whole church is affected and, of course, especially the young who fall in love and want a Christian wedding. By forbidding marriage as well as, presumably, continuing to teach against fornication, the false teachers are preventing the church from growing by normal reproductive methods. Moreover, by enforcing celibacy on the young, the false teachers are creating pressure for surreptitious sexual activity with all the damaging impact this will have on everyone concerned. "Better," Paul had said, "to marry than burn" (1 Cor 7:9), and of course, "if you marry, you do not sin" (v. 28).

Alongside their ban on marriage, the false teachers imposed dietary restrictions or "abstinence from foods." We have no idea exactly what these were, but we do know that discussions about food offered to idols and vegetarianism had already occurred in Paul's letters in answer to queries raised by other churches (1 Cor 8:1-2; Rom 14:2). The restrictions must have been part and parcel of the ascetic lifestyle being promoted by the false teachers[2] and which would have created lines of demarcation between Christians who

---

1. Irenaeus (ca. AD 130-202), *Haer.* 1:28.1, and Clement of Alexandria (ca. AD 150-215), *Strom.* 1:15, both knew of an ascetic sect called "Encratites" who, as here, forbade marriage.

2. Hippolytus (ca. AD 170-235), *Haer.* 8:13, says that the Encratites, (n. 111 above), besides forbidding marriage, also abstained from all animal-based food and alcohol.

abstained from particular foods and Christians who did not with all the potential for intra-congregational quarrels and guilt.

In the second part of the verse, Paul begins his rebuttal of demonic doctrine. He returns to the original condition of the world at creation and the entire purpose for the provision of energy sources for humanity through the intake of food. God created all the different kinds of food "for partaking in." These foods are evidence of God's generosity and ought to be "received thankfully by the faithful." To reject foods on unwarranted, supposedly spiritual grounds is to reject God's goodness, an argument that finds echoes in Paul's address to the people of Lystra: "He has shown kindness by giving you rain from heaven and crops in their seasons" (Acts 14:17). Foods provided by God may be received without false guilt by those "who know the truth," showing how truth sets free rather than binds up (cf. John 8:32).

b. Teaching the goodness of creation (4:4–6)

> For everything which is created by God is good, and nothing should be rejected if it is received with gratitude, for it is made holy by the word of God and by prayer. If you teach these things to the brothers and sisters, you will be a good servant of Jesus Christ, brought up in the words of faith and good teaching that you have followed closely. (1 Tim 4:4–6)

4. Expanding on the rationale and making the reference to Genesis explicit Paul affirms a central biblical truth that "everything which is created by God is good" (Gen 1:9, 12, 21, 25).[3] The only stipulation he makes is that it be "received with gratitude." 5. And he continues "it is made holy," thus not only acceptable, but "holy" and made so by the "word of God and prayer," which probably refers the giving of thanks at the meal table and the gospel itself with the words of Jesus "declaring all foods clean" (Mark 7:19).

6. Timothy's teaching is to expose the origin and baneful effects of false teaching and to point to the gospel and the original goodness of creation as a remedy. Only healthy teaching undoes unhealthy teaching, and so Timothy should "teach these things" (everything from 2:1 to 4:5) regardless of what

---

3. Although the Jew-gentile distinction is probably not in view here, the goodness of creation in Gen 1 was not understood by Jews to have been *negated* by the special laws of Lev 11:7–17 and parallels, which symbolized their *moral* separation from the gentile world (cf. Lev 20:24b–26; Let. Aris. 142–155). Paul was always clear these rules were not applicable to gentiles at all, the situation of many if not most of Timothy's church members.

others may do or say. If he does this, he will be a "good servant of Jesus Christ," to whom his ultimate loyalty lies. It is to the "brothers and sisters" Timothy must speak to the ordinary congregational members who are being duped, though in the next chapter the right approach to elders is spelled out.

The next word (*entrephomenos*) can mean "train" or "nourish" which is why "brought up" is an appropriate translation and, as a present participle, it is "concurrent with the main verb, *you will be*."[4] Consequently, the sentence indicates not only what sort of servant Timothy is through a long upbringing shaped and nurtured by Scripture but also the kind of people the brothers and sisters of the church should be. They also should be shaped and nurtured by Scripture, by "the words of faith and good teaching."[5] "Words of faith" probably refer to the gospel itself. The Scriptures, then, are the antidote to unhealthy teaching and retain the ability to feed Timothy and those who listen to him.

c. Strenuous and exemplary godliness (4:7–11)

> **Reject the empty myths** *of folklore* **and train yourself up in godliness. For while physical training is of some use,** *training in* **godliness is beneficial in every way insofar as it holds promise both for this present life and the life to come. The saying is sure and worthy of all acceptance. For this purpose we toil and endure insults, because we have put our hope in** *the* **living God who is the savior of all and especially** *of the* **faithful. Command these things and teach them. (1 Tim 4:7–11)**

7. Next Paul speaks of "empty myths of folklore." The use of the pejorative *bebēlous* (empty, worthless or profane) may point beyond para-biblical lore to the numerous stories of Greek and Roman mythology. These stories circulated in classical culture, functioning as explanatory tales of the otherwise inexplicable forces in human life. Do you want to know why we have winter and summer? Look at the story of Proserpina. Do you want to know why Athens gained supremacy over other Greek cities? Look at the story of the goddess Athena. Do you want to know why human life is suddenly cut short? Look at the story of the three sisters of fate, and so on. Unlike the embroidering of Jewish law with additional restrictions and outlandish speculations, the myths of Greece and Rome have little in the way of moral content. You would not from them, for example, make any deductions about

---

4. Fee, *1 and 2 Timothy, Titus*, 103
5. Mounce, *Pastoral Epistles*, 249.

forbidden food or forbidden marriage. The protagonists of Greek myths are not much more than human beings writ large. The adventures of Theseus, Odysseus, and Hercules speak of human effort and ingenuity. They were the superheroes of their day, but they offered little to the church and Timothy should leave them well alone.[6]

Paul now changes the metaphor of nurture and upbringing in v. 6 to one of athletic discipline—curiously also very "Greek," but now of much clearer value![7] "Train yourself up (*gymnaze*)" is the word from which we derive gymnasium and gymnast. And what is the goal of Timothy's training? It is none other than godliness (or *eusebeia*). This word denotes religion elsewhere in the Bible and shares a root with words referring to "awe and reverence." Thus, it implies "a worship that befits that awe and a life of active obedience that befits that reverence."[8] It is not just an "inner form" of life but "has an inner power."[9] We should emphasize that "godliness" does not imply walking around with a long face all day and pretending to be holy. Instead, it has affinities of being "in Christ" and sharing his joy.

The command to "train yourself up" introduces the notion of disciplined exercise and draws comparison with athletes who put themselves through a training program to achieve higher levels of excellence.[10] Timothy is to exercise himself in "godliness" which implies spiritual disciplines of prayer and Bible reading with a view to becoming godlier, increasing his inner capacity. This is not the false asceticism of the errant teachers, but it is an answer to any accusations they might make over Timothy or even Paul's apparent laxity. Moreover godliness, unlike false asceticism, allows individuals to participate in their congregations and in secular society without raising artificial barriers brought about by cultish restrictions. It is a practical as well as a spiritual answer to the problems plaguing the Ephesian church.

8. Paul admits "physical training" has "some use" but cannot compare in scope or duration with godliness which touches "this life (*zōēs*)" and "the life to come." Paul speaks of the Christian's life as having an eschatological or eternal dimension and is not simply biological life. Only *zōē* "holds the promise" of the future, and it is *zōē* that is "in Christ Jesus" (2 Tim 1:1) and

---

6. There were, evidently some Christian attempts to compare Jesus to Hercules. See Aune, "Heracles and Christ," 3–19.

7. See Poliakoff and Poliakoff, "Jacob, Job, and Other Wrestlers," 48–65, and more recently, Concannon, "Not for an Olive Wreath," 193–214.

8. Knight, *Pastoral Epistles*, 197.

9. Knight, *Pastoral Epistles*, 197.

10. There had been a long tradition of exploiting this analogy in Greek thought, cf. Reid, *Athletics and Philosophy*.

was brought to light through the gospel (2 Tim 1:10). Physical training may benefit the body, but godliness is "beneficial in every way." 9. This saying is "sure" and is in line with the apostolic tradition and therefore "worthy of full acceptance." Like the others in the Pastoral Epistles (1 Tim 1:15, 1 Tim 3:1, 2 Tim 2:11, and Titus 3:8), this so-called "trustworthy saying" is underlined as true and marked out as "part of the accepted tradition."[11] In this instance, the words in the second part of verse 8 are likely to be the saying because they have the character of a proverb and the words in verse 10, which are the other main option, are explanatory rather than free standing.

10. "For this purpose" (to exercise godliness), "we toil" (which speaks of hard manual, intellectual, and spiritual labor), and "endure insults." The sheer grittiness of Christian ministry is laid bare here. Anyone who thinks being a preacher is merely a matter of speaking for half an hour on Sunday and being treated with automatic respect is badly mistaken. There is labor and struggle in view here, and the variant word for "endure insults" employed in some manuscripts is cognate with "agony" in English.[12] The struggle is only possible "because we have put our hope in the living God." And how bare and spare those words might seem! It is not government or human justice or science or art or scholarship that attract our hope but rather the "living God," the God who is the source of "life" rooted in eternity and glory. And this God is the savior (*sōtēr*) of all and "especially (*malista*) of the faithful." Many commentators point out that *malista* can mean "that is" so that sentence ends by identifying more precisely what has gone before.[13] To render it otherwise would suggest Paul is a universalist, which he is not. The phrase parallels what has already been said earlier (1 Tim 2:3,4) and the reference to "all" may be intended to contrast with the exclusivism of the false teachers.

11. We are commenting on this verse in this section because the instruction to "command" (*parangelle* means "give orders, command, instruct, direct"[14]) refers to what Paul has just been writing about. Not only should Timothy command but he must "teach." Here again the answer to the predicament of the Ephesian church is steady teaching. It is not mass excommunication or prophetic denunciation or even physical restraint. Rather, teaching by Timothy will help turn the tide and eventually return

11. Towner, *Timothy and Titus*, 144.

12. See Knight who prefers *agōnizometha* over the textual variant *oneidisometha* because of slightly better manuscript attestation and a better fit to the context (*Pastoral Epistles*, 202).

13. Knight, *Pastoral Epistles*, 203.

14. Knight, *Pastoral Epistles*, 204.

the church to health. The value of unspectacular ministry of teaching is implicitly underlined at this point.

d. Following through (4:12–5:2)

> Do not let anyone look down on you because you are young, but set the faithful an example in word, conduct, love, faith, and purity. Until I come, concentrate on *church Bible* readings, exhortation, and teaching. Do not neglect the gift that is in you that was given to you through a prophecy and the laying on of hands by the council of elders. Cultivate[15] these things, dwell[16] in them, so that your progress may be evident to all. Subject yourself and your teaching to special scrutiny *and* persevere in them, for by so doing, you will save both yourself and those who listen to you.
>
> Chapter 5
>
> Do not *directly* rebuke an older man, but appeal to him as *if he were your*[17] father, younger men like brothers, older women as mothers, younger women, as sisters in all purity. (1 Tim 4:12–5:2)

12. "Do not let anyone look down on you because you are young." The natural tendency of the existing eldership, many of whom we presume to be among the false teachers (Acts 20:29, 30), would have been to look down on young Timothy even if he was in his thirties. In a highly stratified society, age commanded automatic respect, and Timothy must overcome the tendency to dismiss him out of hand. Paul's words are an encouragement to all young ministers of Christ finding themselves plunged into a resistant congregation. The way that Timothy is to gain respect is by conducting himself in an exemplary fashion. In other words, respect cannot simply be demanded but must also be earned. The principle applies across the board, even within the secular world. The young may find themselves put upon and their opinions treated lightly, but if their conduct is first rate, they will gain a hearing. "Set an example" is what Paul did ("follow my example, as I follow the example of Christ" 1 Cor 11:1) and supremely what Christ himself did.

---

15. Or "practice."
16. Lit. "be."
17. Greek, "as [a] father."

Five areas of life are then given: "word" must refer to conversation, public speaking, and perhaps written communication. The New Testament commends plain, truthful, oath-free, thankful, edifying, and forgiving speech (Matt 5:34; Eph 4:32). There is no room for coarse jokes, swearing, or malicious gossip (Eph 4:31). "Conduct" refers to general behavior and way of life. The Christian is to put off the old man and put on the new man "created in righteousness and holiness" (Eph 4:22–24), and Timothy's behavior is to contrast with that of the false teachers who have brought disrepute on the church (1 Tim 3:15). "Love" (or *agapē*) is the self-sacrificing, Holy Spirit-inspired behavior that God shows to human beings. So, even in the midst of dispute and disruption within the Ephesian church, Timothy is to show the love of Christ to others. "Faith" may refer to trustworthiness or to faith in the sense of a confident expectation of better times ahead. "Purity" has overtones of clean sexual conduct since the same word is used in 1 Tim 5:2 where Timothy is "enjoined to treat younger women like sisters."[18]

13. Paul still expects to reach Ephesus and so tells Timothy to engage in a holding operation and to do so in three main ways: reading, exhortation, and teaching (in Greek, *anagnōsis, paraklēsis, didaskalia*). The first term almost certainly means *Bible readings* at which all were present, of great importance when few church members might be able to read. If he observed the standard synagogue pattern given in Acts 13:15, these three would probably have occurred in very close association. Hence Paul would most likely have followed a reading with an "exhortation" or encouragement to a particular line of action picking up a theme implicit in the words already read. And preaching and teaching would almost certainly have taken the form of expounding Scripture with thoroughness and rigor. The ministry of Apollos, who in Acts shows how a teacher's ministry operates (Acts 18:24–26), was said to "water" the seeds planted by Paul in Corinth (1 Cor 3:6), and this must be one of Timothy's aims.

14. In a further (and probably connected) imperative, Timothy is told "not to neglect the charismatic gift" within him. This *charisma* is a manifestation of the grace of God in Timothy's life functioning in the "reading-preaching-teaching nexus."[19] It is a gift manifested in congregational settings for the common good (1 Cor 12:7). Although *charismata* can refer to the broad gifts given to Israel as a nation (Rom 11:29), the usage here may refer to one of the gifts enumerated in 1 Corinthians 12 and expounded more fully in 1 Corinthians 14. These are gifts *of the Spirit* and not simply natural

---

18. Mounce, *Pastoral Epistles*, 260.

19. We owe this phrase and thought to Lance Pierson (private communication, 2021).

endowments stemming from genetic or educational advantage. Although there is no information about the particular gift Timothy received, we can argue on the basis of other data in the New Testament that it functioned in collaboration with his will rather than by usurping it because Timothy is later told to stir the gift up in himself, which implies it can lie dormant or burn low (2 Tim 1:6).

The gift could simply have been glossolalia by which Timothy could edify himself in prayer as part of his preparation for public ministry (1 Cor 14:4), or it could have been a gift of discernment or healing that would have authenticated his message to the church. Alternatively, because it was given "through a prophecy" (that is, the prophecy declared what Timothy would become in the future), perhaps the gift remained hidden and would only manifest itself over time. But in the context here, the gift might precisely be something to do with teaching, a capability among those listed in Ephesians 4:11. But speculation will not answer this fully, and all we can say is that the gift was important in the circumstances he found himself in and that God had already equipped Timothy for what lay ahead.

There are two implications of the gift that need to be considered. First, the practice of the New Testament church was evidently charismatic. There was a body of elders and during the time when the elders met, prophecy was given and laying on of hands took place. This was a church functioning with plural leadership and at the prompting of the Spirit rather than at the prompting of a liturgical handbook or sacramental manual. The Pentecostal and charismatic movements have consistently argued or implicitly presumed the need for a return to New Testament norms, and this verse, along with others, and without any elaborate argumentation, shows how the early church functioned. It also shows, in passing, that the Pastoral Epistles refer to a time in the life of the church before the powerful "area" bishops of the second century. This is very much a church in tune with the model depicted during the missionary journeys of Paul within the book of Acts (14:23).

Second, the passage is important psychologically for Timothy. He has already been affirmed by the body of elders, the same group of people whose doctrine he must now correct and protect.[20] The errant elders can hardly dismiss Timothy as an upstart or novice if they themselves have publicly brought him to prominence by prayer and prophecy and the laying on of hands. But what is the body of elders? Discussion has circulated round two

20. It is also possible the body of elders referred to is the one first recognizing Timothy in his home church of Lystra. If this is so, we can still be confident the Ephesian elders were appointed by Paul and knew of Paul's connection with Timothy and so indirectly approved of Timothy. Or to put this another way, if their own position in the church was established by Paul, so was Timothy's.

options: either this was a formal presbytery, or this was a loose-knit body of elders, which is more likely.[21] In practical terms for our understanding of this passage, the distinction makes no difference.

And what of the purpose of laying on his hands? Here the options vary between formal ordination or simple commissioning for ministry. Formal ordination is anachronistic[22] and so the most likely parallel is in Acts 13:3 when Paul and Barnabas are commissioned for their first missionary journey. It is not necessary to see the laying on of hands as a recognized procedure to raise Timothy to the status of eldership although this is possible. Among the arguments against assuming Timothy was an elder within the Ephesian church is the mobile, traveling nature of his ministry. Elders, because of their duties to particular congregations, tended to operate within the congregation's catchment area.

We will delay our discussion of the laying on of hands until the commentary on 1 Tim 5:22.

15. Paul urges Timothy to "cultivate" and "dwell in" these things, to make them thoroughly part of his lifestyle and mentality so that his "progress" is evident to everyone. This can only occur if Timothy's public profile is raised and this, in turn, exposes him to public scrutiny and criticism. Spiritual progress may be part of the vocabulary of the false teachers, and Paul may be turning it back on them.

16. Timothy must subject himself to "special scrutiny." He is to be his own first critic and to make a sober estimate of his own life and conduct—something that is anyway enjoined on Christians prior to the breaking of bread or eucharist (1 Cor 11:28). If Timothy ensures he is on track in conduct and doctrine, he will save himself and those who listen to him. In the context of this epistle, these words show how crucial Timothy is to the survival of the church. Paul, by his commands and by urging self-scrutiny, seeks to ensure the double protection of his protégé.

1. The battle for the survival of the Ephesian congregation does not entail a loss of Christian courtesy or respect. Timothy is told not to "rebuke an older man" (*presbyterō*) despite ample grounds for conflict over false teaching. *Presbuteros* can mean both an older man in general as well as an official "elder." However, the fact that the latter case is handled separately (1 Tim 5:19) may mean that just older men are in view here. This would seem to fit with the advice that Timothy should "appeal to him" or exhort him as he would a "father." Custom dictated respect to older members of

---

21. Mounce, *Pastoral Epistles*, 262; Fee, *1 and 2 Timothy, Titus*, 108. See also Campbell's excellent work on this subject (Campbell, *The Elders*).

22. Fee, *1 and 2 Timothy, Titus*, 108.

families and so respect is to remain intact.[23] Timothy is not to be abrasive and start angry rows. "Younger men" are to be treated as "brothers" with all the warmth and familiarity implicit in the relationship. Straight talking in the context of affection is to be Timothy's approach.

2. Older women (*presbyteras*[24]) are to be treated as "mothers," that is, with affection and respect and younger women "as sisters." Again, family values set the tone for relationships within the church and for Timothy's dealings with others. Paul is not thinking here of dysfunctional or fractured families, which obviously existed (2 Tim 3:2-3) but of the Christian norm or ideal where brotherly or sisterly affection (Heb 13:1) and sacrificial love (Eph 5:25) was evident. The only condition is that Timothy's "affection" towards young women should be "in all purity" (*hagneia*) which as a synonym for chastity,[25] implies purity in the sexual realm.

---

23. We might add that if proceedings against an errant elder noted in 1 Tim 5:19 are based on the pattern for other church members in Matt 18:15-17, that the initial accusation occurs in private, and/or with two or three witnesses before it is taken to the whole church (Matt 18:17, 1 Tim 5:20). The cultural sensitivity of 1 Tim 5:1 may thus apply in both cases, in that a first-time public rebuke in the middle of an exhortation or sermon would certainly be inappropriate.

24. Technically, of course, *presbyterai* could mean women *elders*, but the parallel with the treatment of older men above almost certainly means this is not in view here.

25. Knight, *Pastoral Epistles*, 214.

V. WIDOWS, ELDERS AND SLAVES

    a. Widows (5:3–16)
    b. Elders (5:17–25)
    c. Slaves (6:1–2)

V. WIDOWS, ELDERS AND SLAVES

The next section deals with three separate social groups: widows, elders, and slaves. Just as previously Paul has considered criteria for the appointment of elders and deacons separately so now, he addresses the other groupings, attending principally to honor and finance. It is possible to take his instructions and reasoning as free-standing blocks of apostolic guidance, but we prefer to view what he says to the three groups in the overall context of the epistle and the precarious situation in the church at Ephesus. So, we assume the discussion about widows and elders is impacted by the false teaching circulating the church. This is not to say, however, that the instructions Paul gives only apply to that congregation, or set of congregations, because the principles informing what he writes have lasting relevance and value.

a. Widows (5:3–16)

> Honor widows who really are widows[1], but if any have children or grandchildren, they should first learn to exercise the duty of care for their own family and in their turn support the parents *that looked after them*[2], for this is pleasing to[3] God. A "true" widow who has no living relatives can only persist *in bringing* her petitions and prayers *to God* night and day, but a widow living in conspicuous luxury is "dead" even while alive. Command these things so that they may *all*[4] be above reproach. *So*, if someone does not care for their own relatives, particularly in their more immediate family[5],

---

    1. In the strong sense of having no other living relatives, cf. v. 5.

    2. Greek "as a recompense."

    3. Greek "before" or "in the sight of."

    4. I.e., widows in varied situations and their extended families, wholly or partially within the church

    5. Greek "of their household."

they deny the faith and are worse than an unbeliever. A widow can be enrolled *for church support* if she is sixty or above, widowed for the first time, and well known for *her* good work *in* bringing up children, showing hospitality, washing the feet of the saints, helping those who are in trouble and dedicating herself to every good deed. But do not put younger widows on the list, for if they are drawn back by their natural affections and seek to remarry, *and thus step back from being widows "for* Christ"[6], they may experience criticism[7] for having broken a pledge. At the same time, *some of these younger widows* can become creatures of leisure[8], going around from house to house, not only idle, but gossipy and meddlesome, saying things they should not. I would advise younger widows, therefore, to *re-*marry, have children and run a home again, so that *we do* not give *our*[9] adversary[10] an opportunity for criticism. For some have already turned away and "followed Satan" *in this matter*. If any believing woman has relatives who are widows, she should support them *herself* and not over-burden the church so that it can help widows *in* genuine *need*[11]. (1 Tim 5:3–16)

3. "Honor widows who really are widows." Here is the first imperative of the chapter, and it gives the general rule to be followed. As we shall see, there are exceptions and conditions, but this general requirement for the Ephesian church to honor genuine widows demonstrates how seriously the early church took its responsibility for the poor and vulnerable (cf. Gal 2:10). Widows were an exposed social category and had been identified by the Old Testament as needing practical and compassionate financial support (Ps 68:5; Deut 10:18; Isa 1:17; Jer 7:6; Mal 3:5). That was the case here, and it had been the case in the big Jerusalem church early in the book of Acts (6:1–6). There a daily distribution of food had been made to Hebrew-speaking

---

6. The implication here is that older widows with no relatives and no further prospects of marriage might, in accepting church support, regard themselves as "married to Christ," and probably, as strength permitted, available to help in the church in some way. A younger widow using such support merely to tide herself over while looking for a new husband could be viewed as violating the church's trust.

7. "Be condemned" or "feel guilt" are also possible translations.

8. Greek "get into the habit of idleness."

9. Greek "the."

10. "The" adversary probably refers to Satan, as in v. 15.

11. Greek "true."

and Greek-speaking widows, showing the church quickly taking on roles performed by Jewish synagogues for their communities. More than this, in Roman society as a whole, widows were more numerous than they are today because of the ten-to-fifteen year age difference between men and women on marriage.[12] About 19 percent of women aged between thirty and thirty-four had been widowed and 18 percent of those between thirty-five and thirty-nine.[13] Support for the widowed was at least one purpose of the dowry system, where the money provided to the bride by her father on her wedding could be used to support her in the event of her husband's death.

Two questions arise: what does "honoring" mean? And who are "real widows"? Most commentators agree the verb *tīmaō*, used in Greek renderings of the fifth commandment,[14] includes financial or material support as well as respect. The command to honor parents includes being prepared to help them when this is needed, and hence the scathing comments by Jesus on the corban loophole that allowed gifts to the Temple to replace financial care for parents (Mark 7:11–13).

The "real widows" are those the church should support financially, and they are "real" in the sense they have no family support. Other widows have, of course, been genuinely bereaved but they are fortunate in having "children or grandchildren to exercise the duty of care for their own family" (v. 4), sometimes by administering the dowry on their behalf.[15] The family itself is a support network, and those who have been cared for in childhood should "in their turn support the parents that looked after them."

5. "A 'true' widow who has no living relatives can only persist in bringing her petitions and prayers to God night and day." An unsupported godly woman throws herself on God in prayer, and it is the church that should be the answer to her prayer. To put this more bluntly, the church would be hypocritical if it preached the love of Christ but failed to help destitute members in its midst. The widow who calls out to God is spiritually alive and is able to edify others by her testimony to God's faithfulness and any spiritual gifts that are fired by her prayerfulness. She stands in stark contrast to "a widow living in conspicuous luxury" who is spiritually "'dead' even while alive" (v. 6). The idea of being dead in sin and alive to God is found elsewhere in Paul (Rom 6:2, 11).

---

12. Shaw, "Roman Girls," 30–46.
13. Winter, *Roman Wives*, 125.
14. LXX Exod 20:12; cf. Jesus in Mark 7.10 where English translations invariably offer "honor."
15. Winter, *Roman Wives*, 126–7.

7. "Command these things." Commentators disagree about whether the command is addressed to the widows, their families, or both. The point, however, is to ensure that they "all should be above reproach." Since the families are being told to rise to their responsibilities, it is most likely that the command is directed at them although it is possible to envisage situations where the widow is a Christian, but her family is not, thus making her case more difficult. It is probably best to envisage the command as a general directive intended to rectify potentially complicated situations in which some exceptions were inevitable. Moreover, given that Graeco-Roman society expected families to care for widows,[16] the church would be in the position of arousing criticism or reproach if it undermined this principle without replacing it with anything better.

8. In this sense, failure by a Christian family to care for its widow(s) makes it "worse than an unbeliever" for the simple reason that, as noted above, unbelievers normally did look after their widows. The lower standard of care found in some parts of the church than in secular society should have sounded alarm bells in the congregation. If we ask how and why the Ephesian church had begun to lose its way over the welfare of its widows, the most immediate explanation surely lies in the false teaching being spread through its membership. The false teaching, we can surmise, has directed money away from needy widows to other projects and priorities. In such circumstances the faith has been "denied."

The levels of care and honesty within secular society are variable, but Christians can rightly expect Christian communities and institutions to demonstrate better standards than those "in the world." Where a Christian college, for instance, treats it staff worse than an equivalent secular college, or where a Christian community exploits its volunteers, it is reasonable to ask whether something fundamental has gone wrong. Very often the adoption of business principles or slick management signals the overruling of the precepts of the New Testament and the degrading of personal relationships. Pentecostals and charismatics are not immune to these failures.

9-10. Paul now sets out the criteria for enrolling a widow onto church support. Some commentators have suggested the existence of an "order of widows" with specific diaconal responsibilities.[17] A century and more later

---

16. "What Schnaps says of the classical Greek and Hellenistic period was also true of the Roman Empire: 'Legally, then, a woman was never as thoroughly protected as she was in her old age'" (Schaps, *Economic Rights of Women*, 84 quoted by Winter, *Roman Wives*, 126).

17. Kelly (*Pastoral Epistles*, 115) thinks this, but Fee (*1 and 2 Timothy, Titus*, 125) disagrees. Winter points out, "the reading back into the first century of an order of widows is rejected as it is clear that 1 Tim 5:3-16 is intended to assist only those who

in church history such an order appears to have been recognized, but at this point in the church's development, everything is less formalized, and such a ministry does not seem to be mentioned. All we see is an enrolment process marked by good recordkeeping and basic organization so that the congregation knew who was being supported. Presumably, also, the elders or deacons who had the job of handling the finance had to exercise care about who should be added to this list, keeping an eye on the budget as well as honoring the ideals of charity.[18]

In essence, those added to the list must be of good character and "over sixty years of age" which, given the shorter life expectancy in Roman times, might equate to about seventy in a modern western society.[19] Such a widow must have been "faithful to her husband," and we can assume this stipulation applied even if she had been married more than once since younger widows are advised to remarry (v. 14).[20] The criteria given by Paul are intended to refine and limit the list to ensure the church deploys its resources efficiently and does not support those who do not, or should not, need help. So eligible widows are those who have brought up their children (which is classed as "good work"), "shown hospitality" (an important service for the benefit of itinerant ministry), "washed the feet of the saints"[21] (been willing to perform menial tasks often delegated to slaves), helped "those in trouble" (perhaps unemployed, persecuted, homeless and sick) and been dedicated

---

qualify by reason of age for the assistance of the church" (*Roman Wives*, 133).

18. Note, of course, that the story of the creation of the original diaconate in Acts 6:1ff. concerned the support of widows.

19. Hopkins, "On the Probable Age Structure," 245–264. Despite lower life expectancy, the Roman population was similar to other pre-industrial populations and had the structure to enable its continuation.

20. We prefer "faithful to her husband" to "widowed for the first time" for *henos andros gynē*.

21. It is not necessary to assume this refers to ritual foot washing carried out during Holy Communion since the words are part and parcel of a general list of good works. Thomas, *Footwashing*, discusses the matter thoroughly by reference to ancient practices as well as biblical and non-biblical literature. He notes the geographical proximity between the churches of the Pastoral Epistles and the Johannine community. "If the practice in 1 Tim 5:10 is ultimately based on the tradition in John 13, then some of the earliest actual 'readers' of the foot washing pericope, outside the Johannine community, understood the 'text' to call for a literal fulfilment" (138). Thomas and other commentators note the early church may have interpreted foot washing sacramentally and christologically though equally the practice could be indicative of hospitality or an extended metaphor for a posture of service and humility, which is how it is likely to be read in respect of widows (Mounce, *Pastoral Epistles*, 289).

to "every good deed." It is not necessary, however, to assume every widow had carried out every type of good work (some will have been childless, for instance[22]), but the overall principles are clear enough: she had to be a woman of practical generosity, perhaps modeled on the ideal wife of Proverbs 31 or Dorcas (Acts 9:36–39).[23]

11–12. Paul now turns to exclusions. "But do not put younger widows on the list" because they will be "drawn back by their natural affections" and then "remarry." Paul then suggests "they may experience criticism for having broken a pledge" (*pistis*). There have been several views on how this "pledge" might be understood. One suggestion is that widows being added to the list made a pledge to the church to serve faithfully (and celibately?) "as a condition of" the support.[24] To remarry, besides naturally bringing the situation of need to an end, might also be viewed as the breaking of a pledge, i.e., they have "stepped back from being widows 'for Christ.'" Another suggestion is that the criticism concerned younger widows remarrying non-Christians and then being obliged to turn away from their faith in Christ since the beliefs of the husband took precedence.[25] Reminders that Christian widows should only remarry believers (1 Cor 7:39) suggests "marrying out" did sometimes happen. Whilst this entails imagining, somewhat awkwardly, caution on the church's part about younger women's loyalties, it has the advantage of reading *pistis* in its most natural sense as "faith."[26]

13. Whether on or off the list, some of the widows are going from house to house spreading "gossip" and "saying things they should not." The likelihood that the Ephesian false teachers had made inroads among the widows is raised by similarities with earlier descriptions of the words spun by the troublemakers (1 Tim 6:20–21), an eventuality made more probable given the recruiting of women described later (2 Tim 3:6).

14. The advice given by Paul, and largely inherited from Judaism, is that the "younger widows" should "remarry," "have children," and "run"

---

22. About 10 percent of couples are infertile, cf. National Institutes of Health, "Infertility."

23. Whilst this provision appears to be aimed at Christian widows linked to a congregation, it is possible that larger churches were eventually able to offer care like this to the wider community. By AD 251, it is said the church in Rome was supporting "more than 1,500 widows and needy persons" (Chadwick, *The Early Church*, 57–58).

24. Johnson, *Timothy*, 275.

25. "Plutarch says how the wife must follow the gods of her husband and not embrace foreign divinities," (Winter, *Roman Wives*, 137 on Plu. *Conj. praec.* 19) cf. Fee, *1 and 2 Timothy, Titus*, 121.

26. This would of course allow the simultaneous overtone of a baptismal pledge of allegiance to "Jesus is Lord."

their homes. This, indeed, may well be a contributory factor to the growth of the early church.[27] Not only were Christian families likely to be large and extensive because of their resistance to abortion but children were to be purposefully brought up in the faith. By engaging in the domestic sphere Christian women were reducing the "opportunity for criticism" of the church, both through open support for a broader social good,[28] but also because, as Johnson points out, "The church would indeed be the object of severe reviling if it were perceived as a board of elderly men who financially supported a group of younger women who lived in public idleness and self-indulgence."[29]

A feminist interpretation of these verses reads them as suppressing the legitimate activities of women by confining them to the domestic sphere and reducing their opportunities for public activity within the church or beyond (1 Tim 2:12). Although the verses may be read this way, most commentators consider the weight of argument, in its ancient social context, to be directed towards the welfare and happiness of the young widows themselves, sparing them a misplaced life-long dependency on the church's resources, rather than some more sinister patriarchal suppression of their freedoms.[30]

15. As noted above, sadly, some of the widows have already "turned aside (*exetrapēsan*)" or apostatized.[31] They have departed from the faith and in this sense have "followed Satan." It is unlikely this involved literal "devil-worship"[32] although general departures from the faith were anticipated (4:1), and elsewhere Paul calls participation in pagan sacrifices "eating at the table of demons" (1 Cor 10:20–21). Thus, his words could certainly be read as speaking of a reversion to paganism in some cases.[33] Indeed, as a

---

27. Stark notes "the differential fertility of Christians and pagans . . . was taken as a fact by the ancients . . . a major factor in higher fertility of Christians was a culture that sanctified the marital bond" (*Rise*, 122–3).

28. It may be relevant that the Emperor Augustus had legislated against adultery and provided incentives for having children in the *lex Julia* enacted around 17 BC. Although there was push-back against the legislation and although pagan religion had little moral force, it is evident sections of the upper classes in Rome favored traditional marriage, and, with this, the church was in accord (see Winter, *Roman Wives*, 39–58).

29. Johnson, *Timothy*, 275.

30. Johnson, *Timothy*, 270–72, who refers to Schüssler Fiorenza, *In Memory of Her*; Bassler, "The Widow's Tale," 23–41.

31. Johnson, *Timothy*, 268.

32. On the probably hyperbolic use of such language, see comments on 1 Tim 1:20 above.

33. Attending religious rituals at the temple of Artemis would surely remain

continuation of the discussion about "widows," this might sometimes result from remarriage to a non-Christian (cf. on vv. 11-12 above). However, most commentators note the basic concern here is with the way that anti-church sentiments arising from the lifestyle of some young widows might be "doing the devil's work for him" (by "giving our adversary an opportunity for criticism"). If allowing or even promoting this behavior can be laid at the door of the false teachers, then by using the word "Satan," Paul may be reserving his strongest condemnation for them.[34]

16. "Believing women" (some early manuscripts also add "believing men"[35]) are explicitly encouraged to support any of their relatives who are impoverished widows. In this way the church, not being "over-burdened," can provide materially for those in genuine need. Throughout this passage, we gain an insight into the practical nitty-gritty life of the church in Ephesus. Unwarranted demands are being made on church funds while pious widows struggle and others are gallivanting about and spreading false or unhealthy doctrine.

b. Elders (5:17–25)

> Elders who govern *the church* well should be considered worthy of double honor, especially those who labor in speaking and teaching. For Scripture says "you shall not muzzle an ox when it is treading the grain"[36] and "the laborer deserves his wages." Do not accept an accusation against an elder unless it is supported by the evidence of two or three witnesses. Rebuke those who go on sinning with everyone present so that the rest may be struck with fear. I solemnly adjure you before God, Christ Jesus and the elect angels that you

---

alluring, particularly for widowed women wanting to re-build their social networks.

34. Cf. 1 Tim 4:1 regarding the "teachings of demons." That the false teachers are most likely involved here is affirmed by Bassler, "The Widows' Tale," 23–41, 36–37, and n. 52. If the young widows concerned were still notionally attached to the church (albeit damaging its reputation), then they could still be viewed as "Christians" (cf. 2 Thess 3:14–15), meaning Pagan conversion is not the essential worry. This would have the merit of matching Paul's "handed over to Satan" in 1 Cor 5:5, used for a temporary measure placed upon a *Christian* whom the church intends to restore to full fellowship.

35. See Knight (*Pastoral Epistles*, 229) who cites Metzger, *Textual Commentary*.

36. Greek has a single word for "threshing," not a well-known activity today.

observe these *principles*[37] without prejudice, doing nothing out of partiality. Do not lay hands on anyone[38] *too* hastily and do not share in other people's sins; keep yourself without fault. Don't just drink water, but take a little wine for the sake of your stomach and your frequent illnesses. The sins of some people are clear to everyone, and go before them to judgment; but for others, their sins only come to light later. In the same way, good deeds are *usually* well-known, but if not, they will not stay hidden *for long*. (1 Tim 5:17-25)

The next section turns to elders and outlines a disciplinary process and the appointment of new elders. The solemnity and seriousness of Timothy's task is underlined.

17. The instruction here is straightforward. Some elders are worthy of "double honor." The question is which elders and what does double honor mean? We could divide the elders into four groups: those who "govern" (some well and some badly) and those who "teach" (some well and some badly), or we could assume that all elders teach given that capacity to teach is a requirement of the role (3:2). In this case we have two groups: those do the job well and those who do the job badly. Beyond teaching, the basic role of the elders is to manage, govern, lead or direct the church and the same word, *proestōtes*, is also used of the elder's conduct of his family affairs in 3:4.

Before deciding what Paul means, we note the passage moves on to consider the procedure for receiving accusations against elders. It is difficult to imagine circumstances where teaching that was taking place publicly would require the evidence of "two or three witnesses." Poor governance as well as immorality, however, might be concealed and only known to a small number of people who could expose it. We conclude Paul is speaking against the mismanagement and immorality of some elders, a conclusion for which evidence can be found in the slightly later literature with an example of avarice and the misuse of church funds.[39] The rest are worthy of "double honor."

Regarding "double honor," it is unlikely this means double pay or double the amount received by widows or double the average pay of the congregation since this would introduce unpleasant commercial calculations into the ministry of elders and raise temptations of avarice. It is more

---

37. Greek "things" (implied).

38. The phrase "lay hands on" signifies the commissioning of a church member to a role or task.

39. Johnson, *Timothy*, 288, cites Pol. *Phil.* 11:1-2 concerning the misdeeds of Valens.

probable the double (or twofold) honor is respect *and* payment,[40] and the next verse shows how payment for work is scripturally endorsed. "Speaking and teaching," even if they are non-manual, are classed as "laboring," i.e., hard work (*kopiōntes* is thoroughly Pauline and the verb is found in 1 Cor 15:10, Phil 2:16, Gal 4:11).

18. Paul now turns to the scriptural justification for the payment of elders and quotes from Deuteronomy 25:4. At first sight the text appears inappropriate. Yet the notion that the oxen "treading the grain" to thresh it should be allowed to eat from it had been put through the rabbinical hermeneutical grid to formulate the principle "from the lesser to the greater." If animals were allowed to eat while they were working and to benefit from the produce of their labor, then human beings may do so all the more.[41] The second quotation comes from the words of Jesus himself. Its wording is almost identical to that used in Luke's gospel (Luke 10:7) and has the character of a proverb that would have easily circulated independently among early Christians.

19–20. The Ephesian situation will not be resolved by short-cutting due process. Elders must be given the protection of only having to answer "accusations" if "two or three witnesses" concur. This shows how Christians instinctively adopted the legal safeguards of Jewish law (Deut 17:6). This was noted as having caused difficulties during the trial of Jesus because the witnesses disagreed among themselves (Mark 14:55–6). So, here, elders must be given a fair hearing so that only those who have done wrong and "who go on sinning," are subject to the final stage involving public "rebuke." Towner considers this might include "exposure and convincing of wrongdoing, refutation, correction, reprimand, censure, or discipline."[42] The purpose of this was exemplary, so that "the rest may be struck with fear." The enforcement of public discipline in church meetings was practiced by a number of successful Pentecostal congregations in Scandinavia in their early years.

It is possible that elders who were suspected of having done wrong were first privately admonished in line with the stages outlined by Jesus (Matt 18:15–17).[43] If this failed, the process would be escalated by the testimony of witnesses, and only if they continued sinning were they rebuked

---

40. Fee, *1 and 2 Timothy, Titus*, 129.
41. Towner, *Timothy and Titus*, 365.
42. Towner, *Timothy and Titus*, 371.

43. Note how the process Matt 18:15–17 starts with a private one-to-one meeting, moves to another meeting with one or two others present and only after that is the problem "taken to the church." The private meetings would certainly allow any elder so arraigned to be addressed in a courteous manner (5:1).

"with everyone present." We do not have enough evidence to know whether removal from office was within the range of available sanctions although we would argue that verse 22 may imply this, with new elders replacing those so removed. What we can say is that Timothy may have been familiar with such procedures in Corinth (2 Cor 13:1) where a troubled church had also been set back on track. While Paul often speaks of the importance of "restoring" ordinary church members wherever possible (Gal 6:1; cf. 2 Cor 2:5–8) the higher standards to which leaders and teachers are held (1 Tim 3:1–7; cf. Jas 3:1) and the greater damage they can do to the church may mean more permanent exclusion, particularly where false teaching might be involved.[44]

21. So serious and so necessary was the disciplinary procedure that Paul "solemnly adjures" Timothy to carry it out and to do so "without prejudice" or "partiality." Just as two or three witnesses will bear witness to the guilt or innocence of elders so the three witnesses of God, Christ Jesus, and the elect angels are invoked in reference to what must be done.[45] The awesome reality of God as judge of all stands behind this. Timothy must act without prejudging anyone's guilt or innocence and without favoring anyone: the objective testimony of witnesses is the one reliable guide. The deep seriousness of Paul's instruction to Timothy may well indicate Paul's fear that Timothy will not have the courage to act decisively in the current crisis.

22. This instruction, although no doubt of permanent relevance, seems oddly placed unless it is understood as relating to the appointment of new elders after a removal from office (cf. on vv. 19–20 above). In essence, Paul tells Timothy not to fill gaps in the eldership team too quickly: "do not lay hands on anyone too hastily." The epistle has already referred to the laying on of hands (4:14) in connection with the ministry of the eldership body. In the Old Testament, laying on of hands implied transmission or identification. Moses lays hands on Joshua (implying transmission of the Spirit, Deut 34:9) while the priest lays hands on the scapegoat (implying identification, Lev 16:21–2), and sometimes these two functions are joined or indistinguishable as when the elderly Jacob lays hands on his grandchildren Ephraim and Manasseh. Acts 14:23 probably implies laying on of hands to confirm the appointment of elders.[46] This further implies Timothy will, as

---

44. This may have been informed by the teaching of Jesus in Mark 9:42. The condemnation of false teachers in Jude 3–23 also sounds irrecoverable (v. 13) while yet seeking to "snatch from the fire" as many of the affected church *members* as possible (vv. 22–23). When Paul returns to these teachers in 1 Tim 6:3–5, he does not find any redeeming qualities.

45. Mounce, *Pastoral Epistles*, 316.

46. Banks, *Paul's Idea of Community*, 80.

the apostolic emissary or delegate, lay hands on new elders in the absence of Paul himself, providing elements of continuity and identification. Perhaps also other elders participated in the appointment process since in congregations where there was no apostle or representative available, elders were the only people available to transmit or devolve spiritual responsibility. From 4:14 it is reasonable to expect the illuminating exercise of spiritual gifts like prophecy or tongues and interpretation as an appointment was being considered as well as at the moment of its conferment.

The injunction "do not share in other people's sins" implies that, if Timothy had laid hands on eldership candidates who later and unexpectedly turned out to be similarly defective, he would have been party to their sins. Timothy must keep himself pure or "without fault."

23. On the face of it, this verse has nothing to do with what is being said in the section, but if we assume the advice follows on from the command to be "without fault," we can guess Timothy is being told not to succumb to unnecessary ascetic practices. We also have an insight into Timothy's general health, and commentators have concluded he was of a nervous disposition which is why he suffered from frequent digestive complaints. The command to take a "little wine" is medicinal. Wine is acidic and assists digestion, acts as a tonic, and, in an age where water purification was less perfect than ours, was a safer drink, as "widely recognized in antiquity."[47]

24–25. Returning to the emergency replacement of elders, the consideration of new candidates can err in two directions: some may be superficially attractive but conceal sins that only "come to light later"; others are good but are in danger of being overlooked because their deeds are "hidden." Timothy needs to know the candidates thoroughly before making a final decision. He needs to look for weaknesses in the good candidates and strengths in the apparently weaker ones. The reference to "judgement" has led some commentators to understand these words in the light of a final divine judgement (which would add intense solemnity), but in the context, it is more likely *Timothy's* judgement is being highlighted though we could combine these thoughts by seeing Timothy's judgement as prefiguring divine judgement.

---

47. Kelly, *Pastoral Epistles*, 129. Wine was thought by some Pentecostals to disinfect water.

c. Slaves (6:1–2)

> All those who are under the yoke as slaves must *treat*[48] their masters as worthy of all honor so that God's name and our teaching may not be brought into disrepute. Those who have believing owners should not honor them less because they are brothers or sisters, but rather serve them all the more because those who benefit from their service are beloved *fellow*-believers. (1 Tim 6:1–2)

Slavery was an established social fact in the ancient world and had been for hundreds of years. Israel had been slaves in Egypt at least a thousand years before the time of the Pastoral Epistles. It was commonly accepted that captives in battle should be enslaved and treated as any other type of living property with the result that children born to slaves were also slaves. About 30 percent of the population within the Roman Empire belonged to the slave class,[49] and this may explain why the Pauline Epistles do not enter into an extensive critique of the practice. Human rights as we currently conceive them simply did not exist in the ancient world and to declare, as the American *Declaration of Independence* (1776) does, that human beings were "endowed by their Creator with certain inalienable rights" would have been incomprehensible to ancient people. Rights, so far as the classical world was concerned, came from tradition and law and nowhere else. Most of us fail to see the way Christianity shifted the intellectual foundations of the world for the better.[50]

Although there is no explicit critique of slavery in the New Testament there are implicit critiques and re-framings of the concept. Christ describes himself as a servant (Luke 22:27), and in Philippians, he is described as a slave (2:7), and Paul also uses the word of himself (Rom 1:1). Additionally, when Onesimus runs away from his slave master and meets Paul in Rome, Paul converts him and sends him back to his owner with a letter in which Onesimus is now referred to as a "brother" (Phlm 16). By viewing the slave as a brother, as an equal, as a member of a family, the concept of a slave as merely a piece of property is undermined and re-evaluated.

Within the epistle, the connecting thread running between slavery, widows, and elders is honor. Slaves owe respect and honor to their masters just as elders and widows should be honored by the community.

---

48. Greek regard *in practice*.
49. Wright and Bird, *The New Testament in its World*, 148.
50. Holland, *Dominion*.

V. WIDOWS, ELDERS AND SLAVES 111

1–2a. Slaves are divided into two categories: those with unbelieving masters and those with believing masters. In either case, "all those who are under the yoke as slaves" are obligated to treat their masters "as worthy of all honor," and the reason given for this is so that the gospel, "our teaching," may not be "brought into disrepute." As elsewhere in the epistle, it is vital the gospel should avoid giving unnecessary cause for slander or that the behavior of the church bring disrespect to the name of Christ (3:6–7). There are times, as the early church knew all too well, when Christians had to stand tall and refuse compromise with the Roman regime, but this was a last resort. The Christian obeyed the law unless it required the worship of false gods (e.g., including the emperor).[51]

Slaves with "believing masters" should treat their masters with "honor" even though their masters are also their "brothers or sisters" who are "beloved." The temptation to take advantage of the owner because he or she was equal in Christ should be resisted. The slave should serve the believing master "more" and see the "service" given as a benefaction (using the verb *antilambanō*), a benefit, and here Paul "employs a term especially used of wealthy benefactors who bestowed gifts on social inferiors."[52] Paradoxically, then, the slave is able to bestow a favor on the master and in this way the slave is empowered.

It has been suggested[53] that the other link between these verses on slaves and the previous verses on elders is that some slaves were also elders, but even if this is so and that linkage exists, it is still the case that honor is the main thematic connection between all three social groups. Finally, it is important to realize that elsewhere in the Pauline corpus there is a command given to masters as well as to servants. In the Colossian (4:1) and Ephesian (6:9) epistles, masters are told to treat their slaves well so that the commands on both sides of the equation, slaves and masters, are balanced just as they are on other reciprocal relationships like those between husbands and wives.

---

51. See the introduction to this commentary, §II, *Religious Context*.
52. Keener, *Background Commentary*, 613, in reference to 1 Tim 6:2. See also Knight, *Greek Testament Commentary*, 247.
53. Barrett, *The Pastoral Epistles*, 82.

VI. MOTIVATIONS AND JUDGEMENTS
  a. The corruption of false teaching (6:2b-10)
  b. Timothy's battle (6:11-16)
  c. Warning to the rich (6:17-19)
  d. A final charge (6:20)

VI. MOTIVATIONS AND JUDGEMENTS

Here the main imperatives of the epistle are reasserted with the addition of an exposé of the motives of the false teachers: they are after money. A discussion of wealth follows. In the third section, Timothy is reminded of the stand Jesus himself made before Pilate, a stand that he, Timothy, will one day have to make before Jesus. Ultimately, the issues of this epistle will be judged in the radiant light of eternity.

a. The corruption of false teaching (6:2b-10)

> Teach and encourage these things. If anyone teaches differently from this and is not devoted to the sound words of our Lord Jesus Christ and teaching that promotes godliness, he is conceited and knows nothing but has an unhealthy fascination with controversies and disputes about words which *only* lead to jealously, conflict, slander, groundless suspicions[1] and constant wrangling between people who've lost their minds and *any sense of* truth *and who* consider religion as just a way to make a living. Of course, there is great gain to be had in true piety beyond material sufficiency. For we brought nothing into the world and can take nothing out of it. But if we have food and clothing, we can be content with those. But those wanting to get rich fall into temptation, a trap, and many foolish and harmful desires which sink *such* people into ruin and destruction. For the love of money is the root of all kinds of evil, and some people with this very desire have been led astray from the faith and pierced through by many woes. (1 Tim 6:2-10)

---

1. Or suspicions of or about evil.

2b-3. "Teach and encourage these things." The "these things" cover what has been said in 5:1—6:2, and the command to Timothy stands as a transitional summary bridging to what follows. Paul now launches into the false teachers, or anyone tempted to join them and does not mince his words. A single composite word has already been used to describe them (1:3). They are *heterodidaskaloi* or "teachers of 'other' things," and they stand against "the sound words of our Lord Jesus Christ." What they are in fact doing is pitting themselves against Jesus by propagating doctrines which, instead of leading to spiritual health, lead to corruption, trouble, and often tragedy. Again, health metaphors come to the forefront (cf. 1:10). The words of Jesus are "sound" or health-giving and promote "godliness." There is here a continuation of the principle enunciated by Jesus "by their fruits you will know them" (Matt 7:15-20). In other words, by the results of the output of the false teachers, their true nature will be revealed.

If we ask whether the "sound words" are spoken by Jesus or about Jesus, it is not possible to give a definite answer. Stott suggest that the words of Jesus are those spoken through Paul to the church in Ephesus.[2] Paul, inspired by the Spirit, brings the words of Christ to the church as directly as John in the book of Revelation (Rev 2:1—3:21). Otherwise, the apostolic tradition communicated Christ's teaching from memory (in the case of the apostles who had been among the original disciples) or after detailed conversation, as would have been the case when Paul spent time with the apostles face to face in Jerusalem (Acts 15:4; Gal 1:18, 19). Occasionally Paul quotes the words of Jesus verbatim as he did in connection with Holy Communion and marriage (1 Cor 11:23-25; 1 Cor 7:10). But the "sound words" here surely derive from Paul's own authoritative commission to the gentiles of which his extraordinary life was a fulfilment.

4. "He is conceited and knows nothing." He thinks his opinion is more important than the opinion of the apostles of Christ or of Christ himself. Yes, "he is conceited" and knows nothing or, in the words of one translation, is a "pompous ignoramus."[3] This is a more than a random insult because the ignorance it speaks of is profound. Paul and the other apostles had a firm line of transmission from Christ himself to draw upon and had shown by their brave and outspoken lives their willingness to risk all they had for the gospel. The truth of their testimony had been tested in adversity and by judicial inquiry or rougher opposition. These false teachers were lightweights who had never risked anything for Christ. They had become elders after the church had been established and so had avoided the lonely bravery and faith

---

2. Stott, *1 Timothy & Titus*, 147.
3. NEB.

of the pioneers. This pattern of courage and sacrifice in the first generation contrasting with an extravagant sense of entitlement in following generations is all too common and may unfortunately be found in Pentecostal and charismatic churches.

The wrong attitude has an "unhealthy fascination with controversies and disputes about words." The false teacher is thrilled to be embroiled a fierce argument, especially "about words" (as opposed to the realities behind the words). These are *logomachias*, a compound from two Greek words meaning "word" and "battle," and only used here in the NT.[4] In these situations clever and cutting remarks are the order of the day. Nothing is resolved, of course, but the controversies allow the false teacher to win a few points and therefore feel good. The disputes stir up emotions like "jealousy" and lead to "conflict" (within the church but also perhaps outside it) and then "slander," a term quite possibly requiring legal redress. "Groundless suspicions" also emerge. The disputes polarize participants by casting doubt on the good faith of others and before long a harmonious congregation is split into factions.

5. What goes on leads to "constant wrangling" among people who have "lost their minds" (*diephtharmenōn anthrōpōn ton noun*). Here, *diephtharmenōn* means "corrupt" and is "used in a physical sense to describe the effect of rust on iron and moths on clothing."[5] Paul has a great deal to say about the mind and its need for renewal and transformation. It is part of his understanding of the composition of human beings which, while it sees people as psychosomatic unities, also distinguishes heart, mind, body. The corruption of the mind is particularly terrible since it is through the mind that truth is apprehended. Paul speaks of minds being "darkened" (Eph 4:18) and then "renewed" in Christ (Rom 12:2). The disputatious individuals concerned with false teaching have reached a point where they would not recognize the truth if it were to be presented to them, like those in 2 Tim 3:7 who are "always learning but never coming to a knowledge of the truth." Indeed, the people troubling the Ephesian congregation are destitute of "any sense of truth," which is an indictment indeed. To be destitute (*apesterēmenōn*) of truth (*tēs alētheias*) speaks of an inability to conceive of the concept of truth let alone its content. They have no fixed-point and everything is a lie and equally unbelievable. In fact, they have now reached a point where religion is seen primarily as a way to "make a living" so that it has been debased to a grubby trade. In short, Paul, having deconstructed the doctrines and damaging fall-out from the false teachers, now strips bare

---

4. Knight, *Pastoral Epistles*, 395.

5. Mounce, *Pastoral Epistles*, 340.

their ultimate motivation. We could put this another way by saying the only truth these false teachers recognize is the "bottom line" or the "fast buck": for them, religion is all about money. Sections of the Pentecostal movement need to take all this to heart!

6–8. Speaking of gain, Paul turns the motivations of the false teachers upside down. In effect he says, "you thought religious gain was all about money, but the real gain is piety." There is "great gain in true piety" which is "beyond material sufficiency." The gain offered by piety is the capacity to be content with what you have (Phil 4:11–12). The gain, following the example and words of Jesus, is not of material wealth but is a gain of peace and joy and a true evaluation of material possessions which are held lightly (Matt 6:26–34). The church sometimes needs to be reminded the Savior was born in a stable, had very few personal possessions, and was buried in a borrowed grave. Completing this thought, Paul quotes a classical maxim[6] reminding us that we came naked into the world and can take no material possessions out. And so, if we have "food and clothing," this is enough to make us "content." It may seem as if Paul is setting the bar too low here. Just to be content with "food and clothing" when we have a family to house and a job to find and a car to run? There's a hyperbolic minimalism about what Paul says, but there is also a profound truth to be grasped.[7] If Christians can be content with the bare necessities, they have learned how to be satisfied in Christ when their situation is at rock bottom. They have tested the tender mercy of God to the point when they know it reaches them even when everything seems to have gone and gone wrong. Is Paul saying Christians should live permanently at a basic level? Stott thinks not: "what Paul is defining is not the maximum that is permitted to the believer, but the minimum that is compatible with contentment."[8] If you have more than the minimum, you have grounds for thanksgiving.

9. The text turns from contentment to an obsessive desire for wealth: "those wanting to get rich fall into temptation." The sentence hinges on "desire," on motivation and the human will. In the gospels Jesus said, "seek first his kingdom and his righteousness, and all these things will be given to you as well" (Matt 6:33). The focus is on what Christians are seeking, what drives their decision-making, what is their reason for getting up in the morning. If their desire is merely for a bigger bank balance, the unrestricted service of

---

6. Kelly, *Pastoral Epistles*, 136; Towner, *Timothy and Titus*, 399; Johnson, *Timothy*, 294; Mounce, *Pastoral Epistles*, 342. Paul's primary source for this thought is Eccl 5:15.

7. This may go back to important sayings of Jesus such as Matt 6:25–34.

8. Stott, *1 Timothy & Titus*, 150.

Mammon, they are heading for trouble. First there is "temptation," perhaps a special temptation for those hungering for money, but anyway a temptation that leads progressively downhill to a "trap" (*pagida*, a word used of catching animals, often with a net)[9] and many "*foolish desires*," or mindless passions, which "sink," plunge or submerge the possessors into "ruin" and "destruction." According to LSJ, "if [these words] are to be differentiated, [they] may signify material and spiritual disaster respectively."[10] The downward pathway leads to a destination nothing to do with the believer's eschatological destiny in Christ.[11]

10. "For the love of money is the root of all kinds of evil." These words are often misread as "money is the root of all evil," but this is not what Paul says. It is the "love of money," that obsession with glittering precious metal (*philargyria*), which is the root (*rhiza*, from which we derive rhizome, the fleshy underground stem of some plants) of "all kinds of evil," but not precisely of every evil that exists. The phrase is likely to be a proverb or quotation and should not therefore be pressed as the ultimate revelation about the relationship between avarice and evil in the world.[12] And "some people," presumably those following the false teachers in Ephesus, have been "led astray from the faith," phraseology reminiscent of false christs and prophets (Mark 13:22) and implying Satan's stratagems behind the scenes (because the trap, *pagida*, is specifically connected in 1 Tim 3:7 and 2 Tim 2:26 with the devil's devices). Those once good people lured and trapped by their love of money have backslidden, wandered away "from the faith" and "pierced" (or impaled) themselves with many woes. Not only have they caused trouble in the church, but they have brought harm on themselves.

b. Timothy's battle (6:11–16)

> But you, man of God, flee from these things and pursue righteousness, godliness, faith, love, resilience and gentleness. Fight the good fight of the faith, taking hold of the eternal life to which you were called and for *which you* made your "good confession" in the presence of many witnesses. I command you in the presence of God who gives life to all things and Christ Jesus, who made his own "good

---

9. LSJ, 1284.
10. Kelly, *Pastoral Epistles*, 137.
11. Fee, *1 and 2 Timothy, Titus*, 145.
12. Mounce, *Pastoral Epistles*, 346.

> confession" before Pontius Pilate, keep the commandment, spotless and irreproachable until the appearance of our Lord Jesus Christ, which he will manifest at a time of his *choosing*, the blessed and sole ruler, king of kings and lord of lords. He alone is immortal, dwelling in unapproachable light which no one has seen or could see—to him be honor and power forever, Amen. (1 Tim 6:11–16)

This dramatic and solemn section concludes with a charge to Timothy. We hear in these verses the voice of an impassioned speaker whose instructions to Timothy, "flee . . . pursue . . . fight . . . take hold of . . . keep the commandment," reach back to Christ himself and forward to a vision of God.

11. First there is an instruction to Timothy to "flee from these things." He is to shun or run from the tangled lives and doctrines or the false teachers. Here is an instruction many young Christians could heed. There comes a time when it is important to walk out of what is bad and not be associated with it anymore. Of course, in Timothy's case he cannot walk away from the church at Ephesus, but he can separate himself from the fruitless controversies and disputes plaguing the congregation. He is instead to "pursue" six different virtues that will guide his conduct in the trials he will face. He is to "pursue righteousness" and here righteousness does not appear to have the more theological sense associated with justification but rather honest and transparent living with an impartial handling of church matters. Following righteousness is "godliness" or *eusebeia* which is one of the motifs of the epistle (2:2; 4:7, 8; 6:3, 6). Godliness is a lifestyle and attitude that consciously brings every part of a believer's life to God. This, then, is not a righteousness that is hard and impersonal, but a righteousness infused with all the good, kind, and wise things that come from God. And then "faith" follows, which lifts its eyes and sees beyond the present to the fulfilment of prayer and promises. "Faith" is necessary within the context of Timothy's current difficult ministry, and he must not waver. Even in a judgmental situation, he needs "love" in his heart and not anger or bitterness. Love remains the key Christian virtue, and beyond it, he needs "resilience" and "gentleness." "Resilience" will be necessary when he is battered by criticism or obtuse misunderstanding and when progress is slow. He will need "gentleness" when impatience, anger, or sarcasm are his first instinct.

12. Sometimes the metaphors employed by Paul are military, and at other times, he employs sporting or even agricultural ones. Commentators generally agree that "Fight the good fight" is an athletic metaphor with boxing or wrestling in mind. This is because other forms of the verb for fight or struggle, *agōnizomai*, are used elsewhere with athletic connotations

(1 Cor 9:25). The other question concerns "the faith" and whether the idea here is of particular elements of the Christian faith, Timothy's ministry, or the whole Christian life and walk stemming from trust in Christ. It is probably best to take the last option and see this as a general statement with parallels to Paul's confession in 2 Timothy 4:7 where he speaks of finishing his race. The exhortation to Timothy would be to struggle to complete his Christian life victoriously so that the following words, "taking hold of the eternal life," would apply to grasping the prize after winning the fight. Actually, the grasp of eternal life need not only refer to the end of this life but can stem from a recognition eternal life begins during our ordinary biological existence when we accept Christ; our lives then incorporate the dimension of eternal life.

The reference to the "good confession in the presence of many witnesses" is usually thought to be an allusion to Timothy's adult baptism by immersion where he would have testified to his salvation.[13] The New Testament depictions of baptism are always of adults, and the command in Matthew 28:19 is to make disciples, "teach them" and then baptize them, which is why Baptist and Pentecostal churches have followed the custom of waiting until individuals are old enough to *understand* their salvation and testify to it publicly. Some churches, of course baptize infants, and this is traditionally argued by appeal to texts such as Acts 16:33 where entire households are baptized and also via the analogy with circumcision made by Paul in Colossians 2:11–12.[14] Whilst Baptists and Pentecostals do not find these convincing, the key pointer to an adult context here is simply the element of public confession.

Others, however, have interpreted the "good confession" as an allusion to Timothy's ordination since that would also have been a public event with elders present. Yet, ordination, or formal ministerial recognition, can hardly have been the occasion of God's call to "eternal life." Consequently, it is more reasonable to understand the "good confession" as what Timothy said at his baptism.[15]

---

13. Mounce, *Pastoral Epistles*, 356.

14. Heidelberg Shorter Catechism, question 63 (cf. Bierma et al., *Heidelberg Catechism*). This, naturally, poses the question of how baptism is equivalent to circumcision in the case of *women*. There is an irony here, of course, in that Timothy was actually circumcised as a confessing Jewish Christian *as an adult*—by Paul himself (Acts 16:3). However, this was delayed out of respect for his pagan father, so it is still not definitive. In fact, we do not hear explicitly of Timothy's baptism. Perhaps the main point here is that Timothy's embrace of his faith-based upbringing (2 Tim 1:5) and the scriptural teaching he received (2 Tim 3:15) is what "saved" him.

15. Mounce, *Pastoral Epistles*, 356.

13. Paul has already made clear to Timothy what he wants done. In 1:3 and 5:21, he "urged" or commanded Timothy, and now he reverts to similar vocabulary. "I command you in the presence of God." The strong language has military connotations.[16] And the command now comes "in the presence of God" and with reference to Christ. No higher authority exists. Moreover, God "gives life to all things" and is the Lord of life who sustains all and is consequently close at hand, as is "Christ Jesus who made his good confession before Pontius Pilate."

The example of Jesus before Pontius Pilate draws attention to the courage and dignity of Christ as he stood before the highest Roman authority in his land. Jesus is neither daunted nor forgetful of the purpose of his mission but stands as a witness to truth in the face of judicial power and cynicism. Similarly, Timothy is to take heart and not to buckle under the pressure of the challenge ahead. Some commentators,[17] noting that Jesus did not give an extensive speech at his trial, take the *epi* here to mean "in the days of" Pontius Pilate and take his "good confession" as a reference to his death on the cross.

Either way, the curious resonance between Timothy's own confession (v. 12) and that of Jesus made in the presence of or in the days of Pilate, perhaps suggests that the language of baptismal testimony in early Christianity quickly underwent a verbal assimilation to that of *trial and martyrdom*. Besides Jesus' own challenge to "take up your cross and follow" (Matt 16:24–25) and his promise that the Holy Spirit would help us know what to say if arrested (Mark 13:11), it was Paul who pioneered the idea that baptism was "into Christ's death," and that Timothy's descent into the water and coming up again enacted Jesus' burial and resurrection (Rom 6:3).

14. "Keep the commandment (*entolē*)." This is the climax of the instruction. Commentators are divided about what exactly the commandment is and, while some consider it to be a specific instruction deriving from verses 11 to 13 or from the epistle as a whole, others take the commandment to be more general and widely known, an instruction to live the Christian life and preach the gospel: "encompassing Timothy's commitment to Christ and his ministry."[18] One translation, in keeping with the military or imperial connotation of *entolē*, has "obey your orders"[19] and this captures the authoritative urgency of the original.[20]

16. LSJ, 1306.
17. Fee, *1 and 2 Timothy, Titus*, 151; Mounce, *Pastoral Epistles*, 358.
18. Mounce, *Pastoral Epistles*, 359.
19. NEB.
20. Knight, quoting Bauckham, *Jude, 2 Peter*, 278 on 2 Pet 2:21, points out that

"Keep the commandment, spotless and irreproachable." Although the words "spotless and irreproachable" could apply back to the commandment itself and remind readers of the purity of the gospel and the moral perfection of orthodox doctrine, we have taken the words to apply to Timothy himself. He is to keep the commandment without any taint or whiff of scandal, to be "irreproachable," and to be so "until the appearance of our Lord Jesus Christ," an event that may be close at hand. Here then is the apex of history, the return of Christ in glory, the eschatological moment at an unknown point of time, "at a time of his choosing." This is the terminus, and Timothy must be strong until then for he will stand before Christ (2 Cor 5:10) to give an account of himself; everything secret will be revealed (Luke 12:2–5), and a new era will begin.

The "appearance (*epiphaneia*)" is a semi-technical term applying to the return of a king or emperor from abroad or a royal anniversary. The use of this precise word is an "assault on emperor worship,"[21] a religious practice involving temples and statues woven into the Roman Imperial system since the divinization of Julius Caesar. The cult of emperor worship was intended to promote religio-cultural unity across the empire and to elevate the emperor to a sphere beyond political or economic criticism. To speak of the *epiphany* of Christ, his *epiphaneia*, is to assert Jesus', as opposed to Caesar's, authority and rule.

The climactic moment is at the time of God's choosing. It is not only useless but also impious to attempt to calculate the date of the second coming. In Acts 1:7 Jesus told the disciples, "it is not for you to know" the time of his return, so, equally, it is not for Christians today to know the exact time. Any attempt to second-guess God by calendrical calculations from Scripture are, and have historically been shown to be, a failure.[22] Rather Christians should be on the alert[23] but not believe the calculations of maverick Bible teachers, however well-meaning they might seem.

---

entolē is used in 1 Peter as a "description of Christianity considered as a body of ethical teaching" and is thus generalized (*Pastoral Epistles*, 267).

21. Mounce, *Pastoral Epistles*, 360.

22. William Miller (1782–1849) famously persuaded his followers to sell their possessions and wait on a hillside dressed in white for the Lord's return at some point between March 21, 1843 and March 21, 1844. When this did not happen, he went back to check his calculations and announced a new date, April 18, 1844. Similarly, a small number of Pentecostals in the UK thought the return of Christ would occur in or before 1934, that year being the last of the "period of the gentiles." The calculations are usually based on the weeks in the book of Daniel.

23. Luke 21:36.

"The blessed and sole ruler, king of kings and Lord of lords." This declaration about Jesus captures the zeal and faith of the early church. Jesus is the "blessed and only ruler" (cf. 1:11), the one from whom all blessings flow, the source of all blessedness and the "only ruler," that is, not part of a polytheistic pantheon but sole and supreme sovereign and absolutely within the tradition of Jewish monotheism. He is "King of kings and Lord of lords," echoing Old Testament designations of God (Deut 10:17; Ps 136:3). Kings and lords are his subjects. So, however high and mighty the Caesars might be and however much they surrounded themselves with pomp and ceremony, they were in the eyes of the early church under the authority of Christ.

16. God "alone" is "immortal" and has life within himself (John 1:4) and will not and cannot ever die. Human beings are immortal in the sense that they will survive death, but they, unlike God, are not the source and ground of immortality. The Bible teaches that all life comes originally from God who precedes everything and "dwells in unapproachable light." The revelation here is of God within the realm of glory without any darkness or evil. This depiction of God as clothed in uncreated light too bright for human eyes is a marvelous reality almost mystical in its communication to the human mind and partially illustrated in words describing the celestial city, "the city does not need the sun or the moon to shine on it, for the glory of God gives it light, and the Lamb is its lamp" (Rev 21:23).

Such radiance surrounds God that no human being can bear the presence of the glory. Even Moses was not given the privilege of looking on the fullness of God's glory and had only to see his back as he passed by (Exod 33:18–23). This surpassing radiance, brighter than the brightness of the sun, is glimpsed by Paul on the road to Damascus, and is too much even for the cherubim and seraphim who veiled their faces to avoid looking directly at God (Acts 26:13, Isa 6:2).

"To him be honor and power forever, Amen." This burst of high praise for God, or doxology, crystallizes words of worship before the transcendent greatness of God. To give God honor *is* to worship,[24] and the phrase ends with "power" rather than "glory" as might be expected, perhaps to complete the theme of divine authority which was so fitting an ascription in such a city as Ephesus.

---

24. The etymology provides a clue. Worship derives from old English *weorthscipe,* "worthiness, acknowledgement of worth."

c. Warning to the rich (6:17–19)

> Tell those who are rich in this present age not to be proud and not to put their hope in wealth that may prove insecure, but in God who provides us with all things abundantly to enjoy. They should do good, be rich in good works, generous and sharing freely, laying up for themselves a good foundation for the future, so that they may take hold of the life that truly is life. (1 Tim 6:17–19)

Some commentators think this section belongs earlier in the epistle along with reference to other social groups in the church (5:5–15; 6:1–2), but having warned of the dangers of an overriding desire for wealth in the preceding section, Paul turns to those in the congregation who are already rich by giving them instruction and reassurance, and he does so with energetic Greek wordplay: to the rich . . . uncertainty of riches . . . richly for our enjoyment . . . rich in good works. Incidentally, the passage also draws attention to the wide socioeconomic spread within the Christian community.

17. Paul begins with two commands. The rich are not "to be proud," an instruction relevant to our own times. The rich tend to feel they are different from everybody else and live in a world of their own with gated communities, servants, first class travel, fine goods, and excellent health care. Even those who are comfortably off can feel above and apart from the poor and dispossessed. The first words address attitude. The Christian rich should be approachable, willing to rub shoulders with everyone and not to expect constant privilege, especially in the context of the Christian community. Nor should the rich put their "hope in wealth" as if, being rich, they are insulated from trouble. Riches themselves "may prove insecure" by coming and going—the stock market rises and falls—but instead the rich should put their hope "in God" who remains entirely constant over the vicissitudes of economic crises or revolution. Can anything, asks Paul, separate us from the love of God? (Rom 8:35–39)

More, God "provides us with all things abundantly to enjoy." God's generous provision to human beings is a theme within the preaching of Paul (Acts 14:17) and springs out of the words of Jesus (John 10:10). It is a profound mistake to consider God stingy, grudging, or poor or to believe God frowns on our enjoyment of what has been given to us. God is the giver, and "all things" come from him—hence the gratitude and praise of the church—and are given for our enjoyment (i.e., for the express purpose of giving pleasure).²⁵ These words cut against the false teachers whose asceticism effectively denies or limits the goodness of God (cf. 4:3). This goodness indeed is a spur to Christian generosity rather than an excuse for self-indulgence.

18–19. The rich are commanded to "do good" or be "rich in good works," terms harking back to the command of Jesus to be salt and light (Matt 5:13–16), light involving all kinds of charitable, community-based, and humanitarian activities. This is more than a dry Christianity of intellectual affirmation but involves "being generous and sharing freely" where the notion of "sharing (*koinōnikous*)" is connected with the notion of fellowship (*koinōnia*), both coming from the same Greek root, and implying "personal involvement" and the sharing of oneself or "having in common." Therefore, the rich are to use their wealth for the sake of others rather than hoarding it for selfish ends, and if they do this, they also benefit themselves because they lay up "a good foundation for the future," a phrase likely to mean the same as "laying up treasure in heaven" (Matt 6:19–21; Luke 12:33) by referring to the next age. This is not buying salvation or earning salvation but expressing salvation now in actions serving as a "foundation" of what will be completed at the Parousia of Christ. In doing this, the rich "take hold of life that truly is life" or seize or actualize the eternal life to which their faith points (compare verse 12). Theory becomes practice; the possible becomes actual, and their good deeds show the reality of the salvation of the rich.

d. A final charge (6:20)

> Timothy, guard what has been entrusted to you; turn away from pointless and empty talk and the contradictions of what is falsely called "knowledge."²⁶ By professing this, some have departed from the faith. Grace be with you.²⁷ (1 Tim 6:20)

The letter ends with a brief exhortation that may, like the end of Galatians, have been added in Paul's own handwriting. It summarizes the positive and negative themes of the epistle. Timothy is to protect the faith and avoid the outpourings of the false teachers. The brevity of the final words may stem

---

25. Johnson, *Timothy*, 310.

26. Paul may be using the Greek word *gnōsis* in a technical sense to indicate a deviant para-Christian religious system. A book from such quarters known in the second century was actually called "Contradictions." See commentary below.

27. Since the Greek is plural, perhaps "you all" would be a fitting translation. However, some MSS have the singular, pointing to Timothy alone.

from the urgency of the situation. Like Galatians which is also written out of distress over doctrinal error, there is no thanksgiving for the congregation.

20. "Timothy." However much the epistle is written for the church, it remains a personal document. "Guard what has been entrusted to you (*parathēkēn*)" or literally "O Timothy guard the deposit." The *parathēkēn* is a legal term speaking of property assigned for protection by one person to another. The deposit must be the whole apostolic and orthodox Christian faith entrusted to Timothy together with his commission to defend and promote the faith. It remains interesting that the letter does not, in fact, recount a barrage of all-out assaults on key Christian doctrines, so much as it draws attention to a host of tell-tale signs, some quite subtle, that point to malaise within. This is largely blamed on false teachers whose betrayal of the great "deposit" is not always sensed by those they deceive.

"Turn away from" (or shun as in verse 11) "pointless and empty talk," which is reminiscent of the opening chapter's reference to sectaries "not understanding the things they are saying" (1:7). Equally to be avoided are the "contradictions" (*antitheseis*) of what is falsely called "knowledge." It is intriguing that *Antitheseis* became the title of a book by the second-century heretic Marcion, who while not technically a Gnostic, was often viewed by the church as standing within that grouping. What Marcion did do, however, was to reject the role of the Old Testament in the church, a considerable contrast to the frequent recourse to Scripture we have seen from Paul, who later reminds Timothy that "*all* Scripture is inspired by God" (2 Tim 3:16).[28] Whatever the precise nature of the errors of the false teachers here, it led to tragic results: "some have departed from the faith."

So, Paul ends with a blessing: "grace be with you all." Without grace for Timothy and for the congregation as a whole, there was no way they were going to overcome their problems or thwart the unhealthy encroachment of entrapping false doctrine. Grace is what they need, and the apostle's blessing is given to "you" (plural) or the entire congregation. There is nothing strange about the singular address to Timothy and the plurality of the ending since the letter is both personal and congregational, written to Timothy but in the expectation that it will be read aloud to the assembled congregation. And it is fitting for the epistle to begin with a wish for grace for Timothy and to end with a wish for grace to all those who hear.

---

28. Marcion's *Antitheses* or "Contradictions" was a catalogue of well-known places where the Old Testament might be viewed as inconsistent with itself or with the New Testament religion of Jesus. It is highly ironic that he based this stance on an incorrect understanding of Paul. For further details, see Heikki Räisänen, "Marcion," 100–124.

EXCURSUS III.

On Spiritual Warfare

Spiritual warfare has occupied attention in Pentecostal/charismatic circles.[1] The nature of this warfare has been conceived in different ways. One group has spoken about *commanding* in faith certain things to be or to come into existence with the idea that "God's words in our mouths are as effective as God's words in his mouth." In this formulation, warfare is a matter of command in the face of adverse circumstances including the circumstances of illness. Second, warfare may be a matter of *declaration* rather than command. Certain positive statements are made as public or semi-public declarations of God's will with the intention of making current circumstances line-up with Scripture. "You are well" even if you appear to be ill; "you are prosperous" even if you appear to be poor. Third, spiritual warfare may be a matter of simple and intense prayer to the heavenly father of a Christian. It is not a matter of commanding or declaring but of *asking*.

Of the three approaches, the first suffers from the apparent turning upside down of the relationship between the Christian and God: the Christian is now commanding, and God is making sure that the commands of the Christian are obeyed. The second is a reminder to the Christian of circumstances as they might be in the belief that God will then act. The third makes spiritual warfare like any other prayer and ensures the relationship between the Christian and God is filial and gracious. It makes the agonized prayers of Jesus in the garden of Gethsemane the pattern of spiritual warfare.

---

1. Walker, "The Devil You Think You Know," 86–105. See also Collins, *Exorcism and Deliverance*.

Behind spiritual warfare lies the picture of the world as a material place over which invisible spiritual (and therefore immaterial) forces engage in combat.[2] The principalities and powers of Ephesians 6:12–13 control swathes of territory from the air while, on the ground and embodied, are demons. Demons are expelled by exorcism, but principalities and powers are wrestled with but do not have to be exorcized since they never seek embodiment.[3] Jesus's words about Beelzebub (Luke 11:18,19) and Daniel's prayers (Dan 10) are the texts from which this picture of the world is built.

However, it is clear also that Christians should normally obey the injunctions of the state because the state's apparatus is beneficial, "for rulers are not a terror to good works, but to evil" (Rom 13:3). Any exposition of spiritual warfare that neglects these verses is likely to ignore the paradox caused by accepting the reality of political power while denying its image of itself.[4] Christians accept the need to render to Caesar the things that are Caesar's while at the same time perceiving, as Revelation shows, the bestiality of imperial power (Matt 22:21; Rev 13:1).

Regarding historical examples, it is difficult to find in the works of John Wesley, George Whitefield, William Booth or Aimee Semple McPherson any precise reference to spiritual warfare. Ruffians tried to break up their meetings (a bull was once released while Wesley was preaching to an outdoor crowd and Booth was pelted with rotten fruit or eggs) and ridicule and caricature came their way. They overcame with prayer, persistence, and faith rather than by developing a specialist theology of spiritual warfare.

---

2. Gilbert, "Spiritual Warfare," 847–51.
3. Kay and Parry, *Exorcism and Deliverance*.
4. Bauckham, *Theology of the Book of Revelation*, 35–37, et passim.

EXCURSUS IV.

On Holiness or Godliness

Holiness or godliness has long been a concern of the Pentecostal and charismatic movements. In the nineteenth century holiness movements and holiness congregations in the United States and Britain were usually directly or indirectly descended from Methodism.[1] John Wesley as part of his standard teaching and preaching had expounded a doctrine of sanctification.[2] But was this achieved, as later writers asked, by a spiritual crisis or by the gradual, steady and almost imperceptible influence of the Holy Spirit? In the United States Phoebe Palmer (1807–74) taught a shorter way to sanctification by consecration of oneself while others, notably Bishop Handley Moule, spoke of gaining sanctification "by faith."[3] Once sanctification was gained, should it be seen as the eradication of sinful nature within the Christian or merely the suppression of these tendencies? There was scope for theological disagreement.

When the Pentecostal movement began at the start of the twentieth century many of those swept up into it were Methodists who added on Spirit-baptism as a subsequent experience following sanctification. This led to a three-stage gospel: salvation, sanctification, and then empowerment through Spirit baptism. Other Pentecostals, following William Durham (1873–1912), saw sanctification and salvation as being bound up together

---

1. Jones, *Perfectionist Persuasion;* Stephens, *The Fire Spreads.*
2. Rack, *Reasonable Enthusiast,* 395 ff.
3. Palmer, *Promise of the Father;* Moule, "Message."

in a single theological concept. This led to a two-stage gospel: salvation-plus-sanctification and empowerment through Spirit baptism.

In practice sanctification often descended into small-scale discussions about exactly what holy behavior was. As Wacker points out there were restrictions on what people could eat or drink (chewing gum, Coca-Cola, alcohol, tea, coffee, ice cream, and medicinal drugs might all be forbidden)[4] and restrictions on what people could do (going to theatrical entertainments, dances, playing cards, reading novels, newspapers, comic books, listening to ragtime, and classical violin might all be excluded)[5] and restrictions on what people could wear (fashionable, revealing or flamboyant clothes, expensive hairstyles were frowned upon). When holiness became a matter of petty regulation, believers were often forced into a kind of legalism which ignored the radiant glory of God whose otherness—whose holiness—was the basis for the doctrine in the first place.

Holiness might therefore be defined in two ways: by internal piety fostered by prayer reaching out to God; and holiness defined by action which, in the form advocated by Charles Finney, amounted to a quest for social justice and, particularly, the abolition of slavery and any human exploitation.[6] Thus internal pietism and external social action might be seen as the two sides of holiness that sometimes coexisted in the same person or denomination and sometimes settled far apart as two distinct ways of living the Christian life.

---

4. Wacker, *Heaven Below*, 122.
5. Wacker, *Heaven Below*, 124.
6. Dayton, *Evangelical Heritage*, 18.

TITUS

OUTLINE

I. PAUL, TITUS, AND CRETE (1:1–16)
  a. Salutation (1:1–4)
  b. The task: appointing elders (1:5–9)
  c. The task: the situation on Crete (1:10–16)

II. CHRISTIAN LIVING: A RATIONALE (2:1–15)
  a. Separate groups (2:1–10)
  b. Hope and glory (2:11–15)

III. CHRISTIAN LIVING OUTSIDE THE CHURCH: A RATIONALE (3:1–15)
  a. Living in society (3:1–3)
  b. God saves (3:4–7)
  c. Final admonitions (3:8–15)

COMMENTARY

I. PAUL, TITUS, AND CRETE

    a. Salutation (1:1–4)

    b. The task: appointing elders (1:5–9)

    c. The task: the situation on Crete (1:10–16)

I. PAUL, TITUS, AND CRETE

The situation of the church in Crete appears to have been parallel to the one in Ephesus but not so urgent and less advanced. The false teachers were not, as far as we can see, defectors from an existing oversight, but rather, the church had been left without its full complement of elders with the result that it was fresh and new and without much of a governance structure but, at the same time, threatened by mercenary false teachers who might destroy what had already been planted.

a. Salutation (1:1–4)

> Paul, a servant of God and apostle of Jesus Christ for[1] the faith of God's elect and the knowledge of the truth that is according to godliness in the hope of eternal life. God, who does not lie, promised this before the world began but has now revealed it at just the right time. He has done this through his word in the proclamation entrusted to me by the command of God our savior.

---

1. For this use of *kata*, cf. BDAG, 512 (B.4).

> To Titus, my true child in our shared faith—grace and peace
> from God the Father and Christ Jesus our savior. (Titus 1:1–4)

1. As elsewhere in the New Testament, and unlike modern letters where we put our signatures at the end, this one begins by stating who the sender is. Paul speaks of himself as a "servant of God" (lit. "slave"). This is a term familiar from the OT (e.g., Pss 89:3; 105:42; Num 12:7; Neh 9:14; Jer 25:4), but its force needs to be imaginatively grasped by modern readers. It is as if Paul is saying "I am not the important person; the important person is the one I serve. That's what you need to know about me." And he continues "apostle of Jesus Christ." Again, the unvarnished implications need to be realized. The "apostle" is the one sent out, which implies the sender has authority to post his representative. The tendency among some elements of the Pentecostal movement to see the word "apostle" as a title or rank needs to be deconstructed. The apostle is someone who, after a personal encounter with Christ, has been transformed, gifted, and then entrusted with a mission. Apostleship must imply a deep and submissive personal relationship with Christ and is not in any sense conferred by a vote, committee, or ecclesiastical machinery.

"For the faith of God's elect." Although commentators have discussed the variant meanings of the word *for* (*kata*), the most convincing is that Paul's apostleship is for the purpose of bringing the "elect" to "faith," and here "faith" is a personal believing response more than assent to a generalized body of doctrine that one might call "the Christian faith." The "elect" are the body of believers chosen by God. There is no sense here of any conflict between election and free will,[2] perhaps because election is primarily an OT concept applied to the people of God as a whole (e.g., Ps 105:6; Isa 43:20; 65:9) and is not pressed at the individual level. Indeed, if it were, there would be no need to protect believers from the damage of false teachers since their election would automatically render them invulnerable.

"The knowledge of the truth." The gospel Paul preached is true. There was cynicism among the Roman elite ("what is truth?" asks Pilate in John 18:38), and that question remains central to postmodern culture. Yet Christianity asserts the gospel is true and that Christ himself personifies truth. We may understand truth as the correspondence between "what is said" and "how things are" in the ordinary day-to-day sense. Paul would have no truck with abstruse claims, ancient or modern, that truth does not or cannot exist.

"Faith" and "knowledge" go together in Christianity and fit together harmoniously; faith, in one respect, arises from knowledge, whether this

---

2. That is, in the way this might arise in Reformed Theology and/or contemporary Philosophy of Religion.

is knowledge of Scripture or, in the case of the first generation of Christians, a first-hand encounter with the life, death, and resurrection of Christ. Christianity, unlike the sagas of classical gods and goddesses, asserts a truth that is historically based and defensible, and not simply an abstract proposition or claim hanging in the air but a whole interconnected set of historical events supported by evidence of different types—literary, legal, traditional, and even philosophical. This kind of truth is impactful. It is "according to godliness," meaning that it is worked out in the attitudes and behavior of those who grasp it: godliness is "a total commitment of one's life to God,"[3] an ethical lifestyle animated by a living and therefore genuine relationship with God.

2. "in hope of eternal life." The words may denote a further basis or purpose of apostolic preaching. Either way, the proclamation of the gospel brings the "hope of eternal life" into the consciousness of the hearer. Hope in the Pauline sense (Rom 8:24, 25) is not a vague and wistful desire for something that might or might not happen. No! It is rather a confident expectation of a future good. "Eternal life" belongs to the gospel and is the free gift (*charisma*) of God (Rom 6:23) experienced now and completed in the next age.[4] It is rooted in God's own eternal being and was promised "before the world began," that is, before the cosmos came into existence, and it was promised by a God "who does not lie"—indeed it is arguable that God not only does not lie but cannot lie since what God declares to be the case is the case. More, when we think about it, we may ask why God would ever need to lie! So, the promise of eternal life is given by an utterly reliable God before the drama of human life had ever begun.

3. This revelation stemming from eternity is "now revealed"; so, what was timeless is now seen in time, what was part of God's great purposes has now, at a particular historical moment, come to fruition (see Excursus V on Time and Eternity). This eternity-time concept runs through Paul's theology: God sent his Son to the world in the fullness of time (Gal 4:4); God has now disclosed a mystery hidden from ages and generations (Col 1:26). And here, the faith of God's elect and the knowledge of the truth in hope of eternal life is "revealed" at "just the right time," and it is revealed by "proclamation" (see also Excursus V on Time and Eternity). Paul understood himself to be standing at a chosen point in world history with a message

---

3. Mounce, *Pastoral Epistles*, 380.

4. Although the Jewish eschatological term "eternal life" is often imagined to be an exclusively Johannine term, it occurs occasionally in the Synoptic Gospels (e.g., Mark 10:17, 10:30) and in both the undisputed Pauline letters as well as the Pastorals (Rom 2:7; 5:21; 6:22–23; Gal 6:8; 1 Tim 1:16; 6:12; Titus 1:2; 3:7). That "eternal life" might start now rather than only in the age to come is a distinctive emphasis of Christianity.

of significance to everyone on earth.⁵ He preached God's word which had been "entrusted" to him "by the command of God" who is also "our savior." When we read in the next verse that Jesus is our Savior (also Titus 2:13), we have here the beginnings of the doctrine of the Trinity—not of its reality but of its formulation.

Alongside the sense of divine purposes flowing forward is the human responsibility of Paul. He must speak (as his exclamation in 1 Cor 9:16 demonstrates, "Woe to me if I preach not the gospel") because the message he brings has been "entrusted" to him—placed in his care—and he must communicate it in obedience to a "divine command" (the precise meaning of *epitagēn*,⁶ the word used here).

4. "To Titus." The name is Roman (perhaps he was named after the son of the emperor Vespasian) and indicates a gentile ancestry probably from Antioch.⁷ As a trusted member of Paul's team, he had been given the job of sorting out and smoothing over troubles in the Corinthian church (2 Cor 7:13–16). He had been largely successful and was later chosen to transport the large sum of money collected in Corinth for the Jerusalem church (2 Cor 8:16f). That the volatile Corinthians trusted his financial integrity and practical know-how speaks well of his character and the esteem in which he was held. "My true child in our shared faith": the "true child" shows how Paul feels about his role in Titus's conversion and later mentoring. That this establishes a familial bond across the Jew-gentile boundary becomes a striking illustration of Paul's beliefs about the gospel. And that it is their "shared faith" alone that both saves and unites is a potent denial of the claims of ascetic or gnostic-style false teachers.

"Grace and peace." This follows the pattern of most of Paul's epistles by Christianizing the conventional greeting of the day, but it is, of course, profoundly meaningful. "Grace" is that great, sweeping love and benevolence of God along with the peace and inner calm generated by a stance no longer antagonistic to heaven. "From God the Father," words indicating that blessing comes not from mere good fortune or the unreliable favor of the "gods" but from our true heavenly Father, personal and relatable, to whom we cry "Abba" (Rom 8:15). "And Christ Jesus our savior": the exalted position of Jesus is brought out by his association with the Father as the source of grace and peace and by calling Jesus "our savior." Although Paul clearly

---

5. That the "gospel revelation" makes explicit provision for the gentiles is a distinctively Pauline claim (Rom 11:25; 16:25; Eph 3:3–6; Col 1:26–27). Cf. also the acclamation of 1 Tim 3:16.

6. MM, 247.

7. Bruce, *Pauline Circle*, 58. See also Gal 2:1–3.

implies Jesus and the Father act together in salvation, he shows how we may nevertheless and properly call Jesus our "savior," just as we also call him "Lord." Within the context of the epistle and the situation in Crete, this high Christology may well be relevant in Paul's disputes with the false teachers.

b. *The task: appointing elders (1:5–9)*

> I left you behind on Crete for just this reason, that you might sort out the things that still needed to be done and appoint elders in every town as I directed. *An elder should be* someone *who*[8] is above reproach, the husband of but one wife, *the father* of believing children who have never been accused of wild living or failing to respect authority[9]. For the overseer should be blameless as God's steward, not self-regarding, quick-tempered or have problems with alcohol[10]. He should not be violent or corrupt[11], but welcoming to strangers, a lover *of all that is* good, wise, just, devout, *and* self-controlled, holding on to the trustworthy *message that he has been* taught[12], so that he may be able to encourage *others* with sound instruction and reprove those who speak against it. (Titus 1:5–9)

5. "I left you behind in Crete." The implication here is that Paul himself worked with Titus on Crete. We do not have any reference in Acts to a visit by Paul to Crete although there are gaps in the Acts narrative where this could be fitted. We argued (in the introduction) that this visit took place after Acts 28 during Paul's release from his first imprisonment in Rome. Crete itself is the largest of the Greek islands and would have been an obvious place to conduct a mission. It had a long, distinguished history and was the seat of the Minoan civilization. According to Cretan church tradition, Titus was buried in the then capital, Gortyn, a site later chosen for the first Cathedral in the sixth century.[13]

---

8. Lit. "if anyone is . . ."; the sentence is not completed properly.

9. The traditional translations, "dissipation" and "rebellion" would seem to require a more current gloss.

10. Lit. "addicted to wine." The Greek allows that "not in wild living" applies to the father, but the children would be the more meaningful fit here.

11. Greek *aischrokerdē*, traditionally, "greedy for dishonest gain."

12. I.e., the common teaching that Titus himself has received.

13. Bruce, *Pauline Circle*, 64.

"That you might sort out the things that still needed to be done." The setting up of self-sustaining congregations in any area required all kinds of practical details to be resolved. A place for meeting had to be agreed, the frequency of meetings needed to be settled, financial good practice had to be established, and so on. "And appoint elders in every town as I directed." Although each town may initially only have had one Christian congregation, it is possible Paul could foresee a single group of elders looking after a network of house-based gatherings in or around a larger town. That other Pauline letters are addressed to the "saints" in entire towns or cities might also suggest this.[14] Whether Paul and Titus established these gatherings themselves during an evangelistic tour, we do not know. It is possible they did although we are told in Acts 2:11 that Cretans were present in Jerusalem on the day of Pentecost when the Spirit of God was poured out. This might suggest a number of Cretans had been converted, returned home, and taken the initiative themselves,[15] in which case Paul and Titus may have consolidated and extended this work.

"Appoint elders." The process is not laid out in full. In Acts 14:23 it involved prayer, fasting, and the laying on of hands, and Titus must surely have been familiar this. Prayer was obviously petitionary but may also have included an element of discernment. Is this candidate right or not? Fasting intensified and prolonged the quest for certainty. Laying on of hands would have signaled identification with the new elder (see discussion of 1 Tim 5:22), and perhaps empowerment as well.

6. The next verses describe the characteristics of someone eligible to be an elder. They match well those given in 1 Timothy 3:2–7. The main point to notice is the character of elders rather than their completion of sophisticated theological training. They do need appropriate theological and doctrinal knowledge and an ability to communicate this, but that comes after the list of virtues they should show and the vices they must avoid. There is

---

14. Rom 1:7; 1 Cor 1:2; Phil 1:1; Col 1:2, and others. The Greek of v. 5, *katastēsēs kata polin presbyterous*, which means appointing elders on a town-by-town basis, could perhaps allow that each house gathering had its own body of elders but that such appointments could all be made during the same basic visit. It is also likely that churches were only planted in urban areas in this period and so "town-by-town" may simply reflect this practical reality.

15. Note how early converts of John the Baptist had returned to Ephesus in Acts 19:3–4. Many later "foundation tales" concerning Christian churches assume they had come into being through someone returning home and spreading the gospel in this way. In terms of relatively new Christians taking the initiative without apostolic bidding, cf. the role of "men from Cyprus and Cyrene" in the early mission in Antioch in Acts 11:20.

no tick-list process whereby each potential elder was rated on each virtue or vice or, even, that they were drilled word for word in doctrinal formulations. In this respect, the qualifications for eldership were wide enough to ensure a pool of candidates to draw from.

The criteria for eldership are general and coexist with the ministry gifts of Christ (apostle, prophet, evangelist, pastor, and teacher) listed in Ephesians 4:11. This, together with 1 Peter 5:1 where Peter describes himself as a "fellow elder," strongly suggests the ministry gifts functioned in and through the whole body of elders in a local congregation, even if itinerant ministers (like evangelists) were not bound to particular locations (e.g., Stephen in Acts 8). It is, of course, possible to envisage a situation where the most experienced leader functioned as a "first among equals" allowing his (or her) wisdom and experience to carry decisive weight in any eldership discussion, but the text does not require this.[16]

"An elder should be someone who is above reproach." The same requirement is given to Timothy (1 Tim 3:2), using a different though equivalent Greek word.[17] Elders were to be free of any shadow of criminality, immorality, or double dealing. The elder is to be someone of unchallenged personal integrity whose preaching would not arouse skepticism and whose adjudication of disputes would not be attributed to self-interest. The elder should be the "husband of but one wife," ruling out polygamy, infidelity, and probably remarriage after divorce.[18] In later centuries, the church interpreted this to rule out those who had re-married even after the death of a spouse,[19] but this is too severe and contradicts what Paul taught in Romans 7:3. Whether this might permit the appointment of a former divorcee whose spouse had deserted him (1 Cor 7:15) or committed adultery (Matt 5:32; 19:9),[20] both of which Scripture anticipates, remains unclear.

---

16. Cf. the role of James in Acts 15:13–20. Those who favor this idea sometimes suggest that the NT term "overseer" referred to such a role, even if the elders as a body acted in "oversight" together. Cf. further on v. 7 below, where we take the terms as synonyms.

17. Knight, *Pastoral Epistles,* 289.

18. Although some take Titus 1:6 below and 1 Tim 3:4–5 to imply elders should be married with children, we have to assume this did not rule out others, not least because of Timothy and Paul's own involvement in ministry. Although it is often assumed that Paul was a widower, it is not impossible that his wife left him when he converted to Christianity (Bruce, *Paul,* 270).

19. Mounce, *Pastoral Epistles,* 388, in reference to Chrysostom.

20. Under Jewish and Roman law, desertion was understood to amount to a *de-facto* divorce that could, after appropriate verification, be properly formalized.

In more general terms, of course, marriage and family life have seen huge changes in contemporary Western contexts. After more than a thousand years of general agreement between biblical norms and Western law, these now diverge considerably. Living out a life that is "above reproach" and, if necessary, standing apart from secular society is becoming increasingly difficult because long-held social norms and expectations now express many non-religious values.

"The father of believing children." Here is one practical test of an elder's fitness for office. Candidates who are unable to communicate the faith to their children are not going to be able to communicate it to a congregation. Or, to put this another way, the church is made up of families and the qualities needed by a good parent are the same as those needed by an elder. The stipulation, however, should not be read to imply that only those with children can be elders. "Who have never been accused of wild living or failing to respect authority." The good behavior of children was an established pattern and not merely secured for a brief time by threats or punishments. By implication the children of elders have internalized the moral codes of their parents.

7. There is a switch of terminology with the introduction of the word "overseer" (*episkopos*). "For the overseer should be blameless." The previous verse has pointed out that an "elder" should be blameless, and it is blamelessness which ties together the two terms. The terms have already been used interchangeably in Acts 20. There Paul's address begins speaking to his hearers as elders (v. 17) and ends (v. 28) referring to them as overseers. This is because the elders do the job of overseeing.[21] Like many terms that came to have a special Christian meaning, *episkopoi* (pl.), had long been used in pre-Christian times to refer to communal, public, or temple officials with supervisory duties.[22] More than a supervisor, the overseer is "God's steward," the person charged with running and managing God's house. The steward is found in the parables of Jesus (Luke 16:1-13) and fulfilled a well-understood role within the first-century world. The steward was the person to whom the master entrusted the running of the operation whether it was the household, the business, or the farm. Honesty and integrity were crucial to the running of the master's enterprise, and so it is with the church. Those put in charge act for Christ, their master, and not for themselves, and the church they superintend is not theirs but Christ's. For these reasons the blamelessness of overseers is expressed morally, by avoiding vice and showing virtue.

---

21. "An elder should be blameless . . . for as an overseer he must be blameless to serve in God's household" is Towner's (*Timothy and Titus*), paraphrase, 686.

22. MM, 244; LSJ, 657. "Supervisor" and "overseer" are the same word depending on whether the root is taken from Latin or Greek.

The overseer is not "self-regarding" or "self-willed," "arrogant" or "over-bearing" (all words within the semantic range of *authadē*) or "quick-tempered or have problems with alcohol" (*mē paroinon*). These vices often cluster together, and when they form part of the personality of someone with pastoral authority, are destructive and wounding of fellow Christians. To avoid the charge of *paroinon* does not demand teetotalism, but a responsible use of alcohol. The next pair of vices are equally dangerous. "He should not be violent (*plēktēn*) or corrupt (*aischrokerdē*)." Alcohol abuse is often linked to violence, and if the corruption spoken of here is financial, then this grouping paints an all too familiar picture—definitely not the right person to become an elder!

8. The virtues are now listed. "*Welcoming to strangers*" indicates generosity, humanity and a willingness to see a congregation grow, not pushing away newcomers, not influenced by xenophobia.[23] "A lover of all that is good" indicates a loving temperament. This is someone who "loves" the good rather than someone who is grimly dutiful. "Wise, just, devout, and self-controlled" are less extrovert virtues and only become evident over time. They speak of even-handedness (necessary in dealing with disputes), commitment to private prayer as well as public worship, and personal discipline.

9. The ministerial tasks of the elder are straightforward. They should be "holding on to the trustworthy message they have been taught," meaning they understand and retain the gospel; they are not innovators or theological speculators but faithful to the gospel tradition they have received. We also may assume they have experienced forgiveness of sin, an understanding of the mission and sacrifice of Jesus, and an appreciation of the reality of the resurrection. From this strong position, they are able to perform two crucial tasks: they can "encourage others with sound instruction," and they can "reprove those who speak against it." The encouragement of others could be through preaching and teaching or in conversation, prayer, or by charismatic gifts. Thus, they can build up and stabilize the Christian community. Equally importantly, they have the ability to "reprove (*elenchein*)"—and the word carries the wider meanings of "refute," "convince," and "convict"—those who attack apostolic teaching.[24] In other words, elders are able to rebut by rational and detailed reply as well as to rebuke.

The list of virtues and vices to be found in elders parallels the similar list in 1 Timothy 3:1–7. Mounce's careful comparison of all the terms shows

---

23. Hospitality to strangers was emphasized across Mediterranean society but became a key practice for early Christians whose gospel spoke of a new and even more radical sense of inclusiveness, cf. Arterbury, *Entertaining Angels*.

24. Knight, *Pastoral Epistles*, 294.

them to be either word for word the same (as in the first requirement of being "above reproach") or else equivalent (as in the requirement to be "gracious" in 1 Timothy 3:3 and "not arrogant" in Titus 1:7). Only the three final items in the Titus list are not found in 1 Timothy.[25] Three conclusions can be drawn from these lists. First, the traits and qualities required for leadership in the Cretan and Ephesian churches contrast sharply with those of the false teachers. In the main, Paul is looking for people displaying a certain character more than an array of special gifts. He wants holy, faithful, and honest believers to lead the young congregations because he knows such qualities will win through in the end. Second, although there are slight differences in the lists, the similarities between them suggest a roughly standard "template" for leadership in the early church, meaning there is reason to suppose elders in Corinth or any of the other congregations planted by Paul were chosen according to similar criteria. Third, as Stott has convincingly argued, these requirements allowing for the recruitment of plenty of good new Christian leaders and teachers in Crete were Paul's answer to the false teaching circulating on the island.[26] Note that the answer lies not in the dissemination of correct ideas alone, so much as the wholesale deployment of good *people*, of healthy teachers who would be living examples of all they preached. Such a vision of ministerial training, whether in the first century or today, remains vital.

c. *The task: the situation on Crete (1:10–16)*

> For there are many unauthorized *Christian teachers*[27], particularly from a Jewish background who peddle nonsense and deceive souls. These people should be silenced, as they are ruining whole households by teaching things which should not be taught[28]—and making an exorbitant profit in the process. As one of Crete's local prophets[29] once said, "Cretans are perennial liars, evil beasts, *and* lazy gluttons" Never

---

25. Mounce, *Pastoral Epistles*, 156–158.

26. Stott, *1 Timothy & Titus*, 179, 194.

27. The implication here is that these people operate "as teachers" (see context) within and around the Christian community, but without an official role—hence *anypotaktoi* is rendered "unauthorised" rather than the traditional "rebellious."

28. Or possibly "are not authorized to teach."

29. Lit "one of their own."

> a truer word!³⁰ So, reprimand these people severely, so that everyone's³¹ faith may remain healthy, not paying attention to Jewish myths and man-made instructions coming from those who turn away from the truth. To the pure all things are pure, but to the defiled and unbelieving, nothing is pure, as they are defiled in *both* their thinking and their conscience. They profess to know God, but by their actions, they deny him. They are detestable and disobedient, unfit for any good deed. (Titus 1:10–16)

The church on Crete was younger than the church at Ephesus, as suggested not only by the lack of any mention of a mission in Crete in Acts (cf. Acts 19 for Ephesus) but also the un-developed state of the church apparent from this letter. Crete was still without elders while Ephesus already had them (1:5). Although we might imagine that opposition was less developed than at Ephesus, Titus similarly implies a Jewish background for some of the false teachers (1:10, 14; 3:9); others upsetting the church may have been indigenously Cretan.

10. The young church was plagued by "unauthorized Christian teachers," people with recognized position in the church who taught *nonsense*. We have translated *anypotakos* as "unauthorized" rather than "insubordinate" because that better reflects the situation. These free-range, self-appointed teachers, operating within and around the Christian community were nevertheless undermining it. Paul says that many of these teachers had a *Jewish background* (*ek tēs peritomēs*—from the "circumcision"). We know that the Jewish community on Crete was particularly large, and considerable numbers may have been drawn into church circles.³² Unfortunately, in this case, a number of would-be teachers proved nothing more than *mataiologoi*, vain babblers, spouting empty words (cf. 1 Tim 1:6) that "deceive souls."³³ They

---

30. Lit. "this testimony is true." An element of irony is intended not only in this national self-deprecation, but in reverse too as Paul sees it fulfilled in the church's "home grown" false teachers, most likely with origins within the longstanding Jewish Diaspora community on Crete.

31. Lit. "their." This could refer to the teachers alone, but more likely it refers to their hearers and/or both.

32. On the size of the Jewish community, see Kelly who cites Josephus and Philo (*Pastoral Epistles,* 234). We insert the word "background" precisely to hint at the ambiguity as to whether these were infiltrators from "ordinary" synagogues, or (more likely), those who had already identified as Jewish Christians, but who brought a certain expertise with Jewish texts and traditions into the Christian community.

33. One should add that teaching this bad would have been equally unwelcome in an ordinary Jewish synagogue, let alone a messianic one.

may remind us of the "snake oil salesmen" who peddled their products in the nineteenth century in the days before scientific approaches to medicine took hold.[34] Or, as Samuel Ngewa reminds us, "if you want to get rich quickly in Africa, founding a church is supposedly high on the list of ways to do so!"[35] 11. The result of this bombardment of falsehood was the "ruining of whole households," perhaps because Christian worship and teaching took place in household settings and/or that itinerant teachers were being offered lodging with church families.[36] At any rate, the result was serious enough for Paul to say "they should be silenced (lit. muzzled)" because they were teaching "things which should not be taught" which some commentators have thought included magic though there is no textual evidence for this.[37] Early Christian ministers could certainly be financially supported (1 Cor 9:5–12), and itinerant teachers might also be paid, but Paul implies the motive of these false teachers is mercenary—"they are making an exorbitant profit—(*aischrou kerdous charin*)" because they are charging for sham spiritual benefits which "ruined" (lit. turned upside down[38]) those foolish enough to hire them.

12–13a. To support what he is saying, Paul quotes the sixth century BC Cretan prophet Epimenides who called his own countrymen "perennial liars, evil beasts, and lazy gluttons."[39] This popular paradox[40] was no doubt intended somewhat humorously but shows a grasp of local culture on Paul's part. To turn a literary or proverbial put-down against an opponent was a prized device[41] which Paul nicely employs as he exclaims in 13a "never a

---

34. Cf. Anderson, *Snake Oil, Hustlers and Hambones*.

35. Ngewa, *1 & 2 Timothy and Titus*, 350.

36. Itinerant teachers probably spoke in synagogues and in Christianity might go back to Luke 9:1–6; 10:1–12. That this later led to problems is suggested by Gal 1:9; 2 Cor 11:4; 2 John 10–11, and Didache 11–13. Cf. Horrell, "Leadership Patterns," 323–41.

37. Kelly, *Pastoral Epistles*, 234. The inference is presumably made from similarities with Ephesus.

38. Kelly, *Pastoral Epistles*, 234.

39. Epimenides, *Cretica* (cf. Rendel Harris, "Cretans Always Liars"), the same poem that is quoted approvingly in Acts 17:28. Cf. Mounce, *Pastoral Epistles*, 367. This is perhaps reflected in the later Greek usage, *krētizō* or "I cretanise" meaning to "tell a lie" (LSJ, 995).

40. The saying playfully has a *Cretan* attesting that "all Cretans are liars." Such paradoxes were used by popular philosophical teachers to get students thinking. Is the Cretan lying when he says Cretans are liars?

41. Cf. Matt 11:16–17; Jude 14.

truer word!" However, his appeal to a Cretan saying here may affirm that although linked to the Jewish community, the teachers were home grown, i.e., Cretan.

13b. He goes on to tell Titus to "reprimand (*elenche*) these people severely" using the same verb he used in verse 9 when encouraging elders to reprove those who undermined their teaching. This might imply Titus was to provide an example to the elders of how to carry out perhaps the least enjoyable part of any ministry and encourage him to join with them in confronting the false teachers. The urgency of the reprimand suggests the false teachers were still active within the body of the church—for it is hardly likely Titus would have gone to strangers outside the church to rebuke them. The desired consequence, "that everyone's faith should be healthy," is certainly concerned for the church members[42] but may include the false teachers themselves. Either way, the silencing has a redemptive purpose for all involved.[43] The idea of "healthy" faith is not defined but continues a medical metaphor known in the Pastoral Epistles and elsewhere in Paul, contrasting the life-enhancing doctrines of the gospel and the debilitating doctrines of the false teachers.

14. "Not paying attention to Jewish myths." We do not know exactly what these myths were but suspect that Paul's worries in 1 Timothy 1:4 concerned teaching of a broadly similar character.[44] Whether or not this involved para-biblical folklore or Gnostic material,[45] it could not be regarded as anything other than speculative. It clearly ran against the spirit and the "sound teaching" of the gospel. Christianity is and always has been a religion rooted in historical events, open texts, and "public" discourse rather than esoteric lore. If fantastical myths are allowed to overlay the traditions of the church, people can rapidly start putting myths on a par with core teaching. For this reason, Pentecostal preachers need to check the veracity of outlandish stories and testimonies before passing them on in their preaching. Furthermore, and worse, the teaching troubling Crete was accompanied by new "instructions" or commands (*entolais*), which were pressed upon the

---

42. Fee, *1 and 2 Timothy, Titus,* 180; Knight argues the reference here is to the Cretan believers who had been misled rather than to the false teachers (*Pastoral Epistles,* 300).

43. One must admit that v. 15 does not sound optimistic as far as the teachers are concerned.

44. See our comments on 1 Tim 1:4 for further suggestions. There, the mythical material concerned or perhaps was expressed in genealogical terms.

45. Mounce suggests they focused on minor OT characters "that contained their secret knowledge" (Mounce, *Pastoral Epistles,* 400). Jewish myths today are found in the short stories of Isaac Bashevis Singer (1902–1991).

Christian community.⁴⁶ Consequently, the traditional activities making up the Christian life itself were being undermined and altered. We cannot be sure exactly what such "instructions" included,⁴⁷ but far from constituting edifying additions to the faith, Paul emphasizes that not only were these teachings "man-made," they were "coming from those who turn away from the truth."⁴⁸ So the teachers had actively rejected traditional gospel teaching as a result of turning to myths. This sequence was noted in an epigram attributed to the Roman Catholic writer, G. K. Chesterton, "When a man stops believing in God, he doesn't then believe in nothing, he believes anything."⁴⁹

15. The next couple of verses may hint that purity and purification practice was one of the issues at stake. "To the pure all things are pure," suggests that those who have been purified by faith in Christ do not need to seek additional ritual purification. By trying to impose Jewish ritual activities on the whole Christian community, false teachers were effectively nullifying the gospel in the same way that those who troubled the church in Galatia attempted to bring gentile Christians under the Mosaic law (Gal 3:1–14). We do not know exactly what sort of requirements the false teachers were attempting to impose but whatever they were would have been a denial of Christian liberty. "To the defiled and unbelieving, nothing is pure." Here is where the false teachers sit. Nothing is pure and therefore purificatory rites must be performed at every turn. The irony, of course, in moral terms, is that the false teachers themselves are "defiled" (*memiammenois*, a word often used of ritual impurity⁵⁰) both in mind and "conscience." So, they have lost the guidance of conscience, and yet, apparently, detect impurity everywhere. 16. "They profess to know God, but by their actions, they deny him." Fee calls this the "most stinging indictment of all" since, unlike

---

46. Greek *Ioudaikois mythois kai entolais anthrōpōn* ("Jewish myths and man-made instructions"). It is not clear whether the mythology itself somehow led to the new instructions, or whether both are Jewish in character and that the *entolais anthrōpōn* are Jewish *halakhoth*, rabbinical-style judgments about how biblical laws can be followed in contemporary contexts. If the latter, then *man-made* would constitute a slur on this this sort of teaching.

47. Comparing 1 Tim 4:3–5, a commandment about food could conceivably be of Jewish origin, but a denial of marriage could never be, although a form of Jewish Gnosticism might be involved. The mention of purification in v. 15 below would seem to concern an aspect of Jewish practice, such as immersion.

48. "'Truth' here is a technical term in the pastoral epistles for the gospel" (Mounce, *Pastoral Epistles*, 401).

49. Chesterton Society, "When Man Ceases to Worship God."

50. Mounce, *Pastoral Epistles*, 401.

pagans, followers of Judaism profess to know God.[51] Elsewhere in the NT "deny (*arneisthai*)" is used of those who deny Christ.[52]

In short, "they are detestable (*bdelyktos*) and disobedient," and this would especially be the case if they had been part of the Cretan church. They were "detestable" because they deemed the sacrifice of Christ inadequate to cover their sin. *Bdelyktos* (also translated "disgusting" or "abominable"[53]) in the Septuagint commonly describes idolatry and so carries the implication that the false teachers had behaved abominably by turning their own ritualistic asceticism into an idol more worthy of allegiance than Christ.[54] Their disobedience to God renders them "unfit for any good deed," and given the purpose of God is to form a people "passionate about doing good" (Titus 2:14), this leaves them on the outside.

---

51. Fee, *1 and 2 Timothy, Titus*, 182.

52. Fee, *1 and 2 Timothy, Titus*, 182. Compare 1 Thess 4:5; 2 Thess 1:8, and Gal 4:8. Mounce cites 2 Tim 2:12 where the same word for "deny" is used (*Pastoral Epistles*, 402–403).

53. LSJ, 312.

54. Mounce, *Pastoral Epistles*, 403. Cf. also Luke 16:15.

II. CHRISTIAN LIVING: A RATIONALE
   a. Separate groups (2:1–10)
   b. Hope and glory (2:11–15)

II. CHRISTIAN LIVING: A RATIONALE

a. Separate groups (2:1–10)

> But you should speak things which are suitable for sound instruction. Older men should be temperate, worthy of respect, self-controlled, sound in faith, love and endurance. In the same way, older women should behave with reverence, not be slanderous, not taken to drink, teaching what is good so that they may encourage the young women to love their husbands and children, to be self-controlled, pure, hardworking in the home, good, subject to their[1] husbands so that the word of God may not be brought into disrepute.
>
> So too, exhort the young men to be self-controlled. In all things, present yourself as an example of good deeds. Let your teaching be pure and dignified—a sound message beyond reproach so that any opponent will be put to shame because they will have nothing bad to say about us.
>
> Slaves should be subject in everything to their[2] masters, well-pleasing, not given to talking back or stealing, but showing all good faith[3] so that in everything they may bring credit to the teaching of God our savior. (Titus 2:1–10)

Having spoken about the structural and doctrinal needs of the Cretan church and shown how the false teachers are damaging and reprehensible, Paul, in the next two chapters, outlines a vision for the people of God as those who are zealous for doing good (2:14; 3:8). The two chapters bring the realities of the Second Coming and the new birth to the fore and show how both these divine interventions should have the effect of creating an active, loving, and socially effective body of believers. It is important not to see these chapters as spelling out a dusty rule book for Christians but to understand the purpose of stipulations which are worked out in social roles.

1. Lit. "their own."
2. Lit. "their own."
3. Lit. "all good faith."

These roles are how individuals serve their Lord and disarm criticism of both Scripture (2:5) and God (2:10).

1. "But you." You, Titus, ought to be quite different from the false teachers; the pivot to Titus is emphatic. "Speak things which are suitable for sound instruction": the speaking would include the reprimanding of 1:13 as well as the exhortations of 2:15. One of the key words here is "sound" (from the verb *hygiainein*) meaning "to be healthy" and from which the English word "hygienic" is derived. *Sound* is used metaphorically and contrasts with unhealthy, unwholesome teaching. The metaphor has medical overtones and implies a healthy, fit, vibrant, active church as opposed to one that is sick, miserable, inactive or dying. The tonic here is good instruction (*didaskalia*) from Titus and others which will help to form healthy belief, practice, and behavior.

2. The first of the separate groups are addressed. Paul begins by providing a pen portrait of what he wants to see in the *older men*. There are four or six qualities depending on how you count them. The first is temperance (*nēphalious*) or restraint with alcohol but here has the wider meaning of sober-mindedness, clear-headedness, and consequent carefulness in judgement. The second (*semnos*) speaks of dignity with a demeanor "worthy of respect," and the third (*sōphrōn*) means *self-control*. This frequently cited quality runs through the chapter and is applied to the younger women and men (vv. 5–6) as well as the older women (v. 4). "Self-control" is also one of the fruits of the Spirit (Gal 5:23) and is found in the book of Proverbs (16:32). Finally, the older men are to be "sound in faith, love, and endurance," showing how they are to exercise faith and to show love while facing the inevitable challenges of older age.

Though the first three virtues are important (albeit terms shared with Greek moral codes)[4] the last three are arranged in a distinctively "Christian" pattern similar to the well-known triplet of "faith, hope, and love" in 1 Cor 13:13. Tellingly, there is some overlap with the essential characteristics of elders (who may indeed be older men) and deacons in 1 Timothy 3:1–13 because these leaders function as exemplars for everyone else. Such qualities are wholly compatible with Paul's teaching elsewhere on sanctification (e.g., 2 Thess 2:13) and on the lovely fruits of the Spirit (Gal 5:22–25). Or to put this another way, the character traits Titus is to encourage in older men are not simply culturally determined but born of the Spirit's influence on each man's inner life.

3. "In the same way." Just as for the older men, "older women" receive their own pen portrait of four behaviors. They "should behave with

---

4. As we noted in the introduction to this volume; cf. Kelly, *Pastoral Epistles,* 239.

reverence" (*hieroprepeis*, a composite of "temple" and "fitting") which implies dignity and godliness. "Not slanderous" refers to the "sins of the tongue." The older women are not to be hypercritical of others, speaking ill of them or acting as gossips and busybodies like the young Ephesian widows (1 Tim 5:13). Nor are they to be "taken to drink," a fault found in the ancient world where water was imperfectly purified and wine was purer, cheap, cultivated locally, and plentiful. Rather, they are to "teach what is good." Three comments are in order here: first, older women were to be regarded as offering positive role-models in the church and not simply laid aside as irrelevant spectators, but second, this did include "teaching" the younger women, not merely setting them an example. Thus, whatever Paul's statement in 1 Timothy 2:12 means, it cannot amount to an absolute veto on all teaching. Third, lack of self-control and drunkenness, reminiscent of the sexual misbehavior so often associated with the young[5] remains, perhaps in different ways, a danger at every stage of life. In this sense, Paul calls the whole church young and old alike to stand against the proverbially "Cretan" behavior of the false teachers as "liars and gluttons" (1:12).

4. "So that they may encourage." The older women's teaching is purposive and practical and directed to the "young women." In the home, young women are encouraged to love "their husbands and children." At first glance, it would seem completely unnecessary to teach young people to love their husbands and children, but in an age when some marriages were arranged and typically involved older men and younger women, this encouragement makes more sense.[6] Today's emphasis on romance and free choice, yet arguably with a much higher divorce rate, presents quite different challenges from those in Roman times. But at least here, older women were drawing on their experience and helping younger women negotiate family life as they were likely to encounter it. Arranged marriages with larger age-gaps obviously presented special problems, but they were real marriages and intended to succeed. Restoring a measure of parental instruction and support to young people embarking on marriage in a Western culture would scarcely go amiss.

But even if the marriage is a love match from the beginning, encouraging young women to "keep on" loving their husbands and to do so "sincerely" remains important and echoes the likely sense of Ephesians 5:25. Although this certainly involves faithfulness, the essence of a Christian marriage is far more than honoring a contract.[7] Christians have from the

---

5. Towner, *Timothy and Titus*, 724.
6. Stark, *Rise*, 107, quoting Hopkins, *Roman Girls*.
7. The idea of contract or covenant was perhaps the single most important way

outset also understood that the "one flesh" bond involves a genuine sense of "devotion" and symbolizes the mysterious relationship between Christ and the church (Eph 5:31, 32).[8]

5. In common with nearly universal presuppositions at the time, Paul envisaged a primarily domestic sphere of activity for the young women. This did not preclude some degree of education, nor even roles outside the home, but these were more the exception than the rule. Educated women were usually in the upper echelons of society[9] and such women certainly held a variety of public offices, particularly in Asia Minor.[10] However, it is reasonable to assume most supported their husbands and cared for their families as Paul envisaged. Because they were on average younger than their husbands, they often outlived them and some, though not all, were able to inherit property.[11] While the injunction to be "self-controlled (*sōphronas*)" and "pure (*hagnas*)" reflects Roman patriarchal anxieties about married women in the home, these virtues feature positively in Christian teaching for men and women alike in the Pastoral Epistles and elsewhere (e.g., Gal 5:22–23—the fruit of the Spirit; 2 Cor 7:11). That the young women should be "hard-working in the home" (again contrasting with the Ephesian widows, 1 Tim 5:13) shows that Paul knows this really is *work* and that performing this task while maintaining loving relationships with children and husbands is not always easy. Christian women in this cultural context are not encouraged to delegate as many of these responsibilities as they can to allow more time for church activities.

In this role, women should be "subject to their husbands." Although this is a very uncomfortable idea in today's culture, in the Roman period, it was a more or less universal conviction (see commentary on 1 Tim 2:11). But an additional motivation for Christians is that the "word of God may not be brought into disrepute." This may reflect an apologetic concern where a Christian wife is married to an unbelieving husband.[12] If Christian-

---

that marriage was understood in the ancient world.

8. When Jesus spoke about divorce regulations he called attention to "the hardness of your heart" (Matt 19:8), and hard hearts contrast with loving hearts.

9. Winter, *Roman Wives*, 63–68.

10. Kearsley, "Women and Public Life in Imperial Asia Minor," 98–121.

11. The marriage of Cretan women was customarily delayed until they were capable of managing their households (Winter, *Roman Wives*, 160). "A dowager's life interest in her husband's holdings" was based on the understanding she would, at death, pass it on to children from that issue (Winter, *Roman Wives*, 126). Many widows did not inherit property which is why the church made provision for them (1 Tim 5:9).

12. 1 Cor 7:13, 14. The situation in Corinth was surely replicated in Crete. Cf. also 1 Pet 3:1–2.

ity were to gain a reputation as troublesome to, or destructive of, such mixed marriages, negative consequences would surely follow.[13] However, there is ample evidence that the church identified with this principle even in the context of a wholly Christian marriage, where it formed part of a pattern of mutual submission "as unto Christ" (Eph 5:21ff.). Submission for its own sake was not the defining thing, but rather love (v. 4), and opportunities for service in any and every social context with all their inevitable constraints, is understood by Paul to be a working of divine grace (vv. 11–12).

6–8. Turning to "young men," Paul urges once again the now familiar need for self-control. What is applicable to the older generation is also applicable to the younger generation. And, narrowing the focus, Paul comes to Titus himself who is exhorted to stand as a role model for his generation and others (the theme of setting a good example is found elsewhere in Paul: 1 Tim 4:12; 1 Thess 1:7; 2 Thess 3:9; Phil 3:17). Titus is to show "good deeds," and these are to range across "all things." Martin Luther wrote of Titus 2:5, "Because the heathen cannot see our faith, they ought to see our works, then hear our doctrine, then be converted."[14] The "good deeds" (lit. good works) are presumably to fall within the main parameters of Christian charity, meeting the needs of the poor, sick, disadvantaged, needy, outcast, and those to whom Jesus reached out in the pages of the gospels. Care for widows (and orphans) was a central concern in the life of the big Jerusalem church (Acts 6) and was certainly practiced in Ephesus (1 Tim 5:9–10). If this was as yet un-developed in Crete, we surmise that Paul expected Titus to take the initiative and point his congregation in the right direction.

"Let your teaching be pure and dignified." As a teacher, Titus was to avoid gimmicks and showmanship. His style was to be "pure" ("with integrity," lit. "without corruption") and "dignified" (or "serious") and "sound" (lit. "healthy"), picking up the medical motif again. Titus is to be "beyond reproach" since in his disputes with false teachers he should offer no grounds for accusation, so that "any opponent will . . . have nothing bad to say about us." Again, the avoidance of reputational damage is important. If the church is to make headway in a hostile or indifferent society, it must maintain irreproachable standards. Any failing in the messenger will undermine the message. The intention here is that accusations will prove baseless and thus bring "shame" on the "opponents." All we can say is that, either in the church, the local community or wherever else such attacks might occur, the integrity of Christian teachers and the church as a whole (implied by

---

13. A famous and rather public case of this kind is the subject of Justin's *Second Apology*.

14. Quoted by Mounce, *Pastoral Epistles*, 413.

"about us") would shine through. And shine it did during the martyrdoms of Christians in the gladiatorial arena: according to Bruce the killing of the elderly Polycarp "seems to have produced a revulsion of feeling for the time being; . . . the outbreak of persecution cease[d] with his death . . ."[15]

9. The introduction of slaves is somewhat jarring because the other groups have been arranged according to age and gender. The separate category here reflects the sense that slaves, whether old or young or male or female, did not have the freedom to conduct themselves as the other social groups could.

Slavery in classical times was, of course, reprehensible but should not be seen as exactly identical with the slavery of the last few centuries. This is because slavery was a multiracial phenomenon (anyone captured in battle, whatever their skin color, might be enslaved) and included slaves with trusted and important administrative roles within large households or on major estates. Paul himself identified as a slave—a slave to God (Titus 1:1) and a slave to everyone (1 Cor 9:19)—and yet saw an extraordinary paradox realized by the gospel in the sense that every Christian slave was the Lord's freed person, and every free person was the Lord's slave (1 Cor 7:22).

Not only were some Christians slaves, but, as noted in the introduction to this commentary, it is surprising to learn that Christian families continued to *own* slaves. The New Testament records calls for their fair treatment and even emancipation, but for the moment, everyone had a role to fulfill. The fact that slaves are addressed directly here means they were being treated as people of faith in their own right and that their "families" were including them in gatherings for worship where they could hear Paul's letters read out. The slaves are told to be "subject in everything to their masters" so as to "bring credit" to the gospel of "the teaching of God our savior." Once again, the reputation of the gospel is of paramount importance and overrides every other consideration. And it is obvious that if slaves, who composed 30 percent of society, had been encouraged by Christianity to rebel against their masters or run away, the church would have faced huge repercussions and, perhaps, not grown as rapidly as it did.[16]

Slaves are to be "well-pleasing" (and indeed the phrase "in everything" could apply here rather than with the previous words). Christian slaves are to serve without "talking back" or insolence or "stealing" and to demonstrate fidelity. While this may remain incomprehensible or offensive in today's

---

15. Bruce, *Spreading Flame*, 174.

16. This does not mean that slaves did not run away from time to time, but the way Paul handles this in his letter to Philemon is notable for the way that he appeals to the Christian character of Onesimus' master.

terms, the call to behave well in unjust situations unites all Christians in a continuous act of witness.[17]

b. Hope and glory (2:11–15)

> For the grace of God has appeared, bringing salvation to all people. It trains us to turn our backs on impiety and worldly desires and to live self-controlled, righteous and godly lives in the present age. *As we live in this way*[18], we look forward to the blessed hope and appearing of the glory of our great God and savior, Jesus Christ, who gave himself for us so that he might redeem us from all lawlessness and purify for himself a people for his own possession, passionate about doing good.
>
> Speak about these things; exhort and reprove with all authority. Let no one defy you. (Titus 2:11–15)

This section gives us the reasons for the practical targeted teaching in the preceding section. We take the words "the grace of God has appeared" as referring precisely to the life and ministry of Christ himself. This same term comes to John's mind as he comments that Jesus as God's Word is "full of grace and truth" (John 1:14). This grace "instructs" us and although it is possible to see grace itself as a kind of disembodied tutor, it is likely that early accounts of Jesus' teaching are in mind.

As this passage continues, we hear that embracing this grace now points forward to a new age inaugurated by nothing less than the return of Jesus himself. But if so, the question of how we should live in this present age becomes doubly important. The answer given is the same as before, that we should live sober, just and godly lives. Again, although these virtues appear frequently in Hellenistic teaching,[19] for Christians, our motivation stems from the grace we have received and our patient expectation of the coming of Christ. Indeed, we can see these verses as showing us how to live between the first and second comings of Jesus. The first concerns his incarnation and

---

17. Something of the spirit of this is captured in the third century tale of the free-woman Perpetua imprisoned with, most likely,) one of her own slaves, Felicitas, and martyred together in the arena in Carthage as Christians (Heffernan, *Perpetua and Felicity*, 18–20).

18. The Greek runs on in a single sentence. Breaking this up for clarity, the added phrase here signals the continuity of thought.

19. Fee, *1 and 2 Timothy, Titus*, 195; Keener, *Background Commentary*, 629.

ministry on earth and the second concerns his return. Moreover, this time frame undergirded Christian education in succeeding centuries: "the Pastoral Epistles established a narrative framework . . . (Titus 2:11- 12). [It is] the emphasis in the Pastoral Epistles on 'salutary teaching' in the context of a larger narrative about God's universal salvation that produces piety [and] set the tone for how education unfolded."[20]

11. "For (*gar*) the grace (*charis*) of God has appeared (*epephanē*)." The word *for* is a causal link which indicates the content of verses 11–14 provide the reason for verses 2–10. The *grace of God* carries its usual meaning of generalized and undeserving love displayed by God to his creation. Grace is found throughout the Bible and is one of the defining characteristics of the God revealed by the Judeo-Christian Scriptures.[21] God is not tyrannical, impersonal, arbitrary, disinterested, distant, or impassive but gracious in a thousand ways, not least through the loving ministry of Jesus and the outpouring of the Holy Spirit whose gifts beautify and empower the church (1 Cor 12:4–11).

"Bringing salvation to all people." These words cannot be thought to assert universalism (i.e., that every single human automatically received the salvation offered by Christ) since that concept is flatly contradicted elsewhere in Scripture (e.g., Matt 18:6; John 3:16) and, in this context, would make little sense. If the false teachers have received salvation, why take the trouble to oppose them? Bringing salvation to "all people" is best understood here as bringing salvation to all kinds of people including the slaves mentioned in the previous verses. The NIV has, "For the grace of God has appeared that offers salvation to all people" and so distinguishes between the appearance of the grace of God and the "offer" of salvation.

12. "It [grace] trains us." Although some commentators have taken these words to mean that grace as the generalized love of God trains us to turn our back on what is wrong and embrace what is right, we prefer to see it more specifically as the grace that is wrapped up in the life, ministry, and teaching of Jesus. This allows us to speak of a grace that is at once *personalized* in Jesus and which naturally includes his teaching. This makes sense of the idea that this whole "package," is brought through one and the same "appearing." If we see it in this light, then the way that grace "trains us" is not vague but has real content because the teaching of Jesus was direct and specific.

---

20. Coulter and Yong, *Renewing Christian Higher Education* (unpublished manuscript).

21. References to the *loving kindness* of God (Hebrew, *chesed*) are often OT references to grace.

The training works in two ways, negatively to reject bad things and positively to embrace the good. We are trained to "turn our backs on impiety (*asebeian*)" or profanity[22] and "worldly desires" (sometimes translated passions[23]). On one level, these words are easy enough to understand but on another involve a subtle ambiguity. One the one hand, we might wonder whether some things we want are simply too "worldly." Others, however, have asked whether desire can get so strong it becomes ungodly in and of itself. In practice, these are often mixed up. First century Christians certainly stayed away from gladiatorial games, but probably did attend other sporting events, political rallies, music and poetry recitals, and the theatre. Later Christians were to regard many of these as "worldly," sometimes because of their "vain" content, but more often because they risked raising our "passions." Should contemporary Christians keep out of all public and cultural events on such grounds today? Jesus was clearly a passionate person, infuriated at abuses in the temple and moved by the sight of large crowds, the enthusiasm of children, and the loss of a friend.[24] We think the point here concerns contexts and desires where our ability to lead "self-controlled, righteous, and godly lives" in word or deed is seriously undermined. This will inevitably involve steering our own path through the "present age" with all it has to offer, neither shunning the world entirely by retreating into a monastery nor routinely acquiescing to personal weaknesses in the heat of the moment or through peer-group pressure. We need a measure of detachment here, of true circumspection, and of self-knowledge. Staying apart from the "herd" as it pursues out-and-out hedonism or crass commercialism is one thing. Knowing when a "worldly desire" is "crouching at the door" (Gen 4:7) is another altogether.

13. The chapter now moves to its theological climax. The reference to "the present age" implies another age beyond, and it is the inauguration of this we now glimpse. "We look forward to the blessed hope." We await the hope that brings blessing or blessedness; our orientation is towards the future where our hope lies. And, since Jesus personifies our hope (1 Tim 1:1), we look to him. The church directs its attention towards the second coming of Christ which provides a basis for all the moral and spiritual exhortation in the verses earlier in the chapter. We could say that the church is poised between the "appearing" of the grace of God at the first coming of Christ and the "appearing" of the glory of God at the second, and it is these two events that mark the start and end of the "present age." The text here,

---

22. LSJ, 255.
23. Or *passions*; cf. LSJ, 634.
24. Mark 11:15–17; Matt 9:36; Mark 10:13–16; John 11:35.

although difficult to translate, is surely striking. The "appearing of the glory of our great God and Savior, Jesus Christ" seems to make Christ's appearing the appearing of God himself. Paul rarely speaks of the deity of Christ directly[25] (though indirectly on many occasions),[26] but here the words may indicate precisely that.

Although it is often said that the church's expectation of the imminent second coming of Christ faded as the years passed, it is evident from these verses that this hope remained alive and vivid at the time of writing and Paul wanted Titus to keep it that way! Investigations into Pentecostal expectations of the second coming cannot usually speak for the whole movement but anecdotal evidence as well as research into early Pentecostal literature suggest that Adventism was fervent during the early years of the Pentecostal movement at the start of the twenty-first century.[27] The impression given is that more recently expectations have cooled off although most major Pentecostal and other denominations continue to hold fast to their belief in the second coming as such within their doctrinal statements.[28] Even if the sense of imminence has lessened, for contemporary Pentecostals the second coming still provides real hope for the future and an expectation of ultimate justice for the persecuted and downtrodden. For the early church, embedded in an apparently immoveable Pagan culture, the second coming provided strong reasons for perseverance and motivation for a life of doing good.

Returning to the "appearing of the glory of our great God," commentators note all sorts of technical issues and to arrive at this reading, interpretive choices have to be made. Decisions need to be taken on "of the glory."[29]

---

25. Romans 9:5 would be an example where the words can legitimately be translated to affirm the deity of Christ.

26. E.g., Christ is the one in whom and through whom all things were created (Col 1:16) and in whom the fullness of the Godhead dwells (Col 2:9). The judgement seat of God (Rom 14:10) is the judgement seat of Christ (2 Cor 5:10).

27. Cf. Thompson, *Waiting for Antichrist*. In his survey of a large London Pentecostal church only 21 percent of 469 ministers believed the return of Christ would take place within the next fifty years. However, 8 percent of 2,973 church members believed the return of Christ would take place in the next ten years. According to the Pew Survey of ten countries (*Spirit and Power*, 156), 55 percent of Pentecostals and 44 percent of Charismatics in the USA completely or mostly agree "Jesus will return to earth in my lifetime." The equivalent numbers for Brazil are 37 percent and 26 percent and for Kenya 54 percent and 44 percent.

28. Surveying a sample of 930 ministers in four Pentecostal denominations in the UK, Assemblies of God, Elim, The Church of God, and the Apostolics, Kay in *Pentecostals in Britain*, 147, found 99 percent believed "Jesus will return to earth again in the future."

29. The Greek *tēs doxēs* (lit. *of the glory*) presents a classic instance of the

In Greek, this could act descriptively, e.g., "the glorious appearing" (NKJ, NET) or indicate what it is that is appearing, i.e., "the appearing of the glory of our great God and Savior" (ESV, RSV).[30] We, along with many commentators and most translators, have taken the second option both because the glory of God or unapproachable light where God dwells (1 Tim 6:16) is found elsewhere in the Pastoral Epistles and because the Synoptic Gospels consistently speak of the "glory of the Father" manifested at the return of Christ (Matt 16:27; Mark 8:38; Luke 9:26).[31]

Equally, decisions have to be made over whether two divine Persons are in view, "the great God (i.e., the Father) *and* our savior Jesus Christ" or just one, "our great God and Savior, Jesus Christ." We, along with many commentators and translators, have opted for the latter as a single statement about who Jesus is. This is for both grammatical and theological reasons. Grammatically the words God and Savior are governed by the same definite article. Theologically, as noted by Fee, "nowhere else is God the Father understood to be joining the Son in the Second Coming."[32] Indeed, in Paul, the "appearing" (*epiphaneia*) always refers to Jesus and not to the Father (2 Thess 2:8; 1 Tim 6:14; 2 Tim 1:10). This reading also better fits the flow of the paragraph which begins with Jesus when introducing the appearance of the grace of God and continues with Jesus when talking about redemption in the next verse. Lastly, the pleonasm (lit. *filling out*) "God and savior" is frequently "used in pagan texts to refer to a single personage"[33] not least in relation to the Hellenistic Kings as well as in the later Roman context of the imperial cult.[34]

14. "He gave himself for us." The self-giving sacrifice of Christ is central to the New Testament, and we should understand Christ's voluntary surrender of his life ("No one takes my life away from me. I give it up of my

---

subjective vs. objective genitive problem. Similar considerations allow *dia pisteōs Iēsou Christou* in Rom 3:22 to mean "through (our) faith in Jesus Christ" or "through the faithfulness of Jesus (himself)."

30. This latter "objective" sense could *technically* allow the glory to belong to *Jesus*, making "our great God" qualify Jesus rather than the other way round. This suggestion by F. J. A. Hort is discussed by Mounce who rejects it because "glory" is simply too far away from "Jesus Christ" in the sentence (*Pastoral Epistles*, 425, 431).

31. This idea goes back to the Old Testament where beholding the exact form of God is not possible; cf. Exod 16:10; 24:16–18; 33:18–20.

32. Fee, *1 and 2 Timothy, Titus*, 196. This is almost certainly because Paul's understanding of this epiphany scene is based on taking OT verses on the "Day of the Lord" as references to Christ, cf. Phil 1:6.

33. Kelly, *Pastoral Epistles*, 246.

34. As discussed in the introduction to this commentary, see "Religious Context."

own free will" (John 10:18, GNB)) points to what will be expected of the church too. If Christ voluntarily gives himself, this becomes a pattern and stimulus for our own voluntary devotion to doing good. "For us," a very early Christian affirmation, reminds us that the Cretan church, however lying and monstrous the islanders naturally are (1:12), is still within the reach of Christ's personal love. "So that" indicates that the self-giving of Christ is full of purpose, namely "that he might redeem us."

The metaphor of redemption runs through the Scriptures like a scarlet thread. To redeem is to buy something back, something that has been lost and passed into another ownership. The word is most commonly used of slaves who were once free, lost their freedom and find themselves up for sale in the slave market. If they are redeemed, a price is paid, and they become free once again. The imagery is vivid and all too true of the cruelty leading to enslavement and the redeemer's desperate search for those who have been trafficked to misery. Old Testament law (Lev 25:47–55), specified the process whereby a kinsman-redeemer would pay for the release of the slave.[35] The typology here brings home the questing love of Christ who gives himself to free others. Yes, Christianity is about liberation!

This redemption is from all "lawlessness (*anomias*)" which, though there may be some dependence on Old Testament passages (e.g., Ps 130:8 and Ezek 37:23), covers every type of sin by all people, both Jews and gentiles.[36] "And purify":[37] after redemption comes purification. The two-stage process is indicative of God's transformative love that is well understood by holiness denominations (see also Excursus IV). The sinner is not simply freed but begins to undergo all the dramatic and profound consequences of regeneration and justification so carefully spelled out in other parts of the New Testament (e.g., Eph 5:25b-27; Rom 6–8). In the Old Testament Israel is not simply rescued from slavery in Egypt but passes through the Red Sea and into the desert to begin a new and purified style of life in the presence of God. "For himself": only a purified people is acceptable to a holy God. "A people of his own possession": another classic Old Testament description of

---

35. The duty of the kinsman-redeemer (Hebrew, *goel*) in the book of Ruth is different though the payment of money for the benefit of a family member is the same.

36. In Rom 2, Paul has to address the conundrum that gentiles are not under the Mosaic law and therefore could be viewed as *lawless* only by definition. He assures his readers that, just like Jews who disobey their own law, gentiles are certainly sinful and thus "lawless" in the more general sense. Note that in 2 Thess 2:3, the anti-Christ, a figure uniting all of Christ's opponents, is called the "man of lawlessness."

37. It is interesting that if some of the false teachers had had a misguided understanding of purity (e.g., perhaps in Titus 1:15), then Paul does not have to give up using the term but returns here to a classic biblical theme.

God's people (Ex 19:6; Deut 7:6; cf. 1 Pet 2:9) here becomes an image of the church[38] among a number of others given in the New Testament, such as a bride (Rev 21:9), an army (Eph 6:10–17; 2 Cor 10:3–5), and a body (1 Cor 12:27). Christians find their ultimate identity in belonging to God rather than to a nation, a state, a locality, a trade union, a sporting club, or any other organizational construct.

"Passionate (*zēlōtēn*) about doing good (*kalōn ergōn*)." Having been redeemed and purified the people of God are to be passionate—zealous—for doing good. A completely new people is being created within the gigantic and composite structures of Roman society, a people characterized by a passionate desire to do good. These are not men and women with aspirations for military or economic glory but rather with a strong desire to change the world by acting with the compassion of Christ. And the extraordinary thing is that this people, often drawn from the lower echelons of society and without a political philosophy or much rhetorical ability to confront the norms and attitudes of their age, eventually triumphed with the conversion of the Roman emperor himself. Advocacy is important but doing good may be more persuasive.

The word "zealot" had political overtones in the first century and was applied to ardent Jewish nationalists who wished to rid their country of Roman occupiers (cf. Acts 1:13).[39] It is a word that can be applied to God (Isa 59:17; 37:32) but is here applied to good works. Christians were expected to be full of zeal or passion or enthusiasm for particular objectives. Here it is good works, and elsewhere it is for spiritual gifts (1 Cor 14:12). So, Christians are anything but lukewarm about their top priorities, and just as Pentecostals and charismatics are keen to manifest the gifts of the Spirit and to be empowered by them, so also, they should be keen, or "passionate" about doing good. The language of action, of doing, is strong and deliberate.[40] Spiritual gifts and doing good go hand in hand, and each reinforces the other.

15. "Speak about these things." The chapter ends with brief instructions to Titus himself. This verse fittingly concludes chapter 2 but could equally well start chapter 3. "Speak": this would include teaching as well as less formal types of instruction. "These things" may refer to the immediately

---

38. The term "New Israel" is not used here, and elsewhere (Rom 9:6–8, 11:25–32) Paul has to explain rather carefully the sense in which this is and is not a helpful concept.

39. Quinn, *The Letter to Titus*, 174.

40. This is an impression that might accidentally be caused by the image of the "fruit" of the Spirit (Gal 5:22–23). Although outside the Pauline corpus, the importance of *intention* is well expressed by 2 Pet 1:5ff. "for this very reason, make every effort . . ." etc.

preceding section but apply equally well to the whole epistle so far. "Exhort and reprove with all authority." Here the exhortation or encouragement is directed to faithful believers and the reproof to unfaithful believers, and each verb is in the second person singular, i.e., spoken to Titus and not the church as a whole. "Let no one despise you" (*singular*). This sentence speaks directly to him. It would have been impossible for Titus to avoid the contempt of his opponents entirely, and so the instruction is probably best read as telling Titus not to be deterred by the bad opinion of others. Because there is no reference to his youth as there is in the case of Timothy (1 Tim 4:12), it is quite possible Titus was older than Timothy. Even so, his task was a difficult one.

> III.CHRISTIAN LIVING OUTSIDE THE CHURCH: A RATIONALE
> a. Living in society (3:1–3)
> b. God saves (3:4–7)
> c. Final admonitions (3:8–15)

III. CHRISTIAN LIVING OUTSIDE THE CHURCH: A RATIONALE

In the previous chapter an anticipation of the second coming of Christ should provoke a Christian passion for good works. This chapter, with a different theological center, also shows why Christians should do good in society: individual regeneration and renewal should transform human behavior (3:4–8) and lead to true altruism towards all.

Romans 13 provides a far more developed theology of the state than is given here, but certainly bears comparison. This approach can be traced back to the engagements by Jesus with the Roman imperial administration. He spoke of paying taxes to Caesar (Matt 22:15–22) and of "walking the second mile" (Matt 5:38–42).[1] Christians thus sought not only to comply with Roman law and respect the civic authorities, but also actively to do good (3:1, 8).

a. Living in society (3:1–3)

> Remind them to be subject to the rulers and authorities, to be obedient, to be ready for every good work. Do not slander anyone, be peaceable, gentle to all, showing every courtesy to everyone. For we *ourselves* were once foolish, disobedient, led astray, serving various desires and pleasures, spending our time in wickedness and envy, despicable *and* hating one another. (Titus 3:1–3)

1. "Remind them." We can assume that Paul and Titus, during their relatively brief visit to Crete, would have begun teaching about how Christians should behave towards government, including local government. Paul tells Titus to "remind" the Cretans, implying he is to speak of something they already know. Christians accepted the purpose of government as necessary

---

1. Jewish people could be forced to carry the luggage of a Roman for one mile. Consequently, "walking the second mile" is doing more than is required.

in a fallen world.² "To be subject to the rulers and authorities": Paul, even under the polytheistic and brutal rule of Rome, nevertheless endorsed civic obedience because the magistrate was there by God's will to enforce law and order (Rom 13:4). For all the possible problems with this (and there are corrupt regimes in many parts of the world), the benefits of government outweigh anarchy. An adequate government is better than out-and-out gangsterism, and open courts are better than secret police. And government is better than rule by war lords. Moreover, at least one ancient writer (Polybius) reports that Crete had often descended into lawlessness which suggests that many needed to hear this reminder.³

This said, the early Christians differentiated between a government's legitimate oversight of the ordinary affairs of life (property, inheritance, contract, felony, taxation, and so on) and specific attempts to suppress the gospel. In Acts, when commanded by the Sanhedrin to stop preaching the gospel, Peter gave a direct and uncompromising answer, "We must obey God rather than men" (Acts 5:29).

"To be subject to . . . to be obedient." We may distinguish between "being subject to" (accepting the legitimacy of governmental authority without trying to undermine it) and being obedient (complying with particular stipulations). Christianity has never pressed for blood on the streets and barricades in the thoroughfares or had any truck with revolutionary thinkers whose political manifestos wanted to burn everything down and start again. "To be ready for every good work": in this context, these words imply more than caring for those in church circles. They extend to the wider community. In short, Christians are to be benevolent citizens.⁴

2. This verse gives four specific instructions to Cretan Christians. These concern the behavior of converts towards their fellow-Cretans and what is noticeable is the sheer gracious goodness Paul enjoins upon the church. Christians are not to bask in a sense of their own superiority over their fellow islanders but to take a much humbler attitude. They should "not slander" anyone, implying careful speech rather than reckless and opinionated condemnation. During NT mission, robust debate was possible and sometimes necessary. Paul's visits to Athens, for instance, demonstrated this, but this is not the same as speaking evil of those who failed to accept

---

2. This accords with Luther's teaching. See Wolgast, "Luther's Treatment of Political and Societal Life," 397–413.

3. Mounce, *Pastoral Epistles*, 444; Kelly, *Pastoral Epistles,* 249.

4. Guthrie, 214; Kelly, *Pastoral Epistles,* 249 and cf. Winter, Seek the *Welfare of the City.*

the gospel.⁵ "Be peaceable" follows the line of instruction given elsewhere (Rom 12:18) and removes any sense that Christians should be spoiling for a fight with their neighbors. "Gentle to all": in an empire founded on military power, gentleness is hardly likely to have been an idealized virtue, but here Christians are told to display this quality rather than its opposite, "roughness, bad temper, sudden anger, and brusqueness."⁶ "Showing every courtesy to everyone": again, the sense is clear even if translations struggle to find exactly the right word to cover this attitude: "a consistently gentle disposition" (NEB) or "true humility" (NIV).⁷ An emphasis on the *everyone* is indicated by the repetition running through these words (not slander *anyone*, gentle to *all*, and courtesy to *everyone*).

3. Here Paul reminds Titus that they were once stuck in the same immoral morass as most of the Cretans are. The contrast between what Christians were and what they are now is sharp, but it serves to remind Titus and Cretan Christians, to whom the letter would have been read, of the evangelistic potential of their own testimonies. If Paul and Titus could be changed by the gospel, then many others could be too. "For we ourselves were once foolish"—frittering away our time and energy on meaningless, fruitless, and vain *activities—and* "disobedient" (to God rather than civil authorities, cf. Acts 17:30) and "led astray" by all the confused turmoil of the world and the spiritual forces of which we are so often unaware. "Led astray" is used of the Corinthians in their worship of dumb idols (1 Cor 12:2) and of the Ephesians prior to their salvation (Eph 2:2).⁸ "Serving various desires and pleasures (*epithymiais kai hēdonais*)" is as common today as it was then. "Hedonism" (from the Greek *hēdonē*, just noted) is still very much in fashion, and altruism and duty remain less common motivations. The "desires" spoken of here may include cravings and perhaps even addictions.⁹ Consequently, we were "spending our time" or living in "wickedness and envy," were misanthropic and energized by base motives. It is striking to see Paul, a pious Jew, applying such a description to himself, but he humbly

---

5. Why any Christian might veer in this direction is not clear, but it is possible that an over-zealous reading of Matt 10:14, 11:20–24 is involved. Cf. the curious injunction in Jude 8–10 concerning fallen angels.

6. Knight, *Pastoral Epistles*, 334.

7. Quoted from Knight, *Pastoral Epistles*, 334.

8. Note that "led astray" does not imply that every Cretan was a pagan *convert*, as most would have been born into polytheism. The phrase echoes Israel's unfaithfulness in the Old Testament (Deut 4:19, 13:13, 30:17 et sim.), but when applied to the deceptiveness of pagan religion, is still appropriate.

9. Kelly, *Pastoral Epistles*, 336.

uses "I" and "we" in this way elsewhere.[10] His "autobiographical fragments" repeatedly express regret for persecuting the earliest Christians,[11] something reiterated in 1 Tim 1:15. So, when he rounds on being "despicable" and "hating one another," he may be speaking from bitter experience. This may in turn explain the strong emphasis on love in his post-conversion writings (1 Cor 13) and the striking call to be "peaceable to all" made in v. 2. Christian conversion does indeed change people "from the inside out," from the heart.

b. *God saves (3:4–7)*

> But when the goodness and kindness of God our savior appeared—not because of the things we had done in righteousness, but because of his mercy—he saved us through the washing of regeneration and renewal by the Holy Spirit, whom he poured out on us abundantly through Jesus Christ our savior. *He did this* so that, having been justified by his grace, we might become *his* heirs according to the hope of eternal life. (Titus 3:4–7)

4. The sentences that follow describe a dramatic and wonderful series of events. The contrast between the nasty, mean lifestyle of pre-conversion days and what follows is deliberate and far-reaching. "But when": the dire situation changes as God steps in; but signals the contrast and "when" signals a key point in time.[12] "The goodness and kindness of God . . . appeared." These two qualities are often linked together in classical literature in reference to divine favor or royal largesse.[13] Counter to some expectations, God acts not out of anger and judgement but out of pure goodness and with kindness. After taking the initiative to rescue those who are caught up in a circle of destructive emotions, God saves, and saves *us* (v 5). Perhaps looking back to 2:13 ("our God and savior, Jesus Christ") Paul similarly states in close juxtaposition that God is our savior (v. 4) but also that Jesus Christ [is] our savior (v. 6). The whole Godhead is involved in securing our salvation since

---

10. Cf. Rom 3:9–18; 5:8,10; 7:5–25.

11. Cf. 1 Cor 15:9; Gal 1:13; Phil 3:6. See also Acts 7:58—8:3 for the story of Paul's persecuting activity.

12. *Hote de*, "but when" (as here, cf. Gal 1:15; 4:4) and *nyni de*, "*but now*" (Rom 3:21; 6:22; 7:6; 1 Cor 15:20; Eph 2:13) are often used to signal the great turning points in salvation history and in Paul's life.

13. Cf. Kelly, *Pastoral Epistles*, 251; Mounce, *Pastoral Epistles*, 447; Quinn, *The Letter to Titus*, 241; Knight, *Pastoral Epistles*, 338.

we can think of the Father as our savior, Jesus as our savior, and the Spirit as effecting our salvation by a transformation of our inner being.[14]

5. Following a distinctly Pauline theme, the text is now careful to state that God's saving acts are not in any way a response to our own "righteousness." We may like to think that God saved us because there was a spark of goodness or integrity in us, but this is not what the text says. Our own "righteousness"—and here the word carries its normal everyday meaning of uprightness in conduct—did not call forth God's great saving mission. On the contrary, it was "because of his mercy" that the scope of God's love was extended to us. In an age when victimhood demands moral priority and personal responsibility is often occluded, it may be hard to take the epistle's words at face value. God's *mercy* is the initial basis of our salvation, and here mercy includes not only the implication that God has withheld deserved condemnation, but that God remembers his creation of humanity. "Mercy" is often the Septuagintal translation of the Hebrew *hesed* (or *chesed*), a term indicating "covenant love" or acts of "pity and help that are appropriate in a relationship between two people."[15]

The next sentence, "He saved us through the washing of regeneration and renewal by the Holy Spirit," raises important questions of theological interpretation. The Greek words following *through* are all in the same case, explaining how God has put this salvation into effect. We take a little time to unpack this important statement.

We take the "washing of regeneration" to refer to the impartation of new life (because "to generate" is to give life or beget and to "re-generate" is to give life again). This is an alternative expression of the same metaphor of "washing" we find in Ephesians 5:26 and 1 Corinthians 6:11.[16] Although many commentators take this to refer to water baptism,[17] which follows conversion, it is easier here as elsewhere to see a simple reference to a cleansing and life-giving transformation wrought by God. That baptism remains a powerful symbol of this saving act is clear, and it is entirely likely that a reminder of this experience is intended. In Ephesians 5:26, this "washing" is specifically accomplished by the "word," and there is no doubt that powerful

---

14. As Archer points out (*Spirit in the Pastoral Epistles*, 523), "The PE reinforce the traditional systematic theological perspective of the role of the Spirit as active in revelation and the salvation process, and as empowering persons for service."

15. Mounce, *Pastoral Epistles*, 10.

16. Lloyd-Jones, *Life in the Spirit*, 160–7.

17. E.g., Kelly, *Pastoral Epistles*, 252. Although many Pentecostals routinely add "water" as here, baptism already means this and is always assumed in the NT; figurative usages can then be indicated as appropriate, e.g., suffering (implied in Mark 10:39) and "fire and spirit" (Matt 3:11).

III. CHRISTIAN LIVING OUTSIDE THE CHURCH: A RATIONALE

preaching played a role in bringing hearers into this experience. However, that point is omitted here, leaving an emphasis on God's initiative and the work of the Spirit.

To this is added "and renewal by the Holy Spirit."[18] This continues to speak of inner transformation of the individual's heart and mind, but immediately begs the question as to whether the "and" (regeneration *and* renewal) should be taken to imply *one* experience or *two*. The Greek allows both,[19] but for Pentecostals, it naturally refers to an initial conversion followed by a subsequent, but closely associated, work of the Spirit further transforming and renewing the person who has been reborn.[20] Elsewhere, "renewal" is applied in a variety of different contexts, e.g., our mind (Rom 12:2) and our inner being (2 Cor 4:16), so it is not unreasonable to imagine a two-stage process: first of new birth or regeneration, and then, the continuing work of the Spirit which, for Pentecostals, includes the baptism in the Spirit, and for Wesleyans would include progressive sanctification "through" the Spirit as well.[21]

As noted, other commentators take the text another way and see "regeneration and renewal" as one composite event where renewal is a natural accompaniment to regeneration.[22] Whether the text refers to one or two events, however, "cannot be solved by appeal to grammatical and syntactical considerations."[23] In any case, the two lines of interpretation are closely held together as the overall means by which God *saves us*, and by the fact that this is a work of the Spirit from beginning to end.

---

18. Warrington notes the role of the Spirit as a "separate person of the Godhead" and cites Titus 3:5 (*Pentecostal Theology*, 46).

19. *Dia loutrou palingenesias kai anakainōseōs*, employs the standard combination of *dia* plus genitive as an expression of means.

20. Stott, *1 Timothy & Titus*, 204.

21. Some Pentecostals (e.g., William H. Durham, 1873–1912) viewed the new birth and sanctification as part of the same divine action. This is why Pentecostalism later divided between non-Wesleyan and Wesleyan (or Holiness) denominations. Those whoudisagreed with Durham followed Wesley and saw sanctification, even sanctification received in a sudden crisis experience, as distinct from the new birth of John 3. Consequently, the Wesleyan Pentecostal denominations thought of a three-stage process: new birth, sanctification, baptism in the Spirit. Other Pentecostal denominations saw only two stages: new birth-and-sanctification followed by baptism in the Spirit. Both groups, however, believed in a post-conversion experience of the Spirit.

22. Mounce, *Pastoral Epistles*, 448; Stott, *1 Timothy & Titus*, 205. See also, Kärkkäinen, "The Holy Spirit and Justification, 126–39 where he cites Moltmann to this effect. "The 'regeneration' as 'renewal' comes about through the Holy Spirit."

23. Knight, *Pastoral Epistles*, 343.

6. That the experience of the Spirit is uppermost in Paul's thought is clear as he continues "Whom he poured out on us abundantly." The profuse outpouring of the Holy Spirit is a central Christian affirmation and consonant with Pentecostalism's pneumatic theology. "Poured out" (*execheen*) echoes Joel 2:28, a passage quoted by Peter on the Day of Pentecost (Acts 2:17, 33). It is used again of events in the home of Cornelius (Acts 10:45) and is almost certainly reflected in Paul's language in Rom 5:5.[24] Although this does not necessarily imply that the same events are in mind, it is reasonable to say that the outpouring of the Spirit is more than a silent and invisible act. It is the abundance of the outpouring that may strike the reader. This is a rich and powerful divine deluge of the Spirit on the individual who is escaping from all the darkness of a godless life.

The outpouring comes "through Jesus Christ our savior" after he gave himself for human sin (2:14). Jesus now gives the Holy Spirit out of harmonious cooperation within the Trinity. Receiving the Spirit from the Father, Jesus pours out the Spirit on the church. In Peter's words, "Exalted to the right hand of God, he has received from the Father the promised Holy Spirit and has poured out what you now see and hear" (Acts 2:33).

7. "He did this." Our translation inserts these words after breaking up what, in Greek, is one long sentence. "So that (*hina*)" indicates the goal of God's saving intervention in human affairs by introducing the familiar NT concept of justification (i.e., being declared righteous) with the words "having been justified by grace." The earlier reference to "mercy" had already pointed to an escape from divine condemnation, and here the word "justification" transposes the theme into legal language. Some readers may find it odd that justification is mentioned after regeneration and renewal since justification and regeneration are normally imagined to be simultaneous, but the tense of the verb comes into play here: "having been" is an aorist participle; in other words, justification describes what has already taken place. Not all passages involving these concepts press a strict sequence, and a similar list also placing washing before justification occurs in 1 Corinthians 6:11, but where all actions are alike in the aorist: "you were washed; you were sanctified; you were justified." Although here in Titus 3:7, there is no reference to justification by "faith," Paul uses the equally traditional "grace" formulation as he has done elsewhere.[25] As Fee

---

24. Where the same Greek word is used, "God's love has been poured (*ekkechytai*) into our hearts through the Holy Spirit."

25. Here, Paul writes *dikaiōthentes tē ekeinou chariti*; cf. Rom 3:24, *dikaioumenoi dōrean tē autou chariti*, which adds *freely* (*dōrean*).

explains, Paul uses "by faith" to contrast "by works of the Law" "but always means 'by grace through faith.'"[26]

The passage, having begun by focusing on the wicked and sinful state of all human beings—including Paul and Titus—and having moved through a sequence of divine interventions to save an undeserving population, now ends with "eternal life." The scope of divine salvation runs across from a very time-bound humanity caught up in self-destructiveness all the way to an endless life. The endless life is bound up with the concept of inheritance.[27] Paul calls us "heirs" (cf. Rom 8:17; Gal 3:29; 4:1–7; Eph 3:6) which, as is the case today, means those who stand to receive a future benefit coming after the death of the benefactor.[28] "We might become his heirs according to the hope of eternal life." The eternal life is what believers stand to receive because of all that Christ has done for them, and they stand "according to hope" in the sense that eternal life is a future possession even if, at other points in the New Testament, it is received in the present by faith (John 3:16; John 6:47; John 11:25).

c. Final admonitions (3:8–15)

> The saying is sure and I want you to insist on these things, so that those who have believed in God may be careful to engage in good deeds which are good and beneficial for people. But avoid foolish controversies and genealogies and contentions and disputes about biblical laws[29] for they are useless and benefit no one. As for a divisive person, after warning them initially and then a second time, dismiss them from the community knowing that such a person is out of line[30], sinful and self-condemned.
>
> When I send Artemas or Tychicus to you, hurry and come to me in Nicopolis, for I have decided to spend the winter

---

26. Fee, *1 and 2 Timothy, Titus*, 206.

27. This is a traditional Jewish usage; cf. Mark 10:17. See also Excursus V.

28. The situation in the New Testament is slightly more complex because there are instances when inheritance is not obviously linked to the death of the benefactor (e.g., Matt 5:5).

29. Given the Jewish background of the teachers (cf. 1:10), this most likely refers to halakhic debate, i.e., about traditional understandings of biblical laws.

30. Perhaps avoiding the contemporary associations of the traditional translation, "perverted."

> there. Take care to send Zenas the lawyer and Apollos on their way, so that they lack nothing. Our people must learn to engage in good deeds as needs dictate, so that they will not be unfruitful.
>
> Everyone with me sends you their greetings. Greet those who love us in the faith. Grace be with all of you. (Titus 3:8-15)

8. "The saying is sure, and I want you to insist on these things." As noted earlier, this is one of five "trustworthy sayings" in the Pastoral Epistles (1 Tim 1:15; 1 Tim 3:1; 1 Tim 4:9-10; 2 Tim 2:11-13; Titus 3:5-8a or Titus 3:4-7). These uplifting affirmations probably circulated independently in the early church and may have originated in Christian worship. Some suggest they were lines from hymns, but they do not share metrical or rhyming features, so perhaps they were simply short pithy sayings like proverbs. The exact scope of the "saying" in Titus is not clear; Titus 3:5-8a and Titus 3:4-7 are both possible. Either way, many of the words and phrases here are typical of Paul. While this is not true of all the sayings, it could mean Paul coined this one, or that it arose in an area where Paul had preached. It is not impossible that words Paul regularly used (like righteousness and grace) ended up in new sayings of this kind and met with Paul's full approval. "And I want you to insist on these things." The preaching and teaching agenda for Titus is laid out by "these things" which probably includes the content of the trustworthy saying and possibly the whole of the chapter so far. "Insist (*diabebaiousthai*)" is a strong word.

"So that those who have believed in God may be careful to engage in good deeds." Deeds follow belief, which is a reality that runs through the whole epistle. Because we believe X, therefore we do Y. "Those who have believed in God" must refer to Christians. Being "careful to engage (*proistasthai*)"[31] in good deeds may be translated as "practicing honorable occupations," a reading we, along with most commentators, reject because it is too narrow (cf. 2:14). Such "good deeds are good and beneficial for people" or, in other words, they have benefits for the whole of society. The emphasis of this chapter (cf. on 3:1 above) in contrast to the previous one is our impact outside the church where such deeds are fully part of our calling and hopefully, of course, also attract people to the gospel.[32]

9. "But avoid foolish controversies and genealogies." This instruction is like the one found in 1 Timothy 1:4. The possibility of disputes about genealogies again suggests influences from the Jewish community (cf. on

---

31. Mounce explains the verb can mean "to practice a profession" (*Pastoral Epistles*, 452).

32. Fee, *1 and 2 Timothy, Titus*, 208, and as the Salvation Army understands.

1:10) which, in some quarters, showed overly developed interests of this kind. Controversies about such things are "foolish" and time-wasting, especially because they were impossible to resolve in the sense that no ordinary people had any documentary evidence dating back hundreds of years. "And contentions and disputes about biblical laws": nobody knows exactly what sort of disputes these were, but if we look at evidence from Acts (15:1) and Galatians (2:11–21), we might imagine Jews who had accepted Christ insisting on Jewish conversion, identity, and practice for the whole church. This position was vigorously opposed by Paul early on in his ministry (Gal 3:10–14) and rejected firmly by the council of Jerusalem (Acts 15:24–29). It is more likely, therefore, that this involves Jewish Christians seeking to apply the Old Testament to contemporary life and who were indulging *publicly* in an intense and detailed mode of (genealogical) analysis not appropriate for a mixed community. The disputes, while notionally based on biblical laws, may in fact have revolved around mystical or gnostic topics.[33] In any case, such disputes are "useless" and, unlike good deeds, "benefit no one." Those causing them should be restrained, as Paul continues below.

10–11. "As for a divisive person (*hairetikon*)." In later times *hairetikon*, came to mean "heretic," but before then, it was used of a "party" or "school of thought" and is, for instance, applied to a subdivision of the Pharisees (Acts 15:5).[34] The divisive person threatens the unity of the church, either by action or by doctrine. The approach to be taken is remedial but firm. Two warnings are to be given ("after warning them initially and then a second time"). Possibly the warnings were public enough for the whole community to be aware of what to do if the warnings were ignored but perhaps the first warning was private and the second was less so. There must have been a level of formality about the process so that there could be no mistake about the number of warnings issued. There is a similarity here with the steps Jesus put in place in Matthew 18:15–17 where the first stage is in private, the second is in front of witnesses, and the third is before the whole church. We note too some similarity to the process for errant elders in 1 Timothy 5:19–20. The divisive individuals (maybe false teachers or those influenced by them) were given a good chance to change their ways. If they did not do this, then Titus was to "dismiss them from the community." Exactly how this happened is uncertain but was probably less severe than the excommunication of 1 Corinthians 5:4–5. Because congregations met in private homes, it

---

33. See our Introduction, "Religious Context."

34. The mention of vigorous arguments about biblical laws in v. 9 recalls the way that different Jewish sects distinguished themselves from each other and suggests Paul's past experience is coming to mind.

would have been relatively easy to inform divisive persons that they were no longer welcome in church meetings and to refuse them admittance.

There is a deeply uncomfortable dimension to what is being enjoined here because the church is, of course, to be welcoming to sinners and loving to all, but we also note that divisive, factious, argumentative behavior could destroy the church from within and divert it from caring for its weaker members or being effective in society. Titus, together with the elders (presumably they were involved), was given the delicate and important task of striking the right balance between facing down those who threatened the church's unity and leaving the door open to contrition. 11 "Knowing that such a person is out of line, sinful and self-condemned": the divisive individuals are "out of line" (or perverted, lit. turned aside) and "sinful" (not merely mistaken or deluded) as is indicated by an unwillingness to attend to solemn warnings. By claiming to know the way of God's salvation better than Titus and the elders and then denying this by their failure to do good, they are, as before, "self-condemned."

12. "When I send Artemas or Tychicus to you, hurry to come to me in Nicopolis, for I have decided to spend the winter there." We know nothing about Artemas. About Tychicus we know a little more. He is probably the man who carried Paul's letter to Ephesus and may have taken the one to Colossae too (Eph 6:21; Col 4:7).[35] He is described as "a dear brother, a faithful minister, and a fellow servant in the Lord" (Col 4:7). He was part of the constant comings and goings of the Pauline circle and was entrusted with important tasks including, probably, the carrying of money from Asian churches to Jerusalem.[36] But he was more than just a courier and must have had ministerial capabilities for Paul to suggest he relieve Titus. Paul's wording shows how he directed members of his staff across considerable distances to service the operations of his missionary mandate. Presumably Paul was confident Titus had got on top of the situation in Crete and could be replaced by someone else.

Although there are several cities called Nicopolis, scholars agree the place which best fits the situation is on the west coast of Greece close to the Adriatic Sea. This is because we next hear of Titus at work in Dalmatia which was only a little further north up the coast (2 Tim 4:10). Paul generally selected a base of operations for the winter when travel was closed down or heavily restricted. Because Paul was expecting Titus to travel up from

---

35. If the sending of the Ephesian letter occurred after the sending of the letter to Titus, then Tychicus would have traveled to Ephesus, and Artemas would have replaced Titus on Crete.

36. Bruce, *Pauline Circle*, 87.

Crete—roughly five hundred miles, it is probable the letter was written and delivered in the early part of the year.

13. "Take care to send Zenas the lawyer and Apollos on their way." We know nothing about Zenas and, although *nomikos* here can refer to a Jewish "teacher of the law" (Matt 22:35), it is far more likely that Greek and/or Roman law is intended. About Apollos we know a great deal more (Acts 18:24, 27; 19:1; 1 Cor 3; 1 Cor 16:12). In any case, it is possible these two delivered the letter to Titus and would therefore have been on the island with him during his busy period appointing elders and rebutting false teachers. Apollos was a renowned teacher of Scripture and had been helpful to the church at Corinth and Ephesus, and so it is quite possible he assisted Titus with the rebuttals and refutations. There were probably few people in the early church as capable as he was for this kind of work. Zenas and Apollos need not have stayed long, however, because Titus is told to "send [them] on their way so that they lack nothing." This may have entailed collecting money from the Cretan church or equipping them with clothing or luggage to cover them to their next destination. They simply form part of Paul's strategic posting of tested, trusted, and constantly traveling men to meet needs in the network of churches for which he so energetically cared (2 Cor 11:28).

14. "Our people must learn to engage in good deeds as needs dictate." These words reassert the constant theme of the epistle and may have been written by Paul's own hand as he comes to sign off.[37] The good deeds in this instance cover the provisioning of Zenas and Apollos but would also have carried the much wider instruction to those who should be "passionate about doing good" (2:14). "So that they will not be unfruitful": fruitfulness and doing good are equated. Bearing fruit is a mark of the Christian life, a theme going back to the gospels (Matt 21:43; John 15:16).

15. "Everyone with me sends you their greetings." Here the "you" is singular and refers to Titus alone. "Everyone with me"—the whole Pauline entourage—joined in greeting Titus who, presumably, they knew and whose mission they also knew. "Greet those who love us in the faith." The salutation is to be passed on to fellow Christians who love Paul, a love presumably created when he visited the island. The Ephesians wept when Paul left them (Acts 20:37).[38] "Grace be with you all." The "you" here is now plural and refers to the whole church. Grace, as always, is what every Christian needs.

---

37. Stott, *1 Timothy & Titus*, 212; It is possible that Paul only wrote verse 15 with his own hand.

38. This belies the caricature of Paul as a universally divisive person and difficult to like.

2 TIMOTHY

OUTLINE

I. PAUL FROM PRISON (1:1–18)
   a. Salutation (1:1–2)
   b. Thanksgiving (1:3–5)
   c. No shame in the gospel (1:6–14)
   d. Examples of loyalty and disloyalty (1:15–18)

II. PAUL SETS OUT FUTURE PLANS (2:1–26)
   a. Apostolic continuity and training new teachers (2:1–2)
   b. Working for the long-term (2:3–7)
   c. Enduring for the gospel (2:8–13)
   d. Dealing with false teachers (2:14–19)
   e. Being the servant of the Lord (2:20–26)

III. PAUL WARNS AND ENCOURAGES (3:1–17)
   a. A coarsening of society in these days (3:1–9)
   b. Standing firm and holding on to Scripture (3:10–17)

IV. PAUL UNBOWED (4:1–22)
   a. Final charge to Timothy (4:1–5)
   b. Paul faces death and anticipates glory (4:6–8)
   c. A round-up of news with a warning and requests (4:9–15)

d. Fulfilling his ministry in court (4:16–18)
   e. Greetings, information and hope for a final meeting (4:19–22)

COMMENTARY

I. PAUL FROM PRISON
  a. Salutation (1:1–2)
  b. Thanksgiving (1:3–5)
  c. No shame in the gospel (1:6–14)
  d. Examples of loyalty and disloyalty (1:15–18)

I. PAUL FROM PRISON

Writing his last known letter while enchained in a Roman prison,[1] Paul encourages Timothy to be brave and faithful. His words convey no self-pity or regret for his hard and painful life or the suffering he now endures. His purpose does not waver and his confidence in God and the gospel remains unchanged.

a. Salutation (1:1–2)

> Paul, an apostle of Christ Jesus by the will of God according to the promise of life in Christ Jesus to Timothy *my* beloved child. Grace, mercy, *and* peace from God *the* Father and Christ Jesus our Lord. (2 Tim 1:1–2)

1. "Paul, an apostle of Christ Jesus by the will of God." Even in what is predominantly a personal letter, there is formality in the opening words. This is presumably because Paul's identity is inseparable from his apostolic calling and because he expects his words will be read out in numerous

---

1. Traditionally, the Mamertine Prison which is thought to be the location of his imprisonment. The site is now open to visitors and pilgrims.

congregations, as the plural "you" right at the end (4:22) implies. "An apostle of Christ Jesus" is personally sent out by Christ on a specific mission by "the will of God," a phrase repeated many time (e.g., 1 Cor 1:1; 2 Cor 1:1; Eph 1:1; Col 1:1), and which in this case contrasts with the military command at the start of the previous epistle (see comment on 1 Tim 1:1). The will of God is fundamental to Paul's understanding of the way the world works and the kind of activities Christians should pursue. The will of God operates in the world bringing about certain goals (Eph 1:11), and Christians should align themselves with the will of God by prayer and seeking to be full of the Holy Spirit (Eph 5:17–20).

"according (*kata*) to the promise of life (*zōēs*) in Christ Jesus." The goal and purpose of Paul's apostleship is found in the life, the eternal life, in Christ. It is not found in the Mosaic law but in the superabundant life within Christ himself that begins today in the here-and-now and extends into eternity (see Excursus V). It is the life spoken of in the prologue to John's gospel ("in him was life," John 1:4) and in Jesus' declaration "I came that they may have life" (John 10:10). It is another way of presenting the gospel; while he is sitting in a cell awaiting death Paul thinks of life.

2. "To Timothy my beloved child." As with the previous epistle, Timothy is Paul's "son." There he was the "true" son (1 Tim 1:2), and here he is "beloved." Paul visited Lystra at least twice and the implication is that Timothy and his mother and grandmother were converted on the first occasion (Acts 14:8–18) so that, on the second visit, Timothy is described as a "disciple" (Acts 16:1). Converted under Paul's ministry and then trained by him (being taken on the remainder of the missionary journey (Acts 16:3)), Timothy becomes Paul's spiritual child, and Paul becomes "father" to Timothy whose biological father may already have died.[2] The greeting "grace, mercy, and peace," or words very similar, is the Christianized version of conventional greetings in classical letters but should not, for that reason, be skipped quickly over.[3] "Grace" is not only the awesome unmerited favor of God behind the salvation of every believer but also their ongoing experience, and every Christian needs grace right until the end of life. "Mercy" is different in this respect in that it is the cancellation of rightly imposed judgement; every act of divine mercy is an act of grace, but not every act of grace is an act of mercy. "Peace" is internal and external, within the recesses of emotional life and outwardly in the challenges we face in the world around us: it enables the believer to face dark circumstances with equanimity but not indifference, and sometimes it appears irrational or

---

2. Marshall, *Acts*, 259.
3. Mounce, *Pastoral Epistles*, 464.

b. Thanksgiving (1:3–5)

> I thank God, whom I serve with a clear conscience in continuity with my ancestors[4] as I remember you constantly in my prayers, night and day. Recalling your tears, I long to see you so that I may be filled with joy. I am reminded of your sincere faith, which first dwelt in your grandmother, Lois and your mother, Eunice, and I am sure now also dwells in you. (2 Tim 1:3–5)

3. "I thank God." Though thanksgiving is common to Pauline openings (Rom 1:8; 1 Cor 1:4; Phil 1:3), the words should not be taken for granted. Thanksgiving is appropriate at the start of any session of prayer, and here, in straitened circumstances, Paul turns to memory and recalls Timothy's early life and their last meeting together. "Whom I serve with a clear conscience in continuity with my ancestors": despite the prison, the chain, and the pending legal process, Paul has no sense of guilt or shame. His "conscience"—that inner appraisal of one's own actions—is clear, and he is standing in a long line of Jewish forbears who also served God. "I worship the God of our ancestors" he says in court to Felix (Acts 24:14). Every Jewish believer in Jesus can say the same. Paul's reference to his ethnic and faith heritage is in preparation for what he will shortly say about Timothy's heritage. As "I remember you constantly in my prayers, night and day." As an ex-Pharisee Paul may have prayed at set times in the evening and the morning; night may be mentioned before day because the Jewish people counted their days from sunset to sunset. "Constantly" here means Paul prayed regularly for Timothy during his daily prayer times.

4. "Recalling your tears." Again, memory is woven into prayer. A public display of emotion appears to have been more acceptable in Roman times than it is today, and we read of the Ephesian elders weeping when they said goodbye to Paul (Acts 20:37, 38). In their case, tears were shed because they never expected to see Paul again, and perhaps this was the case with Timothy too. "I long to see you so that I may be filled with joy." Although Paul appears to be saying "come and see me to cheer me up," there is more to it than

---

4. The temporal phrase *apo progonōn* here conjures the images of a continuous witness of obedience starting with Abraham and continuing amongst Jewish Christians of the present era.

that. By going to visit Paul in prison—and, as we shall understand shortly, this itself requires tenacity and resistance to shame (1:16, 17)—Timothy will see Paul's steadfastness in the face of impending death (4:6). By visiting Paul, he will assure the old man the future of the church is in good and faithful hands and will bring him joy. Joy is that profound state that strengthens believers (cf. Neh 8:10) and is independent of, and sometimes laughs at, adverse circumstances. The cycle of volatile emotions running through this verse has been observed previously when Paul has waited for news in an agitated and restless state (2 Cor 2:13; 1 Thess 3:5, 6).

5. "I am reminded of your sincere faith." Again, memory is invoked, as it is three or four times in this chapter. Paul sifts through his recollections of Timothy to recall the young man's faith. It is possible "faith" means simple belief in Christ, but it could refer to the kind of faith that can look above and beyond adverse circumstances. Timothy's "sincere" faith contrasts sharply with the insincere faith of others named in this epistle. His is a faith taught by the women of his family since it "first dwelt in your grandmother, Lois and your mother, Eunice." Consequently, Timothy has known the Scriptures since boyhood (3:15).[5] The early education of Jewish children was usually in the hands of the mother and so it was with Timothy, although he must have been reared in a religiously hybrid way because his father was Greek. Timothy remained uncircumcised throughout his youth and presumably could not have formally assumed his adult obligation to the law[6] at the local synagogue even if he believed the Old Testament.[7] Even in this bi-cultural sense, he had the inestimable benefit of a believing home to form his character and shape is mind. When Paul came to Lystra, the two women and the young man must have watched with delight and amazement as the gospel was preached by Paul even if this delight turned to sorrow when they saw Paul stoned and dragged out of the town (Acts 14:8–20). The faith of the whole family must have soared up and plunged down as they first welcomed their salvation in Christ and then were left distraught by the counterattack that led to Paul's stoning and apparent death. Yet, the faith of the Lystrans was strong enough for them to gather round the unconscious Paul and pray

---

5. In this period, of course, this would mean the Hebrew Bible, although available in a Greek translation.

6. There is no evidence of a formal *bar mitzvah* ceremony in this period, but there is some suggestion in the Mishnah (ca. AD 200) that Jewish children were expected to assume adult religious responsibilities at the age of thirteen.

7. Later, presumably after the death of his father, and of course, after meeting Paul, Timothy could feel free to identify himself formally as a Jewish rather than a gentile Christian. This is the most likely explanation of the note in Acts 16:3 about his later circumcision.

for his recovery. "And I am sure now also dwells in you": the same true faith dwelling in Timothy (*enoikein*, lit. to live in, abide in) can cope with reversals in the Roman law courts and judicial execution; it can look beyond setbacks to a brighter future still in God's hands.

c. No shame in the gospel (1:6–14)

> For this reason, I remind you to rekindle the gift of God that is in you through the laying on of my hands. For God has not given us a spirit of timidity, but of power, love, and self-discipline.
>
> Therefore, do not be ashamed of the testimony about our Lord, nor of me[8], his prisoner, but take your share in suffering *with me* for *the sake of* the gospel according to the power of God, who saved us and gave us[9] *our* holy calling, not through anything we had done, but according to his own purpose and grace given to us in Christ Jesus before time began[10] but which has now been manifested through the appearing of our savior, Jesus Christ, who abolished death and brought life and immortality to light through the gospel of which I was appointed a herald and apostle and teacher and for which[11] I suffer these things. But I am not ashamed, for I know whom I have believed and am convinced that he is able to ensure the safety of[12] what he entrusted to me for that day.[13] Hold fast to the pattern of sound words which you have heard from me in *the* faith and love that are in Christ Jesus. *In your turn,* guard the good deposit entrusted to you by the Holy Spirit who dwells within us. (2 Tim 1:6–14)

6. "For this reason." What follows next arises from Timothy's faith. Without it, Timothy will not stir up the gift he has received. "I remind you to

---

8. The Greek allows for "about" . . . or "of" . . . in both cases, but the testimony *about* Jesus and *of* Paul would be the most natural sense.

9. Lit. "called us with."

10. Lit. "before eternal ages."

11. Lit. "which reason."

12. "Watch over" or "guard" are also possible.

13. Here, we are meant to understand the gospel as a sacred charge. However, "what I entrusted to him" might also be understood as a reference to Paul's life (Mounce, *Pastoral Epistles*, 488).

rekindle the gift of God." What Timothy has received, even if it is "through the laying on of [Paul's] hands," is from God, not Paul. Paul may be the agent through whom the gift is given but the gift itself is divine and is *in* Timothy. Here, then, is a reminder of the indwelling Spirit that Timothy has received. Too often and historically for too many years, so Pentecostals and Charismatics think, the church relapsed into formalism and allowed itself to function without attending to Christ's priceless gift of the Spirit. Timothy is to "rekindle" the gift (*anazōpyrein; ana* = again, *zōpyrein* = *to kindle a fire*), a metaphor in keeping with the command not to *quench* the Spirit (1 Thess 5:19) and the baptism with the Spirit *and fire* (Matt 3:11; Luke 3:16). Given that the fire spoken of in the gospels speaks of judgement ("His winnowing fork is in his hand, and he will clear his threshing-floor, gathering the wheat into his barn and burning up the chaff with unquenchable fire"), there may be a warning for the false teachers just as there was for the Pharisees and Sadducees (Matt 3:7–11).

But what is the "gift of God" (*charisma*)? The same Greek word is used of the gifts of the Spirit in 1 Corinthians 12, though there in the plural. Pentecostals and charismatics have traditionally understood the gifts of the Spirit to be manifestations, endowments, or enablings of the Spirit, that is, abilities given to human beings through the action of the Spirit. Sometimes these gifts are thought to be limited to these nine: word of wisdom, word of knowledge, faith, gifts of healing, miraculous powers, prophecy, discerning of spirits, speaking in tongues, interpretation of tongues (1 Cor 12:8–10), and we can imagine Timothy using whatever spiritual gift he had received to help him in the Ephesian situation. But *charisma* can also be used of the gift of teaching. In Romans 12:7–8, Paul writes, "We have different gifts (*charismata*), according to the grace given to each of us . . . If your gift is . . . teaching, then teach." Thus, we could also imagine Timothy employing his powers of exposition—of making Scripture clear and understandable to others—as a way of combatting the false teaching circulating the troubled church of Ephesus.[14] The essential point of Paul's exhortation is to remind the younger man that he had *already* received gracious and divine spiritual gifting and that what he needs to do is to stir it up and rekindle it. In the same way, individual Christians facing challenges today should be able to re-ignite their gifts to help resolve their situations.

The laying on of hands may have occurred when Timothy was baptized or when he was set aside (or ordained) for ministry but may also have taken

---

14. Furthermore, it is possible to combine the ideas of 1 Corinthians 12 and Romans 12 to say that a "word of wisdom," for instance, may be part and parcel of the teaching gift (Cf. Gee, *Concerning Spiritual Gifts*).

place on another occasion, as was the case with the Samaritans who received the Spirit after the laying on of hands by Peter and John (Acts 8:14-17). The text in Acts 8 is taken by many Pentecostals to substantiate their belief in a (second) reception of the Spirit *after* conversion and water baptism.[15] We do not know the precise circumstances of Timothy's conversion or his subsequent spiritual journey, but what is said about the Spirit here can stand alone regardless of historical context.

7. "For God has not given us a Spirit of timidity, but of power, love and self-discipline." Although some commentators have interpreted the word "spirit" here as "attitude" or "disposition" and prefer to see Timothy's gift as that of being an evangelist, we take the word "Spirit" to be the Holy Spirit.[16] We take the Spirit to be an intangible but real force within the church, personal and profound, like an invisible wind that blows (John 3:8), while conveying the reality of the presence of Christ to every believing congregation on earth (John 14:16-18). We take Paul's statement here to be a pneumatological summary indicating the nature or character of the Spirit.

First, the Spirit is not fear-inducing, provoking "timidity" or cowardice. This is evident enough in the Apostolic preaching and outreach of the early church. The Spirit assists in the declarations and proclamations of the church, and although the church did tread carefully in the early Roman Empire, this was not because Christian hearts were perpetually filled with fear. Rather, within the false teaching swirling round the Ephesian church was an insidious legalism (1 Tim 1:7) which, like superstition, frequently builds upon the accumulation of many minor worries. The Spirit is bold and brings freedom.

Turning to the three positive aspects of the Spirit, they can be seen as belonging together with each modifying the other two. The Spirit is not pure power without love or pure self-control without power. Pentecostals have too often emphasized power while forgetting love, but it is the dynamic balance of these three attributes which is descriptive of the Spirit. "But of power (*dynameōs*)": this power is spoken of by Jesus prior to the day of Pentecost ("you will receive power," Acts 1:8) and is then manifested during the unfolding narrative of Acts: there is power to heal (Acts 9:17,18), power to raise the dead (Acts 9:36-41), power in the impulse to mission (Acts 13:1-3), power in the wisdom given to the Jerusalem council (Acts 15:28), power in charismatic gifts like prophecy and speaking with tongues (Acts 2:4; Acts 11:28), and power even in judgement (Acts 5:1-10). The impulse and sustenance of the Spirit bears the church up and carries it along.

---

15. For a discussion see Yong, *Renewing Christian Theology*, 88-92.
16. Mounce, *Pastoral Epistles*, 477-9.

"Love." There are four types of love in the New Testament: friendship, sexual love, family love, and divine love (*agapē*).[17] It is the last of these that is denoted here. The love poured out into the heart of the Christian (Rom 5:5) is a self-giving love, and it is supernatural and not natural in the sense that it includes a love for enemies, outcasts, and unlovable people. What sustains the church in its humanitarian mission is a love that does not originate with all the normal psychological processes but goes above and beyond them.

"Self-discipline (*sōphronismou*)." The word here "combines characteristics of prudence and self-discipline,"[18] and it is similar to the word used for a Christian leader in 1 Timothy 3:2. The wider theological point is that the Holy Spirit does not override the love or the power wrought within the Christian but rather respects human autonomy. Or to put this another way, the Spirit enhances restraint and rational decision-making. Though manifested as intense fire, the Spirit is also manifested as a gentle dove (Acts 2:3; Matt 3:16).

8. "Therefore, do not be ashamed of the testimony about our Lord." We link the "therefore" here to all of verse 7: to be ashamed is to be in a literal sense to be unspiritual. In the light of the power of the Spirit, the love you have (for Christ), and your self-discipline, "do not be ashamed." In the ancient world, shame and honor were drivers of behavior more than they are in much of today's western society which prioritizes self-expression and achievement.[19] Shame is that sense of embarrassing humiliation often arising from activities that clash with the predominant value system. Jesus was a convicted criminal who had died a felon's death, and it was outrageous to commend him as the hero and a savior. Elsewhere Paul speaks of the "scandal" of the cross (1 Cor 1:23). Because it makes more sense in this context, we take the "testimony of the Lord" to refer to testimony about Jesus rather than by him. In effect, Paul is encouraging Timothy to speak about Jesus, as all Christians should be prepared to do, and not to be ashamed either "of me,[20] his prisoner," who had followed in the footsteps of Jesus to the extent of being arraigned before Roman justice. In a telling insight, Paul thinks of himself not as the emperor's prisoner but as the prisoner of Jesus. Or, to put this another way, the emperor could not have chained up Paul but for the permission of Jesus. In this, he echoes Jesus who recognized Pilate's judicial authority came "from above" (John 19:11).

17. Lewis, *Four Loves*.
18. Knight, *Pastoral Epistles*, 372.
19. Johnson, *Timothy*, 346, 358.
20. The Greek allows for "about" . . . or "of" . . . in both cases, but the testimony *about* Jesus and *of* Paul would be the most natural sense.

"but take your share in suffering with me for the sake of the gospel according to the power of God." Not only is Timothy to resist and reject shame but also to "share in suffering" for the sake of the gospel. This theme of the epistle stands against the easy and superficial preaching Pentecostals sometimes hear on their "right" to material blessing. On the contrary, there always has been a strand of suffering for those who stood up for righteousness or proclaimed the gospel (Matt 5:10–12). Such proclamations are almost invariably countercultural and critical of the established political, religious, or social order. No wonder, then, suffering is part of the package. There is no merit in suffering as if it is a good thing in itself, but it can at least strip away non-essentials and focus the attention on God. Suffering can be borne, Paul says, "according to (*kata*) or by the power of God" made present through the Holy Spirit (1:7). The exact way the Spirit upholds suffering believers is not spelled out, but we can think of an intensification of spiritual realities to anaesthetize against grim conditions.

9. "who saved us and gave us[21] our holy calling." This long sentence continues to extend as each part amplifies the last. Close to the thought of suffering is also the thought of eternal life.[22] In fact, Paul's mind here sweeps back into eternity and then forward to the day of judgement. As a man whose life was always spent looking towards the horizon, traveling by land and sea, in his prison cell, he searches beyond the stone walls of his circumstances to eternity.

With the exhortation to "take your share in suffering" comes also the reminder that God has "saved us." It is not that suffering is to save us. No, salvation has already been accomplished and Christians have a holy calling. It may be that the calling is the first step on the road to salvation[23] (Rom 8:30; 1 Tim 6:12), but this distinction in this context is not salient. What matters is that the salvation given by God relates to a vocation, purpose, lifestyle, ministry, and destiny. And this "not through anything we had done," reminding us in a familiar Pauline admonition that what we have received from God is not given on the basis of any of our previous morality or spirituality "but according to his own purpose and grace." Ultimately, it is God's "purpose" that is going to determine the outcome of events, and as the epistle continues, we can infer that Paul's own circumstances and the state of the church are in God's hands. This is so even if God's servants have their own responsibilities to fulfill. The balance between human responsibility

---

21. Lit. "called us with."
22. See also Excursus V.
23. Kelly, *Pastoral Epistles*, 162.

and divine sovereignty, between time and eternity, runs through and behind all that Paul writes here.

"given to us in Christ Jesus before time began (*pro chronōn aiōniōn*)."[24] God's grace was given to Christians at a point outside the current space-time continuum, and it was given "in Christ Jesus," words that point to the pre-existence of Christ, that is, his existence prior to his birth in Bethlehem. Arising from such considerations, Christians understand Christ is, and always has been, part of the Godhead. And "in Christ Jesus" is the characteristic phrase used by Paul to indicate belonging to, believing in, being accepted by, redeemed by, identified with, joined to, and saved by Christ. Elsewhere Paul speaks of the church as being chosen "before the creation of the world" (Eph 1:4). This is way beyond the Emperor or Roman religious politics and might be a source of Christian arrogance were it not for the reality that what is given is grace. Indeed, in Paul's theology grace was given to him to help him cope with his challenges, pains and setbacks and to prevent him becoming proud: he had received an abundance of revelation "but also" a thorn in the flesh (2 Cor 12:7, 9). So here, he fixes on the distinction between receiving grace in eternity and doing time in prison.

10. "but which has now been manifested (*phanerōtheisan*) through the appearing of our savior, Jesus Christ." This grace given "before time began" is "now manifested"; salvation and grace spring from divine interventions breaking in from outside nature. A similar word speaks of the revelation of the glory of God in the miracles of Jesus (John 2:11), the uncovering of what was hidden and invisible by turning on a light (1 Cor 4:5) or the manifestation of charismatic gifts (1 Cor 12:7). Grace comes through "the appearing of our savior"—specifically through Jesus himself who "abolished death." The simplest way of understanding this phrase is by reference to the resurrection of Jesus (cf. Rom 1:4). This is the undoing of death by Christ who not only rose from the dead but remains alive. Other resurrections in Scripture, like Lazarus in the gospels (John 11:43, 44), were temporary because Lazarus eventually died at the end of his natural life. But the resurrection of Jesus continues with the power of an endless life (Heb 7:16), because death, having been overcome, has no claim on Christ at all. "Abolishing (*katargēsantos*)" is used elsewhere in a similar context (1 Cor 15:26). It undoes death but does not imply Jesus himself suffered a "spiritual death" between his crucifixion and resurrection as some Pentecostal preachers

---

24. Lit. "before eternal ages." See also Towner, *Timothy and Titus,* 470. The phrase is similar in meaning to Eph 1:4 *pro katabolēs kosmou,* "before the foundation of the world."

have asserted.[25] The Bible speaks of death in more than one way: the unconverted are dead in their trespasses and sins (Eph 2:1, 5), that is, they are unresponsive to God. Later we read of the eventual abolition of death when, in the Book of Revelation, death and hell are cast into the lake of fire (Rev 20:14), a moment when mortality is swallowed up in immortality. But the fundamental and primary reversal of death takes place at the resurrection of Jesus.

As savior, Jesus "brought life and immortality to light through the gospel." The metaphor of "bringing to light" is found in the Greek word *phōtisantos* and may have special significance in the circumstances of false teaching swirling around the Ephesian church. The light of the gospel dispels the darkness of confusion caused by unhealthy teaching but what is said here is again an emphasis on the "life" available through Christ, reaffirming the first verse of the epistle. What is new in these words is the statement that "immortality" has been brought into the light. "Immortality (*aphtharsian*)" is the term applied to the imperishable body of saints at the general resurrection at the end of 1 Corinthians 15 (vv. 50, 53–54). The dead body is sown in weakness but raised imperishable (*aphtharsian*), thus giving a glimpse of the resurrection body Christians can look forward to in their future state.[26] And all this is "through the gospel," which anchors the theology and reality of these breathtaking expectations in the good news preached by every evangelist.

11. "of which I was appointed a herald and apostle and teacher." Paul has been appointed to proclaim this gospel in every way possible. Theologians have often distinguished between the *kerygma* (preached message) announced by the early church and the *didachē* (teaching) that followed it. So, the herald trumpets the initial proclamation but what follows that proclamation requires other skills and other gifts. Paul is an apostle, one sent out by Christ, and with the specific task of planting new churches and calling gentiles into obedience to the gospel (Rom 1:5), a ministry requiring many qualities including bravery, pastoral sensitivity, and strategic vision. In addition to this, Paul is a teacher, who expounds and explains the text of the Old Testament and writes words that others will later explain and expound as the church proceeds along its historic journey. For Pentecostals and charismatics who have focused on the ministry gifts of Christ (Eph 4:11), what is of special interest here is the breadth of ministry given to Paul. He is undoubtedly an apostle but can function in several modes (including as a

---

25. Atkinson, *Spiritual Death of Jesus*, has examined the matter thoroughly and concluded Kenneth E. Hagin and others are wrong on this matter.

26. Kelly, *Pastoral Epistles*, 164.

teacher) depending on circumstances. Presumably other Christian ministries today can anticipate similar fluidity.

12. "and for which[27] I suffer these things." There is no minimizing the suffering of Paul by glibly glossing over it or attributing it to anything else than his appointment to gospel service. Nor is this suffering "redemptive" in the sense that it makes Paul a better person. All we can say is that Paul's suffering, and the suffering of the first generation of apostles, sets an example for succeeding generations of Christians right up to the present day.

"But I am not ashamed, for I know whom I have believed." Again, Paul affirms that he feels no shame for his imprisonment. This is where "conscience" is vital (1:3). Whatever the public judgement of Roman magistrates or appointees, Paul is inwardly sure of his innocence. Elsewhere he writes, "We have wronged no one; we have corrupted no one; we have exploited no one" (2 Cor 7:2). But Paul's lack of shame has another ground. It is found in his personal knowledge of Christ as he states, "I know whom I have believed." Ultimately, just as Paul can write of the "son of God who loved me and gave himself for me" (Gal 2:20), so he can also write here of the Christ he has known for so many years. In this personal relationship is comfort. His experience, his personal religious experience, is what sustains him—a lesson for those who minimize religious experience and dismiss it as valueless.

"and am convinced (*pepeismai*) that he is able to ensure the safety of[28] (*phylaxai*) what he entrusted to me (*parathēkēn mou*) for that day."[29] All this leaves Paul sure of God's protective power. The sentence, though, is capable of two interpretations. On the one hand, as we have translated it here, it is God who has entrusted the gospel to Paul, and it is God who is able to safeguard this gospel whatever happens to Paul. This reading of the text gains credibility not only because the word *parathēkēn* is used elsewhere of something entrusted by God to others (1 Tim 6:20), but also because two verses later a similar thought and similar meaning is contained in the words about Timothy who is to guard the deposit entrusted to him (v 14). An alternative meaning arises from the idea that it is Paul who speaks of his own deposit (*parathēkēn*). He is confident that everything entrusted to him will be divinely safeguarded because he has entrusted everything—his gospel, his work, his life, his soul—to God and because of his personal knowledge

---

27. Lit. "which reason."

28. Or "watch over," "guard."

29. I.e., the gospel as a sacred charge; but "what I entrusted to him," i.e., Paul's life, is also possible (Mounce, *Pastoral Epistles*, 488).

of God.[30] Whether God entrusts to Paul or Paul entrusts to God, it is clear the words express a confidence that can only encourage Timothy.

As part of the linguistic richness of this passage it is worth noting *parathēkēn mou* literally means *my deposit*. The deposit was a well understood technical term for something (often money or property or even people), entrusted by one person to another when the first person went away on a journey or was otherwise detained. "To be faithful to such a trust, and to return such a deposit unharmed, were among the highest and most sacred obligations which ancient thought recognized."[31] And the notion of guarding from *phyllassō* implies keeping secure (the verb is used of the soldiers who guarded Peter in prison in Acts 12:4) or holding to (the verb is used of the decrees gentiles are to observe in the letter written after the Council of Jerusalem in Acts 16:4).

"for that day or until that day." Here is reference to the day of judgement, the day of the return of Jesus. Paul has already spoken in his sermon to the Athenians about the day when Christ will judge the world (Acts 17:31) and the phrase or thought is present elsewhere in Paul's writings (Rom 2:16; 1 Cor 1:8; 2 Cor 1:14; Phil 2:16; 1 Thess 5:4). So, the entrusted deposit is kept safe until the end of the age, however far off that may be. The expectation of a day of reckoning when everyone will give account of themselves[32] in front of Christ is absolutely integral to Paul's theology. It is not as if history is wandering aimlessly to an unknown destination, but on the contrary, there is an appointed day so that, in this sense, time moves lineally from creation to judgment and is quite different from any Hindu or Buddhist notion of time that goes round in endless circles. Both the other Abrahamic religions, Judaism, and Islam, also consider time to move in a line from the beginning of the world to judgement which, for Christians, is a day of hope even if it is also a day of reckoning.

13–14. In these verses, Timothy is told to "hold fast to the pattern of sound words and to guard the good deposit," two parallel instructions intended to safeguard the future life and progress of the church. Although this epistle reveals Paul's exemplary steadfastness in the face of his approaching death, it is also concerned with the transmission and flourishing of the faith in the next generation. Timothy, as one of Paul's closest associates, is a crucial figure here. Holding fast to the "pattern (*hypotypōsin*) of sound words" is another way of telling Timothy to be faithful to the gospel message he

---

30. Similar, perhaps, to the thought in Col 3:3.

31. Barclay, "Our Security," 324, via Mounce, *Pastoral Epistles*, 487.

32. A day of reckoning is found in the parables of Jesus (e.g., Matt 13:24–30; Matt 25:14–30).

has received. "Pattern" is an interesting word choice since it may refer to an architect's sketch or the draft of a document.[33] In any case, Timothy is to be the authentic transmitter of the apostolic gospel. This is made clear by "which you have heard from me." The *hypotypōsin* has therefore been interpreted as a model or standard, a non-negotiable set of truths.[34] Yet, the communication of the sound words is to be in "the faith and love that are in Christ Jesus" implying graciousness rather than aggressive dogmatism. Fee suggests the meaning of the verse might be rendered, "let what you have learned from me serve as your model for sound teaching but let it do so as you yourself also model faith [or faithfulness] and love."[35]

Timothy in his turn is to "guard the good deposit (*parathēkēn*)," thus continuing the previous metaphor. The valuable deposit God entrusted to Paul (or Paul entrusted to God, whichever way round we read verse 12) is in Timothy's care. The meaning is clear enough: Paul is handing on the baton, ensuring the gospel is in safe hands after his death. It is a "good" deposit implying what Timothy has received is the gospel itself. He is to guard it by "the Holy Spirit." This is the second reference to the Holy Spirit in a few verses. Timothy is therefore to stir up or rekindle the Holy Spirit, and because the Spirit brings power and love and self-discipline, is to protect the gospel. This instruction means that Timothy is not alone in his task (because the Spirit is really present with him). But it also means he has the resources of the Spirit for guarding the gospel, which does not imply locking up the gospel or burying it in the ground but rather being able to propagate it with the assistance of the Spirit. How better to protect it than to proclaim it?[36] And this is the Spirit that "dwells within" both Paul and Timothy. This experience of the Spirit, creating union and communion of hearts and minds, is brought about by the Spirit that infuses believers and enables shared fellowship with God. There is an echo here of the way the glorious stone and gold temple of Jerusalem is being replaced by a new temple composed of living believers, both Jew and gentile (Eph 2.22; cf. 1 Pet 2:5).

---

33. Guthrie, *Pastoral Epistles*, 145.
34. Stott, *1 Timothy & Titus*, 43; Towner, *Timothy and Titus*, 477–8.
35. Fee, *1 and 2 Timothy, Titus*, 233.
36. Given the problems with false teaching, however, it is possible that this includes vigilance about the proper and full contents of the gospel as and when it is passed on to others, hence the importance of 2 Tim 2:2 below.

d. Examples of loyalty and disloyalty (1:15–18)

> You know that[37] everyone in Asia turned away from me, including Phygelus and Hermogenes. May the Lord grant mercy to the household of Onesiphorus because he refreshed me many times and was not ashamed of me when I was in prison,[38] but when he came to Rome, he searched hard and found me—may the Lord grant him to find mercy from the Lord on that day. And you know only too well how much service he rendered in Ephesus. (2 Tim 1:15–18)

Paul is a realist. After speaking about his calling, the gospel, his suffering and his expectation that Timothy will suffer too, he turns to face the current crisis though, selflessly, without any carping about Roman politics or its legal system. As he has already said, he is a prisoner of Christ not the emperor but that is not how everyone sees the situation, as the divergent behavior of several individuals will reveal.

15. "You know that[39] everyone in Asia turned away from me." This astonishing statement shows how well-informed Paul was even in his prison cell. He may be referring to widespread apostasy across Asia brought about by news of his arrest and the very natural attempt of Christians to distance themselves from a man under investigation by the Imperial authorities. Since, however, the church at Ephesus continued to be a major Christian center for centuries after Paul's martyrdom it is unlikely the shunning of Paul points to an Asia-wide defection. So, some commentators think what is meant here is that the Asians in Rome did not stand with Paul during his courtroom defense.[40] Others point out the dissociation appears to be specifically from Paul himself rather than from the gospel. "Turned away from *me*" is what he writes. What supports this reading of personal disassociation is the later comment about Onesiphorus who took the trouble to find Paul in prison, or in other words, was loyal to Paul personally. As becomes apparent, Onesiphorus was a resident of Ephesus which was the chief city of Asia. What seems to have been happening is that the defection from Paul is rippling out from Ephesus, presumably because of the false teachers Timothy

---

37. Lit. "this, that . . ."
38. Lit. "of my chain."
39. Lit. "this, that . . ."
40. Mounce mentions several commentators who wondered whether the reference is to men from Asia who did not come to Rome to speak in Paul's defense (*Pastoral Epistles*, 493).

was sent to deal with. Does this mean that Timothy failed in his mission as it was set out in the first epistle? No, the Ephesian church became a center of orthodoxy for several centuries. But what *is* implied is the repair of the church from the encroachments of false teaching was no quick fix.

"Including Phygelus and Hermogenes." We know nothing about these two people. Presumably they had originally been friends or associates of Paul whose surprising and hurtful defection is mentioned because it contrasts with the altogether more honorable man spoken of next.

16. "May the Lord grant mercy to the household of Onesiphorus because he refreshed me many times and was not ashamed of me when I was in prison."[41]

Onesiphorus came to see Paul in prison and "refreshed" him. Because the nutrition and amenities provided to prisoners were meagre, any food parcels or other comforts provided by visitors were most welcome. Among other things, Paul would have needed letter writing materials and/or an amanuensis to whom he could dictate his words. Any money given to guards might well ease Paul's conditions and there must have been some method of getting his letter out of the prison and across the empire to Timothy. We do not know much about Roman prisons although the reference to a chain suggests that Paul was manacled to a wall in conditions that would have been undignified and probably unsanitary. Ancient prisons were gloomy, cold, and depressing places, but Onesiphorus took the trouble to gain access to Paul "many times" and by his practical love and friendship refreshed the old man. In doing this, Onesiphorus shrugged off any "shame" he might have felt. There is one other consideration here which seems to be a general rule about imprisonment. Anyone who is known to have friends on the outside tends to be treated better by guards than those who have nobody: not for nothing did Jesus say, "I was in prison, and you came to visit me" (Matt 25:36).[42]

Paul wishes the "household of Onesiphorus" be granted "mercy." Some commentators have assumed the household rather than Onesiphorus is wished mercy because Onesiphorus himself has died; but such an inference is not necessary. It is just as likely that Onesiphorus is either in Rome or traveling between Rome and Ephesus while his household remains in Ephesus where Timothy is. Paul's wish for mercy for the household may have the day of judgement in mind or may be more akin to the greeting already extended to Timothy (1:2). That Onesiphorus was a householder indicates his relatively comfortable social and economic status.

---

41. Lit. "of my chain."

42. The cases of Alexander Solzhenitsyn and Natan Sharansky illustrate this point. Both were supported by powerful voices outside the Soviet Union.

17. "but when he came to Rome, he searched hard and found me." The search for Paul indicates this was a very different kind of imprisonment than the house arrest depicted at the end of Acts (28:16–23). There Paul was able to receive visitors, communicate the gospel and was certainly not chained up. The prison regime has worsened greatly, and Paul is difficult to find. "When he came to Rome" may indicate Onesiphorus was in Rome already or that he came to Rome specially to find Paul.

"may the Lord grant him to find mercy from the Lord on that day." There is a play on words here as well as a spiritual point. Just as Onesiphorus found me, says Paul, may he find mercy. The apparent clumsiness in "may the Lord . . . from the Lord" could be intended to distinguish between the Son and the Father. "That day," like verse 12, must refer to the day of judgement (see also 1 Cor 3:13). We do not know whether Onesiphorus was alive or not and so there is insufficient evidence here to build a doctrine advocating prayers for the dead. Indeed, what Paul says is a wish not a prayer. "What Paul wishes for is that the blessing promised to God's faithful servants be fulfilled in the case of his friend."[43]

18. "and you know only too well how much service he rendered in Ephesus." The search for Paul in Rome and the refreshing help Onesiphorus was able to give is a continuation of the service he provided in Ephesus. Onesiphorus is a model of the faithful and diligent supporter of the apostle, going out of his way to be useful and offering an obvious contrast with fair-weather friends. We see here an early polarization of the church between those who keep going during hard times and those who turn back either to worldly pleasures (4:10) or are led astray into doctrinal peculiarities (2:17–18).

---

43. Towner, *Timothy and Titus*, 485.

> II. PAUL SETS OUT FUTURE PLANS
>
>   a. Apostolic continuity and training new teachers (2:1–2)
>   b. Working for the long-term (2:3–7)
>   c. Enduring for the gospel (2:8–13)
>   d. Dealing with false teachers (2:14–19)
>   e. Being the servant of the Lord (2:20–25)

II. PAUL SETS OUT FUTURE PLANS

Even from prison Paul lays out a strategy for the future. This involves training a new cohort while being prepared for suffering and being sustained by grace in the face of contention.

a. Apostolic continuity and training new teachers (2:1–2)

> **You therefore, my child, be strong in the grace that is in Christ Jesus and those things which you have heard from me in the presence of many witnesses, entrust to faithful people who will be competent to teach others. (2 Tim 2:1–2)**

1. "You therefore, my child, be strong in the grace that is in Christ Jesus." It is the word "therefore" that springs out at us as we start this chapter. Just as Onesiphorus has remained loyal in the face of Paul's imprisonment as a criminal, so Timothy should take courage and do the same. And the source of the courage he needs is to be found in the "grace that is in Christ Jesus." At times the command to be strong or brave seems impossible to carry out and yet what enables us to overcome our fears is the grace of Christ. The command to be strong does not stand on its own as if Timothy could confront his weakness by gritting his teeth and straightening his back; it stands because the favor of Christ can become a present reality; it is in Christ that Timothy will find strength. "My child": the tone here is not that of an apostle commanding an ecclesiastical subordinate but that of a father speaking to his son.

2. Paul now outlines his strategy for the Ephesian church. Because at least some elders have defected and begun to teach erroneous doctrine, Timothy is to recruit a new cohort of people, probably elders, who will combat the unhealthy doctrines currently in circulation. If false teachers have been recruited to their damaging cause, the solution must be to recruit

replacements who will argue the case against them. This is an entirely practical solution and demonstrates Paul's resilient mindset. The scale of the Ephesian crisis is too great for Timothy to handle alone but what he can do is to find faithful people—who must be those who have not been fooled by the false teachers—and then "entrust" to them the deposit of the gospel which he has previously received. And here Paul is specific. What must be entrusted has been heard "in the presence of many witnesses" and is therefore public knowledge, preached openly by Paul. But there is a twofold point here. Timothy is to stand in stark contrast to the false teachers by reinforcing the apostolic doctrine everyone has heard since the church's foundation reported in Acts 19. In short, and before Timothy makes the long journey from Ephesus to Rome, he is to employ his time giving intense teaching to selected individuals who will stem the tide of the false teaching and ensure the church is kept safe in his absence.

Some commentators have viewed Paul's instructions as establishing an "apostolic succession." By this they refer to an unbroken chain of belief and practice transmitted through the laying on of hands and going back to the first apostles.[1] There is truth in this claim to the extent that Paul was careful to ensure the undiluted and uncontaminated gospel reached the next generation and beyond: from Paul, to Timothy, to faithful people, to others. These verses, however, do not support claims later developed by the Roman Catholic Church about the succession process because no perpetual cycle of transmission is envisaged by the words "who will be competent to teach others also." Yet, typically, Pentecostals also see a continuity between the early church and today's church, but whereas the Roman Catholic claims depend upon a chain of connection brought about by the laying on of hands down the centuries from one generation to the next and stretching back to the first apostles, Pentecostals understand continuity as being brought about directly by the Holy Spirit (as well as by Scripture itself). The Spirit was at work in the early church and is at work in the contemporary church. The charismatic experiences engendered by the Spirit in the early church are the same as the charismatic experiences engendered in today's church, and this is because the Spirit is the same and has not changed at all. The Spirit is an immaterial entity and part of the eternal nature of the Godhead. To drink from the water of the Spirit today is to drink from the same stream that refreshed the early church (see Excursus V on Time and Eternity).

---

1. O' Collins and Farrugia, *Concise Dictionary of Theology*, 17.

b. Working for the long-term (2:3–7)

> Join in bearing hardship as a good soldier of Christ Jesus. No one who serves in the military *remains* entangled in civilian affairs, so that he may please the one who enlisted him. So too, an athlete is not crowned unless he competes according to the rules. It is the hard-working farmer who must get the first share of the crops. Think about what I am saying, for the Lord will give you understanding in all these things. (2 Tim 2:3–7)

3–4. "Join in bearing hardship as a good soldier of Christ Jesus." Here the command is to act like a soldier of Christ. Not a soldier of the emperor, but a soldier of the savior who led the fight against sin and unrighteousness. The soldier is under discipline and obedient to the orders of the commanding officer. The exhortation is to bear hardship (*synkakopathēson*) in the way that a soldier puts up with a rigorous life, training, battles, and danger. Although some commentators have translated *synkakopathēson* as "share suffering,"[2] we see context as determinative here. Both the soldier and the athlete (verses 4 and 5) are called to endure "hardship" for the purpose of gaining victory. "No one who serves in the military remains entangled in civilian affairs": part of the hardship the soldier is called upon to bear concerns a disentanglement from the comforts of ordinary civilian life—the homelife, regular meals, and children—in the service of the army.[3] The duties imposed by military discipline come down the chain of command through the commanding office to the lower ranks. Just as the soldier wishes to "please the one who enlisted him," so Christians wish to please the "captain" (KJV; Heb 2:10) of their salvation.

5. "So too, an athlete is not crowned." The second example is taken from an athlete who, like the soldier, submits to a rigorous lifestyle for an ulterior purpose. The soldier wishes to please the commanding officer, but the athlete wishes to gain victory. The two are similar in their approach to life. Both put aside immediate pleasure in the interests of long-term gain. The athlete "unless he competes according to the rules" is disqualified or remains uncrowned. It is not certain whether the rules referred to strict

---

2. Fee, *1 and 2 Timothy, Titus*, 241; Mounce, *Pastoral Epistles*, 507. It is surely true that soldiers and athletes are called on to accept hardship rather than suffering pure and simple.

3. The translation of *synkakopathēson* as "share suffering" may be etymologically correct but it seems to overstretch the meaning of *suffering* to apply it to disentanglement from ordinary business and domestic life, which is what is called for in verse 4.

training (athletes had to take an oath before a statue of Zeus, affirming they had been in ten months of training before the Olympic Games[4]) or to the rules of athletic competition itself. But it makes no difference to the general idea. Christians should act according to the rules if they expect to be recognized as legitimate winners. Perhaps there is an implicit recognition here that Christians should be law abiding citizens (Rom 13:1).

6. "It is the hard-working (*kopiōnta*) farmer who must get the first share of the crops." Like the soldier who wants to please the commanding officer and the athlete who strives for victory, so the farmer works for the harvest. Without hard work, the farmer will never see a new season of fruit. Although some commentators have associated this sentence with 1 Corinthians 9:10–11 and interpreted it to refer to remuneration for Christian ministry, that hardly fits the context here. Timothy is not being told to make sure that he is paid before he sets off for Rome. In the context of the instruction to raise up a new cohort of teachers it would be easier to see Paul as telling Timothy to watch out for the effects of his training program on the new recruits. Sow and water well so that the seedlings grow, and the young teachers start their ministries. And this is hard work—*kopiōnta* speaking of toil or physical exertion. No doubt the text can be interpreted eschatologically as well and read as an exhortation to Timothy to keep his eyes on the consequences of his actions in respect of Christ's return, but we take the command to raise up faithful teachers as determining the prime way the three mini-parables should be understood.

7. "Think about what I am saying." Paul has not spelled out the implications of his one sentence parables. They can be variously understood, yet, by reflecting on them, Timothy can reframe his task. He can battle against false doctrine like a soldier, struggle to win like an athlete, and patiently sow and reap like a farmer. The mini-parables break down his task into manageable and familiar roles making the grand plan to win back the Ephesian church easier to grasp.

"The Lord will give you understanding." Jesus promised the Holy Spirit would carry out precisely this function. He would lead disciples into all truth after Jesus had left them (John 16:13). Although the chapters in John (13–17) mainly concern the unique relationship between Jesus and the original disciples, they also spill over to us today.[5] The Holy Spirit can illuminate Scripture for the believer either suddenly and directly or through meditation. This important truth lies behind the way many Christians engage with the Scriptures. They read the Scriptures not because they are static

---

4. Kelly, *Pastoral Epistles*, 176.
5. Cf. the hint in John 17:20 about this.

and distant but because they are alive and, by the Spirit, become relevant in unexpected ways. This is not to say that any random strange idea entering a Christian's head is given by the Spirit but rather that, in keeping with the nature of God and the overall message of Scripture, the Spirit can bring words to mind just as Jesus promised would be the case when Christians were dragged before courts and tribunals (Luke 12:12). Or to put this all another way, the gift of the Spirit to the church provides a priceless personal connection with Jesus himself, a connection that transcends or negates any remoteness in historical time between then and now.

c. Enduring for the gospel (2:8–13)

> Remember Jesus Christ, risen from the dead, of the seed of David, according to my gospel for which I am suffering misfortune to the point of being chained up like a criminal. But the word of God is not bound! Because of this, I endure everything for the sake of the elect, so that they also may find[6] the salvation that is in Christ Jesus with eternal glory. The saying is sure:
>
>   For, if we have died with him, so also, we will live with him
>
>   If we endure, we will also reign with him.
>
>   If we deny him, he will also deny us.
>
>   If we are unfaithful, he remains faithful,
>
>   for he cannot deny himself. (2 Tim 2:8-13)

This section begins, like the previous one (v. 2), with reference to concrete historical events whose implications are then unpacked.

8. "Remember Jesus Christ, risen from the dead, of the seed of David, according to my gospel."[7] The message shared by Paul in the presence of many witnesses (2 Tim 2.2) and the physical resurrection of Jesus are platforms from which Paul takes the argument of the epistle forward. This is characteristic of Christianity which is a religion of historical events that have meaning well beyond what was often apparent to the first observers. The crucifixion was observed by soldiers who gambled for Jesus's clothes

---

6. Or "obtain," "experience," etc.

7. A characteristic epithet is used elsewhere by Paul (Rom 2:16; 16:25, cf. Gal 1:8, 11; 2:2) often linked to his distinctive insistence on gentile inclusion, but certainly other things too. The implication is that some of Paul's concerns and insights were not universally emphasized.

with no idea whatever of the turning point in world history taking place a few feet away from their game of dice. The living Jesus after the resurrection was witnessed not only by Paul who testified to the Ephesians but by more than five hundred people (1 Cor 15:6). The birth of Jesus in David's line links him back to Old Testament prophecy (Acts 2:23–32; 8:32–35; 17:1–3).[8] The impact of these events has spread out, and is spreading out, across human history. In the Ephesian milieu with its airy false teaching, it was important to bring believers back to the basic facts that constitute the gospel.

9. "for which I am suffering misfortune (*kakopathō*) to the point of being chained up like a criminal (*kakourgos*)." The gospel is inevitably associated with suffering given that it includes the trial, humiliation, flogging and crucifixion of Jesus. Here Paul speaks of his suffering on account of the *gospel* rather than on account of Jesus whose prisoner he is (1:8). Suffering for the gospel has been factored into mature Christian thinking from the earliest times ever since Jesus said, "take up your cross and follow me" (Luke 9:23). There is an enormous moral gulf between suffering for the gospel and suffering for wrongdoing but what is clear from Paul's life is that, while he recognized suffering would accompany his ministry, he did not seek pain in any masochistic way. When he was about to be flogged in Jerusalem, he used his Roman citizenship to avoid this harsh treatment (Acts 22:25). We do not see Paul as self-harming but as conducting his ministry wisely. Indeed, he left some cities hurriedly to avoid trouble (Acts 17:10; cf. Matt 10:14). And he only endured pain when it was a consequence of his calling to preach and teach. His last journey to Jerusalem (Acts 21:1–16) which led to his arrest is the only obvious exception to this rule, but we may see his determination to visit Jerusalem as connected with his desire to ensure the racial unity of the church, a desire that had already been shown through the financial generosity of the gentile church to the Jewish believers (Acts 21:17–19; 1 Cor 16:1–4; 2 Cor 8:16–21).

The Roman judicial system had classified Paul as a "criminal (*kakourgos*)" just as it had done to Jesus. There is a vast psychological pressure put on anyone who, through a formal and legal process, is classified in this way and then separated from the rest of society in prison. The Russian show trials of the 1930s similarly used the judicial system to create public disapproval of those who were considered to be a political threat to the communist regime. In Paul's case the category of prisoner into which he has been placed, *kakourgos*, is a harsh one and used in the gospels to describe the men crucified on either side of Jesus (Luke 23:32–3). The word would fit the

---

8. A significant statement in view of the later Marcionite heresy in which Christianity was entirely separated from the faith story of Old Testament.

context of the Neronian persecution under which, according to tradition and the consensus of historians, Paul was executed.[9]

"to the point of being chained up." The point here, presumably, is that most criminals were not actually chained up but were simply confined to prison. But the worst and most dangerous were chained up inside the prison cells.

"But the word of God is not bound!" Paul finds a positive even in the negative. Although he is chained, the word of God is not. Here the "word of God" applies to the gospel, or more widely to the message taught by Jesus, and it applies at a time when the word of God is passed on by word of mouth rather than as a written text. So it may be that Paul's imprisonment encouraged other preachers (cf. Phil 1:12–18) or that Paul, even where he was, excited such interest and comment among other prisoners and guards that they were speaking about Jesus even if they were not yet converted.

10. "Because of this, I endure everything for the sake of the elect." Paul suffers because of the gospel itself or because his suffering is beneficial to the unbound gospel. Some commentators have connected Paul's suffering mystically with the tribulation through which the church must pass.[10] It is more convincing to argue Christ suffers with or through the members of his church (Acts 9:4)[11] and that this brings members of his church into fellowship with Christ in an intimate way (Phil 3:10). To suffer with Christ is not only a badge of honor but a deep bond of fellowship with Christ. Additionally, if we suffer, we are "partners with Christ"[12] while giving an example of patience to other believers. What Paul is certainly not claiming is that he suffers redemptively for the church since only Christ did this.

Whether "the elect" refers to the unconverted who will yet join the church or is a more general term for the people of God has no bearing on the thrust of this sentence. Paul is suffering in order that others might benefit. We can, perhaps, become too focused upon the outer edges of the meaning of this passage. What Paul is doing, and what the other early apostles were doing, is demonstrating by their commitment to the point of martyrdom how the gospel is an ultimate truth. If Paul and the early apostles had conceded any ground at this point to Roman paganism, the

---

9. Ramsay makes this point and Guthrie quotes him with approval (Ramsay, *The Church in the Roman Empire*, 249 quoted in Guthrie, *Pastoral Epistles*, 156).

10. Kelly, *Pastoral Epistles*, 178, mentions Col 1:24 here and finds reference to "a predetermined amount of suffering which the Messianic community, the body of Christ, must undergo before the End can come."

11. Christ identifies with his people and feels for them.

12. Calvin, *Philippians, Colossians, and Thessalonians*, on Col 1:24.

history of the church would have been entirely different. In this sense, the first generation of apostles were foundational to the centuries that followed and unflinchingly demonstrated Christianity is not only a matter of doctrine but of lifestyle and ethical integrity.

"so that they also may find[13] the salvation that is in Christ Jesus with eternal glory." Paul's suffering is for a purpose. Suffering with a purpose is more bearable than suffering without apparent meaning. Whether Paul's suffering underlines the ultimate truth of the gospel or gives an example for others to follow or draws attention to the life and crucifixion of Christ or all these things and more, it assists other people's quest for salvation (by regeneration and justification) and points towards the eternal glory Christ entered after his resurrection (John 17:1–5). The contrast between suffering and glory is an important Pauline theme (Rom 8:18; 2 Cor 4:17) later expounded by Martin Luther.[14]

11–12. "The saying is sure." Because of their rhythm and structure most commentators agree the next few lines probably belong to a hymn or a creedal statement. Paul uses these lines to summarize what he is saying about suffering and in this way copies the textual pattern found elsewhere in his epistles when he completes an argument with a series of Old Testament quotations to buttress his point. Here he uses words that would be known by early Christians in another context; but the literary sequence is similar: historical reference, argument, clinching quotations (e.g., Rom 2:17, 18–23; 24).

> "For, if we have died with him, so also, we will live with him
> If we endure, we will also reign with him."

Many commentators understand the first line as speaking of baptism rather than martyrdom.[15] "If we have died with him" rather than "if we are prepared to die for him" follows the figure of speech in Romans 6:1–13: we are buried with Christ in baptism, an image enacted by being plunged down into water and then raised up again: so "we will live with him." In this sense, the Christian's life is already over and buried, and the Roman authorities cannot kill anyone a second time. Of course, the phrase must also be read for its impact on Paul's current predicament; imminent actual death will lead to eventual actual resurrection. In parallel, the next line contrasts present trials with future triumphs. "If we endure," then we will "reign." There

---

13. Or "obtain," "experience" etc.

14. He contrasts the theology of the cross and the theology of glory in the Heidelberg Disputation.

15. E.g., Kelly, *Pastoral Epistles*, 179. Baptism anticipates martyrdom, however, as suggested by Matt 10:38.

could hardly be a greater incentive for enduring, and it is from words like this that the early Christians derived comfort and strength. Perhaps it is hinted here that the lower Christianized echelons of Roman society will finally turn the tables on their masters and become the ones who reign rather than the ones who are always ruled.[16]

"If we deny him, he will also deny us." This stern saying must have its origins in what Jesus himself said (Matt 10:33). The pointed nature of Christ's words is precisely suited to the Roman demands for uniformity when Christians were required to deny Christ and offer worship with a pinch of incense to a statue of Caesar.[17] It is equally suited to the brainwashing techniques of the Chinese Communist Party when Christians, under duress, were told to repudiate their faith and kowtow to Maoist doctrine. In such extreme situations, Christians are known by their words because these express their ultimate loyalties and the true object of their worship.

13. "If we are unfaithful, he remains faithful, for he cannot deny himself." The possibility of unfaithfulness must be distinguished from the possibility of denying Christ. Unfaithfulness here speaks of a lapse, a drifting away from Christ, rather than apostasy. If we, as Christians, are unfaithful to the Lord, he yet remains faithful. In the other lines of the quotation, if we do something, God does something else. Here if we do something, God remains exactly the same as he was before. He remains faithful to his covenant and his promises because he "cannot deny himself." Christians are sometimes surprised to think of something that God *cannot* do, but what is said here makes perfect sense. God is self-consistent and cannot deny his own being or attributes. So here we have a wonderful affirmation of the rock-solid faithfulness of God. Not only is God faithful, but he also *cannot* be unfaithful. The words are an encouragement to the wavering Christian rather than a condemnation.

d. Dealing with false teachers (2:14–19)

> Keep on reminding everyone about these things, solemnly warning them before the Lord not to quarrel about words, which is of no use at all and only leads to the ruin of those who hear *such things*. Make every effort to present yourself to God as one approved, a worker with no need to be ashamed,

---

16. Cf. Matt 5:5, although an eschatological sense could also be intended, as seen in Rev 2:26–28.

17. Bruce, *Spreading Flame*, 173.

cutting a straight path for the word of truth. But avoid ungodly[18] banter[19] for it will only lead people into greater impiety and their talk will spread like gangrene. Hymenaeus and Philetus are amongst them, men who have deviated from the truth by saying that the resurrection has already happened and destroy[20] some people's faith. However, God's solid foundation stands firm bearing this inscription[21] "The Lord knows those who are his own" and "Let everyone who calls on the name of the Lord[22] turn away from wrongdoing." (2 Tim 2:14–19)

This section contrasts true and false teachers who are distinguished not only by their doctrine but by their demeanor and by the practical effects on their hearers of what they say.

14. "Keep on reminding everyone about these things." Memory continues to be vital. Part of Timothy's job is to remind the Ephesians of what they already know. Timothy himself has already been reminded of Paul's gospel—Christ's descent from David and his resurrection—as well as the charismatic gifts he had received and his own sincere faith. When a congregation goes wrong, there is a need to call it back to its beginnings as happens when the Ephesians are called back to their first love, or the Galatians are called back to their own original reception of the Spirit (Rev 2:4–5; Gal 3:2). The words "these things" refer to the gospel and the other exhortations already given but not to the whole of the epistle so far since some of it is personal to Timothy.[23]

Timothy is also to point to danger by "solemnly warning them before the Lord." The presence and person of Christ is invoked. There are times when believers need to realize how close the head of the church is to his people. He is "the Lord," their master and king, and so they must be warned "not to quarrel about words (*logomachein*)." What fundamentally matters is the reality the words describe. If instead of remembering the gospel the

---

18. Lit. "profane." This can be neutral, in the sense of anything that is not specifically religious, but the negative connotations here suggest something like "worldly."

19. Greek *kenophōnia*, lit. empty talking.

20. A range of possible meanings includes: "upset," "overturn," and "ruin." The strength of condemnation here would suggest a serious impact.

21. Lit. "seal," but in context commonly translated "inscription."

22. Greek *onomazōn to onoma kyriou*, lit. "names the name of the Lord." Although reminiscent of it, the wording differs from LXX Joel 2:32 (3:5) which has *epikalesētai to onoma kyriou*.

23. Mounce, *Pastoral Epistles*, 523.

Ephesians plunge into word battles, as *logomachein* may be translated, they will damage themselves.[24] As we shall see in a moment, a reinterpretation of the word "resurrection" had led some to a total misunderstanding of our present reality.

If, as Paul says, the strife over words "is of no use at all" one might wonder then why the early church later spent so much time and energy debating creeds at the big ecumenical councils of Nicaea and elsewhere. If we take Paul's warnings to heart, it must be that these are not really arguments over words but arguments over the nature of God, the way of salvation, and historicity.[25] Similarly in Ephesus the thrust of what Paul contends for is the gospel itself with all its historical actuality and ramifications and, on these matters, he will rebut the false teachers. Because false teachers have downgraded Christ and obscured his saving work they must be resisted and refuted.

15. "Make every effort to present yourself to God as one approved, a worker with no need to be ashamed." In contrast with those who mishandle Scripture, Timothy is to "make every effort," do his best, and strive earnestly to "present" himself to God. Here the word is used either of presenting oneself as a sacrifice or presenting oneself to a judge.[26] The crucial point here is that Timothy is answerable to God and stands before God in what he does. Nothing is more calculated than this to ensure Timothy strives to acquit himself well. And he is to present himself as one who is "approved," or tested, one who is confident he has mastered the subject matter and understood it thoroughly and so is without any need to be ashamed. The command encourages Timothy to detailed and careful preparation prior to the carrying out of his task. The idea of "studying to present yourself" (KJV, AKJV) found in earlier translations is not entirely misplaced. Given this task of preaching and correcting them is being *heard*, not read, (e.g., 2 Tim 1:13; 2 Tim 2:2) and the close reference to vain chatter or "ungodly banter" (2 Tim 2:16), the context is oral communication: Timothy is to be precise in what he says and preaches.

---

24. Fee, *1 and 2 Timothy, Titus*, 254. Interestingly, British philosophy in the twentieth century, after its infatuation with idealism, passed through logical positivism and then took a linguistic turn and became embroiled in "word battles." It took Wittgenstein to point the whole field in a different direction.

25. "If the formation of concepts can be explained by the facts of nature, should we not be interested, not in grammar, but rather in nature which is the basis of grammar?" (Wittgenstein, *Philosophical Investigations*, 230). Similarly, it is the reality of God that should concern us, not arguments over words.

26. Towner, *Timothy and Titus*, 520.

Moreover, he is to be a "worker" who is "cutting a straight path (*orthotomounta*) for the word of truth" or in other translations "dispensing the word of truth in the right way" (Kelly) or "who correctly handles the word of truth" (Towner). The origins of this metaphor have been lost though the Greek OT (the Septuagint) uses the same word to speak of the "effect of wisdom or righteousness as cutting a straight path . . . for the upright (Prov 3:6; 11:5)."[27] The message Timothy gives must be honest and accurate. To the Corinthians Paul avowed he and his team (which included Timothy at that time) did not use deception or distortion in ministering the word of God (2 Cor 4:2), and that avowal echoes here.

Commentators are almost universally agreed that the "word of truth" is the gospel itself though there has been discussion about whether Paul is speaking of recognized writings of the New Testament Scripture and his own initiation of the collection of the canon.[28] This may or may not be so but does not alter the instruction to Timothy. It is equally reasonable to assume that Paul kept copies of the letters he sent and that these copies, held in Rome, became the origin of the canon of his letters.[29]

16–17. "But avoid ungodly[30] banter[31] for it will only lead people into greater impiety." Paul's warning here concerns the spread and escalation of impiety rather than its origin. "Banter" is one thing, but "ungodly banter" is quite another. Jesus himself warns against idle words (Matt 12:36), and James compares the tongue to a rudder setting the direction of a large ship (Jas 3:4, 5). Ungodly banter, impious in itself, will lead to "greater impiety" that "will spread like gangrene." Without antibiotics and with the prevalence of wounds inflicted by swords and knives, gangrene was one of the most hated and dangerous of medical conditions in the ancient world. The gangrenous limb was first infused with puss and began to give off a foul smell. Death soon followed.

Two culprits are named: "Hymenaeus and Philetus are amongst them," the first of whom was a blasphemer who had been already disciplined (1 Tim 1:20). However, the fact that he was still causing trouble in Ephesus illustrates how difficult the situation was. If the church was large and with many home groups across the city—as was probable because purpose-built church buildings did not exist in the first century—rogue leaders with their

---

27. Towner, *Timothy and Titus*, 522 in reference to the Septuagint.
28. Wall and Steele, *1 and 2 Timothy and Titus*, loc 5881, in reference to Trobisch.
29. Richards, *Paul*, 212 and following.
30. Lit. "profane." This can be neutral, in the sense of anything that is not specifically religious, but the negative connotations here suggest something like "worldly."
31. Greek *kenophōnia*, lit. empty talking.

own circles of influence would have been hard to restrict.³² It is possible Paul was informed by Onesiphorus (2 Tim 1:16–18) about who was doing what in Ephesus, which is why he was able to name the ringleaders.

18. "men who have deviated from (*ēstochēsan*) the truth by saying that the resurrection has already happened." The resurrection of the dead has been integral to Christianity since the resurrection of Christ himself. If we take Hebrews 6:1–2 as an outline of Christian doctrine in a sequence of steps, then after repentance and faith, will come the resurrection of the dead prior to the last judgement. But there would also have been regular reference to resurrection in teaching about water baptism by immersion (Rom 6:1–11), and so, by a deliberate distortion of apostolic doctrine, it is possible to conflate the sacrament or ordinance of baptism with the real event it prefigures. However, false teachers could and did make fundamental errors here by saying something like, "When you were raised from the waters of baptism, you were raised from the dead. You now have a resurrection body and will never grow old or die."³³ Strands in Greek philosophy devalued and despised the body in comparison to the soul it contained. Greeks, like all rationalists, found the resurrection of the dead hard to believe—as was evident when Paul preached in Athens (Act 17:18ff., esp. 32)—and so tended to slide into Gnosticism, a fuzzy and confusing belief system stressing salvation by secret knowledge. Gnosticism could give rise to two reactions, either the suppression and weakening of the body through legalistic asceticism or reckless and often sexual immorality deriving from the belief that whatever was done in the body could not touch and taint the soul.

By saying that "the resurrection has already happened" the false teachers had profoundly undermined "some people's faith" by robbing Christianity of its forward-looking expectations of future events of great divine power and majesty. We do not know what other downgrading of the faith the false teachers propagated, but it is quite possible the resurrection of Christ himself had become in their minds merely a symbolic event bereft of historical actuality.³⁴ To deny the future resurrection of Christians is "to deny our past (Christ's own resurrection on which all else is predicated)."³⁵ Corinth had already been plagued in this way and so what was happening in Ephesus

---

32. As frequently imagined in relation to the comments in 3 John 9–10.

33. For evidence of this kind of statement, cf. Irenaeus *Haer.* 1:23.5, via Kelly, *Pastoral Epistles*, 185.

34. Another possibility is that the new life in the Spirit is being understood as "resurrection" in its own right, as perhaps in Eph 5:14 where Paul reworks the image of Isa 60:1–2.

35. Fee, *1 and 2 Timothy, Titus*, 257.

was a resurgence of a philosophical and doctrinal problem Paul had already encountered and countered. Just as Jewish culture might default into arguments over the role of the Mosaic law so Greek culture might default to philosophical or rational objections to the gospel (cf. 1 Cor 1:22–24). The teaching of Hymenaeus and Philetus was heretical because "to deny the bodily resurrection is to deny Christ's resurrection,"[36] rendering the gospel void (1 Cor 15:12–17).

19. "However, God's solid foundation stands firm bearing this inscription."[37] Against this dangerous threat to the entire Christian mission in Ephesus Paul can make two theological assertions which hark back to a turning point in the life of the people of Israel. When, in the wilderness, Moses had been challenged by a contingent of tribal elders who resented their exclusion from priestly leadership and duties, there was a showdown which was resolved by a divine judgement of the rebels and an endorsement of Aaron and his line. The situation at Ephesus had escalated into a confrontation of similar size and seriousness. Just as Moses had been able to assure the legitimate leaders of God's knowledge of them, so Paul was able to assure Timothy God personally knew those who were his.

First, though, Paul asserts "God's solid foundation stands firm." Commentators discuss whether this refers to Christ himself or the apostles as the foundation of the institution of the church (Eph 2:20) or to the individuals called to Christ, the elect (v 10), in the Ephesian situation. Given the earlier reference to individual defectors, the latter meaning may be preferred. When Paul arrived in Ephesus, he made it his business to lay a strong foundation for the church by ensuring believers, who until that moment had been followers of John the Baptist, understood Christ's fulfilment of all that John had preached (Acts 19:3–5). After that, he laid hands on them and ensured their experience was thoroughly charismatic (Acts 19:6); and after all that, he taught them thoroughly in public settings and from house to house (Acts 20:20). There was nothing for their benefit he withheld (Acts 20:20). Just as he had done in the case of the Corinthians, he laid the foundation of Christ as a good master builder (1 Cor 3:10).

"bearing this inscription." Mounce notes that "the metaphor is based on the practice of inscribing a seal on the foundation of a building" to show who owned it (cf. Rev 21:14).[38]

"The Lord knows those who are his own." These words are taken straight from Numbers 16:5 in the Greek translation of the OT (Septuagint)

---

36. Mounce, *Pastoral Epistles*, 527.
37. Lit. "seal," but in context commonly translated "inscription."
38. Mounce, *Pastoral Epistles*, 529.

which is why the parallel with the rebellion of Korah and 250 others may be confidently identified. Paul draws strength from his detailed knowledge of the Old Testament and obviously sees himself as the legitimate spiritual authority, just as Moses was, who is being challenged by illegitimate men aspiring to leadership positions for which they have not been divinely chosen. Even if other people do not know who belongs to the Lord, the Lord himself does. In the end, the matter revolves around the personal nature of God who knows us inside out. From the very beginning of our lives we are known by God both for what we do and what we think. The Old Testament reveals God to be one who searches our hearts and minds and knows us extensively and intimately. And we, for our part, reciprocate by seeking to know God even if this is an entirely unequal relationship because we are finite and God is infinite (Ps 42:1; 139:2, 13, 17; Je 1:5; 17:10). In short, to be known *by* God is a spiritual state complementing our desire to *know* God and one day, says Paul, he will know God even as God knows him (1 Cor 13:12).

"Let everyone who calls on the name of the Lord[39] turn away from wrongdoing." The second statement does not correspond directly with any quotation from the Old Testament although it expresses ideas found in many verses (e.g., Lev 24:16; Isa 26:13; Ps 34:14; Pro 3:7, and also Num 16:26). The passage in Numbers narrates a knife edge episode in Israel's history when God's people could have fallen into a terrible error. The position in Ephesus was equally serious and precarious. And, as has been pointed out by several commentators, the two texts cited by Paul give us two sides of the equation of divine action (election) and human responsibility or, as Van Neste has it, preserving and persevering.[40]

e. Being the servant of the Lord (2:20–25)

> For in a large house, there are not only vessels[41] made of gold and silver but also of wood and earthenware, some kept for "best," others reserved for less seemly tasks. Therefore, if anyone cleanses him or herself from these things, he or she will be *like* a vessel that is used for the most important

---

39. Greek *onomazōn to onoma kyriou*, lit. "names the name of the Lord." Although reminiscent of it, the wording differs from LXX Joel 2:32 (3:5) which has *epikalesētai to onoma kyriou*.

40. Cited in the ESV Study Bible, loc 313307–16.

41. Greek *skeuos* can mean "item," "tool," "vessel," indeed, almost anything. The use of this word in Rom 9:21–24 where a *potter* is mentioned means it is reasonable to imagine a "vessel" here too.

occasions, useful to the master, ready for every good work. So flee from every youthful craving and pursue righteousness, faith, love, *and* peace within the company of *all* those who call on the Lord out of a pure heart. But avoid foolish or mindless controversies as you know they *only* cause arguments. But as the Lord's servant, you must not quarrel, but be kind towards everyone, an experienced teacher[42], patient, correcting those who oppose you with gentleness, *hoping* that perhaps God might grant them repentance and so come to a knowledge of the truth and that they may come to their senses *and escape* from the devil's snare having been held captive by him to *do* his will. (2 Tim 2:20-25)

The final section of the chapter continues with the contrast between true and false teachers while showing how true teachers, servants of the Lord, should conduct themselves.

20. "For in a large house, there are not only vessels[43] made of gold and silver but also of wood and earthenware, some kept for 'best', others reserved for less seemly tasks." Paul transitions to the metaphor of a large house with different kinds of vessels in it. The house is the church, and the vessels are people and both metaphors are used elsewhere in Pauline writings (for the house 1 Tim 3:5, 15; for vessels Rom 9:20-23; 2 Cor 4:7). Two kinds of vessels are identified, some made of precious metal for noble purposes and others of wood or earthenware for ignoble purposes. For instance, some may be gold plates in a fine dinner service and others may be wooden bowls for rubbish or excrement. Although the master of the house is going to use the expensive vessels for his own purposes, it is notable that the cheap vessels are also among the chattels of the great house. We can think of the cheap vessels as having a purpose even if it is limited and dishonorable. This helps us understand how to think of Hymenaeus and Philetus. They exist within the great all-encompassing purposes of the master of the house just as, in Romans 9:17, Pharaoh, the vessel of dishonor, was raised up to fulfill God's purpose with Israel. God is in overall control and there is a later hint that the ignoble vessels may yet recover themselves into an honorable position (v 21).

21. "Therefore, if anyone cleanses him or herself from these things . . ." Having described the two kinds of vessels, Paul stretches the metaphor in an unexpected direction. Vessels cannot normally clean *themselves*; nevertheless,

---

42. Cf. Himes, "Rethinking the Translation of Διδακτικός," 189-208.

43. As noted above, the Greek *skeuos* can mean "item," "tool," "vessel," indeed, almost anything. The use of this word in Rom 9:21-24 where a *potter* is mentioned means it is reasonable to imagine a "vessel" here too.

if a "vessel" (a member of the church) can cleanse (*ekkatharē*) itself *from these things*, then a good result will follow.[44] Pointing beyond mere "washing up," the word for "cleanse" here is commonly seen in both moral discourse about people's behavior and in relation to the cultic purity of vessels used in temple worship. The "vessel" of particular value, then, is a person, who can "cleanse" *him or herself*. The question arises as to what *these things* are. There are two options. Either they refer to the false teachers and the cleansing involves removing oneself from them or, better in this context, cleansing involves the washing away of false and gangrenous doctrine. "He or she will be like a vessel that is used for the most important occasions." This is the good result. The clean vessel—the sanctified Christian teacher and minister—can be used for the "most important occasions." And here the advice to Timothy goes much wider than him because Paul is talking about *anyone* and in this sense is stipulating a general condition for Christian service.

". . . useful to the master, ready for every good work." It is the master who decides how the vessel should be used in a range of options that covers "every good work." Holiness (see Excursus IV) ought to lead to activity rather than hermit-like seclusion and even if this text might seem to counsel passivity (it is up to the master to decide who will be used for what), elsewhere in the Pastoral Epistles an aspiration of Christians to serve in particular roles is implicitly commended (1 Tim 3:1).

22. "So flee from every youthful craving and pursue righteousness, faith, love, and peace within the company of all those who call on the Lord out of a pure heart." Timothy is to avoid the typical preoccupations of youth, every youthful craving (presumably: sex, extreme fashion, irresponsibility, drunkenness, drugs, and so on), and instead pursue a different path. So, on the one hand, Timothy is to "flee," and on the other hand, he is to "pursue." The Christian path is not one of perpetual shunning and avoidance but one of positive goals. There is a reminder here of Timothy's youth and of the lifestyle he is to follow. In seeking out "the company all those who call on the Lord out of a pure heart," Timothy is to engage in prayer and the picture is of prayer gatherings within the Ephesian church. As elsewhere in the epistle (1 Tim 2:1), Paul wants to see the church coming together in prayer as an important basic feature of its communal life, especially where that life is on the verge of fracturing. Prayer, in this instance, is surely extempore—"call on the Lord"—rather than liturgical.

The four goals of "righteousness," "faith," "love," and "peace" indicate that Timothy is to remain committed to high Christian ideals. Each of these values has a social dimension and is not only a private virtue. Righteousness

---

44. Towner, *Timothy and Titus*, 542.

speaks of the great Christian theme of establishing a community and, beyond this, a society of equity and integrity. "Faith" permeates the Christian life and can be the basis for mission or any number of godly initiatives. "Love" remains fundamental to every aspect of individual and communal life and must never be jettisoned in favor of a business plan or highhanded leadership styles or any other activist agenda. And peace can be expressed both internally as a state of heart and mind and externally by upright relationships with countless others including family, neighbors, and wider society.

23. "But avoid foolish (*mōras*) or mindless (*apaideutous*) controversies (*zētēseis*) as you know they only cause arguments." The four values Timothy is to pursue might lead him into conflict with others. But he is not to go round the church looking for a fight or an argument. Despite the need to correct parts of the church that have being led astray he is to avoid some kinds of controversy or, as *zētēseis* can be translated, speculation. (In this regard, the verse warns against something more serious than was seen in v. 16). Whether it is necessary to write off all speculative theology is a moot point, but it is easy to see how speculation can raise unanswerable questions whose uncertain answers become the grounds for strong disagreement. Some are *apaideutous* or, literally, "uneducated" and therefore ignorant and others are foolish (*mōras*), a word that also carries the sense of being culpable and sinful.[45] Some arguments, in short, are simply not worth having.

24. "But as the Lord's servant, you must not quarrel but be kind towards everyone, an experienced teacher, patient . . ." Over and above the doctrinal contrast between Timothy and his opponents is a difference of character and disposition. Even in the middle of the crisis threatening the future of the Ephesian church Timothy is to maintain his godly kindness and patience. At first sight, this comes as a surprise. Rather than telling Timothy he must be full of righteous anger and power to defeat the men threatening the integrity of the church, Paul draws upon a quite different example. It is probable he has in mind the suffering servant of Isaiah 52 and 53 fulfilled in Jesus himself. The "but" indicates the contrast with what went before; the "Lord" may be read as Jesus; and the "servant" is the usual word for "slave," which is how Paul often describes himself (e.g., Rom 1:1, Phil 1:1). The phrase "the Lord's servant" is wide enough to include every Christian minister and the command "not to quarrel" covers the whole range of his or her activities in home, church, and society. The sentence echoes the personal qualifications for a Christian elder while, highlighting their teaching function (1 Tim 3:2–7; Titus 1:7–9). The genuine Christian minister does not act

---

45. Knight, *Pastoral Epistles*, 422.

in authoritarian ways but is prepared to "teach," to engage with opponents, and patiently show the right way forward. In charismatic congregations, it is important to recognize that charismatic gifts like prophecy are not the only or even best answer to fraught situations of dissent. Character—"be kind toward everyone"—shines, as does being "patient."

25. "correcting (*paideuonta*) those who oppose you with gentleness (*prautēti*)." No one likes to be told that they are wrong so that even when people are forced to admit their errors, they can still nurse resentment at the way they were treated. Timothy is to correct his opponents with *gentleness*, an extraordinary instruction that runs counter to the fighting instincts of most convinced individuals. *Prautēti* carries the broad meaning of "humility, courtesy, gentleness"[46] while *paideuonta* means "instructing, educating," implying Timothy's correction is to be thorough and rational and with a restorative goal in view: *hoping that* perhaps "God might grant (*dōē*) them repentance (*metanoian*) and so come to a knowledge of the truth." Timothy's opponents need to repent. The full force of *metanoian* implies a change of heart and mind that requires a decision or effort of the human will even if it is God who "grants" (*dōē* comes from the ordinary word for "give") repentance. Again, there is the interplay between divine sovereignty and human responsibility here. We may see the opponents of Timothy as needing to take responsibility for the damage they have done and to acknowledge it, perhaps publicly. Given that repentance implies a change of lifestyle as well as a change of mind, there is a moral dimension in play here. And this leads "to a knowledge of the truth" implying we have a two-step process: first repentance and then an intellectual apprehension of "the truth," the gospel. Given the gnostic tendencies of the false teachers, reference to "the truth" hits home to exactly where these false teachers erred. "Truth" in Paul's writings speaks of the gospel (1 Tim 2:4) but philosophically it may be seen as a correspondence between what is asserted and reality.[47] There is thus a correspondence between the gospel and historical and metaphysical reality.

26. The hope is those who oppose Timothy and are damaging the "church may come to their senses and escape from the devil's snare having been held captive by him to do his will." Although the Greek syntax here is

---

46. BDAG, 699, cited by Mounce, *Pastoral Epistles*, 536.

47. The correspondence theory has a long history, e.g., "It is often said that what makes a belief true is its correspondence with reality" (Kenny, *Western Philosophy*, 789). Other definitions of truth include internal coherence within a discourse or a system (e.g., a mathematical or algebraic system); see, Lowe, "Truth," 881.

"slipshod,"[48] it is most satisfactory to read this sentence as saying the false teachers who have been ensnared by the devil may, by repentance and an acknowledgement of the truth, escape the trap into which they have fallen. Timothy's corrective task is also a rescue mission. "You will know the truth," said Jesus, "and the truth will set you free" (John 8:32).

---

48. Kelly, *Pastoral Epistles*, 191; Mounce, *Pastoral Epistles*, 538.

III. PAUL WARNS AND ENCOURAGES
  a. A coarsening of society in these days (3:1–9)
  b. Standing firm and holding on to Scripture (3:10–17)

III. PAUL WARNS AND ENCOURAGES

Having spoken of the gentleness of servants of the Lord in the previous chapter and their willingness to correct men and women caught up in error, Paul now turns to the complexion of society in the last days. After listing its typical vices, Paul, using his own experience, instructs Timothy in the path he should take, and the many-sided resources found in Scripture.

a. A coarsening of society in these days (3:1–9)

> But know this, that in the last days, difficult times will come. For people will be self-centered[1], lovers of money, boastful and arrogant, speaking ill of their parents, disobedient, ungrateful, unholy, hard-hearted, implacable, slanderous, lacking self-control, savage, uninterested in the good, traitors, reckless, conceited, loving pleasure rather than God maintaining *the* form of godliness but denying its power. *You should* avoid such people. For among them are those who insinuate themselves into homes and take control of vulnerable women[2]. Weighed down by *past* failings and led on by all sorts of yearnings, *such women* are permanently studying[3], but never coming to a knowledge of the truth. In the same way that Jannes and Jambres opposed Moses, so these *teachers* also oppose the truth, corrupted in mind and *showing only* counterfeit faith. But they will not get very far,

---

1. Greek *philautoi*, lit. "lovers of themselves."

2. Greek *gÿnaikarion*, pl. *gynaikaria*, a pejorative diminutive sometimes translated "idle," "weak," or "silly" women; the exploitative context here suggests the translation "vulnerable."

3. I.e., by implication under the tutelage of their *abusers*. Commentators generally see this exploitation as based on the offer of *religious instruction* by peripatetic teachers working for profit, like those described in Titus 1:10–11 "those who peddle nonsense and deceive souls ... ruining whole households" etc. cf. Celsus' accusation against Christian missionaries reported by Origen, *Cels.* 3:55.

> for their lack of understanding will become evident to all, as it did in the case of those men. (2 Tim 3:1–9)

1. "But know this, that in the last days (*eschatais hēmerais*), difficult times will come." Paul would have known of Peter's preaching in Jerusalem on the Day of Pentecost and his ringing declaration of the Spirit's outpouring "*in the last days*" (Acts 2:17). This brought an eschatological urgency to the early church because of the anticipated imminent return of Jesus (1 Thess 5:1–3). The "last days," insofar as one can divide up world history into divinely demarcated sections, begin with the outpouring of the Spirit and will continue up until the end of the age. Whether these days are long or short was hardly the issue for the early church. Christians were expected to be like vigilant soldiers ready to welcome their King (Matt 24:42; Luke 21:26). The early church, informed by Jewish literature[4] and prophetic utterance (1 Tim 4:1), and, more than this, the words of Jesus in the gospels themselves (Matt 24), anticipated troublesome and perilous times prior to the end. The consequences of this expectation placed the Ephesian troubles into a wider context. Perhaps there is an implication here that Timothy should not blame himself for his failure to put the Ephesian church immediately back on track. What is interesting to us is that these *last days* spoken of by Paul do not immediately correspond with the plagues and judgments of the Book of Revelation (e.g., Rev 16). We have pictured here a society riddled with personal immorality but not a society on the brink of political and economic collapse.

2. "For people will be self-centered[5], lovers of money, boastful and arrogant, speaking ill of their parents, disobedient, ungrateful, unholy." The Roman Empire had been built on military virtues including respect for political and military hierarchies, a sense of public duty, courage in battle, respect for classical gods, respect for parents, and a willingness to put the greater good of the state before personal gain. To these, after the conquest of Greece, were added Greek philosophical thought including Aristotle's conception of virtue ethics (justice, courage, temperance, etc.) with its valuation of practical wisdom (*phronesis*), developed through experience and critical reflection. The vices listed by Paul contradict traditional Roman morality, Greek virtues, and the theorization supporting them. At the head of the vices are people who are *self-centered* and therefore lack the Roman sense of duty or the Greek behaviors leading to collective human flourishing. Nearly all moral systems emphasize the balance between the individual and society

---

4. For instance, Fee draws attention to 1 En. 80:2–8; 100:1–3; As. Mos. 8:1; 4 Ezra 5:1–12, and 2 Bar. 25–27 (*1 and 2 Timothy, Titus*, 269).

5. Greek *philautoi*, lit. "lovers of themselves."

and some psychological accounts of human morality show how it develops through reciprocal relations first among children and then is later embodied in such things as the law of contract.[6] Self-centeredness takes the advantages conferred by cooperation but gives nothing back in return. It is therefore destructive of morality or public ethics and undermines their purpose.

"Lovers of money." Running through this list of vices is wrongly directed love. Here money itself is an object of love, and therefore a cause of covetousness and ruthless exploitation, and stimulates the glorification of wealth for its own sake rather than for the good it can do. The miser counting his gold while his servants starve is a well-known figure of satire or rebuke in literature,[7] and Paul has already noted the love of money (not money itself) is at the root of much evil (1 Tim 6:10). Money becomes the source of psychological security and replaces God.

"boastful and arrogant." Neither Christianity nor Judaism has ever admired boastfulness and arrogance since such attitudes inevitably belittle God and aggrandize the boaster. Ultimately, all human existence is subject to God and will be judged either in this life or the next with the result that boastfulness often degenerates into a way of expressing atheism. Both in the gospels, where Jesus warns his followers not to take oaths (Matt 5:34) and in James (4:13–16), we are told to be circumspect in what we say about the future. And in Acts 12, where Herod boasts, we read of his rapid and public destruction (vv. 21–23).

"speaking ill of their parents." Respect for parents is built into the moral code of the Old Testament being present in the Ten Commandments (failure here is literally blasphemy), but it is also a feature of human cultures across the world (e.g., Confucian Chinese or Native American). This is a logical belief given the importance of transmitting the values and skills of one generation to the next, and it covers the care parents have of their children that, over time, is transmuted into the care children have of their parents. The insulting and mistreatment of parents by their children is a cause of tragedy[8] such that intergenerational rifts are indicative of dysfunctional societies. No wonder, then, that in preparation for the coming of the Messiah, Malachi calls for intergenerational reconciliation (4:6). Any social group that accepts the slandering of parents by children is also a group that gives overdue importance to the fashions and demands of the young.

"disobedient, ungrateful, unholy." This cluster of vices belongs together. Those who are disobedient are likely to be so because they are ungrateful to

---

6. See for instance, Piaget, *Moral Judgement*.
7. Scrooge (Dickens) or Shylock (Shakespeare) or Felix Grandet (Balzac).
8. E.g., Shakespeare's *King Lear*.

the older generation for what it has handed on and consequently likely also to be unholy since, in classical religion, piety included respect for elders. This type of respect also runs through the Pastoral Epistles given that Timothy has earlier been told to respect the elders he is correcting (1 Tim 5:1). "Unholy" implies offending against the "fundamental decencies of life."[9]

3. "hard-hearted, implacable, invidious [slanderous], lacking self-control, savage, uninterested in the good." The next three vices may be centered on family quarrels. "Hard hearted" is the opposite of natural affection, the affection that would normally be expected to occur between family members. It has no sexual connotation and simply refers to the kind of affection that takes place across all cultures and all times between members of the human race.[10] To be lacking this kind of affection is to be unnatural and psychopathic. *Implacable* refers to those who, literally, will not make treaties with others, who are irreconcilable, unable to find any form of peaceful agreement with others and whose inability to conciliate or compromise renders them asocial.

That the vices listed so far are opposites of virtues (and indicated in the Greek by the negating *a* or "alpha privative") has suggested to some commentators a parallel with classical moral diatribes.[11] This may or may not be the case, as is any arrangement of the vices into lists and sublists for rhetorical purposes (as found in Knight[12]), but we have preferred simply to see the vices as they are and agree with those (e.g., Mounce)[13] who tie the list to the Ephesian situation and understand it as being directly applicable to it. This means that, although Paul is speaking of the "last days," he is also speaking of his own times. Indeed, it is possible to understand Paul as referring to a prophecy or prophecies set in the future tense which, because they are applicable to the current situation, shift into the present tense.[14] Our view, however, assumes the "last days" cover centuries rather than the period immediately before the return of Jesus since, if they started on the Day of Pentecost, this must be the case and, consequently, the warnings of perilous immorality can apply at any point in the present age.[15]

---

9. Barclay quoted by Fee, *1 and 2 Timothy, Titus*, 270.

10. It is the opposite of one of the "four loves" identified by C. S. Lewis in *The Four Loves*.

11. Johnson, *Timothy*, 409.

12. Knight, *Pastoral Epistles*, 430.

13. Mounce, *Pastoral Epistles*, 546.

14. Cf. Kelly, *Pastoral Epistles*, 193.

15. Indeed, a narrow view of the Last Days would make many Scriptural texts meaningless.

"Slanderous (*diaboloi*)" moves the focus away from natural or family relationships to other forms of personal interaction. We might think here of the Roman equivalent of internet trolls, those who spend their free time trying to hurt other people with grotesque insults and accusations. Slanderers are not interested in truth or facts but in falsification and misrepresentation. And, when shown to be wrong, they do not apologize.

"lacking self-control, savage, uninterested in the good." "Self-control" is one of the requirements for church leadership (1 Tim 3:2) and one of the fruits of the Spirit (Gal 5:23) but this virtue is entirely lacking in the individuals identified here. Assuming the Ephesian troublemakers are in view, we note their behavior is not only out of anyone else's control but out of their own control as well. "Savage," like a wild animal, untamed. "Uninterested in the good" refers to those who have no concern with morality or with any ethical ideals; the concepts do not enter their vocabulary or their thoughts; they are cynical pragmatists.

4. "traitors, reckless, conceited, loving pleasure rather than God." "Traitors" is the word applied to Judas Iscariot (Luke 6:16) and more widely to those who abandon people in danger.[16] "Reckless" refers to those who are hasty and rash and therefore needlessly impulsive and unreflective. "Conceited" or "puffed up" describes the false teachers in 1 Timothy 6:4. Overseers must not have these qualities (1 Tim 3:6). It is a state of mind rendering the possessor impervious to correction. "Loving pleasure rather than God" speaks of those who are hedonists to a fault. They love pleasure to the point where God is replaced.

5. "maintaining the form of godliness but denying its power." You would think that people full of all these vices would also be completely irreligious and proudly atheistic, but this is not the case. These people wear a cloak of religiosity, maintaining an outward show of piety and religious observance, though they deny the power of religion and in this sense are ceremonialists. This sin goes back to the early history of the nation of Israel when religious feasts and festivals were celebrated while orphans and widows were neglected or downtrodden (Isa 1:14–17), and it may be detected in the Pharisees who keep the letter of the Mosaic law while avoiding justice and mercy (Matt 23:23). It is a sin particularly found among religious people. Indeed, there are those who are contemptuous of evangelicals for being too pious or serious about their faith. On one occasion, one of the authors knew a man who spoke acidly of evangelicals and did everything he could to exclude them from positions of influence in the church but who was later found out to have been a paedophile. "Heart religion" matters. Pentecostals

---

16. LSJ, 1475.

and charismatics can be equally sinful in the opposite direction. They can worship spiritual power without taking any account of character and godliness. Again, one of the authors knew a Pentecostal preacher who committed adultery regularly over a long period of time and who, when his behavior came to light, thought that his "anointing" was sufficient to excuse his obnoxious behavior. The power of God belongs with integrity, and it is this that will make an impact on the next generation.

"You should avoid such people." There are questions to ask about how Timothy can avoid such people if they are so prevalent within society. But the questions become less thorny if Paul is speaking more narrowly about admitting such people to the church.[17] Yet, given that Timothy has been told to show a gracious attitude towards offenders so that he might win them back to the faith (2:25), it is not easy to understand exactly what Timothy is being told to do. The best explanation, following Stott, seems to be that Timothy is being told to avoid "religious sinners."[18] Indeed Towner thinks the people to avoid are those "completely hardened in their opposition."[19] Kelly, taking a slightly different tack, thinks Timothy's personal attitude to individuals can be constructive even if his "official attitude" can register horror.[20]

6. "For among them are those who insinuate themselves into homes and take control of vulnerable women."[21] Having itemized these general vices, Paul now pivots specifically to the false teachers troubling the Ephesian church by saying "for among them are those who . . ." Thus, the vice list speaks to the crisis facing Timothy and throws light on the nefarious activities of the false teachers. They are out to wreak havoc with the women of the church, a circumstance helping to explain Paul's earlier advice to the young widows to remarry (1 Tim 5:14). Nonetheless, the text does not say all the women concerned were widows, and so we can assume many kinds of women, often lacking in the education available to men, were prey to these fraudsters. Paul's sharp words come hot off the page even at this distance: the false teachers "insinuate (*endynontes*) themselves," implying deception and guile, into homes to "take control (*aichmalōtizontes*)" of "vulnerable women," as if capturing a prisoner of war[22]—this is the force of the verb.

---

17. Guthrie, *Pastoral Epistles*, 170.
18. Stott, *1 Timothy & Titus*, 88.
19. Towner, *Timothy and Titus*, 561.
20. Kelly, *Pastoral Epistles*, 195.
21. As noted above, Greek *gýnaikarion*, pl. *gynaikaria*, a pejorative diminutive sometimes translated "idle," "weak," or "silly" women; the exploitative context here suggests the translation "vulnerable."
22. LSJ, 45.

And why are the women vulnerable? Because they are "weighed down by past failings and led on by all sorts of yearnings." We have no idea what these past failings were, but we can deduce these women have not properly grasped the forgiveness available through Christ. Perhaps the women lack confidence and are plagued by a sense of inadequacy and guilt and are therefore susceptible to quack remedies and fashionable fads. If these women have been part of the church, their understanding of the faith must have been deficient. If they have not been part of the church, then they may be on the fringes as members of households that have converted even if they themselves are still in darkness. Whatever the case, these women are vulnerable, and the false teachers are taking advantage of their vulnerability to profit from them. When scandals within the world of Christian TV were exposed, it was often the poor and uneducated who were naively sending in their dollars to keep celebrity preachers in millionaire lifestyles. In the Ephesian situation, the women concerned are "led on by all sorts of yearnings" which several commentators have cautiously equated with, among other things, sexual exploitation.[23]

7. "such women are permanently studying, but under the tutelage of their abusers never coming to a knowledge of the truth." Many commentators think this exploitation was based on the offer of religious instruction by peripatetic teachers working for profit, like those described in Titus 1:10–11: "those who peddle nonsense and deceive souls . . . ruining whole households."[24] The women are being led in studies that never allow the truth to be reached. Indeed, there have been clever-clever believers who think the only thing which is true is that we do not know what is true, an entirely self-defeating proposition they maintain with a straight face.[25]

8. "In the same way that Jannes and Jambres opposed Moses." Just as Paul had turned to the story of Korah in the book of Numbers (2 Tim 2:19), so now he turns to Exodus and the encounter between Moses and Pharaoh's magicians. The Old Testament does not identify them, but postbiblical Jewish literature calls them "Jannes" and "Jambres" with the result that we know of the situation Paul has in mind.[26] The combat between Moses and Pharaoh's magicians proceeds in stages. First, Moses performs a miracle which the magicians can duplicate (Ex 7:10–12). This carries on over several miracles until the Pharaoh's magicians are unable to replicate what Moses

---

23. Fee, *1 and 2 Timothy, Titus*, 274; Mounce, *Pastoral Epistles*, 549.

24. Cf. the accusation against Christian missionaries in Origen, *Cels* 3:55.

25. A position implicitly taken by the "episcopal ghost" in Lewis's *Great Divorce*.

26. E.g., Towner, *Timothy and Titus*, 564; Guthrie, *Pastoral Epistles*, 171; *OTP* 2:427–442.

does (Ex 8:18). The implication here is that the fraudsters attempt to duplicate the results of the gospel with a counterfeit version of salvation.[27] And, just as Pharaoh's magicians fail, so the false teachers will fail (v. 9). Their prescriptions will not deliver the results they promise.

"so these teachers also oppose the truth, corrupted in mind and showing only counterfeit faith (*adokimoi*)." In case it is thought these teachers are to be pitied, Paul speaks plainly. They "oppose the truth" by speaking against it. The cause of this opposition is mental because the opponents are "corrupted in mind," a comment that goes against much of the relativism prominent in today's world. To accuse someone of being "corrupted in mind" and therefore fundamentally wrong and on the wrong path appears intolerant and, indeed, in later Christian history intolerance certainly existed. Yet Paul is speaking here of those who set out to destroy the church with their own myths and fables. After the Russian revolution of 1917, when the Bolsheviks seized power, Lenin was presented as a Christ-like figure and depicted in paintings and posters teaching little children in the same way that the church had depicted Jesus. Lenin became a "red Messiah." The battle for the faith is a battle of the mind because ideas matter, and ideas are expressed in doctrines. "The truth" in the Pastoral Epistles equates with the gospel itself[28] and those who show only a "counterfeit faith" have "failed the test" (*adokimoi*), being the opposite of Timothy himself who is *dokimon* or "approved" (2 Tim 2:15). A faith in the genuine gospel produces fruit which is evidence of its genuineness (Matt 7:16).

9. "But they will not get very far, for their lack of understanding will become evident to all, as it did in the case of those men." Paul is confident the false teachers will not succeed in the end. Their "lack of understanding" will eventually be exposed to public gaze. How and why Paul is confident of ultimate success must rest on his faith in God and his understanding of divine purposes. If the false teachers are parallel to Pharaoh's magicians, and if the gospel message can be compared to the message of liberation brought by Moses, then God will have his way and the religious charlatans supporting today's equivalent of Pharaoh will be routed. What exactly the process will be that leads to the exposure of the trickery of the false teachers is not explained but one might assume their promises of spiritual benefit will turn

---

27. There are scenes in John Bunyan's *Pilgrim's Progress* when Christian goes looking for Mr. Legality who, he has been told by Mr. Worldly Wiseman, "hath skill to cure those that are somewhat crazed in their wits with their burdens." (p.20). Actually, only when Christian comes to the cross does his burden fall off.

28. Mounce, *Pastoral Epistles*, 550.

out to be empty, and those who have been tricked by them will realize their money has been wasted.

It has been said criminals forge bank notes because they know real money has value. In other words, paradoxically, counterfeiters provide evidence of the value of the real thing. The false teachers are like this, but when exposed, "their lack of understanding will become evident to all." This section began by describing the perilous moral conditions of the "last days"—conditions into which the Ephesian situation fits—but instead of ending with a note of fatalism and despair at evils that cannot be remedied, Paul shows from personal experience how to win through.

b. Standing firm and holding on to Scripture (3:10–17)

> But you have faithfully followed my teaching, way of life, purpose, faith, patience, love, and endurance, *and* the persecutions and sufferings that came upon me in Antioch, Iconium and Lystra, *and indeed*, what sort of persecutions I endured, and yet the Lord delivered me from them all. Certainly, all those who want to live in a godly manner in Christ Jesus will be persecuted. But evil people and charlatans will go from bad to worse, deceiving and being deceived. But you, continue in the things which you have learned and come to trust, knowing those who discipled you personally, having known the Holy Scriptures from childhood. These things are able to make you wise for salvation through faith in Christ Jesus. All Scripture is inspired by God and profitable for teaching, for reproof, for correction and for training in righteousness so that the person *dedicated to* God[29] may be well prepared and equipped for every good work. (2 Tim 3:10–17)

Paul now shows Timothy how to negotiate his way through the dangers of his situation and his era. There is a way to succeed against the odds when you feel you are, or actually are, under attack.

10. "But you have faithfully followed my teaching, way of life, purpose, faith, patience, love, and endurance." Paul is going to ask Timothy to think about those early days on the long circular tour of the first missionary journey because it was then Paul learned, and showed others, how to present the gospel to Jewish and gentile audiences and to deal with adulation as well as with covert verbal and overt physical abuse (Acts 13–14).

---

29. Lit. "person of God."

Over the years Timothy had "faithfully followed" what Paul taught. Paul had presented the gospel to Jews and gentiles in two quite different ways. In the first, he had gone into the synagogues and argued from the Scriptures that Christ is the fulfilment of prophetic promises worked out over a period of historical time while to the gentiles, who had no common or inspired scripture, he had argued from the cyclical process of the seasons in the natural world that God provides food for the human race of which he is the creator (Acts 13:16–41; Acts 14:15–17).

"But you," here and in verse 14, contrasts Timothy with others. Others may be going down another path, *but you*, you have a different calling. "*Have faithfully followed*" (*parēkolouthēsas*) speaks of following as a disciple or tracing out an idea. "My teaching": Paul's teaching included not only the message of Christ's death and resurrection but also the implications of justification, of sanctification, of church dynamics powered by the Holy Spirit, of spiritual gifts, of healing, of the end of time, of the relationship between Israel and the gentiles—all the things Paul preached, and which are canonized within the pages of the New Testament. Timothy could have and surely would have asked Paul hard questions about the faith and practical questions about handling complex moral or social issues in the ancient world. What about food sacrificed to idols or the remarriage of widows or the limits of contemporary prophecy? So, yes, Timothy knew Paul's teaching and understood its nuances and implications.

"way of life, purpose, faith": Paul's "way of life" would have stood in marked contrast with that of the false teachers and the charlatans upsetting the Ephesian church. To know Paul's way of life was to know, among other things, how and when he fasted, how and when he prayed, how he studied, how long he preached, what he did about preparing his sermons, how he treated other people, what he did with his money, how much he worked and rested, and how he adapted to Jewish and gentile environments becoming "all things to all people" (1 Cor 9:22).

"Purpose." Elsewhere Paul uses this word to refer to God's overarching intentions (2 Tim 1:9). As a result, Paul's purpose is fundamental to the direction and strategy of his life. He must have prioritized so that, for instance, he always began by trying to reach the Jewish people through their synagogues but, when he was thrown out of them, turned to the gentiles so that his gospel was to "the Jew first" (Rom 1:16). Additionally, his purpose must have led him to aim for the big cities of the Roman Empire—Antioch, Ephesus, Corinth, Thessalonica, and eventually Rome itself—rather than its rural backwaters. His purpose was to bring the lost to Christ, and he had more than one way to do this telling the Corinthians, for instance, that he caught them "by trickery" (2 Cor 12:16). We may say that Paul's purpose, given to him through an encounter with Christ, determined his basic desire to preach the gospel (Acts 22:21). "Woe unto to me if I preach not the gospel" (1 Cor 9:16), he said and later spoke of preaching it all round from Jerusalem to Illyricum (Rom 15:19). What we understand from this is that Paul's life was not disjointed and haphazard but unified by a constant and single purpose.

"Faith." We can read this to imply the faith, the gospel, or as is more fitting to the context here, Paul's own personal faith which would undoubtedly have been exercised in all the many predicaments (imprisonment, shipwreck, arrest, trial) that beset him. He needed faith—an emotional, spiritual, and intellectual confidence in God—to enable him to rise up from his troubles. He speaks of being brought to the point of despair until he reached total reliance on God (2 Cor 1:8–10).

"patience, love, and endurance." Although Paul may appear to be drawing unnecessary attention to himself, he does so "without the least suggestion of egotism"[30] and almost in a detached and objective sense as he faces the conclusion of his earthly life. Patience speaks of forbearance towards others and a willingness to wait rather than complain that nothing is happening. We think of Paul as an active man full of zeal and passion, but he was also willing to put up with inconvenience and discomfort. "Endurance" is that quality of the marathon athlete or Olympic oarsman who has the stamina to keep going for long periods of time without collapsing. It is an ability that can be developed with training and by gradually building up one's capacity. And these two qualities coexist with "love" and are enabled by it. Because he loved, he was patient; because he loved, he endured.

11. "and the persecutions and sufferings that came upon me in Antioch, Iconium and Lystra." In this reference to these three cities of Asia Minor, we are fortunate in having Luke's account in Acts to fill out our knowledge. In the first city, Paul preaches in the synagogue successfully so that many Jews and gentiles were converted, but after initial success, the opposition organizes itself, pulls political strings, and stirs up persecution against Paul and Barnabas, and so drives them out. While no violence is recorded here, the threat of violence is evident, and Paul and Barnabas have no option but to leave, and they do so with their honor intact and shake the dust from their feet to indicate the Jewish people of the city should no longer be seen as the true Israel.[31] At Iconium, the mission starts well but runs into trouble after a great number of believers, both Jews and gentiles, have been secured. We are told unbelieving Jews stirred up the gentiles which must mean they

---

30. Guthrie, *Pastoral Epistles*, 173.
31. Keener, *Background Commentary*, 361.

agitated them, perhaps by alleging treachery against Caesar (which after all was the tactic against Jesus), and "poisoned their minds" (RSV, NIV). This surely suggests slanderous and unfounded accusations as well as dark hints and perhaps conspiracy theories. Not so different, then, from our current rampant social media age! The apostles rebut the verbal campaign against them and miracles are performed to validate the gospel message (Acts 14:3). Nevertheless, the opposition, having failed with rational argument, now resorts to the threat of violence. Paul and Barnabas are forced to flee, and they go to Lystra, about twenty-five miles away.[32] Again everything begins well, and at least one miracle occurs, but eventually a Jewish delegation from Antioch and Iconium arrives, and this time persuades the people to stone Paul (Acts 14:19). This is not a judicial matter but is mob violence and was a recognized method of killing people—similar to a lynch mob in the USA—since the murder could not be pinned on any single individual. Paul is knocked unconscious, and his apparently dead body is dragged outside the city as if he is a piece of refuse (Acts 14:19).

The believers gather round Paul, presumably to pray, and he gets up and with great courage re-enters the city which has been so unjustly harmed him (Acts 14:20). The recovery of Paul is evidently intended to demonstrate the miraculous power of God and Paul's re-entrance to the hostile city is indicative not only of his legal right to do so but of his concern for the believers who remain there.

When Paul speaks of "the persecutions and sufferings" he endured, his language is precise. "Persecutions (*diōgmois*)" came from frontal verbal attacks as well as the poisoning of minds against him and his "sufferings (*pathēmasin*)" were both psychological and physical. He was persecuted for righteousness' sake in ways Jesus spoke about in the gospels (Matt 5:10). There was no reason to pick up stones against him or to speak against him, and the more honorable course of action would have been to debate with him publicly (as the Athenians did, Acts 17:17), but these cities chose the lower and more underhanded way of trying to block the gospel.

"and yet the Lord delivered (*errysato*) me from them all." Extraordinarily Paul "is delivered" from all these persecutions and sufferings even though he passed through them (cf. Ps 34:19, which is perhaps cited).[33] He is delivered in the sense that he is rescued out of them and recovers and is able to continue and whatever sufferings he receives in body and mind are

---

32. Keener, *Background Commentary*, 362.

33. Fee, *1 and 2 Timothy, Titus*, 277. Or possibly Ps 33:20, cf. Knight, *Pastoral Epistles*, 440.

healed.[34] There is no evidence that he suffered any continued ill effects from the stoning though, as he said, he carried in his body the marks of the Lord Jesus (Gal 6:17), presumably the scars, to his dying day. Some commentators wonder about Paul's citation of his early troubles on that first missionary journey on the grounds that Paul could have referred to the dangers of his later years, but when we consider Timothy and his family were natives of Lystra, it makes sense to refer to this early baptism of fire as something that would have been real to the young man even though he did not start to accompany Paul until the second missionary journey.[35] Timothy would have found out all about the stoning of Paul (he would have known the Christians who gathered round Paul's unconscious body) and would have pieced together the escalating events that led from opposition to persecution.

12. "Certainly all those who want to live in a godly manner (*eusebōs*) in Christ Jesus will be persecuted." Paul now generalizes from his own experience to all Christians though there is an exegetical decision to be made about this sentence because it can be read as applying to all Christians without exception or only to Christians who live "in a godly manner." It is probably best to apply it to *eusebōs* and thus specifically to Christian piety.[36] Pentecostal and charismatics should underline the whole sentence and note how it explodes the idea of perpetual prosperity as a mark of the Christian life. Paul does not say *all* Christians *all* the time will suffer persecution, but he does warn of sporadic persecution directed against the godly. Paul's Ephesian preaching causes a slump in the silversmith trade because new Christians no longer want to buy little silver idols (Acts 19:24-27). Where revivals take place, the sale of alcohol will drop, cinemas and theatres may find attendance decline and nightclubs may close. By way of reaction, commercial interests will stir up anti-Christian sentiment. And it can be worse than this when Christians are perceived to be void of patriotism. By refusing to offer worship to Caesar, Christians were thought to be threatening the unity of the empire. The violence of the state was then turned against them. Nevertheless, one of the tasks of the church is to stand against wrongdoing throughout society even where this is endorsed by fashionable celebrities or vociferous and angry activists.

13. "But evil people and charlatans (*goētes*) will go from bad to worse, deceiving and being deceived." In keeping with the earlier eschatological

---

34. According to LSJ, 694, *ruomai* has a range of meanings including "deliver," "shield," "guard," "protect," "hold back," "free" and even "heal" or "cure."

35. Mounce gives no fewer than eight reasons why Paul chose to cite the experiences in Antioch, Iconium, and Lystra rather than others, (*Pastoral Epistles*, 558).

36. Mounce, *Pastoral Epistles*, 560.

warnings of societal deterioration, Timothy is warned evil people and charlatans (*goētes*) will become progressively worse. The word for *charlatan* can also be used for "sorcerer" potentially linking it to Jannes and Jambres in v. 8 and showing how Paul continues to have the Ephesian situation in mind. The consequence of deceiving others is a predisposition to be deceived oneself. Eventually all notion of truth is lost, and there is no way back for those who lose the capacity to distinguish good and bad, right from wrong. One of the terrible consequences of lying is the devaluation of all communication. As MacIntyre aptly notes: "a lie violates a duty to oneself and to others, because rational beings owe each other truthfulness."[37]

14–15. "But you, continue in the things which you have learned and come to trust, knowing those who discipled you personally." Again, the words, "but you," demand Timothy sharply distinguishes himself from the people in the previous verse. Essentially Timothy is being told to remain firmly connected with Scripture and with the people who taught it to him from childhood. We can identify two principles in these two verses: first trust people of integrity, and second trust Scripture. In keeping with the first principle, we should ask: is the information we are receiving given by faithful and trustworthy people or, to put this another way, what is the moral integrity of the people to whom we listen and who have gained our trust? The character of the giver of information is a crucial test of the information itself. In the case of Timothy, he had learned to trust his mother and grandmother, presumably over many years, and had no reason to doubt either their integrity or love.[38] The second principle regarding the Scripture itself is also crucial and will receive amplification below.

There is always a tendency to rush after new things and therefore to ditch all that is old and unfashionable. The instruction to Timothy is to "continue in" or remain in what he has already learned and come to "trust" and therefore to retain the body of knowledge he had already personally tested. Timothy is assumed to be a reflective person, one who ponders the past and evaluates what he finds. The interesting thing here for Pentecostals and charismatics is Timothy is not being encouraged to seek one new revelation after another but rather to sift his accumulated experience and then rely on the conclusions he reaches. All this draws attention to the inestimable value of a Christian home where Christian parents introduce their children to Scripture.

---

37. See MacIntyre, "Lying," 515.

38. It is possible that Paul, because of the plurality of "*those who*," also has himself in mind here as one of Timothy's Scripture teachers.

15. "having known the Holy Scriptures (*hiera grammata*) from childhood (*apo brephous*[39])." We assume Timothy's family had scrolls at home from which he read or learned to read. As for the Bible, we do not know whether he had access to a Hebrew text or the Greek translation of the Hebrew made in the mid-third century BC and called the Septuagint (or LXX), although the latter is more likely, but, whichever version, what matters is that he engaged with Scripture from a young age and *knew* it, that is, was well informed about the detail of its content and its various genres.[40] The term *hiera grammata* without the definite article was the "stock designation" for the Old Testament in "Greek-speaking Judaism (cf. Philo and Josephus)";[41] it is possible there is an implication here of "a course of religious instruction for which Scripture would be the student's principal text."[42]

"These things are able to make you wise for salvation through faith in Christ Jesus." The "these things" may include the instruction in the gospel Timothy received from others ("those who discipled you personally") in addition to his long-standing knowledge of the Scriptures. Nevertheless, it does not make sense to try to separate knowledge of Scripture from the other kinds of religious instruction Timothy may have received as if one would operate without the other. The Scriptures are precious because they contain practical divine wisdom in the sense that they reveal how "salvation" is found through faith in Christ. "These things are able to . . .": the present tense conveying their continuing effectiveness. Kelly writes, "the key to Scripture is Christ, and it can say nothing to men until they have accepted him as Savior and Lord."[43] Many evangelicals will gladly testify that Scripture came alive to them once they found Christ. The vitality of the church and the vital study of Scripture belong together, and each enhances the other. Conversely, if once any church loses its grip on Scripture and seeks to

---

39. Or "earliest childhood" (Johnson, *Timothy*, 419).

40. Mounce says "since the time frame is Timothy's childhood, it supposedly would have been the Hebrew Scriptures that played a vital role in Timothy's upbringing, even in the non-traditional household of a Jewish mother and a Greek father" (*Pastoral Epistles*, 563). However, Wall and Steele write "According to 2 Timothy 3:14–17, the future of Paul's apostolate depended on Timothy's recognition that God inspires a *particular* holy text, the LXX [Septuagint], for teaching and training . . ." (original italics) (*1 and 2 Timothy and Titus*, loc 6368). The Septuagint includes apocryphal writings, and this therefore has a bearing on the extent of the canon.

41. Kelly, *Pastoral Epistles*, 201. See also Johnson, *Timothy*, 419, for a fuller list of citations.

42. Wall and Steele, *1 and 2 Timothy and Titus*, loc 6261.

43. Kelly, *Pastoral Epistles*, 202.

present itself only as a humanitarian organization or an ancient repository of ecclesial tradition, its days will be numbered.

16. "All Scripture (*pasa graphē*) is inspired by God (*theopneustos*)." These and similar words have been central to twentieth century debates about the authority of Scripture as they are reflected in battles between liberals and fundamentalists.[44] Pentecostals, and often charismatics, though they have certainly tended to conservative understandings of the nature of Scripture, have not generally been party to liberal-fundamentalist controversies. Pentecostals, by emphasizing the power and role of the Holy Spirit, have a natural predisposition to understand the Spirit's connection with divine speech. For this reason, Pentecostals and charismatics have probably found it easier to believe in the inspiration of Scripture than others: they believe their experience of the Spirit is similar to that of Israel's prophets or the Christians of the NT. This is because the Spirit is intimately connected with speaking in tongues and prophecy. Indeed, many Pentecostals would feel a kinship with the whole prophetic stream within the polity of ancient Israel. To hear the "word of the Lord" by revelation from the Spirit and then to declare it with power would be hallmarks of Pentecostalism at its best. In short, Pentecostals have a natural affinity with the concept of divine utterance.[45]

The obvious activity of the Holy Spirit in the New Testament church together with the presence of apostles who had seen the risen Christ led naturally to the production of text that came to be understood as Scripture in the same sense as the Old Testament itself. There are already indications of this when in the same verse a Deuteronomic text and a saying of Jesus found in Luke 10:7 are both called "Scripture" (1 Tim 5:18). Most tellingly Peter brackets Paul's writings with other "Scriptures" (2 Pet 3:15–16).

Their importance in twentieth century debates on inerrancy is reflected by some scholars who translate these words "every inspired scripture is

---

44. Packer, *Fundamentalism*, 77. See also Bebbington and Jones, eds., *Evangelicalism and Fundamentalism*, and Kay's "Pentecostalism and fundamentalism," 309–27. Kay's survey of Pentecostal ministers found only 71 percent believed the Bible contained no verbal errors while over 99 percent believed the Bible to be the infallible word of God; inerrancy and infallibility are therefore differentiated by these ministers.

45. On the other hand, a small number of Pentecostals toppled into the error of assuming Spirit-filled utterances given in their congregations had the same status as Scripture itself. By the 1920s, in Britain at any rate, the great majority of Pentecostal leaders noted the requirement to test and evaluate charismatic utterances (1 Cor 14:29; 1 Thess 5:21). This requirement could only imply the fallibility of charismatic utterances which should *not* therefore be raised to the same level as Scripture.

. . ." and in this way to draw a distinction between inspired and uninspired writings.[46] By way of rebuttal others have pointed to the many times in the NT where *graphē* (a word that literally means "writings") clearly and obviously refers to the OT canon (Rom 4:3; 1 Cor 15:3-4, Gal 3:8, Jas 2:23; 1 Pet 2:6, etc.). As a linguistic parallel, although the English word "scripture" can simply denote "what is written," it now carries an almost technical meaning with the result that, unless qualified by another adjective, it refers to the sacred texts of Christianity. So here, *pasa graphē* refers to the whole of Scripture or all its parts or every Scripture.

But what of *theopneustos*? Also pressed into debate on the nature of Scripture is the question of whether *theopneustos* (literally "God-breathed") is attributive or predicative. If the former, the sentence begins, "All God-breathed scripture . . ."; if the latter, "All Scripture is God-breathed . . ." Together with the majority of commentators and for a variety of reasons, we think the second option is correct. For instance, in the absence of a verb in the Greek, it is natural to construe the several words that follow *all Scripture* in the same way, and thus the sentence continues, " . . . is God-breathed and [is] profitable"; additionally, the sentence is constructed like 1 Tim 4:4 where the adjective "good" is obviously predicative; moreover, if *theopneustos* were attributive we would expect it to be placed before *pasa graphē*.[47] Second, *theopneustos* translates as *inspired by God* because this is a transfer of the words from Greek to Latin and from Latin to English (spiro being the Latin for "I breathe"). Once this has been established, we can attribute the origin of the words of Scripture to God because God breathes or inspires them, and they are indeed the "word of God" (1 Tim 4:5).[48]

It has been objected that Timothy does not need to be reminded that Scripture is inspired because he already believes it; but this is to miss the point that the false teachers are propagating doctrines originating with demons (1 Tim 4:1) and possibly using supportive non-biblical texts. It matters very much that Timothy is dealing with divinely inspired Scripture, and it follows Paul's words here can indeed be building blocks for a doctrine of Scripture itself.

46. Barrett, *Pastoral Epistles*, 114; see also NEB.

47. Knight, *Pastoral Epistles*, 446, 447; Kelly, *Pastoral Epistles*, 203.

48. In this reading, the word "all" assumes a special significance. Given that the later Marcionite heretics would reject a large part of the canon, including the whole of the Old Testament and three of our four gospels, this may be meant very literally. Today, we often neglect parts of Scripture that we find difficult or "boring," but Paul may be reminding us that God has breathed into it *all*, and, as he goes on to emphasize, all of it is *useful*.

"and profitable for teaching, for reproof, for correction and for training in righteousness." The main multi-purpose tool available to Timothy is the Scripture. This is not in any way to neglect the Spirit since the Spirit is implicitly present in the God-breathed or inspired word. Indeed, just as the word of God is the "sword of the Spirit" (Gal 6:17)—the cutting implement wielded by the Spirit—so we and Timothy may expect the Spirit to assist in the deployment of the instructional texts for the task in hand. The word of God is "profitable" or advantageous for "teaching." It is the curriculum of what is taught, and when handled well, directs, refreshes, and nurtures the church (as shown by 1 Cor 3:6, with reference to the ministry of Apollos the teacher). Preachers of all kinds have been found wanting when they spend their time in the pulpit talking about themselves rather than talking about the Scripture, the word of God, which it is their duty to present. "We preach not ourselves" (2 Cor 4:5), states Paul. How many boring sermons have we sat through while the preacher tells us all about his own problems and neglects to unfurl the treasures of Scripture? Because teaching may cover doctrine, ethics, encouragement, history, prayer, hope, warning, and so on, it may also deliver "reproof." "Reproof" is not condemnation and need not be delivered as a rant or, indeed, from the pulpit, and it may be given in the form of measured argument or refutation.[49] "Correction" is "most likely with reference to conduct."[50]

And lastly the Scripture is intended for "training in righteousness." Training may involve discipline as well as tuition and is the ordinary Greek word covering the educational process. Training may form character in addition to the cognitive or intellectual aspect of learning. And the aim and purpose of the education envisaged here is summarized in one word: "righteousness," which results, verse 17, in "well prepared people equipped for every good work." In short, integrity of character born of healthy scriptural teaching will result in a variety of good deeds.

---

49. LSJ, 530.
50. Knight, *Pastoral Epistles*, 449.

> IV. PAUL UNBOWED
>
> a. Final charge to Timothy (4:1–5)
>
> b. Paul faces death and anticipates glory (4:6–8)
>
> c. A round-up of news with a warning and requests (4:9–15)
>
> d. Fulfilling his ministry in court (4:16–18)
>
> e. Greetings, information, and hope for a final meeting (4:19–22)

IV. PAUL UNBOWED

This chapter is the last one Paul ever wrote, and it shows him to be fervent, realistic, and determined. He does everything he can to ensure Timothy will continue the trajectory of evangelical ministry while drawing attention to his own public defense of the gospel—a defense that is the culmination and fulfilment of his own calling—in a Roman court.

a. Final charge to Timothy (4:1–5)

> I solemnly charge you before God and Christ Jesus, who is going to judge the living and the dead, and by his appearing and his kingdom, preach the word, be ready in season *and* out of season, refute[1], rebuke, *and* exhort with all patience and instruction. For there will be a time when people will not bear with sound teaching, *but* with itching ears will draw teachers to themselves who will pander to their own predilections and will turn away from hearing the truth and give their attention to myths[2]. But you, be self-controlled in all things, bear up in suffering, do the work of an evangelist, and fulfill your ministry. (2 Tim 4:1–5)

1. "I solemnly charge (*Diamartyromai*) you before (*enōpion*) God and Christ Jesus." In the light of his own impending death and repeating words and sentiments found elsewhere in the epistle (2 Tim 2:14), Paul "charges" or "admonishes" or "adjures" Timothy by employing a word possibly signifying

---

1. Or possibly "examine," "test," "expose," or "reprove."

2. Cf. 1 Tim 1:3–7, Titus 1:14. These are most likely not Greek myths, but Jewish ones appearing in midrashic speculations about some of the more obscure stories in the Hebrew Bible, as suggested by Mounce (*Pastoral Epistles*, 576).

the formal transfer of office.³ There is no doubting the solemnity and weight of the words written by Paul. These come with the full force of apostolic authority and are spoken before God and Christ or, in some translations, in the "sight of" or in the "presence of" God. Thus, the charge is given with divine witnesses to it and all this despite the fact that Timothy is in Ephesus and Paul is in Rome, that Paul is in prison and Timothy at liberty. None of that makes any difference to the context of the charge which looks beyond the stone prison walls to tremendous future events affirmed in Scripture.

"who is going to judge the living and the dead." The reference to Jesus as the judge of the living and the dead repeats Paul's declaration at the Areopagus (Acts 17:31; see also Acts 10:42). As others have pointed out, Jesus is a fitting judge of the human race because of the Incarnation, because he became human, and so understands the human condition intimately and not from a privileged position. Instead, his life-experience is as a member of a people who had long been oppressed and whose country was occupied by a foreign power. Like his fellow Jews, Jesus experienced discrimination, exploitation, and ethnic intolerance. Indeed, the patron of Pontius Pilate in Rome, Sejanus, was a noted anti-Semite.⁴ Jesus will judge both the living (who are alive when he comes, 1 Thess 4:17) and the dead (who will be raised for the purpose). This climactic point in history will arrive, according to Paul, on a day God "has already appointed," and therefore is certain, future, and fixed, and the judgement will be "righteous" (Acts 17:31) and therefore not arbitrary, impatient, or casual. Human history is inexorably being carried to this point and is not going round in circles (as eastern religions aver) or going to fizzle out in the extinction of the solar system (as philosophers like Bertrand Russell thought).⁵ "And by his appearing and his kingdom": these words, in what is an awkward Greek construction, add the Second Coming of Christ and his "kingdom" as reasons and incentives to carry out what the charge requires.⁶ By putting together the "appearing" of Christ (cf. 2 Thess 2:8; 1 Tim 6:14) with his "kingdom" the future reality of the kingdom is implied. It is both present *and* future, now and hereafter, and in this truth many troubling theological puzzles are answered, especially those concerned with healing, or its lack, and bereavement. Both George Jeffreys and John Wimber understood this tension.⁷

3. Mounce, *Pastoral Epistles*, 572.
4. Lucius Aelius Sejanus (ca.20 BC—AD 31), discussed by Bird, "L. Aelius Seianus."
5. Russell, "A Free Man's Worship," 47–48.
6. Knight, *Pastoral Epistles*, 452.
7. Kay, *George Jeffreys*, 229; Wimber, *Power Healing*.

2. "preach the word (*kēryxon ton logon*)." After this intense and solemn build-up to the "charge," we might be left wondering what it is that is so important for Timothy to do. The answer is so apparently simple. He is to "preach the word," which here must include pre-eminently the gospel[8] but also the wider text of Scripture as it bears on the mission of Christ. To "preach the word," as he has already pointed out (2 Tim 3:16), is to exercise a ministry with several aspects and dimensions. In the first place, not for nothing did Paul, in his parting address, commend the Ephesian elders to the "word of his grace" (NIV) as an antidote to the divisions and doctrinal challenges they would surely face (Acts 20:32). In an age of snappy sermons and short attention spans, Pentecostals and charismatics have bucked the trend by being willing to preach at length. The length of the sermon is, of course, no guarantee of quality: what ensures quality is accurate explanation of the text of Scripture by a preacher for whom it is an experiential reality, and such a reality is pressed home by the Holy Spirit whose presence constitutes "the anointing" (1 John 2:27).

"be ready (*epistēthi*) in season and out of season." Timothy is to "be ready," or "be on hand," "be at his task" at all times, "in season and out of season," whether he feels like it or not. Or, if the following verses determine the meaning, if the hearers feel like it or not. In short, Timothy is to continue preaching and not, as it were, to hold back waiting for what seems like a more convenient or propitious time. Preaching is not an optional extra to church ministry but a central part of it. So how is Timothy to preach? First, he is to "refute" (*elenxon*). Refutation is different from denial since the refuting of a person demands a train of logical reasoning and argument. To deny is to contradict, whereas to refute is to provide argument against. So, we can read Paul as telling Timothy to rebut the arguments of the false teachers and those who come against the gospel. But *elenxon* can also be translated as "confront" which suggests Timothy is to be bold and even outspoken in what he says. In Matthew 18:15, *elenxon* is used in the context of trying to repair a breach between Christians: "go *and show him his fault* in private" and in John 16:8 of the power of the Holy Spirit to convict the world of sin. This strong word describes preaching which will change the attitudes and behavior of listeners.

Second, he is to "rebuke (*epitimēson*)" or give a verbal "telling off." This is not the kind of preaching we like to be at the receiving end of! Yet sometimes it is necessary and can lead to repentance (2 Cor 7:10). In the Ephesian situation strong words were required, and if we see a sequence here, refutation or rebuttal would come before rebuke.

---

8. Mounce, *Pastoral Epistles*, 572.

Third, "exhort (*parakaleson*)" or as it is translated elsewhere "comfort" or "encourage" (2 Cor 1:4; 1 Thess 4:18; 5:11). An early commentator found a medical analogy here: after showing the wound (refuting), the physician makes the incision (rebuking), and then applies the plaster (exhorting).[9] Or, in another view, the preacher's threefold appeal is to reason (refuting), conscience (rebuking) and will (exhorting).[10] The preacher's intention is not to knock people down permanently but ultimately to lift them up.

"with all patience and instruction." Preaching is a continuous flow of words and there is always the danger of being carried away by loquacity. Whatever the mood and mode of preaching, Timothy is to remain patient—which may require explaining himself repeatedly—in all his instruction. The "all" qualifies both the patience and the instruction.

3. "For there will be a time when people will not bear (*anexontai*) with sound (*hygiainousēs*) teaching." One of the prime reasons for the charge given to Timothy is now set out. The link between this verse and the two before it hinges on the word "For." Timothy is to take every opportunity to preach the truth because a time will come when people will not listen. We can read these words as a warning to the Ephesian congregation against a wave of gnostic teaching that will sweep through the city in the future, or we can put Paul's warning in the light of his earlier eschatological forebodings of a widespread period of defection (2 Tim 3:1–9). Either way there is trouble brewing and Timothy should take advantage of the present moment.

The reference to "sound (*hygiainousēs*) teaching" is a familiar one—picking up the health metaphor from chapter 1 (vv. 13–14) because "sound" means healthy. What is added is the word "bear" with the meaning "tolerate"; the social and moral cost of holding onto sound doctrine will become a price people are unwilling to pay. Earlier in the epistle false teachers were castigated (1 Tim 1:3, 4, 7) but this latter warning concerns the people themselves who "with itching ears will draw teachers to themselves who will pander to their own predilections." The itching ears speak of a desire for spicy novelty, a dilettantish curiosity.[11] Populist preachers and teachers, by pandering to fads and fashions, will leave their people bereft of divine revelation.

4. "and will turn away from hearing the truth and give their attention to myths." Instead of the historical and doctrinal substance of the gospel, the content of this populist preaching will turn to "myths" (cf. 1 Tim 4:7). By their very nature myths can never be verified but instead become poetic

---

9. John Chrysostom, *Hom.* 9 on 2 Tim 4:2.

10. Kelly, *Pastoral Epistles*, 206.

11. Fee, *1 and 2 Timothy, Titus,* 286 quoting BDAG, 550.

stories much as the classical tales of gods and goddesses did in ancient times. The myths play on universal themes of the human condition, even as they vary from culture to culture, but they give faith nothing secure on which to build. Hearers of these populist preachers follow a two-stage process: first a "turning away from" and then a "giving attention to." To turn away from the truth involves a rejection of the historical evidence for the life, ministry, crucifixion, and resurrection of Jesus.[12] It also often involves rejecting the testimony of the Old Testament to Israel's history and the messianic theme running through it.

5. "But you," switches to Timothy and tells him to stand out against others and be different. He is to "be self-controlled (*nēphe*) in all things" or sober in all circumstances, or to put this another way, he is not to become wild and unreasoning in an effort to make his hearers see sense. This instruction is in line with what has already been said about the patient way the servant of God (2 Tim 2:24) should act despite provocation and opposition. "Suffering" may follow, but he is to "bear up" by enduring it as part of his job and calling.

More than this he is to "do the work of an evangelist." Alongside his patient teaching ministry aimed to restore the church to gospel doctrine, Timothy is to work as an evangelist. We only have one example of an evangelist identified as such in Acts and this is Philip. We note Phillip's preaching to a city or geographical area and the impact he makes upon it (Acts 8; 21:8). We note his ability to preach Christ and to bring new believers to faith followed by water baptism, but we also note he requires assistance from Peter and John in the big Jerusalem church, and they come down to complete the task and establish the Samaritans in the power of the Holy Spirit. The evangelist introduces men and women and boys and girls to Christ but does not claim to be able to teach all they need to know. Essentially, the evangelist is a person of only one message although this message can be preached from almost any starting point. An evangelist has the ability in meeting after meeting to present Christ and his saving power, and even if he stays for several weeks in one place, he is constantly renewed to preach his message with passion and conviction. It is marvelous to see a real evangelist at work bringing hearers to a point of decision. And, in the case of Philip, we note that after he has stirred the city of Samaria, he is called to bring the gospel to a single individual, the Ethiopian treasurer. Whether to fervent crowds or solitary individuals, the true evangelist has the gift of communicating Christ convincingly.

This passage does not say that Timothy was a natural evangelist and that this was his true gift but rather that he is "to do the work of an evangelist"

---

12. See for instance, Bauckham, *Jesus and the Eyewitnesses*.

or to adapt himself to gospel ministry whereby he would bring new believers into the church. While the teacher can function as an evangelist, the evangelist struggles to function as a teacher. Thus, Timothy is given a double commission: he is to speak into the church and correct its false teachers and its wayward congregation, and he is to speak outside the church to win unbelievers. Timothy's natural ministry is surely found in his ability to teach (which is why he co-authors epistles with Paul and is the right man to tackle the doctrinal problems in Ephesus), but he must also reach out beyond the church community into secular society. By preaching in this comprehensive way, he is to "fulfill" his "ministry" and discharge all the duties of his calling.

The conventional evangelist preaches a gospel message and then seeks a commitment to Christ from his or her hearers, but the Pentecostal evangelist does more than this.[13] In addition to calling for salvation, the Pentecostal evangelist will normally pray for those who are ill sometimes after the call for salvation and sometimes simultaneously with it. Pentecostal evangelists may therefore preach a message of healing in addition to, or mixed in with, their message of salvation. When Paul went to a new place and preached the gospel, he often healed the sick and sometimes did so in the middle of his preaching (Acts 14:8–10), and we must assume Timothy's mode of evangelism would have been similar. Healing outside the church validates the gospel message (Mark 16:20), and in this sense, proceeds on a different theological basis from healing inside the church (Jas 5:14–16).

b. Paul faces death and anticipates glory (4:6–8)

> For I am already being poured out like a drink offering and the time of my departure is at hand. I have fought the good fight. I have finished the race. I have kept the faith. From here on, there is reserved for me the crown of righteousness that the Lord, who judges justly, will give to me on that day—not only to me, but to all those who have loved his appearing. (2 Tim 4:6–8)

Having prepared and encouraged Timothy for future ministry, Paul speaks about his own impending death. Readers now understand the urgency of the commission to Timothy; Paul has not much time left.

6. "For I (*egō gar*) am already (*ēdē*) being poured out like a drink offering (*spendomai*)." After the "but you" of the previous verse, we read "for I" as the focus moves to Paul himself who describes his life as "being poured

---

13. Compare Graham, *Just as I Am*, and Harrell, *Oral Roberts*.

out" in the same way wine was poured out in some OT sacrifices (Ex 29:40; Num 28:7).[14] He has already used the same metaphor and the same word in Philippians 2:17. But what does this tell us about the way Paul thinks of his impending death? It surely shows he conceives of himself as following in Christ's footsteps, though without any sense that his death is an atonement for his or others' sins. Though Paul regards his death as a sacrifice the emphasis is on its value and purpose, as the next few verses will show. There are no regrets or recriminations here, no fear of pain or indignity and no sense of a wasted life. He is "already" (*ēdē*) being "poured out" and thus conceives of this final phase of imprisonment, which is presumably extremely unpleasant, as the start of the extended sacrificial process.

"and the time of my departure (*analyseōs*) is at hand." An *analẏsis* often speaks of a ship loosing its moorings and setting out on a voyage or travelers or soldiers packing up their camps ready to move on. We infer that Paul thinks of his execution as a point of *departure* on a journey. His life is not, as atheists and secularists believe, extinguished to nothingness on death, but on the contrary, his existence will continue, and he is setting out to meet Jesus.

7. Paul now makes three simple and powerful statements summing up his life. "I have fought the good fight." The allusion here may be more athletic than military (following 2 Tim 2:5) although both would apply and are apt metaphors for the intense spiritual, social, religious, and cultural struggle which has occupied him since conversion. The *fight* itself is good, supremely worthwhile, and deserving of all his talent and energy. Paul does not commend his own performance but rather speaks of the nobility of the cause itself.

"I have finished the race (*dromon*)" means he has reached the stadium's finishing line in what has been a marathon rather than a sprint, a course (the literal meaning of *dromon*) requiring endurance and all the discipline of an athlete. And it is *the* race, the one Timothy and every Christian is also competing in, and in which, as individuals, we run. The good fight may be a collective activity alongside colleagues and comrades, but "the race" is solo even if there is a baton to pass on to the next generation.

"I have kept the faith" could mean, in an objective sense, "I held on to the faith, the glorious gospel that was entrusted to me". But the same phase is found in secular contexts meaning "to be loyal to one's oath" and so, if intended here by Paul, would bring out his personal faithfulness to Christ more than preserving the content of the gospel itself. Either way,

---

14. As Kelly, *Pastoral Epistles*, points out, 2 Tim 4:6 and the LXX use the same Greek verb or a related noun. The link with OT sacrifice is not only conceptual but verbal. Note the use of sacrificial language also in Rom 15:16.

and probably both ways, Paul is reaching the end without reneging on his original commitment or changing and losing the gospel. The "fight," the "race," and the "faith" are all purposeful activities brought victoriously to completion. Roman skeptics might only see a foolish and obstinate old man ending his days in a cold and miserable jail, but those skeptics would be astonished to discover that nearly two thousand years later the writings of that old man and his inspiring example are still a source of hope and inestimable value. Readers may bear "in mind T. R. Glover's comment on the Roman Emperor's condemnation of the Apostle to the gentiles—that the day was to come when men would call their dogs Nero and their sons Paul."[15]

8. "From here on, there is reserved for me the crown of righteousness." Greek athletics awarded winners laurel garlands as a sign of victory, and the custom was transferred across to the Roman military realm. There are pictures of Julius Caesar wearing a laurel wreath after subduing the tribes of Gaul and the peoples of Egypt.[16] The laurel was chosen because it did not easily fade and wither even though it did not have intrinsic worth, as it would have done had it been made of precious metal. The point of the laurel crown was to distinguish the winner from all others, and it was coveted for this reason. When Paul speaks of a crown of righteousness, he is making a comparison with the great athletic and military events of his own era. Paul here speaks of a "crown of righteousness" that is "reserved" for him. Commentators have discussed whether this is a crown somehow *made* of righteousness or awarded *for* righteousness. If it is "made" of righteousness this would speak of the final blessed state in heaven when righteousness is completed. But this interpretation seems unlike Paul who, throughout his ministry, insisted righteousness is granted here and now in this life for those who are justified by faith. So, it is better to read the crown as given to signify righteousness and to understand the term to include integrity and uprightness as well as the righteousness that comes by faith. Paul is not saying he will receive a special crown in recognition of the extraordinary success of his apostolic labors because in the same sentence he says this crown is given "to all who love Christ's appearing." Moreover, elsewhere in the NT, there is reference to other crowns being awarded to Christians for service. For instance, there is a "crown of glory" given to those have faithfully completed all the duties and challenges of pastoral work (1 Pet 5:1–4) and a "crown of life" for those who come through tests and temptations (Jas 1:12). In each case the crown indicates Christ's recognition of a type of service rendered by

---

15. Taken from the flyleaf of Bruce, *Paul*.
16. Illustrated Curiosity, "Wreath."

his people. And at the end, the crowns are thrown down before the throne of God as an act of worship (Rev 4:10).

"that the Lord, who judges justly, will give to me on that day." The declaration is solemn, joyful, and poignant all at the same time. The Christ who suffered human injustice at his trial and crucifixion asked many of the first generation of his followers to walk the same path. Paul confidently expects to see Christ himself "on that day," the Day of Judgement (2 Tim 4:1), and to receive his reward from Christ's own hand. There is a higher justice above Nero or, indeed, all earthly justice. The wronged and downtrodden Christian can look for restitution in another world; and many of us could not endure the human condition unless we believed that. "The Lord," indeed, "judges justly" seeing to the depths of every human being (1 Sam 16:7; Luke 12:3; Ps 139).

"all those who have loved (*ēgapēkosi*) his appearing (*epiphaneian*)" refers to all who eagerly look forward to the Second Coming of Christ which also implies (because *epiphaneian* was a term applied to visitation by the Emperor) that the imperial regime will be judged and found wanting.[17] Consequently, to say "I look forward to the Second Coming" is to make a political statement as much as a religious statement.

c. A round-up of news with a warning and requests (4:9–15)

> Hurry and come to me quickly. For Demas has deserted me because he loved the present age and went off to Thessalonica; Crescens *went* to Galatia and Titus *went* to Dalmatia. Only Luke is with me. Take Mark and bring him with you, for he is useful for my ministry. I have sent[18] Tychicus to Ephesus. When you come, bring the cloak that I left with Carpus in Troas, as well as the scrolls, especially *the ones written on parchment*[19]. Alexander the metalworker caused me[20] a lot of harm—the Lord will pay him back for the things he did—so be on your guard against him, too, because he strongly opposed our message[21]. (2 Tim 4:9-15)

---

17. As Mounce notes, "Paul's use of *epiphaneia* with all its divine associations in speaking of Jesus Christ is an assault on the use of the word in emperor worship" (*Pastoral Epistles*, 360).

18. Preceded in Greek by "but" or "and."

19. The others, we presume, would be written on the cheaper medium, papyrus.

20. Lit. "showed."

21. Lit. "words"; thus, "teaching," "preaching," "message," or something similar

There are always practical matters to be handled, and in this roundup of comings and goings, we learn of Paul's continuing organizational energy, of setbacks, and loyalty, and we may gain a flash of insight into the recent judicial hearing.

9. "Hurry and come to me quickly." Timothy is to hurry from Ephesus to Rome bringing John Mark with him. Although other members of the Pauline circle will be kept busy right up until the end of Paul's life, the anticipated meeting with Timothy, judging by what has already been said in the epistle, may have a more personal and spiritual purpose. Face-to-face Paul can further advise and encourage Timothy about the strategy for Ephesus and beyond; and conversely Timothy can encourage Paul. The note of urgency here indicates Paul has calculated the likely delay caused by Roman judicial inertia will be just about sufficient for a messenger (almost certainly Tychicus) to reach Timothy and for Timothy to make his way to Rome via Troas.

10. "For Demas has deserted (*enkatelipen*) me because he loved (*agapēsas*) the present age and went off to Thessalonica." Demas, a trusted co-worker (Col 4:14; Phlm 24), has abandoned Paul, left Rome and gone off to northern Greece to enjoy himself.[22] There is nothing wrong with loving life (1 Tim 6:17), but it is the desertion of a friend in need which hurts: *enkatelipen* in this context is a strong word.

"Crescens went to Galatia." The NT does not mention Crescens elsewhere, and we do not know where he went. Tradition tells us he went north to plant churches in Gaul, southern France, in the area of Vienne and Mayence near Lyons.[23] He did not desert Paul in the way that the Demas did. Alternatively, he may have gone to the Roman province of Galatia where Paul had been involved in the founding churches during the first missionary journey. If Crescens did go north, this would fit in with Paul's desire to reach to the furthest west in his ministry.[24]

---

would also be appropriate translations.

22. This is possible, although Fee, *1 and 2 Timothy, Titus,* 293 notes that Thessalonica was scarcely a "hot spot." Whilst some church fathers imagined true apostasy here (e.g., Pol. *Phil.* 9:1–2), this would be unusual for such a long-serving Christian worker. It is not impossible that Paul is just using theologically "final" language to express his disappointment. Cf. "handed over to Satan" in 1 Cor 5:5 for a temporary exclusion.

23. Mounce, *Pastoral Epistles,* 590. *Galatia* can refer to Gaul or to the Roman province in Asia Minor. A manuscript variant gives "Gallia" at this point, see Knight, *Pastoral Epistles,* 465.

24. Clement writing from Rome only about thirty years after Paul's death speaks of the apostle as reaching "to the limit of the west," (1 Clem. 5:7) an expression applicable to southern France or Spain (cf. Rom 15:24).

"Titus went to Dalmatia." Titus, a trusted right-hand man, is in Dalmatia beyond Illyricum, the furthest point Paul himself had reached on his own missionary journeys (Rom 15:19). Having completed his task on Crete, Titus has traveled to fresh territory, and the fact that Paul knows where he is may indicate the move was at Paul's direction. In any case, Paul must have known his lieutenants well enough to appraise their gifts and aptitudes: some were better suited to traveling ministry and tough assignments and others (like Luke) could be better employed staying with Paul in Rome.

11. "Only Luke is with me." Luke, a gentile Christian physician (Col 4:14), is traditionally the author of the third gospel and Acts. His method of work is outlined in the first chapter of his gospel and shows him to be a careful man verifying facts and testimony and setting them in order. His literary skills make him an ideal amanuensis, or secretary, for Paul.[25] We do not know the exact conditions under which Paul was kept or how easy it was for him to receive visitors to whom he could give dictation. The compressed nature of some of the phrases in this epistle might point to short meetings between Paul and his visitor, and we must be correct in assuming that Luke was not actually a fellow prisoner with Paul since otherwise it would not have been possible to receive and send correspondence: "with me" must mean Luke was staying nearby in Rome.

"Take Mark and bring him with you, for he is useful (or helpful. NIV) for my ministry." Evidently, Timothy is to find Mark and travel with him to Rome. Where was Mark at the time? We do not know, but he was close enough to be contacted and prepared for the journey. Paul had known Mark for many years. The young man had accompanied him and Barnabas on the first missionary journey, but after their visit to Cyprus, Mark took it into his head to return to Antioch and left the other two men without his assistance (Acts 13:13). This led to the conflict between Paul and Barnabas later because Barnabas wanted the young man, his nephew, to join them for the second missionary journey and this Paul refused. So, Paul and Barnabas parted company (Acts 15:37–39). What Paul's request indicates is his complete reconciliation with Mark. This must have taken place some years earlier because Paul and Mark had been fellow prisoners during the first Roman imprisonment (Col 4:10). So, why was Mark so important? It may be because Mark was able to communicate in three languages. He was John Mark or Yohanan Marcus, with Hebrew and Roman names, who, if Richard Bauckham's reconstruction of the method by which Mark's gospel was written is correct, would have taken Peter's Aramaic and translated it

---

25. On the connection between the language and theology of the Pastoral Epistles and Luke-Acts, see Wilson, *Luke and the Pastoral Epistles*.

into Greek—even if Peter was capable of speaking and understanding Greek because of his Galilean upbringing.[26] Equally, Mark may have been able to speak and write Latin. Whether it was during this period in Rome that Mark acted as Peter's "interpreter" and brought his gospel to completion cannot be said with certainty.

12. "I have sent[27] (*apesteila*) Tychicus to Ephesus." The verb *apesteila* is an "epistolary aorist" meaning "'I am sending', from the perspective of the writer or, 'I have sent' from that of the recipient."[28] Quite probably Tychicus brought the letter to Ephesus since he seems to have been a known letter carrier (Col 4:7; Eph 6:21, 22). Hearing these words, the Ephesian church would appreciate Tychicus could act as a temporary replacement for Timothy.

13. "When you come, bring the cloak that I left with Carpus in Troas." Anyone traveling from Ephesus to Rome, even today, would probably pass through Toas before turning west through Thessalonica, catching the boat to Brindisi and then on by road across Italy. If Paul is alive when winter comes, the big circular woolen cloak with a hole for the head (like a cycling cape) would keep him warm. Carpus is otherwise unknown, but Timothy must know him and know where he lives, an indication of the closeness of Paul's team. Important too "are the scrolls, especially the ones written on parchment"[29] which have also been left behind.[30] A credible reconstruction of events puts Paul on his way to Ephesus (1 Tim 3:14) to deal with the heresy when he is arrested and all his plans are disrupted.[31] The scrolls may contain legal documents proving Roman citizenship or biblical texts[32] or codices (as distinct from scrolls)[33] or simply be notes,[34] accounts, memoranda,

---

26. Bauckham, *Jesus and the Eyewitnesses*, 69, 216. Children become bilingual quite easily in cultures where two languages are spoken. This is observed, for instance, in Wales (Welsh and English) and Canada (French and English).

27. Preceded in Greek by "but" or "and."

28. Quoting Fee, *1 and 2 Timothy, Titus*, 295.

29. The others, we presume, would be written on the cheaper medium, papyrus.

30. All of this provides a wonderful glimpse into the practicalities of reading and writing on the move in the first century and ultimately the production of a substantial part of the New Testament as we know it.

31. Mounce, *Pastoral Epistles*, 592.

32. Knight, *Pastoral Epistles*, 467.

33. Kelly, *Pastoral Epistles*, 216.

34. "What we know the rabbis used were not so much books as private notebooks. They were notes of material known in oral transmission and were not in any sense intended to replace the oral traditions but rather to serve as aids to memory precisely in learning and recalling the oral traditions" (Bauckham, 287.)

and blank writing materials. Paul's trust of Timothy is shown by this simple personal request. Pentecostals and charismatics who revel in the power of the Spirit might care to notice the importance of books (scrolls) to Paul. You can be full of the Spirit and still love to study.

14. "Alexander the metalworker caused me[35] (*enedeixato*) a lot of harm." There are two Alexanders we already know about. One is a member of the Ephesian church and was disciplined for blasphemy (1 Tim 1:20) and the other was involved in the riot in Ephesus (Acts 19:33). They may, indeed, be the same person—though this is unlikely—and then there is the Alexander mentioned here who may be a third person or one of the other two. If he is the one who was disciplined, he may have pursued a vendetta against Paul by instigating his arrest since *enedeixato* could be used in a legal sense of "inform against," or even as a witness for the prosecution in Rome.[36] Alexander was a common name which is why an identifier like "the metalworker" was needed.[37]

"for (*apodōsei*) the things he did." Following the example of Jesus, Paul does not retaliate but leaves judgement to the Lord himself who will repay either in this life or at the Second Coming. This is an important principle: "'vengeance is mine, I will repay' says the Lord" (Rom 12:17; cf. Ps 28:4, 62:12).

15. "so be on your guard against him." It makes little sense for Paul to warn Timothy to be on his guard unless there is a likelihood Alexander will cross Timothy's path. So where might this happen? One option is to suppose Troas[38] where Paul was perhaps arrested and so left behind his cloak and books. Another more compelling option is to assume Alexander traveled to Rome[39] on behalf of the prosecution against Paul with the result Timothy, when he arrives, may find himself in danger from Alexander's vehement opposition. The words "be on your guard" imply Timothy can take steps to protect himself (perhaps by keeping out of his way[40]); "because he strongly opposed our message"[41] meaning he strongly opposed the gospel. Alternatively, because "our message (*hēmeterois logois*)" means "our words," there

---

35. Lit. "showed."

36. Fee, *1 and 2 Timothy, Titus*, 296; Kelly, *Pastoral Epistles*, 217.

37. This is exactly the way that the famous Aphrodisias inscription identifies the various godfearers attending a synagogue not very far from Ephesus. Cf. Reynolds and Tannenbaum. *Jews and Godfearers at Aphrodisias*, 116–23.

38. Fee, *1 and 2 Timothy, Titus*, 296.

39. Mounce, *Pastoral Epistles*, 594.

40. Guthrie, *Pastoral Epistles*, 186.

41. Lit. "words"; thus, "teaching," "preaching," "message," or something similar would also be appropriate translations.

may be reference here to Paul's defense at his trial, especially because this is referred to next.

d. Fulfilling his ministry in court (4:16–18)

> At my first defense, no one came to my aid, but everyone abandoned me—may it not be counted against them—but the Lord stood by me and strengthened me, so that through me the proclamation may be brought to full measure and all the gentiles hear. He rescued me from the lion's mouth, *and the Lord will rescue me from every evil deed and will save me for his heavenly kingdom.* (2 Tim 4:16-18)

Now Paul refers to the trial. Commentators have argued over whether Paul is speaking of the cases leading up to his relatively mild house arrest (Acts 28) or—and this is the view we take—to the ongoing proceedings in Rome destined to result in his execution. Because the fire of Rome in AD 64 was blamed by Nero on the Christians, and many were horribly put to death,[42] Paul must have realized the verdict of the Roman court was a foregone conclusion.

16. "At my first defense, no one came to my aid, but everyone abandoned me—may it not be counted against them." Roman legal proceedings took place in a series of steps. There was a preliminary or first investigation (*prima actio*) at which the accused could speak and at which defense could be made either by the accused or by a lawyer. If the judge was unable to come to a decision, the verdict was *Non liquet* ('it is not clear'), and presumably the defendant was freed. If the judge was able to decide, then the verdict of *Amplius* ("more") led to a second investigation or *secunda actio* at which the defendant had to mount a further defense which, if it was unsuccessful, would lead to a condemnatory verdict that could include the death penalty.[43]

The "first defense" is spoken of here. We know from the accounts in Acts of Paul's complex entanglement in a series of legal cases in the Holy

---

42. Gibbon notes, "To divert a suspicion, which the power of despotism was unable to suppress, the emperor [Nero] resolved to substitute in his own place some fictitious criminals. 'With this view' (continues Tacitus) 'he inflicted the most exquisite tortures on those men, who, under the vulgar appellation of Christians, were already branded with deserved infamy. They derived their name and origin from Christ, who, in the reign of Tiberius, had suffered death by the sentence of the procurator Pontius Pilate'" (*Decline and Fall*, 325).

43. Kelly, *Pastoral Epistles*, 217, 218; Towner, *Timothy and Titus*, 637.

Land (Acts 22–26). He is arraigned before the Sanhedrin, and then Felix and then Festus and the appearance before Festus includes King Agrippa who makes the remarkable statement "this man could have been set free had he not appealed to Caesar" (Acts 26:32). The right to appeal to Caesar was one held by every Roman citizen, and this trumped all local and provincial courts. The outlines of the Roman system may be seen in the cases described in the Holy Land. For instance, a lawyer is hired to bring an accusation against Paul before Felix (Acts 24:1–8), but Paul handles his own defense without calling on a legal team, and as he speaks, gives his testimony of conversion while also rebutting the charges manufactured against him (Acts 24:10–21). Paul is able to speak authoritatively and draw attention to points of law, and his line of defense includes reference to the doctrine of resurrection which was part of the legally allowed Jewish faith permitted within the empire (Acts 24:21; cf. 23:6). We assume Paul's "first defense" in Rome followed a pattern similar to his earlier defenses.

Though Paul's defense may have been similar, the court would have been more splendid as befitted the imperial capital. He may have been entitled to legal advice or representation or to call witnesses or simply have expected the moral support of Christian friends but "no one came to my aid, but everyone abandoned me." He was on his own in a courtroom or forum crowded by many people from all over the empire. It is possible Paul spoke before Nero himself, and if this were so, there would have been a huge crowd of onlookers and officials. The accusations now made against him were presumably like those made against other Christians during this period of persecution, i.e., to do with belonging to a group said to be responsible for the fire. Other charges would have focused on sedition or inciting opposition to the state: these, after all, were the political charges against Jesus (John 19:12) which were repeated in a general form against Paul before Felix (Acts 24:5).

Paul's abandonment by friends and colleagues raises queries because he has already told us that Luke is with him (v. 11), and he sends greetings from other Christians in Rome at the end of the letter (v. 21). Maybe Luke arrived late, after the trial, and maybe Christians in Rome kept away from the trial knowing that to associate with Paul would be to risk their own lives (if this is so, that makes Onesiphorus in 1:16 even more outstanding). Maybe also in the frightening round-up of Christians by the authorities, access to legal aid was closed down. We only know Paul was on his own, without help or encouragement, and his reaction "may it not be counted against them" has the hallmark of a man who consciously imitates Stephen, martyred while he watched (Acts 7:58–60). There is probably a deliberate contrast between what he says about Alexander the metalworker ("the Lord will pay him back") and what he says about those who failed to stand with him ("may it not be counted against them"). In any event, Paul has a keen sense of impending divine justice.

Some commentators see the reference to abandonment as echoing passages in the Psalms and, if this is so, it would not be surprising since Paul would have sung and prayed the Psalms from boyhood and might have been expected to interpret his experience in the light of psalmic themes (e.g., Pss 21; 22).[44]

17. "but the Lord stood by me and strengthened me." Despite being comprehensively abandoned—by "everyone in Asia" (1.15), "Demas" (4:10), the generality of Christians in the large church in Rome (4:18)— "the Lord" stands by him and strengthens him. We should not take this as merely a pious expression but see in it a fundamental though subjective affirmation of the empowering presence of Christ faithfully sensed while the court was in session. Called to defend himself publicly in a hostile court, Paul does not capitulate to fear or shame but maintains his inner spiritual poise in circumstances that would have reduced other men to a nervous breakdown. At other points in his ministry when the outlook was tough, Paul received a vision of Christ giving him reassurance (Acts 18:9, 10; cf. Acts 27:23) and we may imagine a similar accession of divine help before and during the trial.

"so that through me the proclamation (*kerygma*) might be brought to full measure (*plērophorēthē*) and all the gentiles hear." We can read these words as the apex and fulfillment of Paul's mission to the gentiles. Rather than being dismissed in a cursory fashion before a minor magistrate, Paul has the opportunity to act as herald (the force of *kerygma*), to proclaim the gospel in its fullness (*plērophorēthē*), to the assembled hearers.[45] Again, if we take the earlier discourses in Acts as indicative of Paul's eloquence in court, we may assume a lengthy and wide-ranging intellectual defense of the gospel full of reasoned passion inspired by the Spirit and pressed home by an experienced preacher. Paul evidently sees this moment as the culmination of his calling dating right back to his conversion on the Damascus Road (Acts 9:15[46]). He really has "finished his race" by proclaiming the gospel to a huge cosmopolitan crowd of gentiles at the heart of the imperial capital. He has played his part, and not failed, on the biggest stage of his lifetime.

"He rescued me from the lion's mouth." Whatever Paul said to the court was sufficient to delay the death sentence so that, during the respite,

---

44. See Towner for a full discussion (*Timothy and Titus,* 639–42).
45. Mounce, *Pastoral Epistles,* 596.
46. We can be confident a full conversation between Ananias and Paul took place.

he can write to Timothy one last time. Some commentators thought the lion was a wild animal in the gladiatorial arena, but given Paul was a Roman citizen, this was never an option. Others have thought Nero was the lion or Satan (1 Pet 5:8), and the metaphor conveys how close Paul came to dying and how narrow was his (temporary) escape: he was in "the lion's mouth" when rescue came.[47]

18. "and the Lord will rescue me from every evil deed and will save me for his heavenly kingdom." Having looked back at his sufferings and escapes (3:11), Paul is able to say with confidence "the Lord will rescue me" and to do so with a wider, broader horizon of hope. He does not expect he will escape from prison again because has already said his life is being poured out (4:6). His mindset remains eschatological—focused on the future arrival of the Kingdom of God. And when he speaks of being saved for the "heavenly kingdom," he is asserting that no "evil deed" performed against him here on earth will obstruct his entrance to the realm where he will receive the "crown of righteousness" (4:8).[48] This statement is one of faith because, as he writes, he is still at the mercy of merciless captors and confined to their stinking prison. Because of what the Lord has done and will do, and regardless of horrible circumstances, Paul can break out into characteristic praise: "to him be the glory for ever and ever Amen."

The church of today may wish to measure itself against the stature of that first generation of Christians whose faith and sacrifice laid foundations for the centuries that followed.

e. Greetings, information, and hope for a final meeting (4:19–22)

> Greet Priscilla and Aquilla and *everyone in* the household of Onesiphorous. Erastus stayed in Corinth, but I left Trophimus behind in Miletus as he was unwell. Hurry up and get here[49] before winter arrives. Eubulus, Pudens, Linus and Claudia and all the brothers and sisters[50] send their greet-

---

47. Note that in 1 Cor 15:32 Paul refers to fighting with "wild beasts at Ephesus," which similarly suggests a figurative referent, albeit, perhaps one, as here, with a genuine element of danger.

48. According to tradition, Paul was beheaded "near Aquae Salviae (now Tre Fontane) near the third milestone on the Ostian Way" (Bruce, *Paul*, 450).

49. Lit. "come."

50. " . . . and sisters" is implied by the Greek since masculine plurals are used for mixed groups.

ings to you. The Lord be with your spirit. Grace be with you *all*[51]. (2 Tim 4:19-22)

Greetings to personal friends in Ephesus, information as to the whereabouts of colleagues, a reiterated hope for a final meeting and greetings from Roman Christians complete the letter.

19. "Greet Priscilla and Aquila." This was a couple, both Jews, with whom Paul had worked for many years and in different places. He met them in Corinth, they went with him to Ephesus, were then in Rome as brave fellow-workers to whom all the gentile churches owed a debt (Rom 16:3, 4), and are now back in Ephesus. They are unusual in that Priscilla is mentioned before her husband four times which has prompted speculation that she was either a Roman aristocrat or a forceful personality or a teacher of Scripture in her own right. The couple were able to correct someone as knowledgeable as Apollos (Acts 18:24-26) which speaks extremely well of their grasp of Scripture and doctrine. Their original move to Corinth had been caused by the expulsion of Jews from Rome during the reign of Claudius (Acts 18:2). That they were in Ephesus during its assault by a wave of false teaching must give Paul reassurance even though this demonstrates just how fragmented or factionalized the Ephesian church had become. If a couple like Priscilla and Aquila with their good reputation and wide experience were not able to stem the advance of the false teachers, the scale of the problem at Ephesus is underlined. The personal greetings to them in a letter that would have been read out to the whole church is an endorsement of their noble standing and doctrinal reliability. Likewise, the greeting to "everyone in the household of Onesiphorous" endorses them. Why Onesiphorous himself is not greeted has given rise to speculation. Perhaps he was still in Rome or traveling or had died (1:16-18).

20. "Erastus stayed in Corinth." We cannot be certain of the circumstances that led Erastus to stay in Corinth. He may have been in Paul's traveling group when Paul was arrested. If so, he took the reasonable decision to return home. He was a seasoned member of Paul's team (Acts 19:22) and is referred to in Romans 16:23 as "the city's director of public works," senior in local government. The point here is that Erastus is not in Rome with Paul, and Timothy should not expect to find him when he arrives.

"but I left Trophimus behind in Miletus as he was unwell (*asthenounta*)." Although traditional scholarship has concerned itself with when Paul was last in Miletus and how this can be fitted into the travel schedule in

---

51. The "you" on the previous two occasions (vv. 21b, 22a) is singular, i.e., referring to Titus alone. The closing "you" is plural, thus bringing the whole church into view and suggesting the addition of *all*.

the Book of Acts, Pentecostals and charismatics are more interested in the reason why Trophimus is left behind sick. Doctrines of healing in the Pentecostal and charismatic movement have been strong and many evangelists have argued for the inclusion of healing within the atonement and therefore for healing as a guaranteed "right" for Christians.[52] Others have been less forceful and seen healing as one of the charismatic gifts available to the church by the gracious work the Holy Spirit. Yet others have emphasized James 5 and the healing that comes after the laying on of hands by elders. We are probably correct in seeing three different doctrines of healing in the New Testament: one in the context of evangelism where signs are given to confirm the preaching of the word (Mark 16:20); one given through the body of a congregation which is open to the moving of the Holy Spirit (1 Cor 12); and one that is more formalized and given through the ministry of particular people identified as elders or evangelists or apostles. But the surprise here is to discover an esteemed colleague of Paul's has been left behind unhealed. And the verb *asthenounta* is used here as well as in James 5:14. So we must conclude not absolutely everybody in the New Testament was healed or healed immediately. Thus, even though certain ministers see many wonderful miracles, healing remains a matter of grace rather than of right. A thoughtful consideration of the whole topic is given by Donald Gee writing in 1952.[53]

21. "Hurry up and get here[54] before winter arrives." This repeats what has already been said in verse 9 but with the added mention of "winter." The periodic storms between November and March made sea travel in the Mediterranean well-nigh impossible during those months.[55] Thus, if Paul is writing during early summer, there is time for the letter to reach Timothy in Ephesus and for him to reach Rome using fast and convenient sea crossings.

---

52. There is far too large a literature on healing to cover thoroughly here. Wacker, *Heaven Below*, offers a good place to start. Bosworth wrote *Christ the Healer* in 1924, and Maria B. Woodworth-Etter, *Divine Healing*, in about 1920. And others like E. W. Kenyon were influential at the beginning (see Simmons, *E. W. Kenyon*). These views were then relaunched a generation later by evangelists like Osborn, *Healing the Sick* and Kenneth Hagin. Like Wacker, Warrington offers a valuable discussion and extensive bibliography (*Pentecostal Theology*, 265–308). In her *Global Pentecostal Healing*, Brown gives an overview of healing in many countries while King in *Regeneration* provides a long historical perspective, with one of the three volumes being entirely devoted to bibliography.

53. Gee, *Trophimus I Left Sick*.

54. Lit. "come."

55. See Casson, *Travel in the Ancient World* for the classic study on this and other practicalities.

"Eubulus, Pudens, Linus, and Claudia and all the brothers and sisters[56] send their greetings to you." Four Christians with Roman names are now listed and presumably these are the people Timothy should ask for once he reaches Rome. They will be able to assist him locate Paul and provide hospitality. There is obviously contact between Paul and the Roman church although it does not seem to have been sufficiently strong for him to rely on its provision (surely someone at Rome could have given him a cloak? v. 13). By listing these Roman church leaders in a friendly way, Paul signals his forgiveness or understanding of their failure to stand with him.[57] The church, of course, survived and early tradition says Linus became the first bishop of Rome.[58] It is easy to imagine a man mentioned in a letter of Paul's, and after the persecution had died down, would have attracted the confidence of the surviving congregation.

22. "The Lord be with your spirit." This is a traditional Christian greeting (Gal 6:18; Phlm 25; Phil 4:23) with a singular "your" and therefore directed to Timothy himself while "grace be with you all" is plural and addressed to the whole congregation at Ephesus. These are the last recorded words of the man who was the apostle to the gentiles (Rom 11:13). Fittingly, they wish us "grace."

Reaching the end of this letter the reader may be struck by the frightening odds ranged against Paul and the early Christians. He was tried and imprisoned on confected charges—there was never any likelihood early Christians would threaten the state—and the efforts made to silence him would, in a culture of "free speech," have never been allowed. As for Nero, he was one of the most obscene, malicious, and narcissistic of individuals and completely unsuited to public office. Undaunted, the early Christians patiently taught their communities and witnessed to Christ and gradually brought about changes in the empire and, through a long complex historical process, the whole world.[59] In the middle of it all, perhaps to our surprise, lay effective mentoring relationships, in which crucial values, qualities and courage were communicated to the next generation.

---

56. As noted above, "and sisters" is implied by the Greek since masculine plurals are used for mixed groups.

57. Mounce, *Pastoral Epistles*, 601,

58. Irenaeus *Haer.* 3:3.3 (via Mounce, *Pastoral Epistles*, 601) and Eusebius *Hist. eccl.* 3:2, who writes "After the martyrdom of Paul and Peter the first man to be appointed Bishop of Rome was Linus. He is mentioned by Paul when writing to Timothy from Rome."

59. Holland, *Dominion*.

EXCURSUS V.

Time and Eternity

Discussion of time and eternity can become complex and philosophically technical, but we would simply wish to assert the proposition that God is eternal and, indeed, created time. This view goes back at least to Saint Augustine who argued that the world was not created *in* time (at some point in eternity) but *with* time so that when the universe came into existence time also came into being.[1] This is because time is measured by movement and change within the universe whereas if we think of God as an eternal and unchanging there is no time associated with him. Even so, while it is clear from Scripture that God foreknows the future, the precise relationship of God with time is open to discussion. We simply believe that God is both outside time and over time; outside time in the sense that God existed before time began and over time in that God can be present across the whole temporal span of the universe. This is why Jesus can say "before Abraham was, I am" (John 8:58), and the book of Revelation can say that Jesus is the lamb "slain before the foundation of the world" (Rev 13:8).

Whether we can say that God made decisions in eternity which are then carried out in time has been a matter of debate although it is certainly not impossible to believe that God from outside time acts to make things happen inside time.[2] To say that God is eternal is to say the Father, the Son

---

1. Augustine, *Civ.* 11.6.
2. For fuller discussion see, Jantzen, "Time and timelessness"; Leftow, "Eternity"; Craig, "Divine Eternity." One point we can draw attention to consists in the conceptualisation of eternity: is it endless duration or is it an "eternal now" in which all time is held? If it is endless duration, can we think of eternity as having a past, present

and the Spirit are co-eternal even though the Son is "begotten" by the Father and the Spirit "proceeds" from the Father and the Son;[3] and there is no problem in saying this because we envisage eternity as being a state where there is no "before" or "after" but in some sense everything is eternally "present." Even so, when we think of what happens in time, we read Jesus came at the right moment in human history and died at the time for prophecies to be fulfilled (Gal 4:4).[4] In other words, theologians have recognized our ability to understand God in eternity is bounded by our limitations as creatures of time. This is why a distinction has been made between the "economic Trinity" as we appreciate God in time and the "immanent Trinity" as God is outside and beyond time.[5] Though these ideas may seem complicated, they enable us to appreciate the greatness of God is way beyond what our minds can conceive. In historical terms we are told in Hebrews 9:14, Jesus offered himself through the "eternal Spirit," that is, there is a wonderful interaction between time and eternity at the cross. Similarly, we believe that when human beings experience the Holy Spirit, they are touching the eternal. The revelation of the Scripture speaks of "tasting of the powers of the world to come" (Heb 6:5) implying that out of the eternal being of God human beings may know something of the limitless horizons of eternity through the Spirit. And human beings can know this because they are spiritual beings as well as physical beings: there is communication by the Spirit of God to the human spirit (1 Cor 2.9–13). One consequence of all this is that Christian (and especially Pauline) understanding of the climactic return of Christ in judgement *both* heightens the importance of the days in which we live *and* causes them to be seen against the backdrop of another and greater order of reality.

There are references in the Pastoral Epistles to eternity or decisions being carried out "before the beginning of time" (2 Tim 1:9) and to "eternal glory" (2 Tim 2:10) and God as the "eternal king" (1 Tim 1:17) as well as other verses with a similar focus (e.g., 1 Tim 1:17; Titus 1:2), and this is why we have included this excursus.

---

and future? We prefer a "both/and" answer to these questions, which is why we have spoken of God as being inside and outside or above time.

3. The Orthodox church believes the Spirit proceeds from the Father alone and not the Father and the Son. See Young, *Making of the Creeds*, 63–65.

4. For the Judaeo-Christian tradition time is linear rather than cyclical. Pertinent to this, distinctions between Greek and Hebraic conceptions of time are found in Cullmann, *Christ and Time*.

5. Atkinson, *Trinity After Pentecost*, 27.

BIBLIOGRAPHY

Al-Yahya, Maha. "Stylometric Analysis of Classical Arabic Texts for Genre Detection." *The Electronic Library* 36, no. 5 (2018) 842–855.
Aland, Barbara, Aland, Kurt et al., eds. *Novum testamentum graece*. 28. revidierte Auflage. Münster: Deutsche Bibelgesellschaft, 2012.
Anderson, Ann. *Snake Oil, Hustlers and Hambones: The American Medicine Show*. Jefferson NC: McFarland, 2015.
Anderson, R. Dean. *Ancient Rhetorical Theory and Paul*. Kampen: Kok Pharos, 1996.
Archer, Kenneth J. *A Pentecostal Hermeneutic for the Twenty-First Century: Spirit, Scripture and Community*. London: T&T Clark, 2004.
———. "The Spirit in the Pastoral Epistles: Inspiring, Gifting, Sanctifying Presence." *Pneuma* 43 no. 3–4 (2021) 532–537.
Archer, Melissa and Archer, Kenneth J. "Complementarianism and Egalitarianism—Whose Side Are You Leaning On?: A Pentecostal Reading of Ephesians 5:21–33." *Pneuma* 41 no. 1 (2019) 66–90.
Arterbury, Andrew Elvis. *Entertaining Angels: Early Christian Hospitality in its Mediterranean Setting*. Sheffield: Phoenix, 2005.
Ascough, Richard S., Harland, Philip A. et al., eds. *Associations in the Greco-Roman World: A Sourcebook*. Berlin: De Gruyter, 2012.
Ashraf, Shaina, Iqbal, Hafiz Rizwan et al. "Cross-Genre Author Profile Prediction Using Stylometry-Based Approach." In *Proceedings of the 4th International Workshop on Uncovering Plagiarism, Authorship, and Social Software Misuse, Évora, Portugal, 5–8 September, 2016*, edited by Krisztian Balog, Linda Cappellato et al., 992–999. Aachen: Sunsite CEUR, 2016.
Asztalos, Monika. "The Faculty of Theology." In *A History of the University in Europe*, edited by W. Rüegg Vol. 1, 409–441. Cambridge: Cambridge University Press, 1992.
Atkinson, William. *The "Spiritual Death" of Jesus: A Pentecostal Investigation*. Leiden: Brill, 2009.
———. *Trinity after Pentecost*. Eugene, OR: Pickwick, 2013.

Aune, David E. "Heracles and Christ: Heracles Imagery in the Christology of Early Christianity." In *Greeks, Romans, and Christians: Essays in Honor of Abraham J. Malherbe*, edited by David Balch, Everett Ferguson et al., 3-19. Minneapolis, MN: Fortress, 1990.

Bailey, Kenneth E. "Women in the New Testament: A Middle Eastern Cultural View." *Anvil* 11 no. 1 (1994) 7-24.

Balch, David L. "Household Codes." In *ABD* 3:318-320.

Banks, Robert. *Paul's Idea of Community: The Early House Churches in their Cultural Setting*. Rev. ed Peabody, MA: Hendrickson, 1994.

Barclay, John M. G. *Jews in the Mediterranean Diaspora: From Alexander to Trajan (323 BCE-117 CE)*. Edinburgh: T&T Clark, 1996.

Barclay, William. "Paul's Certainties VII. Our Security in God—2 Timothy i. 12." *ExpTim* 69 no. 11 (1958) 324-327.

Barr, James. *The Semantics of Biblical Language*. London: Oxford University Press, 1961.

Barrett, Charles Kingsley. *The Pastoral Epistles*. NCB. Oxford: Clarendon Press, 1963.

Bassler, Jouette M. "The Widows' Tale: A Fresh Look at 1 Tim 5: 3-16." *JBL* 103 no. 1 (1984) 23-41.

Bauckham, Richard J. *The Theology of the Book of Revelation*. Cambridge: Cambridge University Press, 1993.

———. *Jude, 2 Peter*. WBC 50. Dallas, TX: Word, 1998.

———. *Jesus and the Eyewitnesses: The Gospels as Eyewitness Testimony*. Grand Rapids, MI: Eerdmans, 2006.

Bauer, Walter, Danker, Frederick W. et al. *A Greek-English Lexicon of the New Testament and Other Early Christian Literature*. 3rd ed. Chicago, IL: University of Chicago Press, 2000.

Beard, Mary. *SPQR: A History of Ancient Rome*. London: Profile, 2016.

Bebbington, David and Jones, David Ceri, eds. *Evangelicalism and Fundamentalism in the United Kingdom during the Twentieth Century*. Oxford: Oxford University Press, 2013.

Berding, Kenneth. "Polycarp of Smyrna's View of the Authorship of 1 and 2 Timothy." *VC* 53 no. 4 (1999) 349-360.

Berger, Peter L. and Luckmann, Thomas. *The Social Construction of Reality: A Treatise in the Sociology of Knowledge*. London: Penguin, 1967.

Berthelot, Katell and Price, Jonathan J. "Introduction." In *In the Crucible of Empire: The Impact of Roman Citizenship upon Greeks, Jews and Christians*, edited by Katell Berthelot and Jonathan J. Price, 1-17. Leuven: Peeters, 2019.

Bettenson, Henry, ed. *The Early Christian Fathers: A Selection from the Writings of the Fathers from St. Clement of Rome to St. Athanasius*. London: Oxford University Press, 1969.

Betz, Hans Dieter. "The Literary Composition and Function of Paul's Letter to the Galatians." *NTS* 21 no. 3 (1975) 353–379.
Bierma, Lyle D., Charles, D. et al. *An Introduction to the Heidelberg Catechism: Sources, History, and Theology.* Grand Rapids, MI: Baker, 2005.
Bird, H. W. "L. Aelius Seianus: Further Observations." *Latomus* 29 no. Fasc. 4 (1970) 1046–1050.
Bosworth, Fred Francis. *Christ, the Healer.* River Forest, IL: Self Published, 1924.
Bowersock, Glen Warren. "The Imperial Cult: Perceptions and Persistence." In *Jewish and Christian Self-Definition*, edited by Ben F. Meyer and E. P. Sanders Vol. 3, 171–182. London: SCM, 1980.
Brown, Candy Gunther. *Global Pentecostal and Charismatic Healing.* Oxford: Oxford University Press, 2011.
Bruce, F. F. *The Spreading Flame.* Exeter: Paternoster, 1958.
———. *Paul: Apostle of the Free Spirit.* Exeter: Paternoster, 1977.
———. *The Pauline Circle.* Exeter: Paternoster, 1985.
Bunyan, John. *The Pilgrim's Progress.* Oxford: Oxford University Press, 2008.
Burgess, Stanley M. and Van der Maas, Ed M., eds. *The New International Dictionary of Pentecostal and Charismatic Movements.* Revd. ed. Grand Rapids, MI: Zondervan, 2002.
Calvin, Jean. *Commentary on Philippians, Colossians, and Thessalonians.* Grand Rapids, MI: CCEL, 1999. (orig. c. 1550; this e-ed. based on W. Pringle, ed., Edinburgh: Calvin Translation Society, 1851). https://ccel.org/ccel/calvin/calcom42/calcom42.i.html.
———. *Commentary on Timothy, Titus, Philemon.* Grand Rapids, MI: CCEL, 1999. (orig. c. 1550; this e-ed. based on W. Pringle, ed., Edinburgh: Calvin Translation Society, 1856). https://ccel.org/ccel/calvin/calcom43/calcom43.i.html.
Campbell, R. Alastair. *The Elders: Seniority Within Earliest Christianity.* Edinburgh: T&T Clark, 1994.
Can, Fazli and Patton, Jon M. "Change of Writing Style with Time." *CHum* 38 no. 1 (2004) 61–82.
Canavan, Joseph E. "Charity in the Early Church." *Studies* 12 no. 45 (1923) 61–77.
Casson, Lionel. *Travel in the Ancient World.* Baltimore, MD: Johns Hopkins University Press, 1994.
Celsus, Aulus Cornelius. *De medicina.* Translated by Walter George Spencer. LCL. 3 vols. Cambridge, MA: Harvard University Press, 1935.
Chadwick, Henry. *The Early Church.* Revd.ed. London: Penguin, 1993.
Charlesworth, James H., ed. *The Old Testament Pseudepigrapha.* 2 vols. Garden City, NY: Doubleday, 1983.

Chesterton Society. "When Man Ceases to Worship God." 2012, https://www.chesterton.org/ceases-to-worship, (accessed

Childs, Brevard S. *The Church's Guide for Reading Paul: The Canonical Shaping of the Pauline Corpus*. Grand Rapids, MI: Eerdmans, 2008.

Clark, Andrew C. "Apostleship: Evidence from the New Testament and Early Christian Literature." *VE* 19 (1989) 49–82.

Collins, Billie Jean, ed. *The SBL Handbook of Style*. 2nd ed. Atlanta, GA: SBL, 2014. http://www.oxford.eblib.com/patron/FullRecord.aspx?p=3118346.

Collins, James Michael and Stackhouse, Ian. *Exorcism and Deliverance Ministry in the Twentieth Century: An Analysis of the Practice and Theology of Exorcism in Modern Western Christianity*. Milton Keynes: Paternoster, 2009.

Collins, John Joseph. "Testaments." In *Jewish Writings of the Second Temple Period: Apocrypha, Pseudepigrapha, Qumran, Sectarian writings, Philo, Josephus*, edited by Michael E. Stone, 325–355. Assen; Philadelphia, PA: Van Gorcum; Fortress, 1984.

Concannon, Cavan W. "'Not for an Olive Wreath, but Our Lives': Gladiators, Athletes, and Early Christian Bodies." *JBL* 133 no. 1 (2014) 193–214.

Craig, William Lane. "Divine Eternity." In *The Oxford Handbook of Philosophical Theology*, edited by Thomas P. Flint and Michael C. Rea, 145–166. Oxford: Oxford University Press, 2009.

Crouch, James E. *The Origin and Intention of the Colossian Haustafel*. Göttingen: Vandenhoeck & Ruprecht, 1972.

Cullmann, Oscar. *Christ and Time: The Primitive Christian Conception of Time and History*. Revd. ed. London: SCM, 1962.

Cunningham, Valentine. *Reading after Theory*. Oxford: Blackwell, 2002.

Curiosity Illustrated. "Why did Julius Caesar wear a Wreath on his Head?" http://www.illustratedcuriosity.com/history/history-ancient-history/why-did-caesar-wear-a-wreath-on-his-head/, (accessed 25.01.2022).

Daelemans, Walter. "Explanation in Computational Stylometry." In *Computational Linguistics and Intelligent Text Processing—Proceedings of the 14th International Conference, CICLing 2013, Samos, Greece, March 24–30, 2013*, edited by Alexander Gelbukh Vol. 1, 451–462. Berlin: Springer, 2013.

Dayton, Donald W. *Discovering an Evangelical Heritage*. New York, NY: Harper & Row, 1976.

de Alminana, Margaret English and Olena, Lois E, eds. *Women in Pentecostal and Charismatic Ministry: Informing a Dialogue on Gender, Church, and Ministry*. Leiden: Brill, 2016.

De Wet, Chris L. *Preaching Bondage: John Chrysostom and the Discourse of Slavery in Early Christianity*. Oakland, CA: University of California Press, 2015.

Engel, Arthur. "Emerging Concepts of the Academic Profession at Oxford 1800–1854." In *The University in Society, Vol. 1: Oxford and Cambridge from the 14th to the Early 19th Century*, edited by Lawrence Stone, 305–351. Princeton, NJ: Princeton University Press, 2019.

Fee, Gordon D. *1 and 2 Timothy, Titus*. NIBC. Rev. ed. Peabody, MA: Hendrickson, 1995.

Ferguson, Everett. *Backgrounds of Early Christianity*. 3rd ed. Grand Rapids, MI: Eerdmans, 2003.

Foerster, Werner. "σέβομαι etc." In *TDNT* 7:168–196. ?DATE NEEDED

Freedman, David Noel, ed. *The Anchor Bible Dictionary*. 6 vols. New York, NY: Doubleday, 1992.

Gabizon, Michael. "The Development of the Matrilineal Principle in Ezra, Jubilees, and Acts." *JSP* 27 no. 2 (2017) 143–160.

Garrison, Irene Peirano. *Persuasion, Rhetoric and Roman Poetry*. Cambridge: Cambridge University Press, 2019.

Gee, Donald. *Concerning Spiritual Gifts: A Series of Bible Studies*. Springfield, MI: Gospel, 1928.

———. *The Ministry-Gifts of Christ*. Nottingham: AoG, 1930.

———. *Trophimus I Left Sick: Our Problems of Divine Healing*. London: Elim, 1952.

Gehring, Roger W. *House Church and Mission: The Importance of Household Structures in Early Christianity*. Peabody, MA: Hendrickson, 2004.

Gibbon, Edward. *The History of the Decline and Fall of the Roman Empire: 28 Selected Chapters*. Edited by A. Lentin and Brian Norman. Ware: Wordsworth, 1998. (orig. 1776–1789; this ed. based on H.H. Milman, ed., Philadelphia, PN: Porter & Coates, 1845).

Gilbert, P. J. "Spiritual Warfare." In *Global Dictionary of Theology: A Resource for the Worldwide Church*, edited by William A. Dyrness and Veli-Matti Kärkkäinen, 847–851. Downers Grove, IL: IVP Academic, 2008.

Gill, David W. J. "Acts and the Urban Elites." In *The Book of Acts in its Graeco-Roman Setting*, edited by Conrad H. Gempf and David W. J. Gill, 105–118. Grand Rapids, MI: Eerdmans, 1994.

Gill, David W. J. and Winter, Bruce. "Acts and Roman Religion." In *The Book of Acts in its Graeco-Roman Setting*, edited by Conrad H. Gempf and David W. J. Gill, 79–104. Grand Rapids, MI: Eerdmans, 1994.

Goldhill, Simon, ed. *Being Greek under Rome: Cultural Identity, the Second Sophistic and the Development of Empire*. Cambridge: Cambridge University Press, 2001.

Gómez-Adorno, Helena, Posadas-Duran, Juan-Pablo et al. "Stylometry-based Approach for Detecting Writing Style Changes in Literary Texts." *Comput. y Sist.* 22 no. 1 (2018) 47–53.

Goodman, Martin. *The Ruling Class of Judaea: The Origins of the Jewish Revolt Against Rome, A.D. 66-70*. Cambridge: Cambridge University Press, 1987.

———. *The Roman World, 44 BC-AD 180*. 2nd ed. London: Routledge, 2012.

Graham, Billy. *Just as I am: The Autobiography of Billy Graham*. 10th ed. New York, NY: HarperOne, 2007.

Guthrie, Donald. *The Pastoral Epistles and the Mind of Paul*. Tyndale, 1956.

———. *New Testament Introduction*. 3rd ed. London: Tyndale, 1970.

———. *The Pastoral Epistles: An Introduction and Commentary*. TNTC. Nottingham: IVP, 2009.

Hagin, Kenneth E. *Seven Things you should Know about Divine Healing*. Tulsa, OK: Faith Library Publications, 1979.

Harland, Philip A. *Associations, Synagogues, and Congregations: Claiming a Place in Ancient Mediterranean Society*. Minneapolis, MN: Fortress, 2003.

Harrell, David Edwin. *Oral Roberts: An American Life*. Bloomington, IN: Indiana University Press, 1985.

Harrison, P. N. *The Problem of the Pastoral Epistles*. London: Oxford University Press, 1921.

Heemstra, Marius. *The Fiscus Judaicus and the Parting of the Ways*. Tübingen: Mohr Siebeck, 2010.

Heffernan, Thomas J. *The Passion of Perpetua and Felicity*. New York, NY: Oxford University Press, 2012.

Hellerman, Joseph H. *The Ancient Church as Family*. Minneapolis, MN: Fortress, 2001.

Hendriksen, William. *1 and 2 Timothy and Titus*. Edinburgh: Banner of Truth, 1953.

Hezser, Catherine. *Jewish Slavery in Antiquity*. Oxford: Oxford University Press, 2005.

Himes, Paul A. "Rethinking the Translation of Διδακτικός in 1 Timothy 3.2 and 2 Timothy 2.24." *BT* 68 no. 2 (2017) 189–208.

Hitchcock, F. R. Montgomery. "Tests for the Pastorals." *JTS* 30 no. 119 (1929) 272–279.

Holland, Tom. *Dynasty: The Rise and Fall of the House of Caesar*. London: Little, Brown, 2015.

———. *Dominion: The Making of the Western Mind*. London: Little, Brown, 2019.

Holmberg, Bengt. *Paul and Power: The Structure of Authority in the Primitive Church as Reflected in the Pauline Epistles*. Philadelphia, PA: Fortress, 1980.

Holmes, David I and Kardos, Judit. "Who was the Author? An Introduction to Stylometry." *Chance* 16 no. 2 (2003) 5–8.

Holmes, M.W., ed. *Greek New Testament: SBL Edition*. Atlanta, GA: Society of Biblical Literature, 2010. https://www.sblgnt.com/.

Holmes, Michael William. *The Greek New Testament: SBL Edition*. 2nd ed. Atlanta, GA: SBL, 2010.

Hopkins, M. Keith. "The Age of Roman Girls at Marriage." *Popul Stud (Camb)* 18 no. 3 (1965) 309–327.

———. "On the Probable Age Structure of the Roman Population." *Popul Stud (Camb)* 20 no. 2 (1966) 245–264.

Horrell, David G. "Leadership Patterns and the Development of Ideology in Early Christianity." *Sociol. Relig.* 58 no. 4 (1997) 323–341.

Hort, Fenton John Anthony. "Lecture XI: Titus and Timothy in the Pastoral Epistles." In *The Christian Ecclesia: A Course of Lectures on the Early History and Early Conceptions of the Ecclesia and one Sermon*, 177–188. London: Macmillan, 1914.

Hübner, Jamin. "Translating αὐθεντέω (authenteō) in 1 Timothy 2: 12." *Priscilla Pap.* 29 no. 2 (2012) 16–26.

Hutson, Christopher R. *First and Second Timothy and Titus*. Grand Rapids, MI: Baker Academic, 2019.

Instone-Brewer, David. *Divorce and Remarriage in the Bible: The Social and Literary Context*. Grand Rapids, MI: Eerdmans, 2002.

Instone, Stephen. *Greek Personal Religion: A Reader*. Oxford: Aris and Phillips, 2009.

Iremonger, F. A. *William Temple, Archbishop of Canterbury: His Life and Letters*. London: OUP, 1948.

Jantzen, Grace. "Time and Timelessness." In *NDCT*571–574.?DATE ?SPACING OF *NDCT*571

Jeffers, James S. *The Greco-Roman World of the New Testament Era: Exploring the Background of Early Christianity*. Downers Grove, IL: IVP, 1999.

Jennings, Theodore W. "Same-sex Relations in the Biblical World." In *The Oxford Handbook of Theology, Sexuality, and Gender*, edited by Adrian Thatcher, 206–220. Oxford: Oxford University Press, 2015.

Johnson, Luke Timothy. *The First and Second Letters to Timothy: A New Translation with Introduction and Commentary*. AB. New York, NY: Doubleday, 2001.

———. *Among the Gentiles: Greco-Roman Religion and Christianity*. New Haven, CT; London: Yale University Press, 2009.

Jones, Charles Edwin. *Perfectionist Persuasion: The Holiness Movement and American Methodism, 1867–1936*. Metuchen, NJ: Scarecrow, 1974.

Josephus. *Works*. Translated by H. St J. Thackeray, Ralph Marcus et al. LCL. 13 vols. Cambridge, MA: Harvard University Press, 1930–1965.

Kalu, Ogbu. *African Pentecostalism: An Introduction*. Oxford: OUP, 2008.

Kärkkäinen, Veli-Matti. "The Holy Spirit and Justification: The Ecumenical Significance of Luther's Doctrine of Salvation." *Pneuma* 24 no. 1 (2002) 26–39.

Kay, William K. "Pentecostalism and Fundamentalism." In *Evangelicalism and Fundamentalism in the United Kingdom during the Twentieth Century*, edited by David Bebbington and David Ceri Jones, 309–327. Oxford: Oxford University Press, 2013.

Kay, William K. *Pentecostals in Britain*. Carlisle: Paternoster, 2000.

———. *Pentecostalism: A Very Short Introduction*. Oxford: Oxford University Press, 2011.

———. *George Jeffreys: Pentecostal Apostle and Revivalist*. Cleveland, TN: CPT, 2017.

Kay, William K. and Parry, Robin, eds. *Exorcism and Deliverance: Multi-Disciplinary Studies*. Milton Keynes: Paternoster, 2011.

Kearsley, Rosalinde A. "Women and Public Life in Imperial Asia Minor: Hellenistic Tradition and Augustan Ideology." *AWE* 4 no. 1 (2005) 98–121.

Keener, Craig S., ed. *The IVP Bible Background Commentary: New Testament*. 2nd ed. Downers Grove, IL: IVP, 2014.

Kelly, John Norman Davidson. *The Pastoral Epistles*. London: Continuum, 1963.

Kenny, Anthony. *A Stylometric Study of the New Testament*. Oxford: Oxford University Press, 1986.

———. *A New History of Western Philosophy*. Oxford: Clarendon Press, 2010.

King, J.D. *Regeneration: A Complete History of Healing in the Christian Church*. 3 vols. Lee's Summit, MO: Christos Publishing, 2017.

Kittel, Gerhard and Friedrich, Gerhard, eds. *The Theological Dictionary of the New Testament*. 10 vols. Grand Rapids, MI: Eerdmans, 1964.

Klauck, Hans-Josef. *The Religious Context of Early Christianity: A Guide to Graeco-Roman Religions*. Edinburgh: T&T Clark, 2000.

Kloppenborg, John S. and Wilson, S. G., eds. *Voluntary Associations in the Graeco-Roman World*. London: Routledge, 1996.

Knight, George W. *The Pastoral Epistles: A Commentary on the Greek Text*. NIGTC. Grand Rapids, MI: Eerdmans, 1992.

Kruger, Michael J. *Canon Revisited: Establishing the Origins and Authority of the New Testament Books*. Kindle ed. Wheaton, IL: Crossway, 2012.

Kümmel, Werner Georg. *Introduction to the New Testament*. Translated by Howard Clark Kee. 2nd ed. Nashville: Abingdon, 1975.

Laird, Andrew. "Approaching Style and Rhetoric." In *The Cambridge Companion to the Greek and Roman novel*, edited by Tim J.D. Whitmarsh, 201–217. Cambridge: Cambridge University Press, 2008.

Land, Steven Jack. *Pentecostal Spirituality: A Passion for the Kingdom*. Sheffield: Sheffield Academic Press, 1993.

Lavan, Myles. "The Foundation of Empire? The Spread of Roman Citizenship from the Fourth Century BCE to the Third Century CE." In *In the Crucible of Empire: The Impact of Roman Citizenship upon Greeks, Jews and Christians*, edited by Katell Berthelot and Jonathan J. Price, 21–54. Leuven: Peeters, 2019.

Leftow, Brian. "Eternity." In *A Companion to Philosophy of Religion*, edited by Charles Taliaferro, Paul Draper et al., 278–284. Chichester: Wiley-Blackwell, 2010.

Lewis, Clive Staples. *The Great Divorce: A Dream*. London: G. Bles, 1945.

———. *The Four Loves*. London: Fontana, 1963.

Liddell, Henry George, Scott, Robert et al. *A Greek–English Lexicon with Revised Supplement*. 9th ed. Oxford: Oxford University Press, 1996.

Lieu, Judith M. "The 'Attraction of Women' in/to Early Judaism and Christianity: Gender and the Politics of Conversion." *JSNT* 21 no. 72 (1999) 5–22.

Lightfoot, J. B. *Saint Paul's Epistle to the Philippians: A Revised Text with Introduction, Notes, and Dissertations*. 4th ed. London: Macmillan, 1891.

Lloyd-Jones, David Martyn. *Life in the Spirit in Marriage, Home & Work: An Exposition of Ephesians 5:18 to 6:9*. Edinburgh: Banner of Truth, 1974.

Loubser, Johannes A. "Media Criticism and the Myth of Paul, the Creative Genius, and his Forgotten Co-Workers." *Neot* 34 no. 2 (2000) 329–345.

Lowe, E. J. "Truth." In *The Oxford Companion to Philosophy*, edited by Ted Honderich, 881–882. Oxford: Oxford University Press, 1995.

Lugo, Luis, Stencel, Sandra et al. *Spirit and Power: A 10-Country Survey of Pentecostals*. Washington, DC: Pew Research Center, 2006.

MacDonald, Margaret Y. *The Pauline Churches: A Socio-Historical Study of Institutionalization in the Pauline and Deutero-Pauline Writings*. Cambridge: Cambridge University Press, 1988.

MacIntyre, Alasdair C. "Lying." In *The Oxford Companion to Philosophy*, edited by Ted Honderich, 515. Oxford: Oxford University Press, 1995.

Madden, John. "Slavery in the Roman Empire Numbers and Origins." *Classics Ireland* 3 (1996) 109–128.

Malherbe, Abraham J., ed. *Moral Exhortation: A Greco-Roman Sourcebook*. Philadelphia, PA: Westminster, 1986.

Marshall, I. Howard. *The Acts of the Apostles: An Introduction and Commentary*. TNTC. Leicester: IVP, 1980.

Maxwell Lyte, H. C. *A History of the University of Oxford: From the Earliest Times to the Year 1530*. London: Macmillan, 1886.

McGrath, Alister E. *Christian History: An Introduction*. Chichester: Wiley-Blackwell, 2013.

McLaren, James S. "Jews and the Imperial Cult: From Augustus to Domitian." *JSNT* 27 no. 3 (2005) 257–278.

Meeks, Wayne A. *The First Urban Christians: The Social World of the Apostle Paul.* New Haven, CT: Yale University Press, 1983.

Metzger, Bruce Manning. *A Textual Commentary on the Greek New Testament: A Companion Volume to the United Bible Societies' Greek New Testament.* 3rd ed. New York, NY: United Bible Society, 1971.

Mickelsen, Alvera. *Women, Authority and the Bible.* Downers Grove, IL: IVP, 1986.

Miller, Donald E. and Yamamori, Tetsunao. *Global Pentecostalism: The New Face of Christian Social Engagement.* Berkeley: University of California Press, 2007.

Mittelstadt, Martin W. "A Century in the Making: Receiving the Samaritan Pentecost (Acts 8: 4–25) in the Pentecostal and Charismatic Traditions: SPS Presidential Address 2021." *Pneuma* 43 no. 2 (2021) 173–198.

Moule, H. C. G. "The Message: Its Scriptural Character." In *The Keswick Convention*, edited by Charles F. Harford, 65–73. London: Marshall Brothers, 1907.

Moulton, James Hope, Howard, Wilbert Francis et al. *A Grammar of New Testament Greek.* 3rd ed. 4 vols. London: T&T Clark, 2006.

Moulton, James Hope and Milligan, George. *The Vocabulary of the Greek Testament: Illustrated from the Papyri and Other Non-literary Sources.* Peabody, MA: Hendrickson, 2004. Repr. of One Vol. ed. London: Hodder and Stoughton, 1930.

Mounce, William D. *Pastoral Epistles.* WBC 46. Nashville, TN: Thomas Nelson, 2000.

Murphy-O'Connor, Jerome. "2 Timothy Contrasted with 1 Timothy and Titus." *Rev. Biblique* (1991) 403–418.

National Institutes of Health. "How Common is infertility?," 2018, https://www.nichd.nih.gov/health/topics/infertility/conditioninfo/common, (accessed 25.01.2022).

Neal, Tempestt, Sundararajan, Kalaivani et al. "Surveying Stylometry Techniques and Applications." *ACM Comput. Surv.* 50 no. 6 (2017) 1–36.

Ngewa, Samuel. *1 & 2 Timothy and Titus.* ABC. Grand Rapids, Mich.: Zondervan/HippoBooks, 2009.

O'Collins, Gerald and Farrugia, Edward G. *A Concise Dictionary of Theology.* London: Harper Collins, 1991.

Osborn, Tommy Lee. *Healing the Sick and Casting Out Devils: The Message and Ministry of a Bible Disciple Now Living.* Tulsa, OK: Harrison House, 1950.

Osiek, Carolyn, MacDonald, Margaret Y. et al. *A Woman's Place: House Churches in Earliest Christianity.* Minneapolis, MN: Fortress, 2006.

Packer, J. I. *Fundamentalism and the Word of God: Some Evangelical Principles.* Leicester: IVP, 1958.

———. "Understanding the Differences." In *Women, Authority & The Bible*, edited by Alvera Mickelsen, 295–299. Downers Grove, IL: IVP, 1986.
Palmer, Phoebe. *Promise of the Father; or, A Neglected Speciality of the Last Days. Addressed to the Clergy and Laity of all Christian Communities.* Boston, MA: H. V. Degen, 1859.
Parker, David C. *An Introduction to the New Testament Manuscripts and their Texts.* Cambridge: Cambridge University Press, 2008.
Philo. *Works.* Translated by Francis Henry Colson, Ralph Marcus et al. LCL. 12 vols. Cambridge, MA: Harvard University Press, 1929–1953.
Piaget, Jean. *The Moral Judgement of the Child.* London: K. Paul, Trench, Trubner, 1932.
Pierson, Lance. *In the Steps of Timothy.* Leicester: IVP, 1995.
Pitts, Andrew W. "Style and Pseudonymity in Pauline Scholarship: A Register Based Configuration." In *Paul and Pseudepigraphy*, edited by Stanley E. Porter and Gregory P. Fewster, 113–152. Leiden: Brill, 2013.
Poliakoff, Clare and Poliakoff, Michael. "Jacob, Job, and other Wrestlers: Reception of Greek Athletics by Jews and Christians in Antiquity." *J Sport Hist* 11 no. 2 (1984) 48–65.
Porter, Stanley E. "Pauline Chronology and the Question of Pseudonymity of the Pastoral Epistles." In *Paul and Pseudepigraphy*, edited by Stanley E. Porter and Gregory P. Fewster, 65–88. Leiden: Brill, 2013.
Porter, Stanley E. and Fewster, Gregory P., eds. *Paul and Pseudepigraphy.* Leiden: Brill, 2013.
Quinn, Jerome D. *The Letter to Titus: A New Translation with Notes and Commentary and an Introduction to Titus, I and II Timothy, the Pastoral Epistles.* AB. New York, NY: Doubleday, 1990.
Rack, Henry D. *Reasonable Enthusiast: John Wesley and the Rise of Methodism.* 2nd ed. London: Epworth, 1992.
Räisänen, Heikki. "Marcion." In *A Companion to Second-Century Christian 'Heretics'*, edited by Antti Marjanen and Petri Luomanen, 100–124. Leiden: Brill, 2005.
Ramsay, William Mitchell. *The Church in the Roman Empire before A.D. 170.* London: Hodder & Stoughton, 1893.
Reid, Heather Lynne. *Athletics and Philosophy in the Ancient World: Contests of Virtue.* London: Routledge, 2011.
Rendel Harris, J. "The Cretans Always Liars." *Expositor (Series 7)* 2 no. 4 (1906) 305–317.
Richards, E. Randolph. *Paul and First-Century Letter Writing: Secretaries, Composition and Collection.* Downers Grove, IL: IVP, 2004.
Richardson, Alan and Bowden, John, eds. *A New Dictionary of Christian Theology.* London: SCM, 1983.

Roberts, Alexander, Donaldson, James et al., eds. *The Ante-Nicene Fathers: Translations of the Writings of the Fathers down to A.D. 325.* 10 vols. Grand Rapids, MI: Eerdmans, 1979. https://www.ccel.org/fathers.

Russell, Bertrand. "A Free Man's Worship." In *Mysticism and Logic: and other Essays*, 46–57. London: Allen & Unwin, 1917. https://www.gutenberg.org/files/25447/25447-h/25447-h.htm#III.

Schaff, Philip, ed. *Nicene and Post-Nicene Fathers. First series.* 14 vols. Peabody, MA: Hendrickson, 1994. https://www.ccel.org/fathers.

Schaff, Philip and Wace, Henry, eds. *Nicene and Post-Nicene Fathers. Second series.* 14 vols. Peabody, MA: Hendrickson, 1995. https://www.ccel.org/fathers.

Schaps, David M. *Economic Rights of Women in Ancient Greece*. Edinburgh: Edinburgh University Press, 1979.

Schneemelcher, Wilhelm and Wilson, R. McL. *New Testament Apocrypha*. Revd. ed. 2 vols. Louisville, KY: Westminster John Knox, 2003.

Schüssler Fiorenza, Elisabeth. *In Memory of Her: A Feminist Theological Reconstruction of Christian Origins*. London: SCM, 1983.

Scott, Benji G. McNair. *Apostles Today: Making Sense of Contemporary Charismatic Apostolates: A Historical and Theological Appraisal*. Eugene, OR: Wipf and Stock, 2014.

Shaw, Brent D. "The Age of Roman Girls at Marriage: Some Reconsiderations." *JRS* 77 (1987) 28–46.

Shaw, Brent D. "The Myth of the Neronian Persecution." *JRS* 105 (2015) 73–100.

Simmons, Dale H. *E. W. Kenyon and the Postbellum Pursuit of Peace, Power and Plenty*. Lanham, MD: Scarecrow, 1997.

Smith, Mark S. "The Heart and Innards in Israelite Emotional Expressions: Notes from Anthropology and Psychobiology." *JBL* 117 no. 3 (1998) 427–436.

Stark, Rodney. *The Rise of Christianity: How the Obscure, Marginal Jesus Movement Became the Dominant Religious Force in the Western World in a Few Centuries*. New York, NY: Harper One, 1997.

Stephens, Randall J. *The Fire Spreads: Holiness and Pentecostalism in the American South*. Cambridge, MA: Harvard University Press, 2008.

Stern, Menahem. *Greek and Latin Authors on Jews and Judaism*. 3 vols. Jerusalem: Ktav, 1974.

Stevenson, James and Frend, W. H. C. *A New Eusebius: Documents Illustrating the History of the Church to A.D. 337*. Revd. ed. London: SPCK, 1987.

Stott, John R. W. *Guard the Truth: The Message of 1 Timothy & Titus*. BST. Downers Grove, IL: IVP, 1996.

Strelan, Rick. "Paul's Work and his Co-Workers." *Lutheran Theol. J.* 50 no. 1 (2016) 17.

Suetonius. *Works*. Translated by John Carew Rolfe, Donna W. Hurley et al. LCL. 2 vols. Cambridge, MA: Harvard University Press, 1997.

Tacitus. *Works*. Translated by E. H. Warmington, Maurice Hutton et al. LCL. 5 vols. Cambridge, MA: Harvard University Press, 1914.

Temple, William. *Christianity and Social Order*. Harmondsworth: Penguin, 1942.

Thomas, John Christopher. "Women, Pentecostals and the Bible: An Experiment in Pentecostal Hermeneutics." *J. Pentecostal Theol.* 5 (1994) 41–56.

———. *Footwashing in John 13 and the Johannine Community*. London: T&T Clark, 2004.

Thompson, Damian. *Waiting for Antichrist: Charisma and Apocalypse in a Pentecostal Church*. Oxford: Oxford University Press, 2005.

Towner, Philip H. *The Goal of our Instruction: The Structure of Theology and Ethics in the Pastoral Epistles*. Sheffield: JSOT, 1989.

———. *The Letters to Timothy and Titus*. NICNT. Grand Rapids, MI: Eerdmans, 2006.

Trobisch, David. *Paul's Letter Collection: Tracing the Origins*. Minneapolis, MI: Fortress, 1994.

van Nes, Jermo. "The Problem of the Pastoral Epistles: An Important Hypothesis Reconsidered." In *Paul and Pseudepigraphy*, edited by Stanley E. Porter and Gregory P. Fewster, 153–169. Leiden: Brill, 2013.

Van Neste, Ray. "Study Notes to 1 and 2 Timothy." In *ESV Study Bible: English Standard Version*.

Wacker, Grant. *Heaven Below: Early Pentecostals and American Culture*. Cambridge, MA: Harvard University Press, 2009.

Walker, Andrew. "The Devil you Think you Know: Demonology and the Charismatic Movement." In *Charismatic Renewal: The Search for a Theology*, edited by Andrew Walker and Nigel Wright, 86–105. London: SPCK, 1995.

Wall, Robert W. and Steele, Richard B. *1 and 2 Timothy and Titus*. THNTC. Kindle ed. Grand Rapids, MI: Eerdmans, 2012.

Warrington, Keith. *Pentecostal Theology : A Theology of Encounter*. London: T&T Clark, 2008.

Waters, Kenneth L. "Saved through Childbearing: Virtues as Children in 1 Timothy 2: 11–15." *JBL* 123 no. 4 (2004) 703–735.

Weber, Max. "The Meaning of Discipline." In *From Max Weber: Essays in Sociology*, edited by Max Weber, Hans Gerth et al., 253–264. New York, NY: Oxford University Press, 1946.

———. "The Social Psychology of the World Religions." In *From Max Weber: Essays in Sociology*, edited by Max Weber, Hans Gerth et al., 267–301. New York, NY: Oxford University Press, 1946.

Weisser, Sharon. "Philo's Therapeutae and Essenes: A Precedent for the Exceptional Condemnation of Slavery in Gregory of Nyssa?." In *The Quest for a Common Humanity: Human Dignity and Otherness in the Religious Traditions of the Mediterranean*, edited by Katell Berthelot and Matthias Morgenstern, 289–310. Leiden: Brill, 2011.

Wilkinson, Michael, Au, Connie et al., eds. *Brill's Encyclopedia of Global Pentecostalism*. Leiden: Brill, 2021.

Wilson, Stephen G. *Luke and the Pastoral Epistles*. London: SPCK, 1979.

Wimber, John and Springer, Kevin. *Power Healing*. Sevenoaks: Hodder, 1986.

Winter, Bruce W. *Seek the Welfare of the City: Christians as Benefactors and Citizens*. Grand Rapids, MI: Eerdmans, 1994.

———. *Roman Wives, Roman Widows: The Appearance of New Women and the Pauline Communities*. Grand Rapids, MI: Eerdmans, 2003.

Witherington, Ben. *Women in the Earliest Churches*. Cambridge: Cambridge University Press, 1988.

Witherington, Ben and Hyatt, Darlene. *Paul's Letter to the Romans: A Socio-Rhetorical Commentary*. SRC. Grand Rapids, MI: Eerdmans, 2004.

Wittgenstein, Ludwig. *Philosophical Investigations*. Translated by G. E. M. Anscombe. 2nd ed. Oxford: Blackwell, 1963.

Wolgast, Eike. "Luther's Treatment of Political and Societal Life." In *The Oxford Handbook of Martin Luther's Theology*, edited by Robert Kolb, Irene Dingel et al., 397–413. Oxford: Oxford University Press, 2014.

Woodworth-Etter, Maria B. *Divine Healing: Health for Body, Soul and Spirit*. Self-published, c.1920.

World Health Organisation. "Intimate Partner Violence and Alcohol." 2006, https://www.who.int/violence_injury_prevention/violence/world_report/factsheets/fs_intimate.pdf, (accessed 25.01.2022).

Wright, Nigel Thomas. *Paul: A Biography*. Kindle ed. London: SPCK, 2018.

Wright, Nigel Thomas and Bird, Michael F. *The New Testament in its World: An Introduction to the History, Literature and Theology of the First Christians*. London: SPCK, 2019.

Wyke, Maria. "Woman in the Mirror: the Rhetoric of Adornment in the Roman World." In *Women in Ancient Societies: An Illusion of the Night*, edited by Léonie J. Archer, Susan Fischler et al., 134–151. Basingstoke: Macmillan, 1994.

Yarbrough, Robert W. *The Letters to Timothy and Titus*. PNTC. Kindle ed. Grand Rapids, MI: Eerdmans, 2018.

Yong, Amos. *Spirit–Word–Community: Theological Hermeneutics in Trinitarian Perspective*. Aldershot: Ashgate, 2002.

———. *Renewing Christian Theology: Systematics for a Global Christianity*. Waco, TX: Baylor University Press, 2014.

Young, Frances M. *The Making of the Creeds*. London: SCM, 1991.

Zeichmann, Christopher B. "Military Forces in Judaea 6–130 CE: The Status Quaestionis and Relevance for New Testament Studies." *CurBR* 17 no. 1 (2018) 86–120.

Zelnick-Abramovitz, Rachel. *Not Wholly Free: The Concept of Manumission and the Status of Manumitted Slaves in the Ancient Greek World.* Leiden: Brill, 2005.

INDEX

Academy, 34, 41-43
Adam, 67, 72, 73
Adventism (see also Second Coming), 155
Agabus, 87
Agrippa, King 244
Alcohol (see also wine), 70, 78, 81, 82, 88, 128, 135, 139, 147, 224
Alexander the Great, 15, 22
Amanuensis, 28, 33, 36, 40, 190, 240
Ananias, 60, 245
Angels, 78, 84, 86, 105, 108, 139, 162
Apollos, 31, 94, 168, 171, 229, 247
Apostles, ix, 5, 43, 47, 48, 56, 57, 76, 113, 132, 186, 193, 198, 199, 205, 223, 227, 248
Apostolic Church of Wales, 155
Apostolic Succession, 193
Apostle to the Gentiles, 237, 249
Aquilla, 8, 247
Artemas, 167, 170
Asceticism, 24, 88, 91, 109, 123, 145, 204
Asia, 19, 29, 31, 149, 170, 189, 222, 239, 245
Assemblies of God, ix, 155
Athens, 90, 161, 204
Augustine, St, 250
Augustus Caesar, 15, 22, 26, 68, 104

Baptism (in water), 86, 103, 118, 119, 164, 181, 199, 204, 234
Baptism (in the Spirit), ix, 56, 127, 128, 165, 180
Barnabas, 9, 48, 59, 96, 222, 223, 240

Barr, James, xiv, 254
Bishop, 11, 13, 29, 30, 76, 81, 82, 95, 127, 249
Bithynia, 83
Booth, William, 126

Caesar, (see also entries for individual emperors) 19, 25, 121, 126, 160, 200, 223, 224, 237, 244
Caligula, 25
Calvin, John, 64, 198, 255
Chains, 175, 177, 182, 189, 190, 191, 197, 198
Charismatic gifts, x, xi, 4-6, 29, 34, 42, 44, 51, 56, 59, 72, 80, 85, 94, 95, 100, 109, 139, 153, 158, 180, 181, 184, 201, 205, 210, 227, 248
Childbirth, 67, 73, 74
Children (also childhood), 9, 10, 25, 39, 49, 58, 67, 75, 77, 78, 80, 81, 100, 102-104, 110, 132, 134, 135, 137, 138, 146, 148, 149, 154, 175, 176, 178, 192, 194, 214, 219, 225, 226, 241
Church of God, 155
Claudius Caesar, 15, 18, 23, 247
Clement of Alexandria, 88
Clement of Rome, 7, 27, 81, 88, 239, 254
Clothing, 51, 68, 112, 114, 115, 128, 171, 196
Complementarianism, 69, 70, 72,
Conscience, 50, 51, 52, 58, 60, 61, 62, 81, 82, 88, 141, 144, 177, 186, 233

269

Corinth, 8, 10, 11, 12, 26, 29, 34, 70, 94, 108, 134, 140, 149, 171, 204, 221, 246, 247
Courts, 50, 161, 177, 179, 189, 196, 230, 243, 244, 245
Crescens, 238, 239
Crete, 7, 11, 13, 14, 33, 34, 129, 131, 135, 140, 141, 143, 149, 150, 160, 161, 170, 171, 240
Crown, 194, 235, 237, 238, 246
Crucifixion, 66, 184, 196, 197, 199, 234, 238
Cyprus, 136, 240

Dalmatia, 11, 170, 238, 240
David, King, 196, 197, 201
Day of Pentecost, 69, 136, 166, 181, 213, 215
Deacon, Deaconess, ix, 5, 21, 25, 29, 45, 76, 84, 98, 102, 147
Demas, 8, 238, 239, 245
Demons, 80, 87-89, 104, 126
Deposit, 25, 124, 179, 186, 187, 188, 193
Devil (see Satan), 58, 60, 75, 79, 80, 99, 104, 105, 116, 125, 210, 211, 239, 246
Didache, 30, 142, 185
Divorce, 24, 77, 88, 137, 148, 149, 207, 218
Domitian, 15,
Dowry, 100
Durham, William, 127, 165

Egalitarianism, 18, 69, 70
Egypt, 22, 110, 157, 237
Elders, ix, 5, 6, 8, 11, 14, 29, 48, 50, 57, 76, 77, 79, 80, 81, 83, 84, 90, 93, 95-98, 102, 105-111, 113, 118, 131, 135-141, 143, 147, 169, 170, 171, 177, 192, 205, 215, 232, 248
Election, 105, 108, 131-133, 196, 198, 205, 206
Elim Pentecostal Church, 155
Epaphroditus, 8
Ephesians chapter 4, ix, 5, 12, 48, 52, 67, 80, 94, 95, 114, 137, 185

Ephesus, 8, 11-14, 23, 24, 26, 29, 33, 48-51, 59, 61, 69, 76, 84, 87, 94, 98, 105, 113, 116, 117, 121, 131, 136, 141, 142, 150, 170, 171, 180, 189, 190, 191, 193, 202-206, 221, 231, 235, 238, 239, 241, 242, 246-249
Ephraim, 108
Erastus, 12, 246, 247
Eternal life, 55, 58, 91, 116, 118, 123, 131, 133, 163, 167, 176, 183
Eternity, 58, 92, 112, 133, 183, 184, 193, 250, 251
Eubulus, 246, 249
Eunice, 177, 178
Euodia, 71
Eusebius, xix, 7, 11, 13, 30, 83, 249
Evangelical, 216, 226, 230
Eve, 67, 72, 73
Exorcism, 23, 34, 82, 125, 126

Fasting, 136
Felix, 177, 214, 244
Festus, 244
Finney, Charles, 128
Fivefold Gospel, x, 5
Foods, 53, 76, 87-89, 91, 99, 112, 115, 144, 190, 221
Foundation, 11, 17, 51, 85, 123, 193, 201, 205, 250

Gallio, 18
Gangrene, 54, 203, 208
Gee, Donald, 80, 180, 248, 257
Gentiles, 9, 11, 15, 22, 48, 52, 64, 66, 67, 70, 82, 84, 86, 89, 113, 120, 134, 144, 157, 178, 185, 187, 188, 196, 197, 220, 221, 222, 237, 243, 245, 247, 249
Glossolalia (see also Tongues), 95
Gnosticism, 23, 24, 28, 29, 51, 65, 124, 134, 143, 144, 169, 204, 210, 233
Godliness (see also Eusebeia), xiv, 6, 45, 62, 63, 67, 68, 90-92, 112, 113, 116, 117, 127, 131, 133, 148, 212, 216, 217
Gortyn, Crete, 135

Healing (see charismatic gifts), x, 5, 34, 72, 80, 95, 180, 221, 231, 235, 248, 255, 257, 258, 260, 262, 266
Hedonism, 154, 162, 216
Hercules, 91
Hitler, Adolf, 42
Holiness, vii, 6, 53, 67, 68, 74, 94, 95, 127, 128, 140, 157, 165, 179, 208
Holy Spirit, ix, x, 6, 29 31, 34, 42, 52, 56, 57, 59, 69, 71, 72, 76, 80, 85-87, 94, 108, 113, 119, 127, 128, 136, 147, 149, 153, 155, 158, 163-166, 176, 179, 181-183, 188, 193, 195, 201, 204, 213, 216, 221, 227, 232, 234, 242, 245, 248, 251
Honor, 4, 22, 31, 35, 54, 55, 58, 98-100, 105-107, 110, 111, 117, 121, 182, 198, 222
Household, 12, 16, 17, 18-21, 50, 75, 78, 84-86, 98, 138, 142, 149, 151, 190, 212, 218, 226, 246, 247
Hymenaeus, 58, 60, 61, 80, 201, 203, 205, 207

Iconium, 9, 220, 222-224
Ignatius, 27, 29, 76
Incarnation, 57, 86, 152, 231
Interpretation of tongues, 71, 109, 180

Jacob, 91, 108
Jambres, 218, 225
Jannes, 218, 225
Jeffreys, George, 231
Jerusalem, 5, 11, 14, 44, 48, 59, 68, 76, 85, 99, 113, 134, 136, 150, 169, 170, 181, 187, 188, 197, 213, 222, 234
John the Baptist, 136, 205
Josephus, 22, 63, 77, 141, 226
Joshua, 108
Julia, 71, 104
Julius Caesar, 120, 237
Junia, 71

Kenny, Anthony, 27, 33, 37, 210
Kerygma, 185, 245
Kingdom of God, 52, 115, 130, 243, 246
Korah, 206, 218

Last days, 212, 213, 215, 220
Laying on of hands, ix, 76, 93, 95, 96, 108, 136, 179-181, 193, 248
Lazarus, 184
Leadership, 5, 8, 12, 14, 34, 48, 51, 55, 59, 60, 63, 69, 70, 76, 77, 79, 80, 84, 95, 108, 137, 140, 142, 147, 182, 205, 206, 209, 216, 227, 249
Lewis, CS (Clive Staples), 39, 182, 215, 218,
Linus, 246, 249
Lois, 177, 178
Luke, St, 5, 8, 9, 19, 55, 56, 222, 240, 244
Luther, Martin, 41, 150, 161, 199
LXX (Septuagint), 100, 201, 206, 226, 236
Lydia, 72
Lystra, 9, 10, 59, 89, 95, 176, 178, 220, 222, 223, 224

Manasseh, 108
Marcion, 30, 124, 197, 228
Mark, John, 238-241
Marriage, 10, 17, 24, 25, 53, 70, 74, 77, 78, 81, 83, 87, 88, 91, 99, 100, 102, 104, 105, 113, 137, 138, 144, 148-150, 221
Martyrdom, 7, 13, 19, 27, 33, 119, 151, 152, 189, 198, 199, 244, 249
Marxism, 42, 44
Mary, 71
Methodism, 69, 79, 127, 259
Miletus, 34, 246, 247
Money, 78, 79, 81, 82, 100, 101, 112, 115, 116, 122, 123, 134, 142, 157, 170, 171, 187, 190, 212-214, 220, 221
Mosaic law, 52, 61, 144, 157, 176, 205, 216

INDEX

Moses, 79, 108, 121, 205, 206, 212, 218, 219
Moule, Handley, 127, 262
Muratorian canon, 3, 4, 30
Mystery, 81, 82, 84, 86, 133
Myths, 22, 50, 51, 53, 54, 90, 91, 141, 143, 144, 219, 230, 233, 234

Nazi Germany, 42
Nero, 15, 18, 25, 31, 33, 198, 237, 238, 243, 244, 246, 249
Nicopolis, 167, 170

Odysseus, 91
Onesimus, 110, 151
Overseer (see Elders), 5, 14, 19, 76, 78, 82, 135, 137-139, 216

Palmer, Phoebe, 127
Paraenesis, 12
Persecution, 18, 19, 23, 56, 151, 155, 198, 222, 223, 244, 249
Persis, 71
Pew Survey, x, 34, 155
Pharisee, 52, 55, 56, 169, 177, 180, 216
Philemon, 4, 8-10, 13, 36, 64, 151
Philetus, 203, 205, 207
Philo, 16, 18, 22, 63, 73, 141, 226
Phoebe, 5, 71, 83
Pierson, Lance, 9, 76, 94
Pilate, Pontius, 16, 112, 117, 119, 132, 182, 231, 243
Pliny the Younger, 17, 23, 25, 83
Polycarp, 12, 27, 151, 254
Prayer, 34, 60, 62-64, 66-69, 76, 80, 84, 89, 91, 95, 98, 100, 117, 125, 126, 128, 136, 139, 176, 177, 191, 208
Preaching, 7, 10, 41, 48, 51, 58, 66, 69, 86, 94, 119, 122, 126, 127, 133, 134, 137, 139, 143, 161, 165, 168, 181, 183-185, 202, 205, 213, 218, 222, 224, 229, 232-235, 238, 242, 248
Priscilla, 8, 71, 72, 246, 247
Prison, 3, 7, 13, 19, 27, 33, 34, 36, 56, 135, 152, 175, 177-179, 181-187, 189, 190-192, 197, 198, 222, 231, 236, 240, 246, 249
Prophecy (see also charismatic gifts), 4, 6, 29, 34, 59, 72, 93, 95, 109, 180, 181, 197, 210, 215, 221, 227
Prophet, ix, 5, 42, 59, 116, 137, 142, 227
Pseudepigrapha, 27, 28, 31, 35
Pudens, 246, 249

Quakers, 79

Regeneration (see new birth), 157, 160, 163-166, 199
Roman Catholic, 4, 29, 144, 193
Russell, Bertrand, 231, 264

Samaritans, 181, 234
Sanctification, x, 127, 128, 147, 165, 166, 208, 221
Sanhedrin, 55, 161, 244
Saphira, 60
Satan (see devil), 58, 60, 80, 99, 104, 105, 116, 146, 151, 239, 246
Savior, x, 49, 63, 64, 90, 92, 115, 131, 132, 134, 155, 156, 163, 164, 166, 182, 185, 194, 226
Scripture, ii, ix, xi, 5, 9, 52, 57, 60, 70, 72, 78, 90, 94, 105, 120, 124, 125, 133, 137, 147, 153, 157, 171, 173, 178, 180, 184, 193, 195, 196, 202, 203, 212, 220, 225-229, 231, 232, 247, 250, 251
Seal, 201, 205
Second Coming (See also Adventism), x, 29, 120, 146, 152, 154, 155, 156, 160, 195, 213, 215, 231, 238, 242, 251
Septuagint (LXX), 9, 38, 145, 100, 164, 201, 203, 205, 206, 226, 236
Shame, 79, 146, 150, 177-179, 182, 183, 186, 190, 202, 245
Shema, 58, 65
Silas, 10, 12, 19

Slavery, 17, 18, 20, 54, 70, 75, 78, 83, 85, 102, 110, 111, 128, 132, 151--153, 157, 209
Sosthenes, 36
Spain, 7, 33, 239
Spirit (see Holy Spirit)
Stark, Rodney, 21, 24, 25, 104, 148
Stylometry, 27, 32, 37, 38
Synoptic Gospels, 133, 156
Syntyche, 71

Tacitus, xix, 18, 243
Teetotalism, 70, 78, 82, 139
Tertullian, 18, 23, 27, 30
Testimony, 55, 58, 66, 69, 70, 72, 86, 100, 108, 113, 119, 141, 143, 162, 179, 182, 234, 240, 244
Theseus, 91
Tiberius Caesar, 15, 16, 25, 243
Timothy, 3, 4, 5, 7-14, 16, 24, 28, 33, 34, 36, 62, 77, 89, 93, 85, 108, 112, 119, 123, 124, 175-180, 181, 187, 190, 192, 193, 201, 210-213, 217, 219, 221, 231, 323-235, 239, 241, 242, 247
Tongues (see also glossolalia), 4, 34, 109, 180, 181, 227
Torah, 52, 70
Trinity, 58, 64, 134, 166, 251
Trophimus, 247, 248

Trump, Donald, 42
Truth, 31, 51, 63, 65, 67, 82, 84-86, 89, 94, 113-115, 119, 132, 133, 144, 152, 188, 193, 195, 198, 199, 201, 203, 204, 210, 211, 216, 218, 219, 225, 231, 233, 234
Tryphena, 71
Tryphosa, 71
Titus, 3-5, 7-10, 12-14, 33, 147, 150, 155, 159, 162, 167-171, 240, 247
Tychicus, 13, 167, 170, 241

Vespasian Caesar, 15, 134
Virtue, 40, 74, 78, 117, 136-139, 147, 149, 152, 162, 208, 213, 215, 216

Warfare, 60, 78, 125, 126
Wesley, John, 126, 127, 165
Widows, 21, 24, 69, 76, 82, 98-106, 110, 148, 149, 150, 216, 217, 221
Wilkinson, Michael, x, xvi
Wimber, John, 231
Wine (see also Alcohol), 10, 81, 109, 136, 148, 236
Wittgenstein, Ludwig, 202
World Health Organisation, 70
Wycliffe, John, 41

Zealots, 158
Zenas, 168, 171

www.ingramcontent.com/pod-product-compliance
Lightning Source LLC
Chambersburg PA
CBHW050433240426
43661CB00055B/2364